Dear Nell:

The True Story of the Haven Sisters

Based on the Haven-Pugh Letter Collection

by Kathleen Langdon-Haven McInerney

To Ellen Eustis Pugh,
Regina Haven Pugh
and
John J. McInerney

Contents

Acknowledgements

I owe particular thanks to my brother, John J. McInerney, Jr., who has worked for years on our family's genealogy, has patiently provided suggestions and advice and has generously given of his time (thanks also to his wife, Victoria).

I also would like to thank the following relatives:

- My cousin, Ann Iverson (Thomas and Regina Pugh's granddaughter) for contributing source materials

- Della Haden-Dirickson (descendant of Walter Pugh) for sharing a great deal of Pugh family history and photos, including the material about the mysterious Madewood fires

- Alyce Harris Rossow (Alice Pugh Stone's granddaughter) who has shared material from Alice's family, including photos

- Robert Pugh (great-great-grandson of W.W. Pugh) for his expertise on the Pughs

- Carl McInerney, another of my brothers, for making the effort to meet and spend time with our Louisiana relations in the 1980's, and for forwarding his research findings to my father

- My father, John J. McInerney, who preserved the Haven-Pugh Letter Collection and without whose interest and perseverance in his wife's family history this book could not have come to fruition

Thanks to Erica L. Bartlett, who gave her time to read an early manuscript. Finally, thanks to Matthew Hock for his fine art work on the covers, inside image placement, suggestions and *Dear Nell* e-book design and production.

Preface

This is the story of Fanny and Ellen, two of the Haven sisters, who grew up in the mid-1800's in Manhattan's Fort Washington, overlooking New York's Hudson River.

Ellen, whom Fanny called Nell, married into a prominent plantation family (the Pughs) in Louisiana just prior to the Civil War, thus entering into a world with a different culture, politics, economy and way of life.

Separated by the terrible division of North and South, and despite the clash of belief systems, the sisters' love and interdependence never wavers. The sisters' story, and that of their families as well as the era itself, is told largely in their words, drawn as it is from over 1400 letters spanning roughly from 1855 to the early 1900's.

The effects of the Civil War on the families, their livelihoods, and, in the South, on their very identity, come alive in their words.

The excerpts in Dear Nell come from the six-volume Haven-Pugh Letter Collection. The letter collection contains the many hundreds of letters written from and to members of the Haven and Pugh families. These letters were saved by Ellen Eustis Haven Pugh ("Nell") and passed down through her youngest son Thomas Pugh, the author's grand-father.

After John J. McInerney (the husband of Ellen's grand-daughter and also the author's father) read through all the letters and documents during the 1970's and 1980's, the letter collection lay largely ignored, stored in brown grocery bags in clothes closets, until the early 2000's.

After reading some of the letters, the author set to transcribing and assembling the letters into the six volume set. Then, a great story, rich with pathos, conflict, love and death, demanded to be told: *Dear Nell* was born.

Genealogical Chart

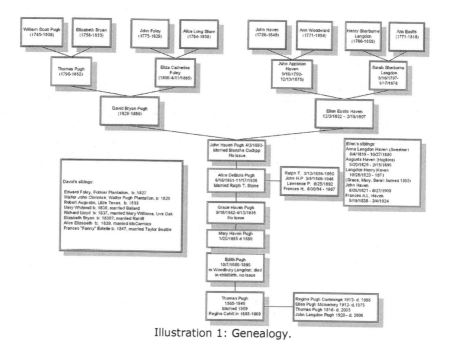

Illustration 1: Genealogy.

Timeline

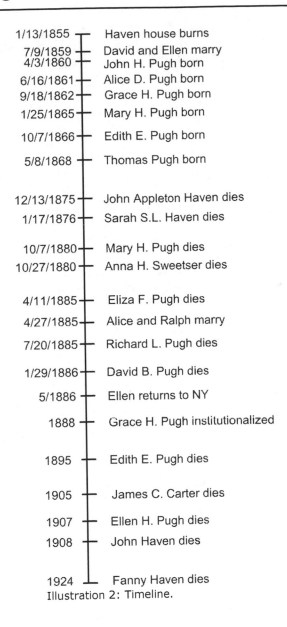

1/13/1855	Haven house burns
7/9/1859	David and Ellen marry
4/3/1860	John H. Pugh born
6/16/1861	Alice D. Pugh born
9/18/1862	Grace H. Pugh born
1/25/1865	Mary H. Pugh born
10/7/1866	Edith E. Pugh born
5/8/1868	Thomas Pugh born
12/13/1875	John Appleton Haven dies
1/17/1876	Sarah S.L. Haven dies
10/7/1880	Mary H. Pugh dies
10/27/1880	Anna H. Sweetser dies
4/11/1885	Eliza F. Pugh dies
4/27/1885	Alice and Ralph marry
7/20/1885	Richard L. Pugh dies
1/29/1886	David B. Pugh dies
5/1886	Ellen returns to NY
1888	Grace H. Pugh institutionalized
1895	Edith E. Pugh dies
1905	James C. Carter dies
1907	Ellen H. Pugh dies
1908	John Haven dies
1924	Fanny Haven dies

Illustration 2: Timeline.

The Patriarch

John Appleton Haven (born in Portsmouth, N.H. 1792, died 1875) was the oldest of ten children of John Haven (see p. Error: Reference source not found)and Ann Woodward (see p.). John Haven (John Appleton Haven's father) was a very successful Portsmouth, N.H. merchant and was himself the son of Rev Samuel Haven, D.D. of Harvard (born 1727, died 1806).

Rev. Samuel Haven was a Unitarian and has been described as a philanthropist who dabbled in chemistry and medicine, and as a much beloved member of the Portsmouth community[1]. He met George Washington during the Revolutionary years, and some twenty years later he acted in a way that might have earned him rancor from the then-President.

In 1797, George Washington was quietly at work trying to recover his wife Martha's escaped personal slave. The Washingtons were living in Philadelphia at the time, and Ona Maria Judge escaped via cargo ship from Philadelphia and landed in Portsmouth, N.H. When Washington learned that Ona had been seen in Portsmouth, he enlisted the help of well-known Portsmouth residents to find her. It is therefore possible that Rev. Haven knew of Washington's effort to recapture her. Nevertheless, Rev. Haven married her in January of 1797 to a Jack Staines in his South Church, Portsmouth[2].

Rev. Haven married twice and fathered 17 children (John Haven was the 7th child of his first wife, Mehitable Appleton). The site of the former home of Rev. Haven is now Haven Park, in Portsmouth.

John Appleton Haven's sister Susan married William Emerson (Ralph Waldo Emerson's brother), and John Appleton Haven's brother George Wallis Haven (born 1808, Dartmouth and Harvard) was a friend of Ralph W. Emerson's. George W. Haven's obituary claimed that between George and his father John Haven, the Portsmouth house had been visited by Mason, Choate, Webster, the younger and older Quincy, Hawthorne, Emerson and Ticknor, and that Holmes, Fields[3] and Longfellow were George's friends. George was said to have met Goethe, Wordsworth and others during his extensive European travels.

John Appleton Haven and his brother, Joseph Woodward Haven, ran Haven & Co., from downtown N.Y.C. Haven & Co. was located on Beaver St., which runs off Wall St. and fronts along the area of the New York Stock

---

[1] Seacoast, NH (http://www.seacoastnh.com)

[2] Historical New Hampshire, Vol 62, No. 1, published by the New Hampshire Historical Society; by Robert B. Dishman (citing records from North Church, Portsmouth held by the Portsmouth Athenaeum)

[3] The Havens, particularly Fanny, were good friends with the Adams family of New York, one of whose daughters, Annie, married James T. Fields. Annie worked on Harriet Beecher Stowe's biography, and knew many other well-known authors of that time (Longfellow, Holmes, Tennyson, Emerson).

Exchange. Haven & Co. was a respected commission merchant, part of whose business involved loaning money to southern planters to purchase land and crop seed.

Illustration 3: Ellen's grandfather, John Haven, by Gilbert Stuart. The 25" x 29" portraits of John Haven (1766-1849) and Ann Woodward Haven (1771-1849) were painted by Gilbert Stuart (1755-1828) in 1824. They were passed down to Ellen's father and then her brother, and then were given to the New York Public Library in 1924 by Fanny's will. The library sold the paintings in 2005.

Illustration 4: Ellen's grandmother, Ann Woodward Haven, by Gilbert Stuart.

The Matriarch

Sarah Sherburne Langdon (born in Portsmouth, N.H. 1797, died 1876) was the daughter of Henry Sherburne Langdon and Ann Eustis.

Henry Sherburne Langdon (born 1766) was the son of Woodbury Langdon and Sarah Sherburne. Woodbury Langdon (1739-1805) was the brother of John Langdon, who served as speaker of the Assembly of New Hampshire, president of New Hampshire, member of the Continental Congress, delegate to the Federal Constitutional Convention, senator from New Hampshire and governor of New Hampshire.

Woodbury, a successful ship captain, ship-builder and merchant, at age 26 married the 16-year old daughter (Sarah) of his business partner Henry Sherburne. Several years after their marriage they traveled to Boston to have their portraits painted by John Singleton Copley.

Woodbury was one of the wealthiest men in his community before the revolutionary war. Woodbury switched allegiance according to which side was winning and was at one point imprisoned in New Hampshire, possibly for his Loyalist leanings. He served as a Judge on the Superior Court and was impeached, and was elected to the General Court. With the help of his brother, Woodbury was appointed by President Washington as a commissioner to settle Revolutionary War claims.

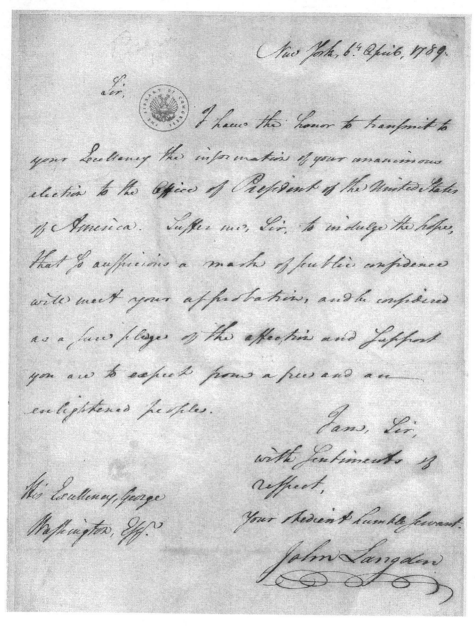

Illustration 5: John Langdon to George Washington, 1789, announcing that Washington was unanimously elected president. John Langdon was Ellen's great grand-uncle.

The Haven Home & the Fire of 1855

John Appleton Haven built the family home, known as Waldenfield, in 1837. Situated on a ten-acre parcel, it overlooked the Hudson River across to the Palisades. On the back side was the Harlem River. An old map in the New York Public Library collection shows the notation "Haven" next to Jeffery's Hook, which was the name given to the point over which the Haven property looked. In 1855, the Fort Washington house was described in a New York City newspaper as "in this city, between Manhattanville and Spuyten Duyvil Creek, on the North River".

The original Haven house was built of wood and was, according to a newspaper account, about 125 feet across the front by 40 feet deep. Another account described it as having a large main structure and two wings, the south wing having been added about 1847 and the north wing, a 3-story tower, had just been built in 1855 and hadn't been furnished by the time of the fire.

On January 13, 1855, Waldenfield burned. At home at the time of the fire were Mr. and Mrs. Haven (aged 63 and 58, respectively), Anna (36), Sarah (26), Mary (24), Ellen (23) and Grace (18). Augusta (29) was a short distance away in her own house with her husband Milt Hopkins, and Fanny (17) was in the city at school. John (34) lived at home but was away. Langdon Haven (32) had married and moved away. Anna had recently married Dr. William Sweetser, and may have been at her parents' house because her husband was away.

The fire began about 20 minutes past three on Saturday morning. John Appleton Haven walked through the house at 10:30 p.m., per his routine, and saw nothing amiss. At midnight he got up to adjust the heat register and went to sleep again. A little after 3 a.m., he again awoke, this time due to smoke. John and his wife Sarah ran through the house alerting the family (their daughters Anna, Sarah, Grace, Mary and Ellen) and servants. John and Sarah, Anna, Mary, Grace and Ellen, as well as the servants ran out and stood on the lawn outside the house. Within 10-15 minutes, Anna, Mary and Grace had gone off somewhere; young Sarah had not been seen at all.

Ellen feared that at least one person had gone back inside: by this time, Ellen's brother-in-law Milt Hopkins (whose house was about 400 feet away) and others had arrived. A ladder was put up against the burning house, and, miraculously, the men pulled an unconscious Anna from a window on the second story.

Meantime, as a servant directed men through the first floor, two bodies were found: Grace and Mary, dead. It is possible that they didn't understand the severity of the fire and went back in to try and rescue valuables, or that they sought warm clothing.

It was after 5 a.m. that the first fire equipment began to arrive from Carmansville and Manhattanville. Finally the house collapsed, and when the flames subsided, the third body was found: that of Sarah, beneath the ruins. Newspaper accounts say she was burned beyond recognition, her limbs entirely destroyed. She may have returned to grab a warm wrap or coat.

The three who perished were Sarah, Mary, and Grace.

From a newspaper account (New York Times, Jan. 15th, 1855):
> Anna is at the residence of Mr. Connolley, and is slowly recovering. Her throat is thought by Dr. Elliott to have been burned, and is quite sore. She has not yet been told of the loss of her sisters. Her sister Ellen visited her this morning, and although quite overcome herself, the brave girl controlled herself so perfectly as to appear cheerful and gave no suspicion of the dreadful reality. When she left Anna's room she very nearly fainted in the arms of Mrs. Connolley.
>
> Yesterday the bodies were at the house of Mr. Hopkins. That of Sarah was not shown. That of Grace was said to be little changed, while the features of Mary were almost lifelike in their expression, with not even the hue of death. She seemed rather to be feigning asleep in tableau, and still retained the remarkable beauty of her life."

The family were devastated: their home was leveled, their belongings gone, yet this was nothing compared to losing the three precious lives. Several days later the funeral and burials were held. The funeral was held at Augusta and Milt's house, and according to the New York Times, upwards of 500 people attended. The girls were buried in a family tomb on the estate. On the 17th, Madame Chegaray's School (where Fanny had been the day of the fire, and from which Grace had graduated the year before) hosted an address honoring the girls. The Rev. Prof. McKee, who knew all three girls, gave the address.

Describing the funeral the day before, Rev. McKee said,
> "There they lay before us. Mary, with the strange, unearthly beauty of the dead, upon her face, calm and placid, as if a deep slumber had fallen upon her; - and Grace, with her grand intellectual head, the "palace of a soul," majestic with thought and feeling; - and Sarah, the single-hearted, frank, and pleasant girl, I loved so well once to meet in these halls, a charred ruin! What a sight! What a scene!"[4]

---

[4] Extract from Rev. Prof. McKee's Lecture, before the Young Ladies of Madame Chegaray's School, the Morning After the Funeral of the Misses Haven, printed by C.S. Francis & Co.,

Fanny and Ellen's sister Augusta and her husband, John (Milt) Hopkins opened their home to the Havens until the Haven house could be rebuilt.

From all accounts, the fire started in the northwest corner where the kitchen and laundry were located. The servants were new, and had been ironing late that night using irons heated on a range that was connected to the boilers. Shortly after the fire alarm was sounded, a neighbor saw the two girls who had been ironing, fully dressed on the side of the road. This led many to believe that they had been careless and were responsible for the fire. John Appleton Haven attributed the fire to a probable overheating of the registers.

Excepting one son, Langdon Henry Haven (who had married and moved out in 1846), Augusta, who lived nearby, and Anna and Dr. Sweetser, the Haven family was now composed of the parents, John Appleton Haven and Sarah Langdon Haven, and John, Ellen and Fanny. It is possible that the bond between Ellen and Fanny grew much stronger after the fire and the deaths of Mary, Grace and Sarah.

Almost immediately, work began on a new house.

252 Broadway, New York

Illustration 6: John Appleton Haven.

Illustration 7: The original Ft. Washington house that burned in 1855.

Illustration 8: Ft. Washington house from the opposite side; the foundation level was a full story in height.

Illustration 9: The rebuilt Ft. Washington house. The figures on the porch may be John Appleton Haven, with one of his daughters to his left.

Illustration 10: Fort Washington, Haven house, the same view as in Illustration 9, but from further away.

Illustration 11: Fort Washington, Haven house, looking down drive. The porch on the left can be seen in Illustrations 9and 10 on the right side of the house.

Illustration 12: Another view of the Fort Washington, Haven house driveway.

Illustration 13: Ft. Washington bedroom (possibly Fanny's) showing photos of the Pugh plantation Madewood on the wall (just to the right of the bed).

Illustration 14: Fort Washington, Haven house interior room.

Illustration 15: Another interior room, Fort Washington, Haven house.

Illustration 16: Ft. Washington, Haven house, stairway and hall to billiard table.

Southern Connection: The Pughs

Years before the fire of 1855, John Appleton Haven established a business relationship with Thomas Pugh of Louisiana.

Thomas Pugh was one of three brothers (Thomas was a half-brother) who came from North Carolina to Louisiana's Bayou Lafourche region to make their fortune in cotton and sugar cane agriculture. The Pugh brothers tried to out-do one another in building their houses.

Thomas' plantation home, Madewood, was designed by the architect Henry Howard in Greek Revival style, took eight years to build, and was constructed of lumber and bricks harvested or made on the property. According to Laughlin's GHOSTS ALONG THE MISSISSIPPI (American Legacy Press, 1968), Madewood's walls are from 18 to 24 inches thick, made of over 600,000 stuccoed bricks fired on the property. Beams are of 14" heart cypress, and the interior has 20 rooms of which two are massive halls.

Thomas Pugh married Eliza Foley, and they had 8 children who survived to adulthood. Before he could see Madewood finished, Thomas succumbed to yellow fever on Oct. 31 1852 (the same year Harriet Beecher Stowe's book Uncle Tom's Cabin was published in Boston). Eliza Foley Pugh successfully managed Madewood for over 30 years after Thomas died.

Thomas and Eliza's second son, David, was born in 1828. At age 18, in 1846, he writes a letter to his mother from New York. At age 21, in 1849, he writes his father Thomas Pugh from New York and mentions that he has seen Mr. Haven. In August of 1850, Thomas and David are in upstate New York, for what was then called "taking a cure". For them, the cure was to rest far away from the horrid heat and mosquitoes of Louisiana in New York: it is quite possible that they saw the Havens along the way. Thomas writes Eliza, and describes David as having chills, which may mean David had malaria:

> "Of David, I will write first, for of him I know you are most anxious to hear. For the last week he has all the time been doing badly. In this time he has had three chills and a fever almost every day. But today he is manifestly better being free of fever and with some appetite.
>
> He began to take quinine yesterday afternoon and will continue to take it every three hours all day today. This course will I hope stop the fever and then we shall have nothing to deal with but his ugly cough and the old complaints. The cough is already some better and I hope after which the other malady will yield likewise."

M

The undersigned respectfully solicit your attendance at the Three Masked Society Balls, to be given at the Orleans Theatre as follows:

Wednesday, 23d February,

Friday,------ 4th March,

Tuesday,---- 8th "

Your obedient Servants:

J. A. BORDUZAT,
A. SHREIBER,
P. W. COLLENS,
C. E. FORTIER,
CARL. WEYSHAM,
E. V. FASSMANN,

} *Committee of Invitation.*

Orleans Theatre,   February 1850.

Illustration 17: Invitation to three events at Orleans Theatre, 1850. On the back Ellen Haven Pugh has written that her brother John Haven attended, which indicates John Haven had come to New Orleans on Haven & Co. business on behalf of his father, John Appleton Haven.

Illustration 18: Madewood, year and source unknown.

Illustration 19: Madewood from the bayou, 1885.

23

Illustration 20: Madewood from the rear.

Illustration 21: Madewood 2009 (photo by John J. McInerney, Jr).

Illustration 22: Detail of a pillar at Madewood 2009 (photo by John J. McInerney, Jr).

Illustration 23: Thomas and Eliza Foley Pugh; Thomas Pugh died in 1852.

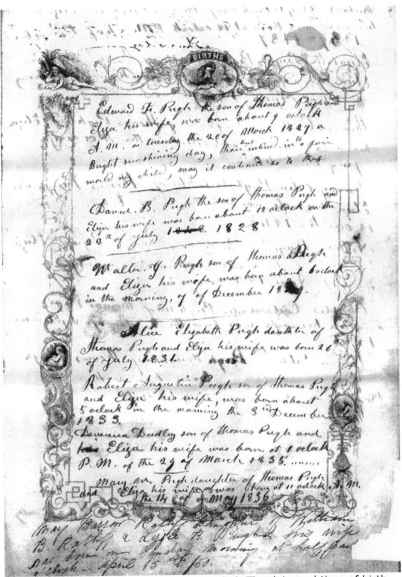

Illustration 24: Madewood: births recorded. The date and time of birth of each of Thomas and Eliza Pugh's children was recorded in the Pugh family bible. David is listed second, and was born on the 27th of July, 1828. The bible was published by Harper & Brothers in New York in 1846, and includes a table of weights, coins and measures. (courtesy of Della Haden-Dirickson).

27

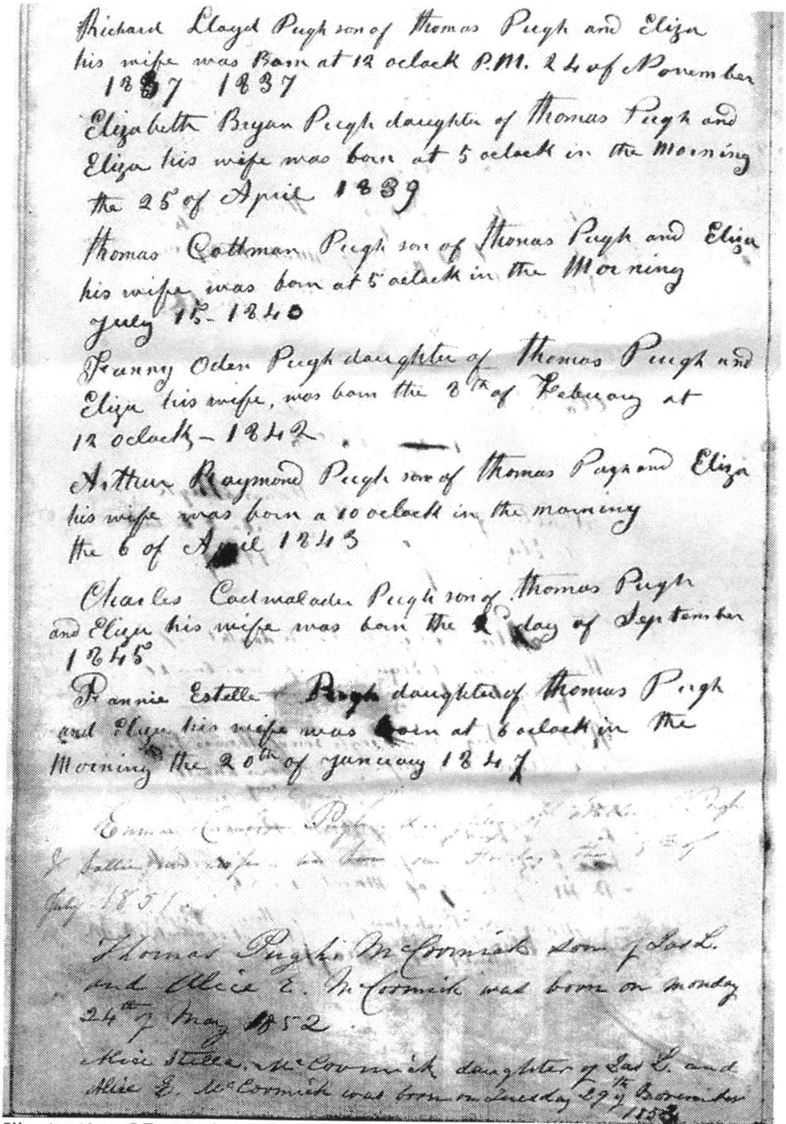

Illustration 25: Madewood births, 2d page (courtesy of Della Haden-Dirickson).

Illustration 26: Eliza C. Foley, photo courtesy Della Haden-Dirickson.

Illustration 27: Eliza Foley Pugh (photo courtesy of Della Haden-Dirickson).

Illustration 28: Eliza Foley Pugh, photo courtesy Della Haden-Dirickson.

Illustration 29: Eliza Foley Pugh, inscription on back: "With Mama's love to Ellen, Eliza May 1888".

Illustration 30: David Bryan Pugh.

David and Ellen (1856-1859)

In the winter of 1856, only about a year after the fire, Sarah (Ellen's mother) writes Ellen,

> "Am very glad that you have heard from Mr. Pugh. He is at home undoubtedly by this time -- if you ever write to him again give our love to him and compliments to his mother."

By the spring of 1856, Ellen and David seem to be corresponding regularly. Sarah writes,

> "I am happy to hear that you have heard from Mr. Pugh. – and hope his letters are agreeable, you will probably hear from "the Bayou" tomorrow."

In July of 1856, Ellen is visiting relatives in Portsmouth, N.H., and she receives a letter from her mother saying that John Haven (Ellen's brother) and David Pugh have just returned from their trip up the Hudson River. Sarah also says there is still work to be done on the house (it has been about 18 months since the fire):

> "The House progresses and many of the doors are hung – there is still a great deal to do."

In a letter from 1856 that has no month or day on it, Sarah writes:

> "...your father and I would like to have you go to the White Mountains, see Lake Winnipesaukee etc. and then see some of the beauty and grandeur of New Hampshire scenery provided, a suitable party is formed. Mr. Treadwell will go and I hope your aunt and Emily – you two, and I have no doubt but David Pugh will go..."

By summer of 1857, there is no additional mention of David Pugh, but the girls were busy with visits with friends and family. Ellen went to Sharon Springs, N.Y. with her aunt and uncles (Alfred and J.Woodward Haven) and cousins on her father's side.
Fanny went to Sheffield, VT and Marblehead and the Swampscott, MA area with friends. The girls' grandfather on their mother's side, Henry Sherburne Langdon, died at age 91, but their mother assured them that they needn't return from their respective summer visits:

> "You have received information of your grandfather's death. I take my pen to tell you not to return - his remains will be taken to Portsmouth - he was always a kind father - I never heard him speak an unkind, or quiet word to one of his children – his temper was a most lovely one ...a more patient, gentle sick and infirm man never breathed in this world...his long life is unstained and not a single vice or bad habit."

From the end of summer 1857 through the beginning of 1858 there are few letters, because the girls were together most of the time at home.

Meantime, in Louisiana, David Pugh bought out his mother and siblings of a half-share in a plantation located about a mile above Thibodaux (about 17 miles below Napoleonville, where Madewood was located). The half-share was part of Thomas Pugh's (David's father's) estate, and David paid his mother Eliza $15,000 down with notes to pay her the rest ($67,000) in the form of annual payments over the next eight years[5]. Thomas Pugh and Richard Darden had purchased the plantation, known as Energy Plantation, in 1840 for $39,800. It was described as follows: "13 by 80 arpents, 1 mile above Thibodeaux i.e., 1100 acres, 700 of them arable." This purchase may have been David's attempt to establish himself as a legitimate grower in his own right, in preparation for asking for Ellen's hand in marriage.

In January, Fanny visited with her mother's relatives in Albany, the Judge Amasa Parker family. By the summer of 1858, Fanny visited Sharon Springs, N.Y., where Ellen had been the year before.

In November of 1858 David Pugh writes Ellen from St. Louis while on the way to Louisiana from N.Y. (his trip took 10 days, including 18 hours stuck on a sand bar). His tone is intimate, calling her "dear Ellen" and describing "those sad feelings constantly arising, from quitting you". The first of a string of love letters, Ellen numbers each in light pencil ("No. 1", "No. 2", and so on). By this time they are engaged to be married in July of 1859.

In his letter (labeled "No. 3"), David reveals that he has told his mother of their plans:

"She not only gives her consent to our engagement, but bid me to assure you, that she will be very happy to receive you as a daughter and will do everything in her power to make her home a pleasant one for you. Her only fear is, lest the sudden change from such a one as yours to ours, may prove too great for you."

Eliza Pugh's comment about the "sudden change" was prescient, as were some comments in letter "No. 8", Dec. 29th, 1858 from David to Ellen ("they" refers to Ellen's parents):

"I did not know they would find it so hard to part with you. And yet, there is a reason why I should wish to remain with my mother, of which I have never informed you.

My father, when on his deathbed, told mother, that if I ever returned from France, I would be the one to look after her interests... But she is willing that I should go away for the summer

---

[5] According to www.measuringworth.com, the purchasing power of the half-share, which totaled $82,000, equates to over $2 million dollars in 2008 dollars.

months… So we can arrange to pass the time, from the first of June, till the first of October, near your father and mother."

In February 1859, Ellen's uncle and aunt, J. Woodward Haven[6] and Cornelia Griswold Haven, visited Louisiana. David met them and spent a significant amount of time with them, taking them to two operas and a grand ball, and then to Madewood. Mrs. Haven stayed with Eliza Pugh while David and Mr. Haven traveled to meet planters with whom Haven & Co. had business.

By June 2nd, 1859, David writes from New Orleans that he is on the way to Fort Washington, and he states that his sister and her husband hope to arrive in New York by the 1st of July (the wedding date was July 7). This is the final letter from David to Ellen before their marriage and Ellen labels it in light pencil "No. 34".

---

[6] J. Woodward Haven was John Appleton Haven's youngest brother and partner in Haven & Co.; the J. Woodward Haven's lived in New York City.

Illustration 31: David Bryan Pugh.

Illustration 32: Ellen Haven Pugh.

39

Separations (1859 -1860)

On July 9th 1859, two days after the wedding, Ellen's older sister Augusta writes that they eagerly anticipate seeing Ellen in about two weeks. She describes the Havens and the family friends as missing Ellen terribly:

> "Carter[7] said there seemed a great void, which could not be filled, that he did not remember ever being at the house when Fan was home without you."

On July 10th, Fanny writes Ellen at one of Ellen and David's planned stops on their honeymoon, "I shall not tell you how much I miss you as I am afraid you would drown yourself if you knew it."

Ellen paints a word picture for Fanny in her letter from Niagara of July 31st:

> "The edge of the rocks seemed to be scalloped in that the water fell off in a number of Falls all joined together. We were made aware of our nearness to them by a gentle misty spray that seemed to envelope us. At our feet the rainbow was arched and I really believed myself in the clouds as I looked down upon what before I have always looked up to the Heavens for and the spray increased my illusion as forming the cloud through which I was peering.
> The roaring of the waters as they rushed through the rapids and down the fall, the sunlight rendering some of the water brilliant and dazzling in the extreme, the mist, the rainbow, and the heavy green of the water showing the depth, giving an idea by color of the great mass and force of the water, all made an impression of the sublimity of the Divine presence which the services of the most impressive churches, a hundred in a day, could never produce…
> The (rain)bow from here was beautiful. It was a bow upon spray. Each curl and roll of the spray as it swept so gracefully and majestically away carried with it a section of the bow, a curve of mist crowned with a halo, faded only to be succeeded instantaneously with another.
> It was one of the most fairy sights I ever witnessed, it was a rainbow and yet it was no rainbow, only mist and colors. I wished so much that you were with me dear Fan."

From Niagara, Ellen and David went to the White Mountains, Quebec, and to Portsmouth, N.H., where there were many relatives on both the Haven and Langdon sides. At the conclusion of their honeymoon travels, roughly the end of August, they returned to New York for a final visit of about six

---

[7] James Coolidge Carter, founder of the N.Y. law firm Carter, Ledyard, was a very close friend of the entire Haven family. Carter attended Harvard with John Haven (Ellen's brother) and tutored the Haven children. He visited the Haven house at least weekly for many years, was considered a son and brother, and the family friendship endured to his death.

41

weeks before heading south to Madewood in Louisiana in October. Although David had purchased Energy, he was still at Madewood, helping his mother manage the plantation, and it was understood that he and Ellen would live at Madewood.

In mid-August, Ellen writes Fanny from Quebec, touching on the impending separation:
> "I cannot bear the thoughts of going so far from you all. If we were going to live in New York I should be very happy but to go so far this winter worries me terribly whenever I think of it.
> I do not tell David how much I dread it for he is very fond of his Mother, it is his <u>home</u> and he says he is looking forward so much to taking me there. Perhaps it won't seem so difficult after I have been home this time."

On Oct. 3d, 1859, Ellen leaves New York for Louisiana. She, David and Fanny spend the last few days together in New York City.
Fanny writes on Oct. 5th,
> "It seems so strange my dear Nell to think that this letter must go off so many, many miles before it reaches you ...However I shall send it off in hopes that it will be at the plantation awaiting your arrival."

Ellen and David pass through Cincinnati to Louisville, KY by Oct. 8th. Ellen feels the loss of Fanny acutely, writing,
> "I did long so to have you with me...the very quiet and beauty of everything made me feel homesick...a few quiet tears in the dark made me feel better when no one could see me. I wished so much that you were coming down to pass the winter with me."

Ellen's mother tells her on Oct. 11th to have courage as she embarks on a new life:
> "...my dear Ellen Eustis, you have gone away from us, have formed new connections and have to call a strange country your home...- but keep up a brave heart..."

On Oct. 16th, Fanny writes Ellen that
> "We have been imagining you today at Mrs Pugh's and I suppose you had a family gathering."
About the rooms they shared at home, Fanny
> "...arranged them as best to suit my widowed condition. I have lots of room but I would willingly give up some of the drawers and nails to have my old Nell back again. I came very near crying over some of your old hair bows..."

On Oct. 30th, Fanny reveals how much losing Ellen means to her as she describes her feelings of a month ago, when she and Ellen shared a room in N.Y.C. just before David and Ellen's departure.

"I lying in a graceful attitude on the bed was watching you (though you did not know it) with half shut eyes and wondering if I should remember every line and shadow of your face till I saw you next June. I didn't tell you how full my heart was then, or all the evening for fear of dissipating the little courage I had left and moreover it would not have been very flattering or pleasant for David to know how much I dreaded your departure."

As late as February 1860, Fanny still feels the loss acutely:
"You don't know dear Nell how much I missed you when I returned home last Friday. Mother was very glad to see me but when I went up to take off my things it seemed as if you ought to come rushing into our room. You see I am not even yet reconciled to your marriage."

By early April, Ellen had given birth to their first son, named John Haven Pugh after Ellen's brother[8]. Fanny may not understand the demands of Ellen's new charge, writing, on April 4th,
"If you can possess yourself of Dickens' last book do read it. I think parts of it very beautiful, there is more pathos in one page of his than sixty of Thackeray's, though I suppose the latter does not aspire to any such reputation, his forte being satire. The book is called "A Tale of Two Cities"."

The burden of a new baby was not expected to prevent Ellen's journey North in June. Fanny writes on April 7th,
"I keep counting the weeks and Sundays now before you will be here. Be sure you start as soon as possible, for we are all very anxious to embrace Baby and his Mama."

On April 14th, Ellen's mother Sarah suggests that Ellen come North by water rather than by land.
"Why don't you come on in the steamship, I would not, but, you all like any mode of traveling and therefore I ask the question. You would have much less fatigue and I think you would be more comfortable with the baby than by coming on by land."

Ellen's father weighs in on April 22nd:
"I hope this will find you fully restored to health, and making your preparation for an early journey to Fort Washington. You must be careful not to make too much haste. Have your health well-established before you leave home, choose the best and most comfortable route and do not fatigue yourself on the journey."

---

[8] All references to child-bearing are couched in euphemisms (pregnant as "sick", for example). Sarah's advice about baby's garments, each of which had to be made: "Be very careful that you never have any of your little garments lying around. And never sew on them in the presence of the gentlemen."

And on April 27th, despite the Haven house being in somewhat of an uproar due to its being painted, cleaned, rugs being laid and carpenters at work, Sarah promises Ellen that by June,

> "I shall have the South room upstairs arranged for you and your husband, then you will have your nurse and child around you and we shall get along very nicely." And, Sarah has "had my Crib brought in to arrange for your baby, I hope he will enjoy it and have as many pleasant, healthy naps in it as his ancestors have, rather his uncles and aunts."

By May 19th Ellen writes Fanny that she has recovered from a bout with dysentery and that her trip will be a bit delayed. On May 26th, Ellen is literally counting the days till her trip home. She is particularly anxious to see her father, because he was seriously bruised when thrown out of his carriage.

> "In twenty one days now we start. I should start right off for I want to see Father so much but I have no nurse for the baby and then I thought that the idea of my coming would worry you and Mother as I have to bring David, a nurse and child... I dread the journey but I look forward to the arrival."

Fanny writes Ellen on June 8th but suspects that Ellen has already left for the trip North, which she expects will take about 12 days. Fanny jokes,

> "We are so busying ourselves preparing for a family from the south whom we expect to pass the summer with us. Mother seems to take great interest in the arrangements, I can't conceive why unless because they are southerners."

She closes her letter with,

> "Our next communication will be on our front steps – just think of it."

There are no letters during the period of Ellen's first visit North, but by August 11th, they had left Fort Washington for Rye Beach and Portsmouth, N.H. David made side trips to Portland and Winthrop, Maine. After they returned to Fort Washington, David made a trip to Syracuse, N.Y. and returned to the Fort[9] the 3d week of September. David, Ellen and the baby left N.Y. for Louisiana Oct. 1st 1860.

---

[9] The family often referred to the Haven home and surroundings as "the Fort".

Signs of Strife (1860-1861)

Shortly after Ellen's return to Louisiana following her first visit to N.Y., on Nov. 15[10] 1860, she writes openly about the rift between North and South to Fanny[10]:

> "...But what use is there in my dwelling upon such trivial matters when there is so much hanging over our heads.
> Fanny there is now no doubt but that we are two different nations. You cannot imagine the deep concentrated feeling that exists here. In N. Orleans the excitement is intense and it is increasing every day. The Governor of Louisiana has his proclamation written, although it is not out yet, to call an extra session and even the Bell men[11] all say the state is doomed to follow the others."

On Dec. 2nd, Sarah tells Ellen,

> "There is now a great deal of excitement and trouble. God grant in his great mercy that it may all be removed and that our country may continue to be the great country it is now."

Sarah again touches upon the issue on Dec. 13th:

> "Everybody is anxious and troubled as well we may be, the amount of the matter seems to be that the country is governed and has been for a long time, by its passions. However, I cannot help it one way or another, so I will say no more."

Ellen writes Fanny, probably in late 1859 or early 1860 based on the content, describing how incendiary events had become down South. Ellen has been caught up in the southern sentiment:

> "A rumor instantly spread that there was an abolitionist in the cars. The excitement was very great and the people rushed to the cars in a body to take him out and kill him. The conductor seeing the great crowd coming, sounded his whistle and started before his time but fearing that the next station would be telegraphed he passed through without stopping and took the gentleman safe out of Mississippi, thus saving the man's life.
> A meeting of the South Carolinians in N. Orleans was called at the St. Charles. Mr. Darden was invited to attend. He says every man signed his name to die for Carolina rather than submit to Lincoln for president.

---

[10] In this same letter, Ellen mentions that she put "the baby's christening dress upon him" and took him visiting." The christening dress has been restored by a textile conservation company that described the dress: "This beautiful christening gown is made of cotton fabric and embroidered cutwork...All of the stitching is done by hand with tiny and even stitches. The back closes with 4 tiny buttons. There is a drawstring at the neckline and there are 4 drawstrings to cinch the waist."

[11] Presidential candidate John Bell of Tennessee, of the Constitutional Union Party, which supported Union and slavery.

...Thibodaux is up in arms, the excitement round the post office was as if some matter of life and death was pending. A law is going to be passed that all the free negroes are to be turned out of the state immediately.

All this will produce great suffering at the North while the South feels perfectly independent.

Her cotton saves her while all the factories at the North will be stopped. They already talk here of what Forts they are going to arm, etc. I believe a great deal of suffering and trouble are pending.

Everybody is more savage and more savage and I do wish that N. York had not disgraced herself by going for Lincoln or else that I was not a New Yorker for I don't think the Lincoln party are right and I shall be caught up next."

On Jan. 1st 1861, Fanny makes it clear that she doesn't want to get into a discussion about the difficult topic:

"About politics dear Nell I shall not speak – of course we should differ and there is no use in discussing the subject. Of course we are all intensely interested in these gloomy times. Father feels it very much, is really unhappy about it."

On Jan. 6th, Sarah writes,

"I think more quiet, peaceable exhortations are needed, no one needs any stirring up. War is a very serious calamity and a civil war frightful."

After Sarah writes urging Ellen to come North by summer so Ellen can give birth to her second child in the comfort of the northern climate and surrounded by family, Ellen writes Fanny (Jan. 8th) that David doesn't approve. Her feelings may have been swayed by his feelings, which were as strong for the South as they were against the North. In any event, it is clear that Ellen feels David, as the husband, has the final say:

"Our movements are so uncertain that I am very much afraid that we will not come on this summer. I hope against hope. David says I must remember that I have but one home which I do not seem to consider. That this is his home which he has for me. He would certainly take me north but that in case of sickness he thinks his wife's place is at her home.

I suppose that he is right but I liked mother's plan and I do not look upon it in the light that he does but I think it is unreasonable in me to persist in what my husband thinks had better not be."

By early February 1861, conditions have deteriorated to the point that Sarah is concerned about whether their letters will be opened, and she touches on the idea of using a "flag of truce" to get letters through:

"I presume you will write as soon as you have decided on your plans for the summer. If things remain as they are, I presume no letters will be private, as one liberty after another is taken and should there be war, of course all communication will be cut off. A flag of truce might venture with the letter, but, it is not likely you or I can avail ourselves of this way of communicating."

Meantime John Appleton Haven is enough concerned about conditions that he tells Fanny she must cancel a trip to Washington:

"...comes Father to my room, says that as there is so much political trouble at Washington and at the South that he does not think it a pleasant or a safe time for me to go, that he should be anxious about me and in fact preferred that I should give it up."

On Feb. 14th Sarah reiterates her concern about their ability to communicate:

"Now too, when each letter you receive or we receive may be the last certainly for the present and I certainly shall not write if my letters are to be opened or pried into in any way."

By March 11th, Sarah has heard enough from Ellen and David that she feels she must weigh in (happily her instruction to burn the letter was not met):

"...My dear Ellen, we have avoided purposely writing to you and David on this sad, very sad state of our country, sad it is that we should throw away the many and wonderful blessings God has given us. We know that any remarks made now, on either side, tend only to increase the irritability that is already upon many minds and perhaps create bad feeling.

We love you and David and your dear child too dearly to risk any statement of that affection, we can retain it for one another and yet differ in many of our opinions.

You have pursued a different course, you write to each of us on this subject. I will make a few remarks, then write of something else, though I wish you to understand that we are thinking and talking of nothing else.

There was a great deal of forbearance shown and kind feeling evinced toward the south, till she took forcible possession of U.S. property of every description, threw down, trampled on, insulted and fired on our flag, thus disgracing us, north and south, all over the world. Then there was a great change came over the feelings of all, men and women (be quiet and listen to me, your mother). Remember Ellen, I lost a dear, darling brother defending that very flag against foreign enemies. That flag which our great uncles and grandfathers still held over their heads, though suffering from hunger, thirst, nakedness and cold, never faltering in its defense, it never touching the ground unless the poor fellows who have it lay down to die. I don't care whether there were stars and stripes upon it, or, lions or dogs, or, trees that were on it. It was our glorious flag, the flag of the Union, which George Washington fought under and for, and gave it to us to keep unsullied forever, with his parting blessing.

...We think it better not to write on this subject and it is decidedly better that you should not.

...Now, my dear, dear child, you know I am no politician, but, I know right and wrong and now is the time to show ourselves Christians, if we are such. Try to quiet ruffled spirits. Judge no one, let us soothe the wounded feelings, if we do not, where is this to end? I do not ask you to change your views, but, I do desire you to reflect and after so doing, I know you will think with me that it is best not to write about these things.

If you read the little I have written quietly, I'm sure you will think I am right and that I have written you the truth. What motive could I have in thus writing but, the love I share to my children.

...When you come to New York my dear children, you must come loving north and south alike -- you will burn this letter."

On April 11th, Sarah urges Ellen to write about her feelings, but to stay calm:

"If you feel at times as though you wished to write to me concerning the awful state of our beloved country, it is best you should do so, endeavor not to become much excited on the subject, either in thinking, speaking or in writing to me. I know it is very difficult so to do, but, try, for your own sake."

In the same letter Sarah digresses to revisit the subject of war:

"Of course, my dear children, no one is thinking or speaking of anything but of our poor destroyed country, of probable war and its train of horrid evils, therefore, it is very difficult to refrain from speaking to you of it all, but, it will do no good, therefore, we must be still and resigned to whatever we have invited to come upon us.

...We all wish very earnestly to see you, but, I don't believe we shall, for I apprehend a great trouble in the country, still men's minds may come down and we may be as we once were."

War (1861- 1865)

By April 16th 1861, the war is adversely affecting parts of the South. David writes Ellen from New Orleans,

> "The city is all in confusion since the war news from the north, and companies are leaving fast for Pensacola. You will have seen from the papers that Lincoln has called out the northern militia, so that we shall now have fighting in earnest – God alone knows where it will end.
> Money matters are worse than during the panic. Particularly bad for me, having to borrow money."

That same day, April 16th, Sarah tells Ellen to

> "...remember, even if we cannot write to you, that we all love you with our whole hearts and your dear husband too..."

Two days later, David writes Ellen again from New Orleans,

> "We are in for it now, my dearest Ellen, and shall fight hard for our homes and rights. Ultimate success depends upon the action of Virginia -- whose convention is now in secret session, and must decide within a few hours. It has already, according to the telegraph of last night, refused a contingent of men to Lincoln, and decided that northern troops shall not pass through her boundaries.
> This is a good move, and if she will join us within Forty eight hours (such a standstill will make Lincoln pause) in less than 60 days we shall have 150,000 men concentrated in the vicinity of Washington under President Davis."

David continues, writing of business and domestic issues, and adds a sentence at the close:

> "There has just come in a dispatch that Virginia has seceded. Hurrah!"

Fanny, who has just returned from a visit to Albany on April 30th 1861, writes Ellen in earnest about the war:

> "This horrible war occupies all my thoughts, indeed we think and talk and read of nothing else. There seems so little for a woman to do at such times, she seems so helpless compared to men.
> A society has been formed out here of all the ladies with very few exceptions, called "The Fort Washington Army Relief Association", the object being to make garments of all kinds for the sick and wounded at the hospitals as well as those in service, also lint bandages etc. etc. The first meeting was at our house last Thursday, some forty ladies being present.
> The next was at Mrs. Smith's on Monday and hereafter we are to meet in the basement of the Presbyterian Church, that being the depot for the reception of work garments, hospital stores etc.

Tomorrow I shall get my supply of work and do all I can in the way of sewing. Mother is deeply interested and intends to sew at home, if she does not meet with the society.

An immense meeting of the ladies of the city was held yesterday at Cooper Institute, some five thousand being present. Perhaps ours will be a branch of this, which is very systematically organized.

All our friends and many even of our neighbors are sending husbands, fathers and brothers to this war, scarcely a family but has some member either in Washington or on his way there. Charles and Washington Connolly have gone, the latter as Surgeon's mate, Ben Church and three of Mrs. William Ward's sons.

Henry Elliott[12] has enlisted and will leave in a week or two, also Melville and Shep Knapp. Colonel Asboth has either joined a regiment or is recruiting one himself. I am not sure which, not having seen him for some time.

The greatest interest is felt by all classes and the enthusiasm and excitement are intense. Anyone who is not here can form no idea of it, it is really fearful. It makes me perfectly wretched and heartsick. I have such a dread and horror of war, and yet now there seems no other alternative."

David reports on May 2nd that federal ships are rumored to be on their way to blockade the port of New Orleans, and two weeks later Fanny laments to Ellen,

"How little we thought two years ago at this time that we should ever be placed in such a position, that a terrible civil war was to come between you and us. Even now I can hardly realize it and the events of the last month seem like a terrible dream to me. Though the excitement of the first week after the attack on Fort Sumter[13] has subsided, yet the deep settled purpose of the people far and wide increases every day.

The war is in every one's heart and on every one's tongue, nothing else is thought of or cared for. It is very, very hard that we should have to be on opposite sides."

On May 18th, John Appleton Haven still believes Ellen will be able to visit them at Fort Washington by late summer. May 20th, Fanny writes a long letter in which she touches upon the difficulties of being on different sides, as well as about her acceptance of Ellen's embrace of the southern position:

"There is no use in my discussing the causes of this terrible war, for we view the question from such totally different points of view.

---

[12] The Elliotts were good friends of the Haven's.

[13] April 12th, 1861, South Carolina's Fort Sumter was a federal (Union) fort in a Southern state. The Confederates attacked Fort Sumter, and the fort was surrendered. This marked the start of the civil war.

Of course there are and will be many things said and done on both sides that true, sensible people will condemn, but it seems to me as if the South must be willfully blind when it accuses the North of commencing the war, when the North has actually done nothing but bear and bear with the South and let them do everything their own way, till the flag of the Union was actually fired on and then you surely cannot wonder that the whole country rose to a man to defend it.

I not only think Lincoln has done everything that he ought to, as the President of the United States, and not as the head of the Republican party, but I consider James Buchanan a traitor to the trust reposed in him, that he did not at once and decidedly put down secession when that detestable little South Carolina first started it months ago.

But I have so often resolved that I would not speak on this subject with you that I must stop at once, before I say anything that should wound your feelings, for there is no use in disguising the fact that my dear old Nell has utterly and entirely espoused the cause of her new home and that the feelings, convictions and prejudices of a life time have vanished to give place to the new principles that two short years of southern life have inculcated. It seems very hard for me to realize the fact but I suppose it is natural and it certainly is best that you should be able to do so, you would be very unhappy I fear if it were otherwise."

Sarah, apparently upset at comments Ellen has made, writes on 22d May, "Can you so easily be made ashamed of your relations, that "were it not for your father and mother" you would be entirely alienated from the north –".

Responding to Ellen about the April 19th confrontation in Baltimore, when federal troops attempting to pass through the city on the way to Washington were obstructed, harassed and jeered by secessionists, Sarah claims,

"As to the firing on those brave men who were marching through Baltimore to Washington, under a flag of truce, which I always thought even Satan himself respected (perhaps I may in some cases except the English) you say they were attacked by the mob. Who incited them and threw gold amongst them to encourage them -- who turned out to assist them but, the Maryland guards, who are in Baltimore, but the seventh Regiment is here -- one gentleman wrote to the lady in New York, to whom he was engaged, boasting of the part he had taken against them, she answered him that he could not have offered him a greater insult and she had nothing more to say to him.

I think they were the bravest men I ever heard of -- having offered no provocation, being without one unkind feeling at first, toward them -- with arms in their hands that they could have defended themselves with and yet not doing so -- seeing their friends killed by their side -- and yet not defend themselves, because, they were without orders so to do -- they shew that self-control, forbearance and capacity to govern themselves, more than any set of men I ever heard of."

By May 27th, word has reached Fanny that letters may not get through. She writes her "Dearest Nell":

"A few days ago we saw in the papers that the southern mails would be stopped, if not at once certainly by the first of June. This seemed really too hard to bear, it is bad enough to be separated, but not even to hear from each other is too much. Even now I cannot realize it and it seems as if letters must pass between the North and South some way or other. John told us on his return from the city just now that letters would be sent till the thirtieth of this month, so I rushed up stairs to write at once..."

May 28, 1861, Fanny writes from Fort Washington,

"My darling Nell,

I feel as if this may be my last chance to write to you and my heart is so full and we have been thinking and talking of you so much today that I must send a few lines by tomorrow's mail. I cannot think even now that we shall not hear from each other, people say that the mail will pass through Tennessee or come by Houma. I intend to hope for the best. If not (I mean if we do not hear from each other for long months) do not allow anything, never mind what happens, darling sister to come between you and us, you have been ours through long, long years and we cannot give you up. I never can, come what may. Our thoughts will be constantly with you through this summer and I shall have faith that the good God who has been my consolation and support through so many hard trials, will bring us together again in his own good time."

At the bottom of Fanny's letter, Sarah adds a note:

"After tomorrow, I see there is no communication even by my poor pen. Whatever happens, remember to the last gasp of my breath, I am your loving mother.

May God forgive Jeff Davis for all the ties he has separated, all the hearts he has broken -- surely I never can."

Sarah alludes to something Ellen wrote,

"...and I do wish very much to see you again -- now it is best that we do not meet, with our different feelings and views for we should be very unhappy. We must wait for a great change in all of us -- I have not heard from Portsmouth for some time, I presume they were all occupied as we are.

The first New Hampshire regiment passed through here last Sunday. A flag was presented them here... -- poor fellows, they have all left good comfortable homes, country homes what for?

My dear, dear child good bye – may the Almighty being, who has us all in his holy keeping, guide and guard us and in his own good time permit us to meet again in all full affection.
Tell David with my love to think well and what for, before he resigns his liberty, life and property.
Always your dear mother of my children."

On May 31st John Appleton Haven expresses concern about Ellen's coming confinement with her second child, and hopes she will come North as soon as she and the new baby are able, despite the Civil War:

"...We feel exceedingly anxious for you in this time of great trial and we pray that you may have strength and fortitude to carry you safely through your confinement. In what way we are to receive tidings of you, now that the mail will be discontinued I know not, but your husband must endeavor to devise some plan, either by private hands, or by writing to some friend in Cincinnati, or in some of the states to forward to us the news of your confinement and of the condition of yourself – and of the little stranger.
...I cannot believe that it will be your plan, or the wish of your husband that you should endure the effect of your climate for a single day after your confinement and recovery of strength enable you to leave the Bayou."

Ellen received her father's letter of the 31st, and writes Fanny on June 11th that,

"The mail from the North I see is now returned to the dead letter office at Washington but Southern letters may get North. I pay the Confederate postage and they go as far as Virginia. I also put on a northern stamp and this will take the letters through the North, provided it can drop from one mail into the other. I will continue writing in this way until I am sick."

About her father's suggestion that she come North, she tells Fanny it is impossible:

"Father wants me to come on in August. Why Fanny, it is utterly impossible. Southerners are not going north this summer. They cannot get there, if they wanted to. The rooms Father tells me that there are engaged, there must be some mistake about. People who have always passed their winters in New Orleans and their summers north may have gone on but real Southerners are not going north from this state...Besides if everything else was feasible David has no money and next year things, in this respect, will probably be worse, for sugar, if saleable at all, will bring nothing. I am gradually making up my mind to two years separation certainly."

On June 30th, Fanny writes Ellen that they have received news in a letter from David that Ellen gave birth to her second child, a girl (Alice). It has been a month since Fanny has tried to send a letter and she (Fanny) last received a letter from Ellen on June 14th, that was dated the 4th:

> "I do not see why if that letter came through, others could not have done so since, but we read in the papers how daily hundreds of letters to and from the seceded states, were stopped and sent to the dead letter office.
>
> ...Mother and I had been discussing for some days the chances of getting a letter to you by express and on this very day we found in the paper, that it is to be allowed to Adams' Express company to carry private and business letters to the south. So perhaps after all we shall sometimes hear from each other, which is a comfort that only those who have been four weeks without hearing from loved ones can appreciate."

Ellen writes Fanny Sunday July 21st 1861 to say she is,

> "...very thankful to God for those three precious letters received through Adam's Express. When our little baby was born David wrote to a gentleman in the city asking him either to telegraph or send by express his enclosed letter, and if there was any doubt about either mode of communication, to try both. I know I should know whether you had received the letter by a return answer. If you received it I know you would send a letter to me by the same conveyance. We have now only one boat a week so David waited for her return trip to send his letter. He said he had no idea that it would ever reach you."

Later in this letter, Ellen worries that it will be a long time before she sees Fanny again:

> "Dearest Fanny I do not expect to be able to see you all for several years. You have not thought of this but I am trying to look it bravely in the face. This war is going to impoverish North and South.
>
> The expenses must be met. Father may not pay anything but the depreciation of property and the heavy taxations which you will have to sustain of course reduce his property. New York is never going to be what it has been even if the South is subjugated for southern trade and opulence will be extinguished.
>
> We must, individually, meet the expenses of the war and the revenues from our places must necessarily cease. All we can make must be expended upon our places and upon the war expenses. We shall have to stay at home for several years and live upon the produce of our place I know. (I speak of David and myself individually). This is my view of the subject, be the war long or short.
>
> I long to see the face of each one of you but the Almighty wills it otherwise. Never cease in your affection for me my dearest sister, for you will always have my very warmest love and when you can write to me remember how precious and valuable your letters are

to me. It is too expensive for me to write you often and therefore we can hear from each other seldom."

Ellen misses Fanny despite the war and despite having a new baby, as she makes clear near the end of the letter:

"I should like this Sunday afternoon to be able to walk into our room (you see I cannot but keep saying our) and find you at your writing desk."

Sarah sends a letter on July 22nd 1861 in which she laments,

"...I see nothing pleasant or good to look forward to, our own individual blessings we have great cause of gratitude for, but, we are forced to think of the thousands, yea, tens of thousands of our countrymen and women whose homes are destroyed, whose lives are in jeopardy every hour, little innocent children's fathers being killed every day, everybody's business destroyed, not laid aside, to be taken up again when, if ever, or for long years, this horrid, unnecessary, infamous war shall cease. It is a very sad thought that we cannot hear from you.

...We are all well, still the one engrossing subject fills all our hearts and minds -- may heaven help us in all my dear child, we are all passing rapidly to our eternal home. ...Your father is very unhappy about our country -- he takes hardly any interest in anything else, it disturbs me greatly to see him so, as, I feel about as bad, we bear our burdens as well as we can."

On August 14th, Fanny writes Ellen that the Havens just received letters from Ellen and says,

"I too Nell have tried to reconcile myself to what is quite clear to me, that we shall not see each other for a long time, but I shall not mind it so very much, if I can have the consciousness that you are well and happy and that David is with you. If it were otherwise I should be very miserable, but I have seen so much unhappiness in the world, that I like to gather up all the crumbs of happiness that I see scattered about and I think you have a goodly share. So we must be content or try to be with the knowledge of each other's physical welfare and we shall appreciate more highly the joy of being together one of these days in this world or some other."

By late summer 1861, Fanny writes that their father's income has been seriously affected by the war: his real estate holdings have plummeted in value, and he suffers from non-payment of Southern debts and the interest on mortgages he holds.

Sarah is increasingly disturbed by the war, describing, at the end of August,

"Men's blood spilled like water, women turned to fiends, children educated to hate each other and revenge is the foundation of their education instead of "goodwill to all men"."

In mid-September Ellen writes that she and David plan to leave Eliza Pugh's Madewood by spring, because they are tired of living under Eliza's roof. David has been managing things for his mother at Madewood, and feels he has been criticized by his siblings and misunderstood and under-appreciated by his mother.

On Oct 19th, Fanny writes Ellen that

"This separation dear sister is indeed very hard to bear, but I comfort myself with knowing that you are well and happy and have your husband with you and try to look forward to the time when we shall be together again for I know the day will come sooner or later.

Let us keep up brave hearts Nell and hope for the best in this trial as we have had to do in so many others."

In her letter of May 11th 1862, Fanny expresses concern that she has not heard from Ellen in eight months:

"Your last dear letter is dated the 17th of September received by us on the 19th of October. I wrote that very day having an opportunity to send by private hand to Fortress Monroe and to you under flag of truce by Norfolk.

... These eight months of silence and separation have been very long dear Nell especially as other people have heard occasionally from their relatives and friends. But I am sure your silence has been obligatory and now that you can write you will dear Nell, for, a Mother yourself, you can tell how a Mother's heart yearns after the child so far away and so very dear.

I am sure the darling sister whose face looks up at me now from my desk, in the room where we have passed so many happy hours together, still loves me as in those old days and will never let anything separate her in heart and affection from those to whom she is so dear. We think and speak of you so often Nell, and I am glad that I can tell you that we have been well and are so now and I earnestly hope that we may soon hear the same news of you and yours. I shall look for a letter by each mail that arrives, and even if none comes I shall think that it is some powerful necessity that prevents you from writing and shall (I think) write you as often as I can.

... Not knowing if this will reach you or not, I enter into no home details, but look forward to the time when our correspondence can be free and unrestrained again.

Good bye dear Nell and God bless you and all dear to you.

Your ever loving sister

Fanny"

From a letter of June 10th, Fanny and the rest of the family learn that Ellen had indeed been sending letters during the intervening months:

"I wrote a letter to Mother some two weeks ago which I sent by private hand to the city and it was to be forwarded from there by private hand to New York as I did not wish to send any letters through any mail which Butler[14] had opened.

Since I received your letter, however, my mind has changed for this reason. I wrote home to you all many letters during the fall and winter, I sent by flag of truce, by certain other routes which I heard of and which were expensive and lastly by Tampico, paying two dollars for one letter.

You have never received any of these letters; now I will write by your direct mail fearing that this last effort of two weeks since may prove unreliable likewise. I received your letter of the 25th of January, the last which I did receive, likewise another sent by flag of truce.

We are cut off entirely from the city, Butler having stopped the boats and to day I hear no one is allowed to go in or come out of the city. A friend of ours brought this news yesterday on his return from the city where he went, I presume, in his own buggy. How this letter is to go I do not know but I shall write it, hoping some one may be able to slip down. We have no mails of any kind now. The occupation of N.O. is a sad thing to us all but of course you look upon it in a contrary light. Butler tightens things around us every day and we feel it as we are so near him and his gunboats, the latter having been in the Bayou, but away from the water courses the state is still free."

Ellen goes on to explain that they are delaying their plans to leave Madewood and move into Energy (located about 17 miles south of Madewood) because General Butler's actions prevent Ellen from getting a nurse for her confinement. If she stays at Madewood, Eliza can help her through the birth. Because the boats aren't moving, Ellen and David might not be able to move furniture and possessions down to Energy anyway.

"I have refrained heretofore from mentioning my expected sickness in order to save you all from anxiety but now N.O. is taken I see no reason why I should not have a chance of letting you hear from me after my sickness.

I shall continue to write to you all, dear sister, so if you do not hear from me remember it is not from any want of affection on my part but that the fates are against my letter, either by communication being cut off or something of a very similar character, sheer necessity only."

---

[14] General Butler, whose Northern troops occupied New Orleans, was hated by the Southerners.

Ellen has her family very much in mind:

> "I dream about you all so much in the night dear Fan that I hate to wake up. Mother is with me often just like life and I get many a secret kiss from her in this way which lasts me for a long time.
> I am going to keep your room ready for you for I know that you will be the only one to come and see me. Kiss dearest Father and Mother warmly for me, tell Anna I shall answer her letter by the next opportunity offering and give my love to the Dr and Milt. Kiss Augusta, the children and tell John if he does not want the infliction of a kiss to accept my warmest love. My love to Lizzie Gray.
> As to you dearest Fanny you know you have my unalterable affection always. Write me as often as you can and remember that I shall do the same.
> If anything should happen to me before we meet, my little Alice[15] I give you. I have told David this. He will support her if something is left to him..."

By mid-August, tensions are running high between David and Eliza at Madewood, but he and Ellen can't move to Energy until Ellen has her baby. Ellen wishes Fanny could come to visit once she and David move into Energy, but she expresses concerns:

> "I wish that I could have you for the rest of the summer. One of my rooms upstairs I have designed for you and if ever I can get it fixed as I want to I shall try to keep it for you.
> I have wanted you so much to come this winter but I am afraid to indulge the idea for you will not want to come among rebels as things might be said to hurt your feelings and that would hurt mine too. I mean unintentional little things, and besides unless matters change I do not believe you could get up here very comfortably. As long as warfare is being carried on in this neighborhood I would not consider it a safe home for you.
> I am in my own home, my children's interests are here, so are David's and as I have taken him "for better or for worse" my interests and my feelings are here. We are happy in each other, we are pledged to each other for life and for death, eternal life, and we must take our fate together. I leave everything else in the hands of God...Dearest Fan write me as often as possible for you do not know how pleasant it is to me to receive your letters."

On September 2nd 1862, Fanny opines about some of the war troubles Ellen has written about, and asks Ellen to consider asking their mutual friend, Henry Elliott, who is a Northern soldier and is in the New Orleans area, for help if and when things get bad:

> "After some consideration dear Nell I have decided not to answer what you call your "bulletin" as my first impulse prompted me to. I

---

[15] Ellen's first daughter and second child, Alice DeBlois Pugh.

made up my mind long ago that I should never write on the subject, you asked me not to and I told you I should not: I think it was injudicious, though quite natural in Augusta to do so, though I do not know what she wrote and I know she did not mean to say anything to wound you, still nothing can be said on the subject without wounding.

Do not imagine my dear sister, however, that I or any of us were in the least hurt by your letter to me, indeed, we were all glad that you write it and were much interested in every word you wrote.

It is sad and terrible to read as much misery and ruin, but they are the unavoidable results of any war and you must remember that they are not confined to your section but that sorrow, bereavement, misery and suffering too terrible to think of are now wide spread and almost universal throughout our unhappy country and that it is the mad action of the South that has brought us to this state, but for that we might still be a happy, peaceful, united country.

But it grieves me more than I can express that you, my darling sister, should be exposed to any of the actual miseries of the war. I do so wish that we had you safe with us again, though by and by to be sure we may be in the same condition. Is it quite madness in me to wish or ask that you and the children, if David cannot leave, should come on to us for the present. I don't think there would be any difficulty now in getting on from New Orleans and back again in case of any emergency. Do you think it would be practicable? Nell, also I want you to remember that in case you should get in any trouble there, where the aid of any of our officers would serve you, that Henry Elliott is now in New Orleans, Lieut. Col. of the 1st Regt. Louisiana Volunteers, promoted after the battle of Baton Rouge, from his former position on Gen. William's staff. He is a personal and particular friend of mine and I think would do anything, consistent with his duty, for a sister of mine so keep this in mind in case of any emergency, he knows Gen. Butler, Com. Farragut and many other of our officers. Speaking of General Butler I want to say that I did not and have not at any time approved of his famous proclamation[16] of which you have spoken several times.

On September 18th, Ellen gave birth to her third child, a daughter, Grace Haven Pugh.

On Nov. 5th 1862 there is a report from Brigadier General G. Weitzel about insurrection in Thibodaux[17] that affects David and Ellen:

---

[16] Possibly Butler's General Order 28, which was intended to force Southern women to show appropriate respect for Northern soldiers, failing which a woman would be treated like a common prostitute.

[17] The War of the Rebellion By United States War Dept, Robert Nicholson Scott

Brigadier General, U. 8. Vols., Comdg. Reserve Brigade. Maj. George C. Strong, Asst. Adjt. Gen., Deft, of the Gulf, New Orleans, La.

Headquarters Reserve Brigade, In Camp, near Thibodeaux, La., November 5, 1862.

Major: In still further confirmation of what I wrote to you in my dispatches of this morning relative to servile insurrection, I have the honor to inform you that on the plantation of Mr. David Pugh, a short distance above here, the negroes who had returned under the terms fixed upon by Major-General Butler, without provocation or cause of any kind, refused this morning to work, and assaulted the overseer and Mr. Pugh, injuring them severely; also a gentleman who came to the assistance of Mr. Pugh.

...the entire community thereabout are in hourly expectation and terror of a general rising.

I am, sir. very respectfully, your obedient servant,

G. Weitzel, Brigadier-General, U. S. Vols., Comdg. Reserve Brigade.

Meantime on Nov. 24th, Sarah also mentions Henry Elliott:
"You remember your old acquaintance Henry Elliott. He is in New Orleans, he is lieutenant colonel of the first Regiment Louisiana volunteers (whites of course), his regiment went on this expedition to your Bayou. Whether that remained at Donaldsonville or continued up the Bayou I do not know, when he went away we told him and his mother told me she would write to him to tell him where you were and if he could by any accident of war serve you or you and your husband would befriend him it must be so -- I heard last evening that he was ill in New Orleans when his regiment left, he could not therefore go with it, he however gave a letter to an officer, with whom he is particularly acquainted to either your husband or to you -- that if you could be any protection to each other you would be - - Colonel Elliott will join his regiment as soon as he is able to do so."

On December 4, 1862, John Appleton Haven writes what is for him a lengthy letter to Ellen. He has heard of the incident on the Pugh place, but he doesn't know whether it occurred at Madewood or Energy:
"A few evenings since Mr. John Adams called and read to us a letter from his brother in New Orleans, informing us of the terrible affair on Mrs. Pugh's plantation, your husband beaten, the overseer killed, the interference of the U.S. soldiers, who protected your husband and, restored order, after shooting some of the insurgents and although this story may not be correct, yet is sufficiently terrific to cause us all intense anxiety - we do not know

if you are at Mrs. Pugh's, or on your own estate, or in fact, we are ignorant of your whereabouts, of your health and that of your children, in fact we are without any information about you and your family. "

He urges Ellen to come North:

"I do not suppose that David would leave his plantation and his mother at this time, but he will be willing to have you and the children come on and stay with us till the times are more settled and peaceful, when he will be able to come for you. He certainly will wish you to visit us if he has the least fears of any personal danger to you or the children.

Thinking there is a possibility of you coming to New York I have written to Mr. Adams to look out for a good opportunity, probably a steamer, and to place you under the care of some gentleman, who will undertake to see you are made comfortable on the voyage. If you have an infant, we suppose you have, you will have to take some woman to attend you on the passage - not knowing how you are provided with money I have requested Mr. Adams to supply you the needful to procure such articles as may be really necessary to make you and the children comfortable on board and further to pay your passage, if required to be paid before reaching New York. Your mother has written to care of Mr. Adams, and has furnished with directions for your guidance when you arrive in the city.

When I heard of our Army penetrating the Bayou, I wrote to Lieutenant Colonel Elliott of the Louisiana Volunteers, to extend to you all the aid and protection he could. He wrote however that he was not well enough to accompany his regiment to the Bayou but he had written to an officer, a friend of his, and requested him to do you any service in his power.

I shall write to Mr. Bell, the provost marshal, whose sister Ellen was the first wife of my brother George, and ask him to leave a protecting eye over you..."

He closes with a warning:

"...it may be a long time before you could return, you must think of all this and do what you think best, you know we write for your good only and that we should rejoice to see you.

You would be required to take the oath of allegiance to the U.S. and you must be very cautious not to express any opinion to favor the other side – this must be carefully received in New Orleans and on board ship. Otherwise you may have trouble."

The very next day, Dec. 5, Sarah writes,

"...a night or two since Mr. Thomas Adams, of New Orleans, sent us word that you had met with great trouble, that your husband had escaped with his life, but that your overseer had died of the injuries he had received -- we presume this occurred on Mrs.

Pugh's plantation, whether you were there, or, alone on your own plantation we do not know.

Events have now taken so serious a character I must write in earnest -- if this is true you better come home to us with your children and remain till your home is settled again, when you can be safe and comfortable there -- when your husband can either come or send for you, whether this separation will be for a shorter or longer time, he knows better than I do.

Every year increases the danger of your return voyage unless there should be peace -- which seems to me farther off than ever. You must stare these evils in the face."

After giving Ellen instructions and information about how she might come and whom to stay with in N.Y., Sarah warns Ellen:

"If you come don't get into any trouble expressing your sentiments during your voyage or, on your arrival. Let nothing provoke you to this."

Fanny also makes a pitch to Ellen in a letter of Dec. 28th. She begins by saying that none of the family have heard any word from Ellen in over four months, and they are very worried.

"Your letters made us very sad and anxious and we are in hopes that you will consent to come to us for the present with the children and even if David could not come with you, in a little while perhaps he could join you or come to take you home."

Fanny also mentions that their brother John Haven is leaving for New Orleans Dec. 30th, and she says they have given him items to bring to Ellen in hopes he will see her.

With John gone, Fanny adds that,

"...I do hope he will be spared to come safely back to us again. Last night I sat up late over the fire in my room thinking mournfully over the happy times of long ago and hardly able to realize that of all our large family I was left alone here – and so alone, you don't know how very lonely and sad and old I feel when I get by myself in my room."

By early February 1863, Ellen has written her father to ask whether she can sell some lots of land in New York City that her father gave her. He explains in a letter of Feb 12th, that given the current conditions in the country, she would stand to lose the property altogether:

..."It is not possible for you to have them sold at present, it being subject to confiscation under the United States law. The deed was legally executed and put on record in your name at the time I gave you the property. I have paid the taxes up to present time, but I do not think that anyone, except some of our immediate family knows that you are the real owner of it.

It is best to keep the matter quiet, and it is possible that it may be overlooked by government and escape confiscation. It certainly would not answer for you now to attempt the sale of that, as no one would take a title from you, and the attempt to give a title would at once expose it to immediate confiscation. I have taken legal advice on this question and have been confirmed in my opinion. I am also advised that if I have made a will, devising to you any property, that it is not valid, in case the law of confiscation is enforced.

We must keep silent about these matters and trust that better times will soon return. At all events, if the lots of land are preserved to you, they will in a few years be very valuable and afford you a fund that will put little John through Harvard College, besides an education for your other children."

This letter also clarifies why Ellen's brother John left for New Orleans:

"In requesting John to go to New Orleans I was interested not only with the hope that he might access some of the debts due to us, but also by the wish, that he should see you and David and the children, and thus be able to inform us of all the particulars of your situation and your plans and prospects for the future. From a personal interview he would be able to furnish us with much more satisfactory accounts, than we would receive by letters.

I doubt if John realizes much, if any sum, from those who owe us, but he will be able to furnish me information about our accounts with Mr. Hewes and others, who have never written us a line since the rebellion was hatched.

As far as I am individually interested, as I am now over 70 years of age, it matters but little to me if I am cheated of large sums by them, but for my children and for your sake I would like to secure what belongs to me..."

Finally in February, the Havens hear news: Fanny writes that Lt. Col. Henry Elliott returned to N.Y. and told them he didn't see Ellen but he saw David. Then a letter arrives from John Haven saying he has seen David and Ellen at their home.

In her letter of Feb. 22nd, Fanny interjects some humor as well as pathos by quoting a letter Ellen wrote when Ellen was twelve:

"I was looking over some old letters last week (crying over them too) when I came across one from you to Grace dated Portsmouth 1844 – nearly twenty years ago. It is printed[18] and changed my tears to laughter.

I make an extract for your benefit: "While I am here I am going to read "Goody Two Shoes". Mind, don't you and Frances fight together".

You mention "Goody Two Shoes" as if it were Rollins[19] History and your allusion to me is anything but complimentary.

---

[18] Fanny means it is not written in the longhand that an adult would use.
[19] Charles Rollins (1661-1741), French historian

O my dear, darling old Nell I wish I had you here in my room again. I was not half good to you in those old times and perhaps I shall never have a chance to prove to you how much in my heart I love you."

On March 3rd, 1863, Ellen writes to Fanny,

"I am very bitter in my feelings I am afraid, if you only knew what an abolitionist is here and how little is done like the general orders which you all see published, seemingly very fair and right.

You will not believe that it is an abolition war and Lincoln tries to deceive you by exempting accepted parishes. I consider it a disgrace to this parish to have been accepted but since she is, do you suppose the acception does us any good? No, all our slaves had left and the army is expressly forbidden to return us any, which law is obeyed very strictly. They are also forbidden to feed them but this law is very strictly disobeyed. Their rations are given out regularly by abolition quartermasters, this we have seen with our own eyes. We have some slaves back but they do not earn the food we give them. David is going to raise some corn so as to be able to pay our own way as we go along, hoping thus to keep things together until the Confederacy gets Louisiana again, I mean this lower part, when I hope for better times.

Mr. William Pugh took the oath because he could not leave here with his family. My sickness[20] was what made David take it. He held out until about the last person on the bayou. His place then began to be sacked, he went four times to the office and back again before he could make up his mind and finally took it to save this place for a home for me and the children. He did not tell me until it was done for he knew that I would never have allowed it."

In the same letter, Ellen describes what her life has become:

"The freight on everything is so very high that I do with as little as possible. You will laugh when I tell you what I had for dinner today. Fried bacon and eggs, also rice. We are out of potatoes, the soldiers digging all. David bought me some Irish potatoes, some mackerel, tripe and pigs tongues but they are detained in Donaldson, why I know not. David has gone up to see about them. We have just enough chickens to lay eggs and set. It is impossible to buy any, the soldiers have emptied the country. My pigeons are all too young yet.

I never liked bacon or rice but I am learning a great many things. I save my pigeons and kill a laying hen when John comes for I want to make him comfortable, I enjoy so much having him with me. He has made me several little visits in his way to and from Mrs. Connolly's. When he goes I shall feel terribly.

---

[20] Pregnancy

We have had some little trouble here with the people, John will tell you about it when he sees you.

When David is away (as he has been trying to get his slaves and fooling about for nothing) I sleep with his big pistol under my pillow. I have learned to fire it. I expect to blow myself up some night.

...I have a lamp from Mrs. Williams' house as no one could procure oil this last year. I made my woman put up all my butter without salt and then boil it and put it away in jars like lard. This I burned in my lamp."

Life in the Northeast must have sounded very different to Ellen. In early April her mother writes about their friends the Fields (of the publisher's Ticknor and Fields) and their travels as well as their relationship with Charles Dickens:

"Mr. and Mrs. Fields and Mr. and Mrs. Beals, reside in Boston. Sarah went with her mother. They board at the Norfolk House in Roxbury in winter and travel in summer, or, pass their time at some beach. They have been devoted to Dickens since he has been in this country, (thrice), Mrs. Fields wrote me of him as he was in private life, as, he was a great deal with them. Sarah likewise, wrote me a long letter about him, it was a very fine letter and a very interesting one."

And from Fanny, April 20th, comes confirmation that social life goes on despite the war:

"Tomorrow evening I expect to go to a wedding and reception. Miss Sara Le Roy is to be married and I am invited. I shall go with Lizzie and shall wear a white muslin dress made with puffs on the skirt and waist and a pink silk sash and pink flowers in my hair. It is so long since I have been to any sort of a party that I already begin to feel nervous and frightened. Mr. Carter will be there and I don't expect to know another man in the room."

By the end of August, Sarah says Fanny will be returning shortly from a visit to Marblehead, MA. She says she would be happier if Fanny delayed her return for a bit due to the residue of tension in New York City from the Draft Riots of July. Sarah is astute enough to observe that politics played a role in the draft riots:

"I am almost sorry she is coming home, for though New York is quiet now, it has been so stirred up that the bad elements which you know have ever been so vile are so brought out that it will take time to make me feel easy. Stirred up too by politicians, who have their own purposes to serve and by very vile men. The draft had nothing to do with creating the riot, it was made a handle of to excite the rioters."[21]

---

[21] The riots were a result of the National Conscription Act, which provided that a citizen would be drafted unless he could either pay $300.00 or provide a substitute. While the war

65

By Sept. 20th 1863, Sarah is disturbed to learn that Ellen is unwell. This Sarah attributes to Ellen's nursing the baby despite a return of her "monthly troubles", i.e. menstruation:

> "In the first place you must wean your little girl immediately, you should have done so the moment there was the slightest appearance of your monthly troubles. You cannot have that and try to nurse a child. You are fighting against nature one way or the other[22]."

She gives Ellen some advice, and then asks Dr. William Sweetser, Anna's husband, to write. The letter below, of Oct 19th, is the only extant letter written by Dr. Sweetser[23].

> My dear Mrs. Pugh
> In compliance with the request of your mother I write you on the subject of your health. The difficulty you describe may arise from different causes, for the discovery of which a fuller account than your letter affords of all the circumstances attending are necessary.
> If you suffer unusual bodily and mentally langour, and depression, undue nervous irritability, and susceptibility to cold and atmospheric changes, with a pale and bloodless complexion, and uncertain and capricious appetite, I should conclude you were suffering from what, in medical language, we term Anaemia, that is from a watery or impoverished condition of your blood. From which I would advise the following treatment. Medical superoxide of iron, called also some carbonate of iron, beginning with 10 grains of this powder three times per day, which may be increased to 15 or 20 grains. Two or three weeks will be sufficient to test its effects. If the bowels are constipated, some stimulating laxative

was viewed by some as a war against slavery, African Americans were not citizens and thus could not be drafted (they were, however, competing with Irishmen for low paying jobs). Many Irish Americans had become citizens in response to promptings from Tammany Hall politicians (who in turn wanted the Irish vote). These Irish citizens found themselves eligible for the draft, and few of them had the financial resources to buy their way out of the draft (more likely they were living in discouragingly squalid conditions). They were furious, and they turned their anger on the easy target: the African Americans with whom they competed for work.

[22] In a subsequent letter of Oct. 29th, Sarah explains why it is important to wean: "You ask me about weaning your dear little baby, I think you ought to wean her at once, if you are regular in your monthly troubles you are liable at any moment to be in a family way again."

[23] Sweetser, William, physician, born in Boston, Massachusetts, 8 September, 1797; died in New York City, 14 October, 1875. He was graduated at Harvard in 1815, received his medical degree there in 1818, and practiced in Boston, Burlington, Vermont, and. New York City. From 1825 till 1832 he was professor of medicine in the University of Vermont, and from 1845 till 1861 he held the same chair in Bowdoin. He also lectured in Jefferson Medical College, Philadelphia, and in the medical schools of Castleton, Vermont, and was professor of medicine in Hobart College, Geneva, from 1848 till 1855. Copyright © 2001 Virtualology™

will be occasionally indicated, as for example, the compound rhubarb pill -- or the pill of Aloe and Myrrh, take no more cathartic medicine than is urgently demanded. If you can do without any it will be all the better.

Diet. Nourishing and an easy digestion, as beef steak or venison steak if to be had. Or fresh eggs, if they suit your taste and agree with you – good bread and fresh butter, or cream toast. Wheat flour is better than Indian. London Porter, a wine glass full three or four times a day -- fresh air and moderate exercise, as by riding etc., added to present amusements and as cheerful and happy a state of mind as circumstances will allow.

Keep the surface of your body and especially your feet warm, and excited by frequent frictions -- and by all means wean your child. Assuming the condition of your system, or of your blood, I have suggested, the above is the best general treatment I can advise. And I sincerely hope that may contribute to your relief.

I sincerely regret the unhappy circumstances to which you have been and are still subjected, and truly hope that more prosperous and happy times may dawn upon you. I often hear from you through Anna and with her deeply sympathize in your sufferings, but the present unhappy conditions of our country must bring suffering to a greater or lesser degree upon us all -- as Anna says she is writing to you, I will leave to her the detailed domestic matters -- Trusting that your children are well and are to you all that you can desire, and with kind remembrances to Mr. Pugh, I am truly your friend

Dr. William Sweetser"

Ellen tells Fanny in a letter of Nov. 17th about her concerns with the coming election:

"I hear it is pretty well understood that Lincoln is to be reelected. This worries me, a four years war I looked upon as something too long but eight years-oh dear, an abolition administration. We shall all be finished up finely by that time."

In this same letter she touches upon their financial struggle:

"The proceeds of our crop, after paying the expenses, we are going to take to pay every debt standing. We mean common debts, not the interest and notes due on our disappeared Negroes and on the land. We never shall be able to pay these.

In Confederate times we had to pay Confederate prices for clothing and feeding our Negroes, for things we purchased for housekeeping and those debts we are going to settle up if we have anything to settle with..."

By the end of November, Fanny receives another letter from Ellen in which Ellen says that while it has been over three years since she has seen any of the family (other than John), it is likely to be longer if Lincoln is reelected. Ellen then delves into the hardship caused by recent "orders" and the oath (oath of allegiance[24]).

"An order has come out in Thibodeaux which is very trying. I do not know what I will do. A foolish order too. All the stores in Thibodeaux are to be closed but six, no one is allowed to purchase anything without getting a permit and a permit is not given unless the person has taken the oath.

If they have not taken the oath they are obliged to take a terrible oath. No man here can take it without disgracing himself. I cannot tell you now all that is in the oath but I know it says you will make no mental reservation, that you will never assist at the Confederates by thought or word and so on. They say it is to bring people "up to the scratch", this is what the Brigade Provost Marshal says.

David says this brigade Provost Marshall told him (Captain Colville) that everybody was going to be made to take the oath. Even those who had taken the old oath, if they were supposed not to be loyal would have to take this new oath if they wanted a permit to buy anything. David is well known, his sentiments are well known to all the officers but they will trust him as he has taken one oath.

I am very much afraid about myself however. I have heretofore got a pass without having any questions asked through the Provost Marshal who is friendly to David. These permits are given through Captain Colville and I am afraid that if they find out I have not taken the oath they will force me to do so or leave.

For instance I have one of those dresses mother sent me at the dressmakers, it was to be done tonight but I could not bring it out without a permit. If I send David to get me one I am afraid they will ask him if I have taken the oath. If I could get a permit like a pass which would last me a month it would be a different thing. If I go into a store to buy a paper of pins I cannot buy them until this passes. The storekeeper says, "I cannot sell the pins without you show me your permit to buy them," I show him my permit. He then opens a book, asks me my name, puts it down, with the pins and the amount of money received for them. I then say a piece of braid, the same scene. All of a sudden I think of a skein of silk, it is not specified in the permit, I forgot it when with the Provost Marshal. I go right back to get a permit and hurry back but will find the store closed perhaps. (The stores have to close the

---

[24] While the original oath of allegiance to which Ellen refers may have differed somewhat from the following, this is probably close to the text of the oath: "…do solemnly swear, in presence of Almighty God, that I will henceforth faithfully support, protect, and defend the Constitution of the United States, and the Union of the States thereunder; and that I will, in like manner, abide by and faithfully support all acts of Congress passed during the existing rebellion with reference to slaves, so long and so far as not repealed, modified or held void by Congress, or by decision of the Supreme Court; and that I will, in like manner, abide by and faithfully support all proclamations of the President made during the existing rebellion having reference to slaves, so long and so far as not modified or declared void by decision of the Supreme Court: So help me God."

moment the sun sinks, sometimes before dark, or they are confiscated). The next day the permit I have for the skein of silk do not hold good, I must get another bearing that days date. Now if I am not caught for a week I am sure to be caught for the next week so I do not see how I am to escape at all. I cannot bring out the smallest thing or make the smallest purchase.

All this is to prevent goods being taken out to the Confederates. Now if I got a permit to buy I do not see but what I could slip them out just as well is if I did not have a permit.

Butler ordered everybody last fall to take the oath or they would have their houses and property confiscated, in fact published that everything on Bayou Lafourche was confiscated and people got their property back by taking the oath. Now it says everybody must take the oath and people are notified to do so, what will be done to them if they refuse, we are all anxious to know. Next week will determine."

John Appleton Haven warns Ellen in a letter of Dec. 1st 1863 that the war is certain to be over soon, and that she and David should position themselves accordingly:

"You may be assured that the contest is a hopeless one on the part of the South, and the sooner you can believe this and adapt yourself to the change of position the more you will advance your own comfort and that of your husband and children."

His real purpose in writing her is to ask her to deliver an enclosed letter to a Mrs. Connolly, who owes him money. He writes again on the same subject on Dec. 23rd , enclosing a copy of the Connolly letter and asking about other clients:

"...inform me what crop is made this year on Mulberry farm, and what has been done with it. Also what crop Dr. Kittredge makes. I would like to hear about him and his family. And how he is managing his plantation. Also please tell me what has become of Mr. and Mrs. Hewitt. I have not heard of them since the rebellion commenced."

He is also concerned about how their plantation is doing:

"I am very sorry that David has had so much trouble with his sugar making but I hope it is now over and that the results of his crop as to quantity and prices will realize his expectations. You must let us know how much sugar he makes and what it can be sold for."

Beneath Mr. Haven's signature, Ellen's mother adds the following, which likely was not well-received:

"My dear Child, I know you are, both of you, thinking as earnestly of us, as we are of you all at this season of the year. Missing each other. Oh how earnestly I wish that you had kept your faith to your country and to your flag, that you had kept your homes and means, your means and I will say and believe, your own self satisfaction. You have lost all these my children so far as I see and gained not even a friend, how many you have lost I know not, if any, you have not lost us, for I firmly believe that in the citadel of each of your hearts, stands loyalty, to the Union, and to the Constitution, like an armed man that no trouble, no losses, no dictator or leaders, can ever conquer. Yet, I have only this entire conviction, neither your language or your acts sustain me in this belief I assure you.

How I wished last evening that you were all here around Augusta's Christmas tree with our other grandchildren. I am afraid your father and I thought more of our absent ones than those that were present.

We enter into none of these things, our hearts are with our faraway brothers, husbands and children and others in your vile holes you call your prisons, starved and frozen even unto that merciful friend called death, and continue to be heartbroken, frozen and starved, we see enough and hear enough and I know enough, without looking in the papers. I hope those men who have ordered and caused our brave, enduring, patient soldiers to thus suffer may endure the same themselves and see all they pretend to love suffer the same, I cannot pray for them. They are in holier hands than mine I am glad to know. I cannot but write thus for only my heart is bursting with all this cruelty. May God in his mercy protect all of you from such rulers, from such power that you have even given to them.

All this weary suffering, wicked war that is almost killing your dear father. His heart is with every wounded, ill man and around every desolate hearth.

War, pain, aboveboard war, we can stand up to bravely, with our whole hearts, if necessary, but malice, cruelty and unheard-of barbarism is too sad even to speak of.

I send you my whole, my true hearted blessing and love, to you, my deluded children and to your precious children.

Mother Christmas Day 1863

May all this calamity soon pass away and may you and David see many happy Christmas days, and your dear children the same."

Ellen writes her father that she believes there has been a sinister plot foisted on them by the Northerners. Sarah writes Ellen on New Year's Day 1864, saying that her father is too ill to reply to Ellen's letter but that he is deeply disturbed that she could believe in such a plot.

In fact, Ellen's father manages to write a postscript to Sarah's letter, after Sarah lets loose:

"He thinks a great deal of your letter, is very much disturbed that you believe such a plot existed as you have written him of. No union officer would dare know of and tell you of such a thing being organized and to be put in operation without causing each person to be arrested and then they ought to be punished severely.

I do not believe there is a person belonging to the North who would know of such a plot, but, would turn the earth upside down to prevent it, what any sane man can tell you such stories for passes my comprehension.

According to your accounts and according to facts your slaves are free, they can come and go as they please, they consider themselves free. What do the abolitionists wish to murder you all for, we cannot imagine.

Your husband and you have strong good sense and know better than to believe these lies. We believe Mr. Lincoln to be an honest and upright man, if nothing else. The whole war has proved him to be this and that he is not malicious or bloodthirsty. Your hating him cannot make him either of these and you know so. You know likewise, my dear child, that if he and his supporters had wished when he went into office, to free your slaves, the Northern states would not have permitted him to do so. All they ever expected was to prevent the <u>extension</u> of slavery. No new state should be a slave state.

The South have had the control of government affairs for very many years. The North consented, because it was right they should do so, they were elected by the people, not because we were cowards. But, when you found the North were to elect their president, determined we should not. Therefore, laid your plans to murder him, if his inauguration could not be other ways prevented by bullying, or, other rough methods. You know all this as well and better than we do.

You know likewise, how few abolitionists there were and how destitute of power they were. The North would not have permitted them to free your slaves. This war has made many more. Nobody wants the slaves here neither did we wish to support them there. The Southern states were never meant to be meddled with - but, the extension of slavery, carried into new states was to be prevented. Your plan is to extend slavery, open the slave trade and govern the north. We will prevent it if we can.

For several years past, if any man (northern man) dared to speak in Congress, he was at once blackguarded - shot, abused and beaten. Since the war commenced there has not been an approbrious, insulting epithet that human imagination could devise that has not been bestowed upon every northern man and shaman. Language used toward them that the lowest fellow at the North would use, but, no one who called himself a man. Much less a gentleman. You have no reason to hate the north, they never wished, never dreamed of injuring you or, depriving you of a penny, or a privilege, you forced them to do so as they have done. Mind my dear Ellen, I uphold not one atom of cruelty from either side and every act of the kind on either side ought to be punished severely, you know it has not been. I think Dr. Dewey or Dr. Parker would have given that man a cup of cold water (the wounded soldier) either friend or foe, if they could have got to him. All the bullying majors on the face of this earth would not have prevented them.

I have written this dear Ellen mainly to tell you not to believe all the stories of plots etc. that make-believe union officers entertain you with. You both know better, this one has too little common sense in it to disturb you for a moment. No tongue can tell how I have entered into your trials and troubles and privations and we still do. You must however keep yourself, for all our sakes, as quiet as you can. You seem to forget that "all power belongeth unto God", that we ought to trust in him. You will make yourself very conspicuous in all this trouble, you must keep yourself composed and prepared for any events you cannot control and prevent. This takes care of yourself, your husband and your children.

You know we love you very much, know that your character and principles are of the very highest order. Don't lose these, or, depart from all self possession. You must hate no one.

A happy new year to you, dear child, to David and your dear little children. How earnestly I feel this wish, I cannot express to you. When you see Mrs. Pugh, remember me kindly to her. She is also meeting with many sad trials."

Below Sarah's message is a note written in John Appleton Haven's hand:

"My very dear child. It is New Year's night, your mother, Fanny, John and I are around the marble center table in the drawing room and all talk of you and your husband and children and wish you were here, but that cannot be at present and can only wish you a happy new year. Trusting that ere its close you will have peace in your borders, and be in the enjoyment of more tranquility of mind than you seem now to have.

I am glad you had my letter for Mrs. Connolly, hope she sees it and will give me a satisfactory answer. I wrote you a week since enclosing a duplicate, if she has sent an answer to my first one, you need not send my second. I am too unwell to write much, or I would comment upon the contents of your last letter.

Will now say only, do not allow your mind to be so muddled, excited, as nothing can be more absurd, than the ridiculous reports, hints and surmises that have been poured into your ears by that wonderful Captain Colville. And the other wise man who hints that abolitionists at Washington were concocting a conspiracy to have you all murdered...it is too foolish even to contradict it.
As ever your father
JAH"

Due to the poor crop on David's plantation and the ill effects of the war on all economic activities, David has made arrangements to lease his plantation and is trying to find work outside the plantation.

Then, on March 28th 1864, John Appleton Haven urges Ellen to consider coming North for the summer:

> "From your remarks in your late letters, I learn that your plantation will be rented this season, that David will be much of his time away from home, and that you will necessarily be left alone with your little ones for most of the summer - Your own health, and the constitutions of the children, after a siege of the measles, whooping cough, and other ills, with which your situation is surrounded, seem to make it desirable that you should make a visit to us this summer, if agreeable to you, and you can arrange to do so."

He warns her that if she comes, she must keep her Southern sentiments to herself:

> "...In case you visit us, I must caution you to be most careful not to give utterance before any persons here of your sentiments in relation to the rebellion, the administration, the war, or any of the topics connected therewith.
> Any remarks coming from you will be eagerly listened to, caught up, and circulated in this neighborhood. Where we have enemies of the Union and the administration I must enjoin upon you to be most reserved and careful on your voyage, and while here, not to give utterance of any expression, that would commit you to the reproach of being a <u>rebel</u>, or the <u>disgrace</u> as you would think it, of being a <u>Unionist</u> –
> For your own interest, as well as for the sake of your father and mother and all of us here, it is most necessary that you be most careful and guarded in what you say – otherwise you will do us great harm."

Fanny replies on May 12th, 1864 to a letter of Ellen's, saying that Ellen has completely misunderstood her father's letter to her of March 28th:

> "...your letter came and grieved us very much. I do not see how you interpreted Father's letter to make out of it what you do. You have misunderstood it and turned and twisted it from beginning to end.
> If he had not desired and wanted you to come of course he would not have asked you. And if we all had not wanted you, we should not have said so. I think it was quite natural in Father to say that he hoped you would not express yourself openly about the war or your views of it. There could be no use your doing so and it would only be unpleasant for us to be discussing the subject all the time when our opinions are so entirely different.

If I came to Louisiana I should expect to keep quiet on the subject and not obtrude it. That is all he wanted you to do I presume. Of course we should never allow you to be insulted in our house, though I do not see who there is to do it. I don't know what harm you do us in any way, and Father never imagined for a moment that you could.

If I was going out to L- I should think it quite natural for a person to say to me "You will have to keep quiet about the war, if you are going out there; be careful that you don't get into trouble". I am sure we all said so to John before he went.

Father and Mother felt very badly about the letter. I told them I thought you had written hastily, having just received his letter, that when you came to read it over you would probably understand it differently and write again in a few days, but no other letter has come till mine by Mrs A."

On May 20th, Sarah sends a long letter to Ellen in which she speaks at length about their sorrow over Ellen's feelings; on religion; on bringing up Ellen's children; and she adds a final word about David:

"Tell David I am sure the time will come when he will love us all again. I believe he will even better than before. When this time will come depends on your rulers. They cannot but see the sorrow, the suffering in the wickedness of this war. What they have done and accomplished whether of vice, or, virtue has been done for all eternity. Their hearts must break or become human ere long. When you see Madame Pugh give her my kindest wishes and best respects.

Let there be no recrimination my dear child. What I have said about the letters need not be referred to again. Let all our words and feelings be pleasant ones. We know not, but, that each letter may be our last."

By June of 1864, Ellen is pregnant again, with her fourth child: Sarah writes how sorry she is to hear about it, especially given the situation with the war and economic hardship.

On June 17th, Fanny includes some war news about mutual friends of theirs:

"Speaking of Boston puts me in mind that poor Mrs. Adams is suffering great anxiety about Boylston, who was wounded and taken prisoner on the 6th of May in the battle of the Wilderness. He was shot in the leg and was trying to limp off the field when another ball struck his other knee and he fell on his face and was instantly taken.

For three weeks she heard nothing of him and then came a letter from him from the rebel hospital at Gordonsville. It was three weeks getting to her or nearly as long. He said he had just been put in there and was kindly treated, but owing to his wound having been so long unattended to and he being out on the field without proper food and shelter, the wound looked dreadfully and he feared he should lose his leg. Perhaps by this time he has died. The papers say that all the officers have been sent to Mason, Georgia and they say there is no hope of an exchange of prisoners till the campaign is ended.

Did you see that Tom Stevenson, Hannah's brother was killed? He was Brig. General[25]. Lizzie felt his death very much."

On July 9th, David writes Ellen from New Orleans, with war news about their horses and ponies:

"It was only yesterday that I succeeded in getting "Laidie" clear, and now I shall remain for today to get back that little pony of Uncle Patrick's which was taken off from us when the Federals left in June of 1863 (you may recollect that our guard Colbert rode him off).

I found him by accident, in the hands of the merchant here, and shall take out an order for him, in one of the courts.

Nothing of great moment going on here -- except the departure of the 19th Army Corps for the North, which is now going on -- I presume they will go to Richmond."

Sarah writes on July 19th 1864 that she is sorry about the pregnancy as well as about the troops who are ever-present:

"I do not understand why all those troops are placed around you continually. I am well aware that you are near the terminus of the railroad and presume this must be the reason.

I am very sorry that you are to look forward to another confinement next spring. I earnestly hoped you would have no addition to your family, certainly till all these calamities are over."

Sarah adds,

"One thing I regret and ever have, that I allowed you to go back to Louisiana when you were last here. I have wished you here ever since on my own account only, for I know you would have been very unhappy if you had been here through all these horrid times. I feel now as if you had endured enough for your share of this war..."

Finally, Sarah admonishes Ellen for having assumed that the Havens believed a published story about an altercation on the Pugh place:

"In your last letter to me, you are very severe and accuse us of not believing your account of that shameful, violent attack on David. You must desire to create trouble out of everything we write you about, to draw such an inference.

---

[25] From: Report of Maj. Gen. George G. Meade, U.S. Army, commanding Army of the Potomac. May 4-June 12, 1864--Campaign from the Rapidan to the James River, "... Fredericksburg road, and, finding the enemy on it, had handsomely driven him across the Ny, losing on the 10th the distinguished Brigadier-General Stevenson."

You (neither of you) must do so anymore. I have always reflected with great comfort on the perfect truthfulness of my dear children, every one of them, with the one dreadful exception[26]. You possess that virtue faithfully my child and because you have thus written and you seem to believe that we doubt your word, I thus write."

July 21 1864, Ellen describes some of the devastation she incurs from the war for Fanny:

"...At first, after great politeness to the Major in command who, by the by, got down from his horse and tried to kill a fine hen of mine with a long stick when he came up to ride around our pasture to select it for his camp, I procured a guard and the Major promised Mr. Guillot one at the sugar house which he ought to have furnished but which he did not although promising every night and every morning he would. I was finally thoroughly disgusted.

David did not come home until Tuesday not being successful in his business. I telegraphed him Sunday but he never received his telegraph until 10 o'clock Monday night.

Meanwhile our fences were all burned up from the Bayou to the sugar house, our warehouse, a fine large building, stripped of the outside planking and the underpinning of brick and mortar pulled away so that the building tottered. Most of all my chickens and my young turkeys with which I had taken so much pains having seventy odd (turkeys I mean) were most all killed, the pickles of our garden pulled down and our melons and tomatoes stripped, our water cistern emptied and everything turned topsy-turvy.

Mr Guillot set up night and day at the sugar house, the soldiers coming down five or six hundred a day. They broke into the sugar house and stole about 40 gallons of very fine molasses put up for use and most all that was in the cistern which was left for the Negroes.

A Capt. happened to come down when some were in the cistern and Mr. Guillot took him in the sugar house. He never even reprimanded the men. At night they went down armed with axes and poles and tried to kill our hogs. Mr. Guillot and I went most distracted.

I fed my guards finely, gave them a decanter of whiskey and a pot of strong coffee each night and the consequence was that all was pretty safe, they catching some men at night, carrying them up to headquarters etc. but the Major withdrew them promising to send me fresh ones.

This he never did and scenes were enacted in front of my window which were perfectly disgusting. Tuesday I made Abram sentinel and Mr. Guillot and I after consultation decided one of us must go and see the General! Mr. Guillot said he could not leave and he wanted me to go. Meanwhile our Negroes, after their dinners were

---

[26] The "one dreadful exception" is her son Langdon Henry Haven, who apparently shamed the family in 1859.

stolen, buckets and all, the first day, refused to work and went into their cabins. They excited the soldiers by telling them we were rebels and so were Julia and Abram (my standbys) as they refused take money from us.

The roads were awful, the mud most up to the horse's knees. I started, determined if David did not come to see the General and ask for a guard at least. David came and we drove at once to headquarters, David made his statement but the General wanted to see me so I dismounted and entered into particulars.

We received no satisfaction, I saw at one glance the General was no gentleman, a foolish and self-important man. He sent us to the Colonel commanding the post. No satisfaction. We went home.

The men all fell sick, the commanders did not mind this but when their horses began to get a disease called the rot they then moved up above us to general Weitzel's old camp.

While David was absent a Captain brought his sick boy and wanted me to keep him in the house, at first I refused but the Captain said so much that at length I admitted him, then the quartermaster came and wanted to hire a room. I refused but finally I found he was the man from whom David got our horse so I admitted him. After they left the smell was so awful that David wanted me to go up to his mothers, said that I might be taken sick any minute but I refused to go. He went to help mend our yard fence and it made him sick.

The smell is still horrible but we have had all hands up at work for nearly a week trenching and opening our large ditches which the troops filled up.

Our pasture is ruined, it is now a mud hole, I have turned all our stock into Mr. Williams' pasture on consent of the lessee.

It will take a good many hundred dollars to repair our damages. Our new corn was stripped likewise. You can imagine I had my hands full until David came home, I never was so glad to see anybody in all my life."

Adding injury to insult was the state of the crop and the weather, as Ellen describes near the end of this letter:

"...Our cotton is good for nothing, David is not even going to spend the time hoeing it. The only crop we shall make will be corn. We have had a daily rain now for nearly 2 months."

Ellen adds a postscript July 22d:

"David has just returned from the Provost's. They will seize David's riding horse but our three year colts are exempted and our mares with young colts. We shall have lost three horses but we exchanged one with this quartermaster and paid him some to boot so that we might have one horse to drive every day."

In August, Sarah writes of her concerns regarding the presence of the soldiers and Ellen's pregnancy, and expresses regret that Ellen ever went south:

> "I wish you to write to me and say whether you intend to remain where you are through the autumn and winter months, exposed to the trial of having these troops continually on your premises and in your neighborhood, why is it?
>
> Is it because you are at the terminus of the railroad? I do not think your position is one for a lady in your situation and to anticipate giving birth to a child in.
>
> ...I do not think your situation is even a respectable one. Why in the name of wonder must you go to these Majors, Colonels, and what not? I do not understand this at all. Your husband is in New Orleans a great deal of the time and you entirely alone. Obliged to have a sick man in your house for you to take care of. Completely in the power of these lawless men night and day.
>
> I am very sorry you went to the plantation, for the life you have endured has been a terrible and lasting injury, I fear, to your health. I cannot bear to look forward to the next year for you."

John Appleton Haven sends a letter to Ellen Dec. 16th 1864, indicating that he is hurt that David doesn't write him, and that he (Mr. Haven) is looking out for their welfare. He suggests that he is willing to have David take on his Connolly account and profit from collecting on it. In this way, Mr. Haven imagines that some of his money can be recovered and left to his daughters, and that David can earn some money.

> "But you know you have much of my love for yourself and children, and for David, whether he wishes it or not. I wish he would sometime write to me, he need not speak of the war, but he can have no difficulty in finding enough else, in which I should be very glad to hear from him.
>
> He and you know that there is a large debt to do to me from Mr. Connolly - now if David is disposed to take charge of my interest there I should be very glad to have him do so. Mrs. Connolly has always expressed her wish and her intention to discharge this debt and I think if David would see her, he could ascertain whether it is in her power to make my payment this year, and also ascertain what are her plans and her prospects for the future.
>
> Now if he can obtain anything now, or hereafter, from the Connolly estate, I wish to give it to my daughters - Anna, Augusta, Ellen and Fanny or say in five shares, one to David for his management of the business and one share to each of the four daughters."

By early February 1865, Fanny wonders if Ellen is "in her room", meaning that she is close to giving birth again. In fact, Ellen gave birth January 25th to her fourth child, another daughter, Mary Haven Pugh.

On Feb 16th, John Appleton Haven writes Ellen again on the subject of David and the Connolly debt: David has misconstrued Mr. Haven's initial letter to mean that he (David) should pursue legal action. Mr. Haven says he meant no such thing:

"...It was not my wish, or intention, that he should resort to any legal steps for coercion of payment, nor for him ever to intimate, or threaten any measures of that sort. But for him, as a neighbor, and in a friendly spirit to approach Mrs. Connolly and say to her, that if it were in her power to make any payment on account of the debt, it would be for his and your interest that she would do so and that you had my written authority for saying so. And further that I had written that it was not my intention to resort to any legal steps to enforce any payment. Certainly not, if she evinced a disposition to pay as far as she was able, even if it were a small sum for the reduction of the debt.

I think David might in this way manage the business so as to benefit you and him and without exciting any unfriendly feelings - but you and he must be the best judges - I confess I see nothing to object to in such a course.

When you write again let me know something of the condition of Mr. Connolly's estate. Whether any and how much crop was made last year, and … How many hands are retained on the place, and what will be done on it the present year."

In the same letter, Mr. Haven says that they have gotten the news about Ellen's having given birth again:

"We were all delighted to receive David's letter announcing the birth of your third daughter."

By mid-March, 1865, Fanny is optimistic that Ellen will come North soon:

"We are all quite excited at the prospect of your coming on and talk about it every day. The other evening Mother was very busy at work on a queer little flannel blanket that she was adorning with a large patch. John asked her what she was fixing and she said it was a blanket for Ellen to wash the baby on. John was much amused and I asked her if I should get out a cake of soap and a towel.

You mustn't leave any of the children behind, we want to see them all."

On March 26th, 1865, about two weeks before the civil war ended, David was drafted and was doing what he could to be exempted from service. He had either to come up with a medical excuse or to purchase a substitute. He writes Ellen from New Orleans:

"...He (a Colonel) contented himself with writing a recommendation for an examination and turned this over to a medical board, which board contented itself on Wednesday with denying any authority -- and what is more any disposition -- to act. My application here was made through Mr. Ross, who knew the chief surgeon, then I hunted up a substitute -- found one at $500 and was thinking of raising the money to pay them, when Mr. M. came to me, saying that he had "pitched into" the old general for breach of faith, (I had given Mr. M. some emphatic talk) and had been promised an exemption.

So I got my certificates and handed them over to him. ...Thus I have been kept from day to day, waiting and trying to save the $500 which we can scarcely spare. And the result is as you see. An exemption would clear me altogether, whilst I am told that parties here are so much in fear of being drafted again at the end of this year, as to be purchasing substitutes -- at high figures -- for the war."

On top of this worry, David had no luck in finding someone to rent their land:

"...Now for our place. There is not a man to be found to take it. I have tried everywhere -- not only myself, but all my acquaintances. Not an individual, who even had an idea of renting, has escaped me, but all to no purpose. Yesterday I hunted up a couple of Irish men who had been anxious to spend a lot of money, and am to receive an answer from them this morning -- scarcely think it will be satisfactory however. There is plenty who would like to cut the wood off the place but that is all."

David secures an imperfect medical letter on March 27th[27]:

"New Orleans
LA March 27, 1865
Captain,
My friend Mr. David B. Pugh has been drafted in the parish of Lafourche. He is utterly incapable of performing military duty and a short session in bad weather would destroy him. He is suffering from an internal injury received at sea some years since. His certificates which I deliver to an officer have been misplaced. I ask it as a personal favor that he may be exempt. This I do because I find no officer here who can act in the case. I am Sir very perpetually yours..."

---

[27] Based on a letter from Fanny in May of 1865, David apparently paid the money for a substitute, only to find it was not needed: "I am so provoked to think that David had to pay such a price for a substitute and a few weeks later none were needed, it is certainly very aggravating."

Illustration 33: Energy plantation, site of Ellen's greatest struggles during and after The Civil War.

PARISH OF LAFOURCHE La.

Provost Marshal and Judge's Office.

Thibodaux, _____ 1863.

Instructions to Guards upon Plantations.

Guards will not interfere in any way, with the management of slaves upon Plantations, (the owners of which have signed the Contract with the United States Government) or with rules or regulations made by the owner, or overseers, except so far as may be necessary to enforce the terms of the contract, keep order, and insure discipline ; Negroes upon such Plantations, will not be allowed to go beyond the limits of the place without the written permission of the owner or overseer ; but must remain upon the Plantation, and work well and faithfully six days in the week, and maintain a respectful and subordinate deportment to those having charge of them ; and on the other hand, the negroes must be well fed ; comfortably clothed and provided with proper quarters, and, if any negro shall return to, or remain upon the Plantation, after the signing of the Contract before alluded to and shall leave the Plantation without written permission before mentioned, the Guard is instructed to cause such negro to be taken back to the Plantation, and to be put at work, and no parties either Civil or Military, will be permitted to harbor or employ such negro.

Obedient and willing negroes are not to do the work of refractory or idle ones, and the Guard will not fail to bring or report turbulent or indolent negroes to me for punishment.

Guards are directed to offer all fair and legal inducements to negroes, in whatever condition of service they may ~~have formed~~ be found, to return to the families and Plantations to which they belong.

No cruel or inhuman punishment to negroes will be permitted, and if the Guard shall neglect to report such cases to me, and it shall afterwards come to my knowledge, they will be severely dealt with.

The negroes are to be made to understand that they are at work under the protection of the General Government, and that they are not to be abused or illtreated, and on the other hand, that the Government will expect from all able-bodied negroes full days work each week, and that the same punishment will be inflicted to disorderly negroes upon Plantations as if they were in the army.

Dr. Allen Dedrick, of Thibodaux, has been employed by me to attend the sick upon Government Plantations worked by me, and, upon application of any of the Guards will furnish such medicine as may be needed. Food, and clothing, will be supplied by myself in necessary cases.

I will give written orders for the recovery of stolen horses, mules, carts &c., belonging to Plantations, and all doubtful or disputed cases of identity of ownership will be submitted to me for arbitration, and in no case are soldiers to be permitted to take property from loyal citizens within this parish, without written authority.

Enlisted men will not be allowed to visit any of the plantations, without permission from those having charge of the place, unless they have written permission from me, and, I would more plainly caution the Guard to avoid too great familiarity with the negroes, but that they will faithfully perform such duties as have been set for them, and maintain the dignity of a soldier.

ADJ'T ELI C. KINSLEY,
Provost Marshal and Judge, Parish of Lafourche.

Illustration 34: Instructions to guards upon plantations, 1863. Plantation owners who were willing to sign a contract with the United States Government received help in the form of guards who protected the interests of slaves and owners. Some owners experienced difficulty maintaining order. At the same time the guards were instructed to ensure that slaves were treated fairly according to the terms of the instructions.There is no evidence that David signed such a contract, but this document, which details the role of guards on plantations in the area that would have included Energy, was found amongst the many papers that were saved with the letters.

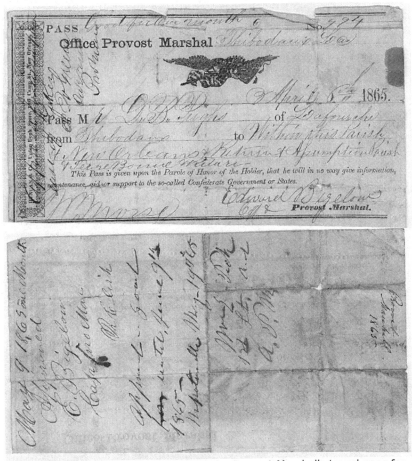

Illustration 35: This document shows the Provost Marshal's travel pass for David, good for one month commencing March 6, 1865. The permit allows David to travel within the parish of La Fourche and New Orleans and to return, and to travel to Assumption Parish and Terrebonne and return. On the back side it appears to have been modified to permit travel beginning May 9th for one month, and again for travel to Napoleanville May 19th.

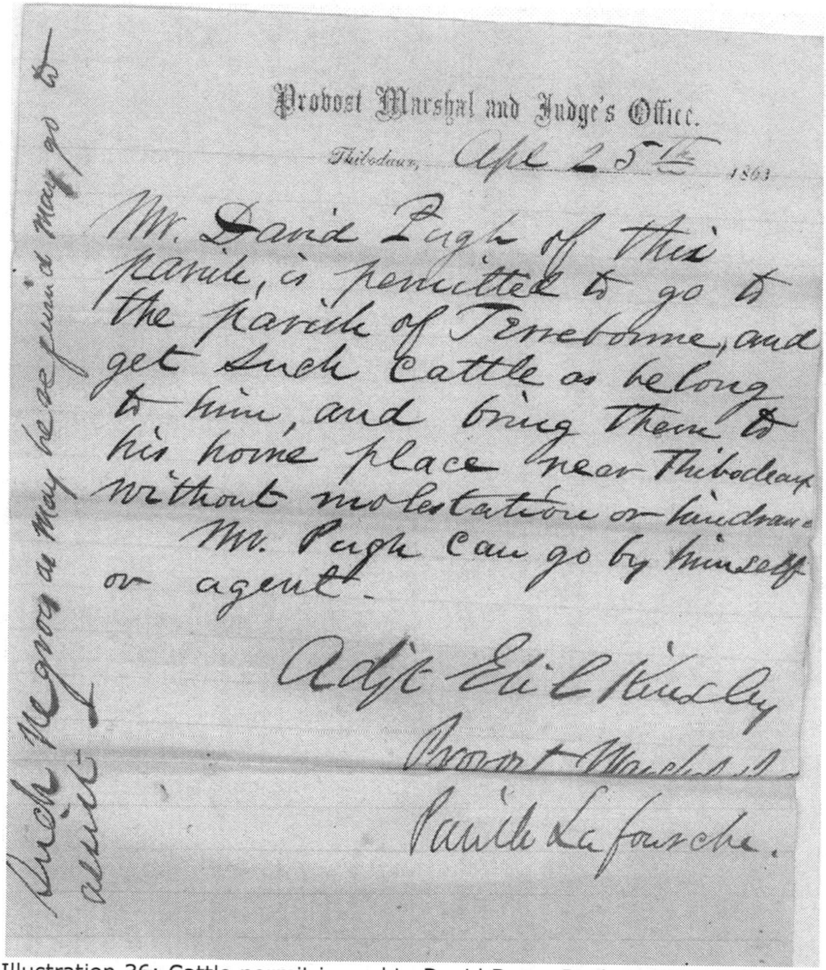
Provost Marshal and Judge's Office.

Thibodaux, Apl 25th 1863

Mr. David Pugh of this parish, is permitted to go to the parish of Terrebonne, and get such cattle as belong to him, and bring them to his home place near Thibodeaux without molestation or hindrance.

Mr. Pugh can go by himself or agent.

Adjt Eli C Kinsley
Provost Marshal
Parish Lafourche.

Such Negroes as may be required may go to assist

Illustration 36: Cattle permit issued to David Bryan Pugh, 1863. David was issued this permit in order to retrieve cattle he was caring for, or had been given, by the Williams', his and Ellen's neighbors. When this region of Louisiana came under control of the Union, permits were used to regulate and control behavior on and off the plantation.

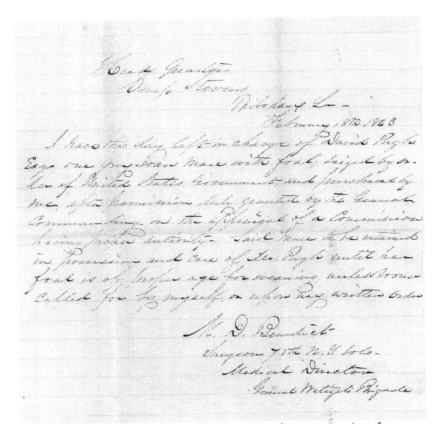

Illustration 37: Official note permitting David to keep possession of a mare and foal until the foal can be weaned. The note was written by Gen. Weitzel's Medical Director (of the 70th NY Volunteers).See the transcription of this note on the following page.

Headquarters

Camp Stevens

Thibodaux La.

Feb 16th 1863

I have this day left in charge of David Pugh Esq. one gray-roan mare with foal; seized by order of United States Government and purchased by me, after permission duly granted by the General Commanding on the appraisal of the Commission having proper authority. Said mare to be retained in possession and care of Mr. Pugh until her foal is of proper age for weaning, unless sooner called for by myself or upon my written order.

M D Benedict

Surgeon 70th NY Vols

Medical Director

Gen. Weitzel's Brigade

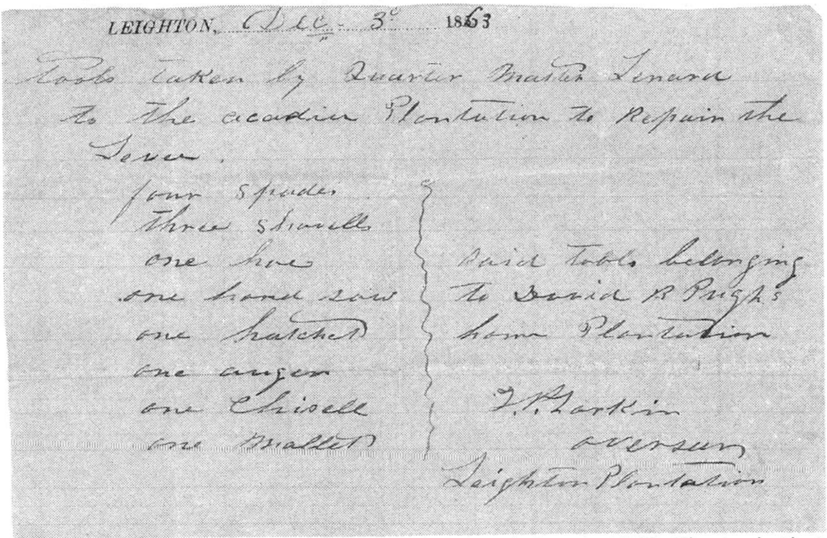

LEIGHTON, Dec 3d 1863

Tools taken by Quarter Master Lenard
to The acadia Plantation to Repair the
Levee.

four Spades
Three shovells
one hoe
one hand saw
one hatchet
one auger
one Chisell
one mallet

Said Tools belonging
to David R Pugh's
home Plantation

T. Larkin
overseer
Leighton Plantation

Illustration 38: Tools taken from David to repair levee, 1863. The tools that are listed in the document were taken by the overseer of Leighton, the plantation next to Energy that belonged to David's brother Richard and his family. However, the levee repairs were apparently being done at the Acadia plantation. When a levee was damaged by floods, it was in everyone's best interest to repair it as soon as possible. It is not apparent why the overseer of Leighton was employed repairing the levee at Acadia.

A Disparate Peace (1865-1866)

By April 11th 1865, Fanny writes that she is "glad indeed" that Ellen will be coming North to visit provided everything works out. There is no mention of the war, and no indication of whether they had heard that the war was over.

But on May 3rd, Sarah writes Ellen, "You are hesitating, I see, about coming on here this summer." Apparently the baby, Mary, has some trouble with her navel, perhaps to do with the healing that must occur where the umbilical cord was cut. Further along in the letter she adds,

> "The frightful horrible murder of President Lincoln has made all hearts ache, although we should think of nothing but his private virtues. The wretched young man who was put up to this deed we do indeed abhor, but, our detestation, abhorrence and all one can despise rests with the villainous murderers who planned, instigated and urged on their chosen instruments to commit this infamous, devilish, murder, rests where we know it belongs. May God have mercy on them hereafter." [28]

On May 23rd, Sarah writes Ellen that they still have not heard whether Ellen will be coming to visit this summer. In the next extant letter, written July 1st 1865, Sarah says,

> "...Your brother received a letter from you yesterday for which we were very thankful as it is the first word we have heard from you since the very sad letter you sent us, written immediately after you heard of Jefferson Davis's arrest.[29]
>
> I am not surprised to hear that you have been ill, if your feelings are always under such excitement you will kill yourself. You must not worry yourself about him, he is no personal friend of yours, never exercised a compassionate or kind thought toward you, he brought about this war and has made it as cruel, heartless, horrible and savage as he could possibly contrive to make it, therefore, he is not worthy of your life being thrown away for him. Some of your views I can make allowance for, though I see no reason for them, but, your exceeding violence of feelings I cannot conceive of. I know you have been allowed to know only one side of this four years fighting and that story has been cruelly untruly set before you.
>
> Now, the fighting is over they say, and you must take care of yourself. Your own troubles are enough for one man and woman to

---

[28] Lincoln was shot April 14th, about 5 days after Lee surrendered; Lincoln was buried on May 4th 1865.

[29] On May 16th 1865, the New York Times reported that Davis' arrest occurred in Georgia, on May 10th. It further said that Jefferson Davis tried to escape by putting on his wife's clothes and wearing a hood. His wife took his arm and pretended he was her mother, but a guard challenged him and he was charged with owning his true identity or being shot. The Times correspondent described Davis as looking "wan, gaunt and depressed." See Mrs. Davis to Ellen on page 283.

---

encounter, you are, however, not alone. There is misery, poverty and, broken hearts, these are all over our land. We ought, each one of us, to try to bear bravely what has come upon us. We are bound to do this for our own interest, if, for no higher motive. You must not express any more such opinions as you have done, in every way, it will serve you no good purpose now surely and may yet cause much evil to your husband and yourself.

We believe a great many of your troubles have arisen from this cause. You have been very violent and open in expressing your opinions and you must not, my dear child, do it any longer, for your own sakes I speak."

Ellen and the children left for Fort Washington for two months on August 25th, traveling by steam ship. On August 30th, David writes Ellen that he misses her already. By Sept. 16th 1865, David has not received any word from Ellen, nor has he been able to learn that her steamer arrived safely in New York:

"Another week since I wrote last dearest wife! And still no news from you! ... yet I am anxious to learn of your safe arrival, with our dear little ones, and cannot be quiet until I hear from you. I have been going to Thibodaux every day since Sunday last, eagerly watching the post office for a letter, and every day scanning the newspaper to learn something of your ship. And each time returning disappointed.

...How much I think about you dear wife -- every waking moment brings me back to you -- and oh how I like to dwell upon those thoughts! Then when I look back upon those years of our married life and see how bright and how short you have made them for me, it seems almost like a dream -- yes it is the true dream of life, and one which stands before me as the bright light of the future, and growing more brilliant with the certainty of its endurance forever."

The Civil War has brought them down greatly: their income now comes not from the soil so much as from livestock and poultry:

"We sell 3 pounds of butter every other day, and get the same quantity of milk, 35 quarts. Cows are falling off a little however."

On Sept 23d, David acknowledges how different it must be for Ellen to be back in Fort Washington:

"I am afraid they will pet you so much at home that our little old house will indeed be a miserable place to you when you come back.

In jest, he adds,

"And I would recommend furthermore, that your mother had your dinner served in the kitchen occasionally, so as to remind you from time to time of our own establishment."

In the same letter, David says that a superintendent of abandoned plantations has come and taken some of their cows on the grounds that the cows belonged to a nearby plantation owned by the Williams (Mr. Williams was David's brother Richard's father-in-law). David found his affidavits of ownership for the cows (that he had been given by the Williams) and is in New Orleans trying to find the appropriate person to whom to appeal. They need the cows for the milk:

"The annoyance is very great, and besides it cut short our milk receipts nearly one half – I only get two dollars per day now."

On Sept. 28th 1865, Ellen writes David that she is feeling wonderful as a result of being in New York. She finds herself in a different world:

"It is quite a treat to have my old friends declare that I am as fascinating as ever etc., it quite rejuvenates me. In fact it makes me bright and I never get cross now. The scenery is lovely so that you may say I enjoy pictures all the time. Not having any dirty work to see to and clean floors and (perhaps I should say carpeted floors) which keep my clothes always nice, the pretty china and glass, the easy chairs, the looking glasses, the comforts of the room furniture and nameless pretty things and comforts around me, all can do so much to pleasant thoughts and also so much to my happiness that I often wonder how we get along, or have got along, with the barrenness of our own house and surroundings."

Perhaps a deeper yearning to return home can be found in this comment,

"There is a cemetery opened out here facing the road as you go from McCombs Dam around to come out just below Kingsbridge. I told the assembled family last night that when I died if you did not insist upon holding to my body where you were I wanted to be buried in that cemetery among my native hills."

On Oct. 8th, Ellen writes David that she has gone to Central Park[30].

"Thursday Augusta made me drive with her to Central Park. It is beautiful there, the roads are perfection and the grounds faultless in picturesque beauty. I enjoyed my drive exceedingly."

She returned to the park a couple of days later, as she describes:

"Just after dinner Mrs. Lowry came in a very stylish turnout, Mr. Lowry driving, for Fan and me to take a drive into the park. I dressed myself in Fanny's little round black hat called a turban and was declared to be quite bewitching in appearance (can you imagine me so?) and away we went. I was perfectly charmed and bewildered with the stream of carriages and equipages, the handsome dresses, the brilliancy and gaiety of the scene and last

---

[30] Opened to the public in 1859, by 1865 the park was predominantly used by the well-off, who rode in carriages. Central Park is considered by many to be one of Frederick Law Olmsted's greatest works; lesser known and sadly overlooked by many is his work as a writer and journalist. In the 1850's Olmsted traveled through the South, directly observing the slave states and their "peculiar institution" of slavery, and writing a great body of work published as "The Cotton Kingdom" in 1861.

but not least, the band of music. We returned by gaslight and found Mr. Carter awaiting us here after an absence of several weeks."

On Oct. 10th, Ellen writes David to say that she has had a long talk with her father and John, and has more information about her father's offer about the Connolly business. She describes the details of the Connolly situation:

"Father says he will give to me the Connolly plantation and make over all of his claims to me if you will act as trustee for me. If you will do so he will send you all the papers."

"...The claim against Mulberry Farm amounts to 60 or $70,000, $30,000[31] of which is represented by a 12-month bond, long past due -- bearing 10% interest and the holder of this bond can sell the plantation at any time after advertising the place for, I believe, 30 days. The plantation consists of about 3000 acres of land, good buildings, a good house, fine, accessible timberland, and soil adapted for sugar, cotton or rice."

She adds that her brother John would already have sold the property the last time he was in Louisiana but for a "bank's order forbidding the sale of plantations" that may have been war-related.

Her father holds additional mortgage notes on the Connolly place that he will sign over to Ellen. While there are two other parties who have claims on the Connolly place, a Dr. Kittredge and Mr. McCollum, their claims are subservient to Haven & Co.

Ellen explains why it is being signed over to her rather than to David and Ellen jointly:

"I want to know as soon as possible if you will act for me, it would have been given to you and me but I told Father then your creditors could seize the place and we would be as bad off as ever."

She ends by saying that she has asked her father and John whether they can think of any work David could do but,

"There is no business here you could enter into that Father or John see."

Meantime, David admonishes her (Oct. 13th 1865),

"...I must give you some advice -- you are receiving calls from all your old acquaintances, and will be expected to return them. Of course most of these people are "out and out Yankees", some of them may possibly be considerate, but the majority will be just like Mrs. Adams -- either ask you unpleasant questions -- or make

---

[31] According to measuringworth.com, the purchasing power of $30,000 in 1875 is over $600,000 in 2008 dollars.

remarks like Lyman. So it is my wish that you pay no regard to conventional usage, about returning visits, and only go to see your old <u>personal</u> friends. Furthermore, you must not let any of these people come to your father's and talk about the war to you -- you must leave the room."

On Oct. 24th, David writes that he has received her letter about the Connolly business. For a man who can get no work, has barely any income nor any prospects, his reaction is a bit odd:

"Now for your second letter! The proposition from your father is most kind. But it comes so suddenly upon me that I scarcely know what to say, and should like to reflect a little before deciding positively. So you must consider this last letter as not yet received, and I shall answer it in time for this Saturday's steamer, as if it had just come to hand. I may possibly take a run down to the Connelly place, and reconnoiter. As it concerns so deeply your fate, my darling! I must weigh everything well, but you shall certainly have an answer on Saturday.

On Nov. 3rd, David refers to an earlier letter of his (which is lost),

"Of one thing I am sure! In my valuation of the plantation, my idea was simply to let your father know of the great depreciation of all property here, and the manner of expressing this -- to the best of my recollection now -- must appear to you more like a dogmatic assertion, with a "view to business", instead of a grateful thanks to your father for so kind an offer."

David writes again on Nov. 4th 1865, having just received letters from Ellen. He addresses the discrepancy between what property used to be worth and what it is worth now:

"This much however is plain to me. Your father has no idea of the terrible depreciation of property in the "sugar region" of this state -- the "cotton country" is not quite so bad. I can best explain this, by quoting the valuation placed upon mother's plantation by the assessor, who was ordered to take the cash market value. The place contains 3000 acres, 1000 of which are fit for cultivation -- and the land of fine quality. The buildings in general condition -- to say nothing of the stock, implements etc., which are all complete -- as well as the location, would give it a value of at least double that of the Connolly place, yet the assessment was twenty one thousand dollars ($21,000)."

..." This must look like "nothing" to your father, yet it is the lamentable truth. Whether property will ever increase in value again, depends upon a change in labor system, of which we have no reasonable prospect."

David writes on Nov. 19th 1865 that Ellen should stay in New York a bit longer, because he feels things are not stable or safe.

"Much as I long for you, dearest wife, it is best that you remain in New York until we are sure here of tranquility. One curse, the military, has just been taken away from us -- the last troops left this morning -- but our Negro population is in an unsettled state, and until Colonel Bush can organize the militia, and arm them the country cannot be looked upon as safe. Our state legislature meets on the day after tomorrow, and will probably take steps toward authorizing volunteer companies..."

But he has some encouraging news about the confiscated cows:
"Mr. Williams has got back his place -- that is, will receive possession on the first of January. He was offered those cows, but refused to take them, on the ground they were mine, not his. He says all that is necessary is for me to see General Baird and claim them, which I shall of course do."

Ellen had almost certainly left New York before David's letter of the 19th arrived, based on Fanny's letter of Nov. 20th:
"It seems strange enough to be writing to you again instead of going into the parlor to talk with you or following you up to your room. How I wish I could look in upon you now and see how you and the dear little ones are getting along, we think and speak of you all the time. I can't begin to tell you how much I miss you or how dreary the house seemed when I came back to it Saturday night and every now and then I think I hear the patter of little feet and shrill little voices calling "Aunt Fan"."

A week after Ellen leaves, Fanny writes and describes a visit by the colorful U.S. Brigadier General Alexander Asboth. Meanwhile, Ellen and the children have encountered trouble getting home. Their steamboat engine suffered a broken piston rod off South Carolina, as a storm bore down on them. Eventually they were towed into Charleston, and they arrived in New Orleans fully three weeks after leaving New York.
"...The Saturday after you left Gen. Asboth[32] came tearing out on his war horse, he stayed to tea and to my amazement Father invited him to dine on the following Tuesday.
Gen. A- accepted and I think Father was very much frightened to think what he had done. John went to Thorndale and though I had asked Carter to come he did not manage to. So we had Augusta down and made the best of it. Mother and I set the table with the best china and raced about all the morning.
We had oyster soup, roast turkey, partridges and celery, quince pudding, ice cream, peaches and cake, then coffee in the parlor.

[32] Alexander Asboth was a Hungarian soldier who came to America in 1851 and lived in New York. He became a good friend of the Haven family, and by the beginning of the war was visiting on a regular basis. Early in the civil war he was promoted to Brigadier General and then Major General. After a successful war career he was appointed U.S. Minister to Argentina. He died there in 1868 but was returned to Arlington Cemetery over 100 years later, where he was re-buried with honors.

We had hock and sherry and a bottle of champagne!! As Mary was handing this to Father she let it fall and it rolled all along the floor on its side, up to the Gen.'s chair, with Mary after it, very much to my amusement and at the same time annoyance. Finally Father received it, but couldn't get it open, he pushed and he fussed and grew redder and redder, then the Gen. said "allow me sir" and as soon as he put his great strong thumb on it the cork broke off close to the neck, then Father took the corkscrew and drew the cork, just as Judge Phillips used to. I suppose the Gen. thought we had never had a bottle before.

Just as we were eating desert a young man came racing up on horseback with a little bob-tailed jacket covered with silver lace, skin tights, calvary boots edged and ornamented with silver and a scarlet cap. He was a friend of the Gen.'s, a young Hungarian in cavalry uniform, very handsome and gentlemanly but could not speak a word of English which was rather a drawback to conversation. However they stayed ever so long and after dark went racing off followed by their servants.

How would you like the Gen. for a brother in law?"

Ellen describes her ill-fated trip home in a letter to Fanny of Dec. 15th, 1865:

"...I wrote Mother about the rain all coming in my state room on account of the canvas not being painted overhead and how I was forced to put the children on the floor in the cabin while I sat upon the sofa all night to keep John and Alice covered. Tuesday morning the ship stopped and we were told she was taking soundings, which I did not believe, and the next evening about 10 o'clock there was some explosion and the ship stopped.

She then laid to all night and we were told the piston had come out of the packing, the ship could not be fixed and she must turn round and go back to Savanna. The steam or the engine upon starting emitted a very wheezing sound which I did not like. About half past seven I was on deck with John and Alice when a succession of explosions took place and we were told the cylinder head exploded.

From that time until Saturday afternoon we drifted about, rolling terribly much of the time, out of the course of all ships and fearing a storm or gale would founder us.

On Saturday we got into the Gulf Stream in the course of vessels on their way from New Orleans to New York, men were kept at the mast's head to watch and the passengers offered a reward to the first man who saw a ship which would help us. The Kensington finally towed us to Charleston and here we had another week of suspense.

...That night at nine o'clock (it was Saturday night, a week) we received a dispatch to go in a steamboat out to the bar and await the Costa Rica. Fortunately the next morning about twelve she came, the two ships were brought together and we had to jump, as the sea brought our ship up, upon the other ship.

It was fortunate the sea was smooth or we would have been transferred in small boats which would have been very disagreeable and difficult with so many little children and packages. The natural swell of the Sea prevented a plank being placed. We had some sensations on the Costa Rica..."

January 7th, 1866, Ellen's father writes David that they have received word of Ellen's safe return, and he adds a cautionary final word:

"My dear sir,

A letter of the 11th has been received, you may imagine the satisfaction all experienced, and the great pleasure it afforded us, to learn that our daughter and her dear children had at last reached home in safety – we all here now join in wishing you all a happy new year in the hopes that health may be presented to you and that no troubles or interruption may hereafter occur, to prevent you from peacefully pursuing the cultivation of improvement of your estate -- I need give no advice, for you and your wife understand your position in the new order of things, and have good sense enough to regulate your conduct in conformity to it."

Feb 4 and 5th, 1866, John Appleton Haven writes Ellen that he has sent paperwork, including a power of attorney, to David, probably to facilitate the arrangement whereby David will act on behalf of Ellen in recovering the Connolly business.

"I want very much to know what are your plans for the present year - will nothing be done on the plantation - no cane planted - no crops of any kind - if such is the case, and you do not succeed in renting, whence are to come your means of living?"

October 7th, 1866, Ellen has again given birth, to a baby girl, Edith. By the 3rd week of November, David is involved with the Connolly case: he has engaged lawyers, and they are trying to get testimony from several people in hopes of going to trial soon.

Less than a month later, on December 10, 1866, John Appleton Haven writes of his concerns to David:

"... I want you to inform me particularly of the position of your own affairs and plans for the future -- I hope you may be able to retain and work to advantage your plantation this present year and that you may have no serious trouble from your creditors."

Two Worlds (1867-1875)

By early 1867, the Connolly business is temporarily on hold due to legal delays, and David is seeking employment but has no luck. He writes Ellen from New Orleans on Jan. 15th,

> "...Tuesday has long passed, and yet I am not ready to go up -- simply from the fact of my not having found any employment, business is terribly dull as scarcely to afford occupation for those already here.
>
> On Monday I learned that two of the appointees to the office of layers of hay -- offices created by the last legislature -- were going to resign, so I called upon Governor Wells -- told him frankly that I was in need of employment -- and asked for the first vacancy. He promised me that I should have it, and I shall probably know tomorrow something definite about the resignations. Walter has found here... an old schoolmate, who intimated to him that he might get him (Walter) an appointment. We will go to see him in the morning, and learn something about the hay business.
>
> If that fails, it is possible I may obtain a situation of Secretary to the Levee Board. Mr. Kelly, who knows Governor Wells son-in-law is to use his influence also, so amongst them all something may be done -- I hope so at any rate. I do not wish to go home until the matter is arranged in some way."

On January 23rd 1867, Sarah adds a note at the bottom of her letter to Ellen suggesting that David continues to struggle:

> "I enclose in this $30 for you. Don't buy anything with it that your creditors will snatch away from you. Kisses to the children."

John Appleton Haven writes on Jan. 26th 1867 that he is trying to find a way to provide income to Ellen without subjecting the money to any risk of capture by creditors:

> "I have been thinking much of your many troubles and trying to devise some method of relief so as to place you in a more comfortable position. As yet I do not see any satisfactory plan. I would like to arrange matters, so as to make your lots produce you some income, without encroaching on the principle. And this, so far as I see, can only be done by a sale of the lots, and investing the amount of the sale and putting it in care of trustees, for a given time and for your benefit and beyond reach and any attachment."

Fanny writes, on Feb 9th 1867, that she is of two minds about David going into the city to look for work:

> "...Mother said you mentioned in Anna's letter that David thought of going to the City to get something to do. I suppose this is the best he can do and for some reasons it seems to me like a good plan if it is carried out. I mean if he can find a place and step right

into it, well and good, but if he has got to go there and be fiddling round for months in hopes of something turning up, I don't think it is worth while.

Of course it will be hard for you to be left alone and it will bring a great deal of care upon you, but I think it will be a satisfaction for you to feel that he is doing something and earning something even if ever so little."

On Feb. 17th 1867, John Appleton Haven writes Ellen about the lots of land he has held for her: he wants to provide her with some income, yet protect the investment from being borrowed against or being sold to meet immediate needs. He believes the property can get $12,000.

"I therefore propose, and I think it very necessary for your security and benefit that you execute to me a deed of the property at the price of $12,000 and I will at once put that sum in trust for you, during your life, the interest on the same to be paid to you every six months. In this way you will make a sale of the lots at their present value, and you and your husband will have the benefit of the income during your life, and the principal, say $12,000, is made secure for your children, after your decease...

"I need not say that my only object in this proposal is for the benefit of my daughter and her children – I shall probably sell the lots within the present year, and if more than $12,000 shall be realized, all liabilities for taxes, assessments being deducted, you shall have the benefit – as I do not take the property with a view of any profit to myself – my object being for your good –..."

Ellen apparently took offense at her father's letter. On March 20th, John Appleton Haven writes again, in response to the reply from Ellen.

"I have your letter of the 10th and am very glad you have written so frankly about the disposal of your lots, but am sorry you for a moment supposed that I had my fears, that your husband would ever, in any way, wish you to part with them for his benefit. I had in view only your and his joint interest, in proposing to take charge of the lots..."

He cautions Ellen,

"My wish is that you keep the property entire, and on no account sell lot by lot to meet any contingencies. But when necessary to make a sale, let it be for the whole property. And have the whole proceeds invested in good securities - you and your husband to receive the interest during your lives, and keeping the principal entire for the benefit of your children... Knowing now your feelings and wishes, I think you had better at present do nothing. But wait a while, and when you deem it necessary to have the lots, empower me or John to sell and invest for you the proceeds..."

At the end of a letter to Ellen April 16th, Fanny responds to a comment made by Ellen in a previous letter regarding her concern about David's performance in taking care of the Connolly business:

"...I am very sorry that you should worry any about David's part in the Connolly business, I dislike business with relations as much as you do, more I guess, but I think this will not result in trouble and will probably be settled satisfactorily."

On April 29th, David writes Ellen that the Connolly case is once again on hold and that he has put a protest into motion to the effect that they (Haven & Co.) cannot get justice in the state courts. He goes on to say that he is also still looking for work:

"...I wish to stay too, to try and find something else to do, have not succeeded as yet, but wish to continue the attempt until I do, there is so little business doing just now --as all tell me to whom I speak -- that is a somewhat difficult matter."

May 2nd, 1867, David writes that things are not looking any better on the work front:

"...I am still hanging on about my appointment -- nothing but promises as yet. However, Mr. Julian Neville goes to see Governor Wells for me today, and as he has strong influence with him, hope to know something this morning. The secretaryship of new levee board, of which I wrote you, cannot be had -- from the fact that the old board will not consent to give up its power, and the matter will probably be referred to the military. I believe one of the appointees to office of Weigher of Hay is about to resign -- Mr. Neville will inquire into that for me.

In regard to obtaining a clerkship, in any office (private office I mean) it is impossible now -- except at a salary of $40 or 50 per month. Business is almost at a stand still -- worse times than have been known since the war, and there will be many failures soon. Walter is doing nothing as yet -- is afraid to go into anything, until matters look brighter.

This is the first time since our marriage that I have been away from you so long -- except when you went to New York -- and my thoughts are continually with you."

A week later on May 9th, David writes again:

"...I have been earnestly engaged since Saturday last endeavoring to secure the secretaryship to the levee board appointed by Sheridan.

...Mr. Burnside promised me his vote, Mr. Oglesby said he would take in my application, the third -- Mr. Lawrence, who married Mrs. Osgoods daughter, you recollect -- wishes to have the secretary of the old board, although he has promised to do what he can for me. Mr. Kenner, Mr. Mandeville and Mr. Williams are to go to see him for me today, and if possible secure his interest. I shall try to find someone who knows the two other members -- they are expected here today -- and see what can be done with them. The board meets for the first time tomorrow..."

David expresses his regret that Ellen is in the situation she is:
"...I go to Aunt Fanny's once in awhile, but my evenings are spent either at Walters or at Mr. Williams office -- quietly, and my thoughts are always away -- running upon the little old woman in the country, who is surrounded by a flock of little children, and whose time is constantly taken up with a thousand annoyances of managing a household -- which household her husband ought to attend to -- and cares of making both ends meet when there is no money to do it with. I would rather spend one hour with that little woman than a week here..."

Also in this letter he mentions that his mother has given him money, and that Haven & Co. has petitioned to move the Connolly case from state to U.S. courts:
"...Mother gave me the $500 out and out, and although I expect to pay the taxes from it her half will only be about $70 so we shall have the rest ourselves.
...In regard to the Connolly business, we received on Sunday from New York, the petition of Haven & Co., for removal of our suit into the U.S. court -- setting forth that they could not obtain justice in the state courts."

By May 15th 1867, it is apparent from Fanny's letter to Ellen that there is tension about David and the Connolly case:
"...In one of your letters you speak of the Connolly business and of Dr Oliphant's bill etc., etc.
After some deliberation I determined it was best to read some portions of the letter to Father, for I thought it much better that he should understand some things about it and thus avoid future trouble, for instance if David found it hard to pay the bill it was Haven and Co.'s business to, I knew Father would certainly wish to do it, I knew he would not mind forwarding money for the expenses etc., if he only understood about it.
I only read some passages here and there. I do not think you would have objected to his hearing it in the least.
He did not say much; my impression is that he said that you did not understand about it altogether, that it would not answer at all for him to pay Dr O's bill, it was proper as the business stood that David should, that he had collected some money, perhaps $100.00 or so and would doubtless defray the necessary expenses from this, that he and David heard frequently from each other in relation to it and it was all right.
I think this is the amount of what he said.

As to Father writing a letter to David and <u>taunting</u> him about his poverty you surely know Father better than to imagine that he would do anything of the kind, it is the very last thing he would do to anyone especially to one whom he likes as much as he does David. Don't suppose such a thought ever crossed his mind and it ought never to have crossed yours in regard to him."

On May 17th, David writes Ellen:
"I have had the blues all the week, or should have written you before. My application for the secretaryship of the Levee board failed. The election was held on Monday last, and although I had the direct promise of the vote from two of the five members and a partial one from another, those three members were the ones who proposed the party elected.
...In private business there is no chance at all, from the fact that nobody is doing anything. Money is more scarce than at any time since the war commenced. The banks are beginning to fail, and everyone dreading a terrible crash before long.
...I <u>ought</u> to go up home at once -- to say nothing of the desire to see you my darling wife and our dear children -- and regulate all those affairs you wish me to attend to, but am loath to do so, until some employment is obtained. Shall continue here for a few days longer, and when I am forced to give up all idea of a situation, will go up for good, but wish to hold on to the last."

David is still in the city on May 25th, 1867:
"I did not write you yesterday, thinking that I should certainly go home in the morning, but meeting Governor Wells today learned from him that there would probably be something opened by Monday morning, and that I had best come in to see him then, so concluded to stay over.
...I believe, unless Wells can give me an appointment, there is no chance otherwise, for business is so terribly dull here that hundreds are out of employment."
David did not get the appointment or any other work.

By December Ellen tells Fanny she is pregnant again. Fanny makes her views clear regarding a woman's lack of control over her body when she writes Ellen on Dec. 20th, 1867:
"...What you wrote me of your own self dear Nell, shocked me very much. Do men think of nothing but their own selfish wishes? Don't be angry with me but I really think it is wicked in men to bring children into the world unless they have means to take care of and educate them properly, without worry, worry, worry.
I go even further than this and my idea is, to quote the words of one of England's first and deepest thinkers, on the subject of

woman's rights "her most sacred right is surely the control of her own person in the matter of child-bearing."[33]

I dare say you will be shocked at my speaking on such subjects, but I don't know why a woman has to bear such things she should not think or speak of them. I think it is wicked, positively wicked, for a woman to have to have children if she will or not. If she wishes for them, longs for them, has the means and desire and strength to take care of them, then let them come and be the blessing and comfort and joy of the home as God surely means they shall be.

Under other conditions, when the hands and home are full and tapped already beyond their capacity the child does not, cannot take its rightful place in the Mother's heart and the man not only wrongs his child but does a far more cruel wrong to the wife whom he pretends to love and whom at the altar he promises not only to love, but to cherish and honor.

I know you will think it is dreadful in me to write so, but I can't help it, it makes me angry when I think on the subject in relation to the world in general and especially when I think of your having any more babies to take care of; as if five wasn't enough for any woman without having a single other care or anxiety in the world."

By January of 1868, David is back in New Orleans, trying to locate documentation to help with the Connolly business and looking for work. He is also waiting for an opportune moment to ask his brother Walter for a loan. He writes, Jan. 12th:

"...I have not applied to Judge Baker for any situation, for Mr. Fellows tells me that everyone appointed must take the "Test Oath[34]", and this I cannot do.

As for obtaining any other employment here, it is almost impossible, most of the merchants are discharging their clerks now -- from want of business.

So I must look for an overseer's berth.

...And how much relieved I should be if we could get the Connolly business closed up! Or get some work to do.

... and as I look around me, am continually rejoicing that I have such a faithful and noble wife. And my great regret is that I should have brought her down to such poverty."

Jan. 16th, Ellen describes their situation to David:

"...Our milk falls off. I believe there are three cows we have thrown off which have run quite dry.

We average about 19 quarts of new milk. I sell all the night's milk, after skimming, say 10 quarts at $.10 a quart, so this helps along

---

[33] Fanny may be quoting Mary Wollstonecroft.

[34] The Test Oath required civil servants and military officers to swear not only to future loyalty but also to affirm that they had never previously engaged in disloyal conduct toward the Union.

well but with all our present expenses it takes up nearly everything.

I am keeping an account of every cent to show you. I have flour, meal, oil soap and sacks of corn continually to buy. One sack of corn lasts Julia and Willis together just 2 1/2 days. Julia quarreled with Willis for giving out too much, so, on Monday, I gave them each a sack, $3.50 a piece, and told them they must make it go through the week."

Ellen continues,

"...I hope Walter can give you your loan. I wrote father yesterday to sell in February for me if he could get my price of $20,000.

I calculate my confinement about the fifth of May, dating from the 20th of December which is just half of the time, and I must write to Mrs. Bolen, perhaps aunt Fanny can tell you her direction for me.

I don't want to hire her for more than three weeks for I think I can get some black woman here for much less price to do the last week for me, perhaps if I get Mrs. Bolen for two weeks it will answer.

...I wish you success to all your enterprises. If you really want to place as overseer or manager, you must be energetic in your applications, for everybody is applying now for this very thing and employers look especially for energy."

January 18th 1868, David writes from New Orleans to say that his mother, Eliza Pugh, may help him:

"...I have not asked Walter for money, because W.W Pugh called me aside a few days ago, and told me mother had talked with him about assisting me -- and he had advised her to do so, telling her that there was no reason in the world why she should not do something for me.

So I shall -- as soon as that steamer's mails are opened -- probably take a boat to mothers and obtain money enough to pay off our servants. I am much gratified that mother should think of me at this time -- it is certainly no more than she ought, considering that I attended so closely to her business for so long."

Life for Ellen has become nearly impossible, with the cares of the place, the bills, all the children and lack of help. She writes David a long letter on Jan. 26th, after stating that she can't afford to take the time to write a letter:

"...I cannot nurse her and all of them through the itch and do all the work I have to do, it is out of the question so if you can find anybody that can, you had better get her -- I have lighted the nursery fire myself and I can't dress the children, skin the cream, stay awake all night and run all day so I might as well give up first as last. I enclose a note sent to you, that man has been dunning me for $15 for corn, I promised to pay him this coming week, how,

> I scarcely know myself. He has been promised your return daily and weekly by Abram until I have felt mortified to let Abram see how things went and how uncertain you are, for the man thinks Abram is fooling him and Abram thinks I am fooling him. ...I can't have so much to worry my mind."

Ellen expresses her exasperation with David, who leaves her for long periods, and seems unable to deal effectively or efficiently with business matters:

> "...I asked you twice, after mature deliberation with myself, before you went to the city, what your plans were. You would not tell me or else you had none, said you were going to get money to pay the servants. At the last minute I asked you if you are going to be gone a month and your answer was, of course not. It is a month today. If you would only tell me your plans if you have any and not keep up such an unnecessary silence, or, if you have none, if you would only make some and act up to them it would appear much better for you and me. This want of prominence and method in business matters is doing you an irreparable injury and through you, your family.
>
> No one will ever want a man for business who is never up to his time and don't know his own mind two days. You had better come home and pay your people and then return to the city, saying you are going for an indefinite period. We shall all then understand. I can take hold of my work with a better will if I could only feel you were to be prompt. If John spent a <u>month</u> in the city working with all his energies, his <u>business habits and punctuality</u> looking for those papers, it will take you a year. Besides if I were Haven & Co. I should think you and Mr. Belcher had waked up of a very late hour to look for what was deemed very important, in the beginning. This is my view of the case..."

Ellen is also frantic about the baby Edith, because she worries that one of the girls who has been helping with Edith has been abusing her. Facing yet another baby in May, Ellen is overwhelmed: "I am most discouraged about everything."

She manages to send her love to David despite her frustration:

> "It is late and I must close, I am very tired. Accept many kisses and much love dearest husband from your wife. I am very sorry you are sick. I know you look awfully shabby for your clothes were all in tatters when you left here. I suspect Sally thinks I am an awful wife to let you go away with such shirts and waistcoats.

Fanny's life in New York has settled back to normal. Fanny tells Ellen on Feb. 10th 1868 that:

"...On Saturday last Mr. Carter came out and took a splendid sleigh ride with me, the sleighing has been capital for the past two weeks in town and out, which is unusual here."

And Sarah writes Ellen Feb. 17th that the neighbors are once again socializing:
"...The neighbors and others around have met once a fortnight at each other's houses through the winter, they have music, dancing, supper etc."

But light-hearted news is scarce in Ellen's world. With her baby due in about 3 months, she receives a letter from David Feb. 29th 1868 saying,
"...I have been engaged, yesterday and today, in making out my tableau and petition for bankruptcy -- just completed it. Have had no time as yet, to look up my Connolly papers."

On March 1, Ellen tells David of more worries:
"...How am I to meet our expenses of this week I therefore do not know. I have Mr Taylor's meat to buy, soap for the week, John's schooling of $5.75 for his philosophy, the butcher, $5 for potatoes, Henrietta who must be paid, Grace, Cely, Elizabeth etc., corn (I sent for sack of corn on credit to Mr. Thompson the day after you left) and what else I don't know, with only $16 on our milk account from which we must take Mr. Binnings, Larkin, Butcher etc.
It takes a sharper head and a braver one than I have this week to be equal to the emergencies coming. There has been almost a hurricane all day today and the stovepipe to our stove has been blown all on one side and the stays bent up, so I suppose it will take all the remainder of tomorrow for the man to repair this. I was obliged to have the fire put out in the still at one o'clock, fearing the pipe would go over and a strong wind would blow the fire and catch the building on fire.
...When I am well I can work all day but I am not well and had not been for a good while. This morning after dressing the baby and all of the children I felt so badly I could not eat any breakfast but laid down while the children eat and I have managed to stumble through the day somehow."
After much discussion about her need to have help in the form of a suitable servant or nurse as the baby's birth approaches, she closes with,
"We live simply and sell our milk. This is all that is necessary to say. I have yet a list of all the clothes to take for I shall have the children to dress in the morning so I must close.
Yours with love
Ellen"

The very next day, March 2nd, David writes Ellen to say,

"I am truly sorry my darling wife you should be sick with so much trouble too, on your hands. I hope to be home soon, and will try to relieve you."

Also on March 2nd 1868, in a letter to Fanny, Ellen attributes David's absence to his work with the Connolly matters. She comments on an offer Fanny has made to help with making baby clothes:

"...Your kind offer dear Fan would assist me very much and I will comply with it if you are really anxious to do any sewing, but I should think you had enough to keep you busy."

Ellen speaks openly about how she feels, and how things are for her. She explains the difficulty of finding a nurse, and says she can't afford to provide the standard of living a white nurse would expect.

"...I am miserable myself, every now and then have nervous attacks, and last night had to get up in the night and walk the floor and suffered so from cramps in my limbs.

Not having any nurse uses me all up, bathing and dressing the children, fretting with them and carrying Edith tires me out so I can scarcely do anything else.

I am as thin as a rail and have frequent faint turns. The woman I have hired by the day is sick and I wrote David last night that he must get me a white nurse in the city.

Black nurses are much less expensive, in the way of feeding etc., but it is impossible to get a black woman, I have been trying now all winter. In two months at least I shall be in my room without a soul to look after the children and I shall never get well and out again if I have this worry on my mind.

I shall have to pay a black woman $8 a month but I can't get her. A white woman I suppose will not come a bit under $10 or $12. Then our kitchen is a rough plank room out doors as the custom is here, there are no chairs, nothing but a table, rations for breakfast are corn meal, molasses and beef (we used to give coffee but now we have none for our own table and cannot give it in the kitchen)...

...David told me a white nurse would involve a pot of coffee for her breakfast, butter, an extra supply of flour, supper to be prepared for her at night, a constant fuss with the black servants. She would not want to go to the well for bath water, wipe up the slops, and attend to the menial part of the children.

All this is true but what can I do? I must have someone.

...This is what I mean by saying rich people can have babies much easier, They don't have all these things to worry their minds about and need not get nervous sure enough. I don't know what David will say to my white nurse proposition but if he gets one I shall dread her advent more than he does.

...I did not mean however, when I began to write to enlarge so upon my subject of nursing so skip it in your mind when thinking of my letter."

March 5th 1868, still struggling without David, Ellen writes him another letter describing all the bills that need paying, plants and seed that need planting, and other matters that need attention.

> "...This morning we needed another sack of corn and I have been trying this week to sell some eggs to meet this sack...The cabbages are gone and we have nothing but beef and potatoes to eat...What can you get a bag of that cracked corn for, it would help out the table...Our lard is also out. What a mental worry and stretch it is all of the time to be so limited in means. As we get no coffee, milk, or pork in the kitchen I should like something else for the table but we cannot help it, that I see..."

In an undated letter that is probably from this period, Ellen unloads on David:

> "Dear David,
> I received your letter this morning about six o'clock after sending for it. I fully expected you today as I had not received any letter since last Saturday and had sent to the mail every day.
> You have not treated me well David, and I don't think you ought to do so. I have been anxious all the week to know if you got the appointment and in trouble or joy I should think your wife would be the first person to turn to. Who has got to pass through the dreary years of anxiety, dredging and working which are in the future but your wife? You are very queer.
> I am working and striving at home, annoyed and harassed in a thousand ways, the chief anxiety money, everybody wanting money, so many things needed and not enough money and you, my husband, start off and leave me without telling me of your plans and stay two months in the city.
> Next when some of your purposes do eke out you keep me in suspense because you have the blues. You and I have no time for the blues, we have a family dependent upon us, social relations dependent upon us, and relations towards each other. If I have to bear the burden and heat of the day I don't want to be treated like one of the children.
> Everybody naturally comes to me to know of you and your plans and I appear like a fool...You must remember you leave debts behind you. This is what is wearing me down, we owe so much and are plunging deeper in debt every day.
> Moreover I want you to write and send my letters through the post unless you happen to send by Mr. Williams besides. He brings up your letters and I have to send to them to know if you have condescended to write to me as they all know Mr. W. brought up the last letter received.
> All this is very trying and disagreeable to me. After Willis's questions to me and my answers of utter ignorance of your plans, Frank says before him that you have not thoughts of coming home

yet a while, that you are having a nice time, dining out etc. etc. that we need not listen or look for you for some time.

I believe I worry and have worried more about the future than you do. Mr. Delas sent me a bill and letter which I think I handed to you when last home for nine or $10, he has sent again for the money and says he needs and wants it. As I did not hear from you I told them you would be home and he should have it Monday. Now I must pay him and it's very difficult for me to do.

I hate this dunning. I am ashamed to show my face. I have Mrs. Young to pay next week, the butcher and meal to buy, for we are out.

...We must pay up back dues and give up our pew from all I can see and I must send out and tell father to sell my land at a sacrifice. We must have something to live on and I have been making a rough estimate of the bare necessaries of life and I will enclose it to show you what we must spend and what our milk brings.

Don't get the blues my dearest husband, and believe me when I tell you I am your best friend, I love you more and counsel you more for your own good than anybody else.

You are very fond of Mr. Conger but I believe that I know him better than you. He likes you but if you were to die tomorrow he would not miss you nor care much. He is intensely selfish in his affections.

All that I tell you is to show you how other people are viewing and judging of you. One day when I, after some of Richard's teasing at your absence, said with a sigh "oh well, it is easy to laugh now but if David really gets business, which he ought to do, I shall not be able to laugh. I shall feel so badly". Mary [Richard Pugh's wife] to comfort me said, "Oh, he has really no thoughts of it, Father [Mr. Williams] says David talks about it but he is not going really to do it." I knew better for I believed you but you see what Mr. W. thought.

...Remember I have paid you out at times $25 of the $30 mother sent me so you owe me that sum. Take it and don't come home without something for coats and pants and waistcoats. I want you to do this. Let us work together dear and we will weather through this, if my hair had not been gray it would now turn so it don't make much difference..."

Ellen's mother sent her $10.00 enclosed in a letter, and urged her to buy something special for herself, but, Ellen tells David, she has spent most of it paying bills and getting necessaries. David probably returned home soon after Ellen's letter (above), and was definitely at home by the end of April because Ellen refers to him being home in a letter to Fanny.

In March and April of 1868, Ellen and her father exchange letters about the sale of the lots in N.Y.C. Her father sends her a power of attorney to sign that will allow her brother John to act in her behalf in selling the lots.

By the end of April, Ellen has received a box of items to help her with her new baby. Fanny, Sarah and Augusta contributed, and Fanny and Sarah did the bulk of the sewing. On May 8th, Ellen gave birth to her last child, a boy: Thomas Pugh. Ellen was 36 years old. From a comment in a letter of June 14th from Sarah to Ellen, we learn that Eliza Pugh came down from Madewood to visit Ellen at Energy ("I was pleased to hear that Madame Pugh had visited you...").

Ellen writes Fanny July 12th 1868 about the lots of land, saying that her brother John wrote her saying she would receive some money for them in July. She says she
> "... wrote him if he was certain it would be paid this month I would come on and pass mother's golden wedding with her and father."

She says she will need to fix up some clothing if she makes the trip.

Fanny writes back on the 16th that they are all looking forward to seeing Ellen and the children, and maybe David. She urges Ellen not to bother fixing up clothing for their visit, because they can do the work after she arrives.
> "Couldn't David possibly come too? We should love to have him and I think it would be pleasant for him. We shall hope to hear in a few weeks that you have decided to come and when and which children and all about it.
> We have now a very smart dressmaker who comes to cut and fit and then we make the clothes, so if you want anything leave it till you get here.
> Mother and Father are delighted at the prospect of having you."

Ellen decides to come by steamer at the end of August. She leaves John, Grace and Mary with David, and brings Alice, Edith and baby Thomas to New York. David writes her often from Thibodaux: he brings the children to various relatives for visits along the bayou, and is attending to various matters. He advises her to let John (her brother) invest the proceeds of the sale of her lots in New York, because he believes the rate of return in N.Y. may be better than they could get in New Orleans. He writes of his love for Ellen, claiming that he first realized he loved her in 1852 (when Ellen was 20), and he begs forgiveness for any "harsh moods and speeches". He imagines Ellen and the rest of the Haven family as they celebrate Mr. and Mrs. Haven's 50th wedding anniversary, and says,
> "And then, I have known how much I owed to you my darling! -- that you should leave all that was right to you, and your dear parents too, to share your lot with a poor miserable husband -- one who often abuses you, for faults of his own."

David's feelings about the South and North have not moderated. He says, Sept 29th 1868,

> "When you see Mrs. Augustus Smith make my respects to her -- I believe she and her husband were <u>Confederates</u>, and of course we all ought to have a kindly feeling for those.
>
> ...I wish you would tell Fanny or John, that it would be quite as well not to send us any more Putnam's -- this of course in a quiet way -- not to offend your father -- we who belong to the south, ought not to receive such a rascally works in our house."

Ellen responds to David's renewed proclamation of love by admitting that she felt his love for her had lessened over the last year or two.

> "Darling I have felt sure for the last year, and was even a little doubtful the year before, that your love for me was dwindling away. I knew that it had not gone right off and I knew a certain sort of love still remained but the real, true, deep affection which you once felt for me I knew, or thought to have gradually passed away.
>
> Your words had told me so and your actions likewise. In pleasant times when nothing ruffled you or me you thought you cared for me but when the test of that affection came it was wanting.
>
> The pieces of the vase, as I said before, were about and the perfume of the flowers had not been washed away, it would take time to do this, but I did not think you cared much for the pretty thing, the pieces answered your purpose just as well.
>
> Your letter says your vase is perfect to you and you once more want to make it whole to me. Let it be so –
>
> Your letter seems to speak from your heart. If ever we come together again we will endeavor to begin anew and as I am sure I have loved you with all my heart I feel sure I can keep my compact if you will yours."

As to David's potential role in politics, Ellen is stern:

> "I want you to keep very clear of any political troubles. I don't want you to join societies at all. If your neighbors are attacked it is then time to run in and defend them and I believe this riot mania is kept up first by one side and then the other.
>
> You see how matters stood the other day, you went to Thibodaux at the ordering of other people to join in a riot if there was the least provocation. You would have been no protection to anybody, you would have just helped to swell the mob.
>
> I should probably have been left a widow and the children fatherless for what? I should have had no protector the rest of my days and you would not have protected anyone in particular, you would not have fired and helped one party fight the other.
>
> Each side is on the alert and one pistol shot from one is now the sign of the general fight and all this is arranged by clubs and societies."

Oct 3rd 1868, David strikes out at Ellen over politics. In the presidential election of 1868, both Louisiana and New York (the latter by a small margin) voted democratic. Democrat Seymour lost to General Ulysses Grant, the latter representing the "radical" republicans who wanted to punish the South and advance the rights of freedmen while garnering the black vote. For David there is no tolerable Reconstruction platform, only the lesser of two evils.

> "...Your political inquires, dearest wife, have put me out. And in answer, I shall ask you -- whether you wish to see all Negroes in the legislature and in our offices of trust and power, whether you want our taxes increased to such a point that no white can own real estate -- this is now the radical boast, and is likely to be accomplished, in case Grant is elected.
> Whether you wish to be forced to send your children to school with Negroes. Whether you want a Negro woman placed in the same state room with you on the steamer, -- or on a steamboat here -- and a Negro man to sit beside you at breakfast and dinner and in the parlors of our hotels, whether you wish to be crowded out of an opera house by men and women of that color, whether you want them to take the best cars on the railroads from you -- in time whether you wish to have them the superior class in our churches, and you to have a seat in the corner?
> Yet all this was regulated by the Legislature 10 days since, and nothing but the personal fear of Warmoth[35] the governor, during the excitement last week -- he knowing that when the row commenced, the white radicals and carpetbaggers, and not the Negroes, would be the first killed -- for he had been warned -- prevented his signing such a bill.
> It is only to prevent this, that people here are willing to side with the Democratic Party, and put down all radicals. The Negro vote is forced upon them, and if they can use that vote to defeat the Reconstruction acts, then they will have their rights, and only then. Now if you wish for all this to come and want to see not only General Hampton, but every other man here literally blacking boots for Negroes, then ask me such questions.
> I knew you were going amongst a set of radicals, but did not expect such a result as this. I shall not vote myself, but will certainly try to influence any Negroes vote that I can."

In his next letter David describes how he has spent the available weekly funds:

> "You ask about my expenditure of the weekly funds. I have been paying for fencing, purchasing some articles -- wearing apparel and luxuries, for myself -- buying some 30 barrels of corn -- and in some useful way or other most of the money is gone. We do not

---

[35] Warmoth, a carpetbagger from Illinois, ran as a Republican and served as the first Reconstruction governor of Louisiana.

receive quite as much however, as when you left. Last upon this topic, I will mention the purchase of a couple of fine heifers from Mr. Lyall, for which I paid $50, and think the money well laid out, as they will probably have calves in the spring."

On Oct. 8th 1868, Ellen writes David with instructions about paying bills with the money she is receiving from the sale of the lots:

"John has gone to the city and I asked him to send you a check for $450 which I wish you would dispose of as follows. I send $95 to pay you for Mrs. Bolen to whoever you owe it to, $50 for Dr. Dancereau's attendance upon me, $100 I want you to pay to the church for last year's rent and this year and take a receipt, and I wish you would pay for my piano and release that. I thought Mr. Hall said it would be $175, at any rate if it is $200 don't ask them if there is anything more -- this will settle all three matters."

The sale of the lots brought Ellen a total of some $24,000 in trust:

"John has gone in to see about my sale today. I told him last night to invest $3000 more in trust for me which would make an investment of $20,000 in trust. The other $4000 I think you had better invest in New Orleans for a higher percentage."

There had been talk of Ellen leaving Alice at Fort Washington for a while, but Ellen writes David that it will not be practical for a number of reasons:

"Fanny says she is perfectly willing to take her and it would be a pleasure to her to have the child but all now that she is living for is to make mother happy the rest of her days and anything interfering with this she could not undertake.
She says if when she and mother were sitting together and she found Alice worried or annoyed mother, she should be obliged to send Alice out of the room and then she would be entirely by herself.
If mother should be taken sick again, if only for a few days, she says she does not know what the child would do.
I know mother would take her but she is not strong enough to take her, for the least little thing excites her and she would make an anxiety out of it at once, whether there was any occasion for it or not.
...Fanny and I had a very plain talk and I have taken everything into consideration and I don't see how I can arrange it."

Oct 10th 1868, David makes an interesting comment about his role in the Connolly business, and about Mr. Haven and the recent election:

"I am very glad you told your father it would make no difference in my zeal for his service whether the Connolly place was to be given to you or not. I am not sure I should have worked as hard, had the matter belonged to me solely. Shall of course however be exceedingly glad of your father's gift to you.

He (your father) is certainly entirely ignorant of matters in the South, or would not say that Grant's election will bring quiet and prosperity. Were he only obliged to live here for six months his ideas would change vastly."

David writes on politics:

"You tell me not to mix up in political troubles. God knows I am willing enough to keep out of them. But this is more than a political question. The Negroes are continually inflamed by outrageous speeches until they are now almost ready for anything. You do not know what caused the excitement in New Orleans, of which I wrote, it was the sacking, by a Negro gang, of one of those handsome confectionery shops on Canal Street.

An outrage which three years ago would have cost almost every Negro in the city his life.

Nothing but strong determination on the part of every white man prevented a riot in the Thibodaux affair, it was a threat on the part of the Negroes to take possession of the sheriff's office, which caused our preparations.

Now when a Negro, Pinchback[36], gets up in the Senate, and openly threatens to burn down the city. And when another (Poindexter, the husband of Mary Ballard's woman Matilda -- and also a senator) tells the Negroes from the courthouse steps, and Napoleonville -- it was when the Negroes undertook to break up that barbecue of which I wrote you -- that he wished the trouble would come, for then he would go in for killing every white man woman and child in the country, that he would begin upon the women and children, do you not think it is time to take action? Nothing but a bold front on our part will prevent a collision, and we must show the Negroes we are ready.

How long do you think white men would be allowed to make such speeches in New York?"

David urges Ellen not to return home before the elections, because he is concerned about violence:

"You speak of starting home about November 1st. Now that is just about the election time, and we are almost certain to have trouble here."

On Oct 14th, David writes of the early election results:

"The whole country has the blues today, my darling. Four telegrams of last night bring returns of elections in Pennsylvania,

---

[36] Pinchback, a republican, served as lieutenant governor and acting governor of Louisiana. Born in Georgia, Pinchback commanded a Union Guard company during the civil war. After Reconstruction, he accepted a presidential appointment as surveyor of customs in New Orleans, earned a law degree in New Orleans and lived in N.Y.C. and Washington, D.C.

Ohio and Indiana, and show clearly that Grant and the Negroes are
to be our rulers henceforth.
It would seem as if the Almighty had really cursed us all here --
the devil certainly reigns now, and with such satellites as Grant, I
am not sure that living directly under the old one would not be
preferable -- would it really be hotter with him in there?"

October 17th 1868, David says
"We all still have the "blues", about the result of Tuesday's
elections, and feel almost sure of Grant's success. There will not
be much thanksgiving in the South -- on Mr. Johnson's appointed
day."

Ellen writes David on Oct 19th 1868 that John has invested most of the
proceeds from the sale of the lots in a trust, and that she is having her
brother send $4,000.00 to David for him to invest in New Orleans. About
the potential election trouble, Ellen says,
"If you are to be in trouble at election time my place is with you.
You say you are sure there will be trouble and you wish me to stay
away, but dearest, remember that you are all and everything to
me and don't seek trouble -- for my sake keep quiet.
You are more precious to me than you understand and nobody
else will thank you for your zeal as much as I shall regret it if
anything should happen to you."

She adds that even though she has fallen back into the lap of luxury and
embraced it, she nevertheless looks forward to going back to David:
"I have enjoyed myself very much here, not only in being with,
and seeing, all at home, but in the nameless little ways one can
here. I have fallen back easily into all, what I now call luxuries, but
which I used to deem as essentials, and they are all very pleasant.
I always enjoyed them and knew that I was enjoying them in old
times, I thought then I never could live without them but birds,
when they fly from their nest, must look out for themselves and
build their own nests and I have been happy in my own even if it is
not well feathered.
I am ready this very evening, comfortable as I am, to fly back to
my dear husband and flutter about again among the cheeses and
mosquitoes -- but I would only do this for the sake of one person.
Dear, I love you very dearly and I want to be a good wife to you
and do all I can to make you happy."

On Oct 26th 1868, as Ellen's return to Thibodaux approaches, David writes
that he is worried about the election, as well as about its effect on the
economy ("We do not know how money matters may look -- might
possibly have a crash like 1857 and 60..."). He then alludes to his
relationship with whiskey:

"Nor would there be any whiskey to disturb you, for -- can you believe it -- with whiskey here all the time, I have not touched any for more than three weeks -- and but on three occasions outside."

On Oct 28th 1868, David describes violence in St. Bernard Parish:
"I was rather premature in writing you, on Monday, that the chances were, we might escape trouble with the Negroes.
At that moment fighting was going on below the city -- Parish St. Bernard, in New Orleans there has been constant excitement, with much shooting, since Saturday night.
You are probably informed of this already, by the telegraph, so it is not necessary for me to enter into particulars.
Mr. Moore, who came from New Orleans today, tells me that Warmoth has been compelled to dismiss all his black police, and during the organization of a new set of whites, the city is being patrolled by volunteers from the different clubs. Every man goes armed -- ready for an emergency.
What a state of things to come to! Whether any row will be made here, we of course cannot say but I am truly glad you are away from here."

David writes again of the election on Nov. 3rd:
"The election has passed quickly here, and we shall know by Saturday or Sunday next, whether there will be a disturbance, of course a good deal depends upon the general result -- if the Negroes carry the state, which I doubt, we may certainly look for it. All are anxious here for news from the north, and the papers of tomorrow will be watched for with great interest. You, of course, can know who is elected, by tomorrow afternoon, as all the returns ought to be telegraphed by that time, perhaps even the dispatches of tonight will be sufficient."

On Nov. 5th 1868, David expresses surprise at the election returns. New York narrowly voted democratic (for Seymour), as did New Jersey, again by a very narrow margin. California voted republican by a margin of less than a half a percent:
"Yesterday's news ends all the hopes which had sprung up within the last 10 days, from the strong assertions of Northern Democrats -- that their party was in better position now to succeed than before the October elections. Of course those hopes were wild and foolish at best, but still the wish was so strong, that people could not help entertaining the belief in the success of Seymour. I did not go to Thibodaux -- feeling so sure the news would be bad -- but learned the result from Mr. Anthon. And must say I am surprised.
After all the talk of Northern Democrats, to think they could not carry Connecticut, New Jersey, California, West Virginia and possibly not even New York, is, to say the least, astonishing.

Of course the radical party is now ten times stronger than before, and we may look for every persecution possible. This much can be said however, Louisiana is democratic. Our parish gave a majority of 177, against 600 radical at the last election. Assumption (parish) gives 25 Democratic majority, and almost every other county parish much larger numbers. Whilst the city gives over 20,000. A great many Negroes voted our ticket."

By the next day, David has received a letter from Ellen in which she describes catching her hoop skirt while stepping off the cars (by 1868, New York used a combination of horse-drawn and steam-powered street cars). David inserts a short line rather than write the word "hell" or "hades":

"What an escape you have had! I thank the Almighty God that you are spared to me! But I tremble as I think of it. It seems certainly a special intervention of divine providence. And that you should not even be injured! You must have caught just as that poor Mrs. Knight did, last summer. Oh these horrid hoops! I always did hate them, and now shall never like to see you wear one again -- as also long dresses, which are almost as dangerous. Besides, you look infinitely better in that traveling dress, than since I first saw you in 1849. As for the hoops -- I wish heartily they were all in _____ that place where I hope the Abolitionists are going.
...when you see Mr Taintor please give him my best thanks for his attention to you, and the presence of mind he displayed in supporting you as he did -- many men would have been frightened and let go a lady, under similar circumstances. Oh how thankful I am that you are now safe! Don't Dear, be trying anymore such experiments, and wait until you are sure the cars have stopped."

On Nov. 8th 1868, Ellen writes David,

"This is my last Sunday here. I feel very sad to think it is my last Sunday here at home and the next minute I am thinking how much I want to see you, so I am very divided."

Ellen adds that her father has met with Carter regarding the Connolly business, and says her father assured her that David will get at least a quarter of any recovered amount. Then Ellen touches upon politics, and her relationship with David:

"There is nothing new out here. There was not much excitement at the election. Many rabid Democrats here are beginning to talk Grant-ish. I told them you would have to change the color of his actions entirely at the South before I could agree with them at all -- they said he had not talked any, I said no but he had acted aplenty.
Now mind and keep your eyes open as I come up the Mississippi and remember you are my own dear husband whatever may happen. If I am drowned, my last thought will be of you and the

remembrance of your love shall be my support in the hour of
danger.
If I live and reach our home my love will be stronger than when
we first landed from the steamer nine years ago and I want to
keep it ever fresh and brighter every year."

Nov. 11th, Ellen says,
"I am very busy these last few days and I don't like to steal one
minute from father, mother and Fan."

By Nov. 17th 1868, Fanny writes Ellen to say,
"The house is forlorn without you and the children and I have
wished you back fifty times since Saturday."
When she and the others came home from the pier, where they said
goodbye to Ellen and the children, Fanny says,
"...you can't imagine how lonely it was nor how much I missed
you."

And on the 27th, Fanny says,
"You have only been gone two weeks but it seems like six and I
continue to miss you all and often think I hear the baby crying."
She describes the Thanksgiving dinner she, her parents and John passed
at Augusta and Milt's, which almost certainly presented a contrast to Ellen
and David's table:
"Mr. Carter was invited, making fourteen at table. The first course
was boiled turkey and oyster sauce, then roast turkey etc; then
ducks and chicken salad, boiled plum pudding, pumpkin and apple
pies, then nuts, raisins and apples."

Less than month after seeing her family and working out the details of the
sale of the lots, Ellen appeals to her father for a loan. On Dec. 13th 1868,
her father explains why he must turn her down:
"John has communicated to me your request, that I loan you
$1000, provided you shall require that sum to enable you to effect
a purchase of half the plantation on which you now reside - and
that I await the refunding of this sum of the interest that will be
collected from the $20,000 mortgages that are held by John and
me in trust for you.
I must decline your proposal. The trust of the $20,000 is intended
to secure to you an income of $700 semi-annually and I am not
willing that you should anticipate the receipt of that for any
purpose of business or speculation. There can be little doubt that
you will have and receive from the use of it when it falls due, and
if you begin by encroaching upon the interest months before it is
due, you may soon be tempted to anticipate payment of the
principal. And in this way defeat the sole object for which the trust
was created.

> I trust you will see that I have solely your interest at heart in declining to comply with your request."

On Dec. 17th 1868, Sarah weighs in with a characteristically moralistic bent:

> "So far as I know you have property enough to bring you in a pretty income, so that you and your children, with strict economy, can live within it. Save five dollars of that, rather than anticipate what is not yet in your hands.
>
> I know it requires a good deal of management, that you have within yourself.
>
> You have suffered mortification and pride enough for you to think of this without my speaking, I do so, because it is mine bounden duty so to do. Anything that has an "If" or "But" to it you ought not to meddle with. It is too late to regret when disappointment and debt comes.
>
> You can be economical if you so will and I see the importance of your so doing, then, if trouble comes you have the consciousness of knowing that you did all in your power to prevent it."

Fanny wonders what David proposes to do, in a letter to Ellen on Feb. 16th 1869:

> "What has he done about getting cattle in order to raise stock or have you given up that idea, by your not speaking of it.
>
> I suppose you have. Is David purposing to do anything particular on the place if he keeps it?"

David tells Ellen (Feb. 18th 1869) that his efforts to secure the plantation (presumably Energy) have failed despite his mother's and brother Robert's collaboration and financial help. Whether the property that went to auction is the matching half to the half he owned (the matching half was originally owned by Darden), or the half he owned but lost in bankruptcy proceedings is not clear (probably the latter). In any event, the property went to auction. At the auction, David, Robert Pugh and Eliza had planned for Eliza to take the property (with Ellen contributing her recently acquired $4,000.00, and Eliza ultimately holding a mortgage note for the amount David would owe). But the bank outbid Eliza for the half interest and took it for $10,400. David says,

> "Now the question will come up in our district court, for a sale of the whole property. This suit can possibly be delayed by mother for a year, but scarcely longer, at the end of which time the plantation must be sold. So there is an end to all our plans for ownership. It is true I can still buy mothers half, if I wished to do so."

David writes Ellen on March 26th that he is having trouble finding and keeping appropriate legal counsel at affordable rates for the Connolly business. He spends a significant amount of time traveling to different lawyers' offices, getting recommendations, speaking to them, finding they are unable or unwilling to take the case, or that they charge too much.

David expresses frustration with what he feels is a lack of understanding by Ellen's father. He writes, April 5th 1869:

"Your father's letter was of inquiry in regard to the Connolly business, and a strong injunction to be energetic in hurrying it on -- stating also, that it was of vital importance to you and our children -- meaning of course a satisfactory settlement.

He little knows how much trouble and worry it has cost me. He also said it was his wish, and that of JWH (J. Woodward Haven, the other partner in Haven & Co.), to have additional counsel, and they were both willing to allow fees for this.

All this is very well, but how those additional fees are to be met, when it has been almost impossible to persuade attorneys into undertaking the case, with an offer of 10%, is not very clear to me."

David tells Ellen that he has written a letter to Ellen's father explaining the details of his work on the case:

" I sat down and gave him a detailed account of everything from December last.

...In fine, my account was so prolix, I'm afraid your father will be tired out before finishing it. But he can send it to JWH. At all events, he can scarcely now think I have been idle in the matter. (It took me five hours to write out, condense and copy off my letter)."

David is still in New Orleans on April 15th, dealing with lawyers and auditors, with missing papers and court issues. There seem to be countless variables involved, but David says he has,

"... made a statement of the origin of the debt to Haven & Co., and description of the steps, reductions and different changes in it from year to year up to 1866, which I propose showing to Mr. Baque, our auditor, tomorrow."

David is back in New Orleans June 1st 1869, where he learns that the Connolly case won't come up before November. He is making various purchases for their place, including a purchase of nine sacks of corn that were damaged by weevils, at a reduced price. He says first-rate coffee is 24 cents per pound, as against oolong tea, which is $1.75 per pound. He is sending by steamer along the bayou, mosquito netting, a stove, a saddle, bridle, groceries, material and whiskey. He continues to work on the Connolly business through June 10th, and feels he must go to Toronto soon to take potentially useful testimony from a doctor who had been involved with the Connolly matter.

On August 11th, David is again in New Orleans working on the Connolly case. On August 14th, Fanny describes Newport, R.I. where she is visiting her best friend, Lizzie.

> "The house is about two miles out of Newport on the beach, a very pleasant situation and I enjoyed the sea ever so much, the air was perfectly delightful. Lizzie has a phaeton and horse and we drove into Newport every day to have a peep at the fashionable world and it was a pretty sight on the avenue to see all the turn-outs and the ladies in their beautiful dresses.
>
> The low phaetons are all the fashion this summer, the lady drives and the groom is perched up behind, generally two ladies go together, if a gentleman goes with a lady he does not drive.
>
> Lizzie's phaeton is a neat one and her groom is a little boy about twelve years old who wears a coat with silver buttons and a beaver hat as tall as he is."

Fanny adds that the Havens await David's arrival in Fort Washington, on the way to his Toronto engagement:

> "We are hoping each day to hear from you when to expect David (and John), though the latter I have not mentioned. Mother is already preparing the room for him."

Fanny closes with a comment about a mutual friend of theirs who is married to an alcoholic:

> "Isn't it horrid to have it in a man's power so to ruin a woman's happiness."

On Sept. 3rd 1869, Fanny writes that they expect David to arrive by September 20th. On Oct 1st, she explains to Ellen that their brother John did all that he could to try to meet Mr. Williams in N.Y.C., but that their schedules prevented them from meeting. The Williams' had come up from Louisiana to investigate hiring Chinese laborers, whom they called "coolies". The Williams' were close friends of Ellen and David, and David's brother Richard married a Williams. Ellen took offense at what she perceived was a lack of effort on John's part, spurring this reply from Fanny:

> "It seems a great pity that having gone through the war and with our intense feeling on one side and yours on the other, that any disagreement should now arise in regard to a subject in which one can have an opinion without hurting any one, though whether it is always expedient to express that opinion is another question."

Oct 3rd, Sarah weighs in on the Williams matter. She describes in detail how John did everything in his power to see the Williams' and to provide them with the information they sought.

> "I would merely say that I cannot imagine what possessed you to write such a letter as you did to your brother, or worse, to harbor the feelings and views you expressed in it. I hope you will get rid of them as soon as you can, my poor child, and never allow yourself to write such a letter to any human being again.

We will say no more on this subject."

David writes Ellen from New Orleans Oct. 10th, before he leaves for Toronto to collect testimony from a Dr. Oliphant regarding the Connolly case:

> "...and hope to be in Toronto on Wednesday night -- will write you from Cincinnati however."

He hopes to be back home within two weeks, even with a stop in New York where he will see the Havens. He writes again from Toronto on Oct. 14th to say things are not going well with Dr. Oliphant, and he is being held up as a result. David had hoped that Mr. Haven would prevail upon Carter to meet David in Toronto and serve as Haven & Co's lawyer in gathering the testimony from Oliphant, but it was not to be. David laments several times not having Carter's expertise, and on the 15th says:

> "Now if Carter were only here, he could frame every answer skillfully and concisely, and could easily get to the consul and have all certificates etc. arranged without reading. But your father will not send Carter, and I am really nonplussed."

Carter, as luck would have it, was on vacation, and when he returned, his own practice demanded all his time.

Fanny says on Oct. 18th 1869,

> "Father had a telegram from David saying he should be in Toronto on Thursday AM the 14th. Father sent a telegram and letter and we expect him here hourly and daily."

Also on the 18th, David writes from Toronto, describing his frustration with Oliphant and the seemingly endless obstacles to getting the testimony. David has learned that Oliphant is reluctant to subject himself to questioning because it might reveal that he does not have a medical degree.

> "So although a doctor in name, he has no diploma. Of course he does not wish this known here, as it might ruin his "hard fought for" practice, and it certainly will be made known, if we employ a lawyer here, and very probably, if we go before the US consul, for a proper certificate of his (O's) testimony ... Then, as he still looks forward to a future practice in New Orleans, he is unwilling to have all this made known there, by means of his own answers."

On Oct. 21st, David is still trying to get Oliphant to finish writing out the testimony. The last task is for them to go before the U.S. Consul, and for Oliphant to read out the testimony before the Consul in order for the testimony to be certified.

By Oct. 24th, David writes from the New York Hotel. He has not yet been out to the Fort to see the Havens, and is still getting matters in hand to make the testimony admissible.

Fanny writes Ellen on Oct. 26th 1869, to say that David has finally arrived, and she finds it hard to believe it has been ten years since he has been to New York.

> "I believe I told you that we had taken up whist during the last year and play every evening, Father enjoying the game very much. John being away he persuaded David to take a hand and though he said he had not played for ten years he and I beat them three games.
> This morning he and Father went off on a ride together and Anna and Dr came out to see him...You don't know how it takes me back to old times to have him here, it seems as if the ten years were only a dream only it makes me miss you, it seems so as if you ought to be here too. He has not changed I think, some think he looks older. I don't see any difference."

The next day, Oct. 27th 1869, David tells Ellen his impression of everyone:

> "Your mother is looking so very well -- just as in 1860, not a bit older -- and much more lively and cheerful in fact just as she was in 1858. Your father looks much younger than your photograph shows him. John just the same, but Fanny not so well -- being thinner. Augusta looks splendidly, almost as young as when she was first married...Anna much older."

On the 28th, Fanny writes Ellen saying that she has taken David in to New York City to see some of the new stores and to visit Anna:

> "It was very dusty windy and cold yesterday. I made David walk all about the city and most killed him, then he had nothing to eat till we got home at 3.30. I was not at all surprised that he should want to go to the Barretto's today. He was afraid I should get hold of him again. He intends to stay all night."

On Oct. 31st 1869, David writes Ellen from the Fort to say that he is hopeful he will be able to conclude the testimony soon. He will have to go to Toronto again.

> "Here I am sitting in the green room, where you used to write to me a year ago, and thinking of what you are doing at this moment...if my papers come tomorrow, from New Orleans, shall leave at once for Toronto -- spend one day there, and continue on to Chicago etc."

Mr. Haven has shown him the location of Ellen's lots, and said it is very fortunate that John sold them for Ellen when he did: because of the construction,

> (Ellen's) "... former lots are 15 feet below it (the new boulevard) -- which has taken one half from their value."

On Nov. 2nd, David writes that he hopes to have the papers in order by the next day, so he can leave for Toronto, and be back home within a week.

David finally returns to New Orleans Nov. 12th, but he must see the lawyers before coming home to Energy.

At the end of 1869, Fanny describes her visit to Albany (her description may have reminded Ellen of what she left behind):

"Mrs Parker gave me a handsome dinner one evening. There were fourteen at table, there was nothing placed on the table, which was set out with silver, flowers, fruit and confectionary. Anna's English waiter assisted Mrs Parker's and all the dishes were carved in the pantry.

The first course after soup and fish, was a dish of pates (chicken or veal), next turkey, filet de boeuf, fried oysters and salad, then ice cream, then desert, all the dishes I mentioned were made separate courses. The wines were hock, sherry, madiera, claret and champagne; coffee in the parlor."

By Feb. 23rd 1870, David is working on the Connolly case, which involves running around to various lawyers with papers, trying to negotiate reasonable fees as well as compromises, and trying to ensure that the auditors will be finished before the case comes before the circuit court. David says he has little to do in between appointments, and he expresses his continued love for Ellen:

"I have a terribly dull time, only something to do for perhaps a half hour or at most an hour -- during the day. And I am continually wishing myself back home with you.

You say, " I love you now, but that I could soon forget you and learn to love another woman".

Oh my darling I can never tell you how much my love for you grows from year to year. My heart may be small, in capacity, in comparison with yours, but one thing I am certain of, it can never be open to any but you -- no matter what might ever happen."

He has undertaken the delicate task of appealing to Ellen's father for guidance, because he is fearful of incurring (and being responsible for paying) legal expenses in the case if they prosecute rather than accept a compromise they have been offered:

"That if all the expense -- in case of loss -- were to fall upon you, I should scarcely feel as doing right in risking your interest by prosecuting -- now that a compromise was offered."

March 1st, David is in New Orleans, trying to get the accounts reviewed by the auditors. He makes purchases for their place, including garden seed, hominy, cornmeal, sewing patterns and thread. He writes of Mardi Gras and his wish to get the Connolly place for Ellen:

"This is "Mardi Gras", and the city literally swarming with strangers, to see the Maskers, who paraded Canal and the adjoining streets today. I have never seen so many people on Canal Street before.

All the hotels are full, ... There is to be, this evening, a grand procession of the "mystic Krew of Cornus" -- Frank Marshall says -- finer than ever before. I think of going up to Mr. Congers to see it. But have hesitated all day, whether I ought to do so, when I cannot have you to witness it with me. And only the desire to be able to tell you of it, has finally decided me to go. For really, my darling, with you, I like and enjoy everything, but without you, nothing.

Even in walking through the streets, I am continually thinking -- why is it that I am here and my little wife toiling and slaving at home. If we can only get the Connolly place, then I might hope for some rest and pleasure for you."

David attends Mardi Gras, writes that it was wonderful, and says on March 3rd 1870 that one of the claims has been paid. Although he is entitled to pay himself from the proceeds, he says,

"as I owe debt to Haven & Co. for that sum sent out by your father in 1867, and some money paid me by Tom Hewes, I preferred to send on the $4950. And if your father thinks proper to wait for those sums due by me, until the Connolly business is settled, he can then return me my portion. I preferred to do this, lest he might think me mercenary -- particularly after my letter to him, of last week."

David returned to Energy several days later, but was back in New Orleans at the end of March 1870. The beginning of April finds him again working with testimony and waiting for auditors. On April 4th he says he is writing out papers, talking to the auditor, and waiting to be "cross-questioned" by one of the lawyers. David explains to Ellen why the Connolly matter is so complex, involving as it does several parties, multiple claims, plenty of gray areas and debtors with no funds.

Sarah writes Ellen on the 17th April 1870, and refers to John Haven's impending marriage to Lydia Mason:

"You know that your brother is engaged to be married. I presume they will be married this summer for I have not heard of any time being thought of. They will be here for the present at least. We have never seen her parents and have seen her only once, that, for a few hours only, when she came out here. I understand she is amiable -- she is pretty, not handsome..."

David is in New Orleans on the Connolly business on May 27th. He says the compromise offers have not been nearly good enough to accept, so they must assume they will go to trial in June. He continues making purchases for them, including hominy, hair dye, crash toweling, curry powders, tea, crushed sugar, coffee cups, groceries, a sponge and some linen sheeting samples.

On June 16th, 1870, Anna sends Ellen news of John's wedding (he was 49), which she, Fanny and Augusta attended in Philadelphia.

By mid-December, David is back in New Orleans, the case is at trial, and he is still working with various lawyers and auditors. David has come to New Orleans with Edith (age four), who needs to have a small tumor removed from her eye. He writes Ellen several times in detail about Edith and the operation, assuring her that things have gone well. But Ellen's letter of Dec. 17th 1870 makes clear that she is distraught about not being there with Edith:

> "I ought to have gone with my own child and I shall never forgive you for not letting me go with her if anything happens to her. You ought to have asked your sister Lizzie to have come here and stayed and taken me with you. My poor little girl! If she is going to suffer and needs a nurse and the oversight of the doctor I am coming down to attend to her if it takes every cent I have in the world."

Dec. 18th, she writes again. She is worried about Edith, and she struggles with bills.

> "...I shall await with anxiety to know the nature of the tumor, whether it is cancerous and whether there is any danger of a return.
> ...I have just received a note from Richard [David's brother] asking me for all the money I have in the house, never mind how small the amount, as he was paying off the China men and was short. I wrote him I had not one dollar. I did not tell him I was in debt to Abram for corn.
> ...Willis just came to say that somebody ought to mend the fence down by the sugar house. It was down flat with the post broke. (I think the butcher's cattle do this) and all our horses and cows were over in Mr. Ledet's field trampling his cane down in the wet and some cows were up by the House.
> I told him to tell Nelson to mend the fence tomorrow morning and that I was writing you and I should tell you I had sent him, Nelson, that order. I suppose this is right.
> I think your business very uncertain for I don't understand it. Does the umpire decide at once? At any rate you must come up on Saturday to be here Christmas even if you go back."

Dec. 21st 1870, David writes that Edith is doing very well, and the Connolly case should be decided soon. Meantime, he thinks he has a means of raising some cash:

> "If this Connolly business is not decided next week, I shall see Robert -- I believe he is expected down here in a day or two --and will sell him my filly which will help us out considerably."

David writes on Friday, Dec. 23rd that the Connolly case will come before the umpire "tomorrow", i.e. Saturday Dec. 24th, Christmas Eve day. David manages to be at home with Ellen on Christmas, but leaves again the next day for New Orleans. He writes that Edith is doing very well, and regarding the case, he says,

> "Today we had a meeting before the umpire, but as no one was quite ready - nothing was done except to finish my testimony – all taken down in writing. Tomorrow however the two auditors will be heard…"

On Dec. 30th, David says he feels that Edith is well enough to return home, but:

> "I say bring her up, but really am not sure whether I can leave -- on account of the Connolly business, which keeps me constantly busy. Every day, testimony has been taken in writing, and with the squabbling of the lawyers, matters progressed slowly."

Meantime the case has become even more complex. There is some question about whether a lawyer mis-handled things years ago, and the defense now plans to argue that Connolly was insane at the time he signed certain papers. Witnesses and testimony seem to disappear, the lawyers disagree, and so on.

David says on Dec. 31st 1870,

> "I believe I have given you all the bad news possible for the moment, besides I am much vexed at not being able to go home and see you tomorrow -- so will close for the present."

Early January 1871 finds David again in New Orleans, where Edith is almost cleared by the doctors to come home. The Connolly case drags on.

There is trouble at Madewood, where Eliza has engaged a manager whom David thinks is incompetent. An exchange between David and Ellen shows where Ellen's sympathies lie. On Jan. 3rd 1871, she writes David,

> "… I told him [David's brother Richard] that you had seen Mr. Ratliff in the city and that he had told you things were working very badly on your mother's place and that he feared she would lose part of her crop.
> He said he had been before hand. He had written a letter to Robert [another of David's brothers] saying that he offered Mr. McFall for the plantation and that if his suggestions were not heeded he would never speak again another word, as there were others older than himself to act.
> … I do not think in this matter you act manly, or rather, I mean, assume the position which you occupy morally and naturally. You are now the eldest representative of your father, your mother's

oldest son and oldest child, your younger brothers all look to see what you do and your sisters naturally turn to you.

Your mother has shown you that she recognized your position by giving your child Edwards [another Pugh brother] watch -- I think you ought at once to take your stand. Speak to your mother and tell her that as long as Edward lived you felt she had a counselor, now, as her eldest child, you offered your services and advice to her at all times or at any time.

You have not said this to her and she may think that as you threw up her business you would never wish to have anything more to do with it. I thought when you told Robert that you gave him advice as his eldest brother that that very position made much encumbered upon you and I think he thought the same.

All three of your brothers rely much upon your integrity and they look to you for example. I would like to see you with dignity fall into the position which God has given you, which your mother's widowhood seems to make and which a large family requires should be filled -- you cannot throw off this position and duty upon anyone else that I see -- Richard's remark, that all of you brothers were older than him made me say what I have been thinking ever since Edward's death.

I think it would be a great comfort to your mother for you to say this to her and she would feel at once that she had one firm prop to lean upon whenever she wished. You would also feel better yourself. Make your offer to them and if your mother don't choose to avail herself of you, you have done your duty.

And I shall be very much mistaken if she does not only feel grateful but much relieved at finding that you know what she may require."

Ellen gets another reminder of life in the well-to-do North, when she reads Fanny's letter of Jan. 5th 1871. Fanny is visiting the Parkers in Albany:

"I have had a very pleasant visit, received calls with Anna on Monday the 2nd, about 130 in all. I wore my black silk which is lovely.

Anna lives with much style and spends money like water. She has sobered down and is a fine character, a trifle worldly, but no one is perfect. The house is full of beautiful things.

We breakfast at ten or even eleven, dine at six, all the dinner service is silver and a stately English butler officiates."

Fanny lists the items she was served for dinner the previous night:

"Soup, Chicken pates, Salmon, Sweet breads a la something, Boiled Turkey and tongue, Filet de Boeuf, Fried Oysters and salad, Roman Punch in glasses, Game, Venison, Pudding glace, Ice cream in the form of a bird's nest, the nest of spun sugar, the birds inside of ice cream, flowers outside of ices, Bon bons, candied grapes and orange (fresh) Brandied pears and plums, Cakes, oranges apples and grapes, seven kinds of wine."

On Jan. 6th 1871, David clarifies his feelings about Madewood and his mother for Ellen: he is still feeling the sting from his previous involvement.
"As for taking the position of head of the family -- when mother consults me, it will be time enough. She has not done so, and I have no intention of volunteering my services. It involves more than I care about undertaking -- having had enough before."

The next day he writes again, with more detail about the Connolly saga. Each day brings new developments, new postponements due to no-shows or missing documents, and most recently, the surfacing of documents from 1855 in Haven & Co.'s favor. The war years play a part as well, because they interrupted the time period that would constitute a statutory span of time:
"But the ruling of the New Orleans court has been that proscription was interrupted from beginning of the war in 1861 to the date at the president's proclamation of peace in 1866. If this is so, then we must be all right in the matter, and I am consequently in much better spirits."

On January 9th, David and Edith are still in New Orleans: Edith has not been home for nearly a month, and is eager to see her mother. David is swamped with work to do with the case, and says, on Jan. 11th:
"One thing is certain -- the umpire, if he does his duty, will have a file of papers equal to a dozen books, to go over before he reaches a conclusion."

By early February, David and his lawyers have finished presenting their case, and the defense will present their response. David dares not leave.

Ellen is at the end of her rope. She writes, Feb. 2nd 1871:
"I thought today certainly would bring a letter and I sent Harry for the mail but no letter came.
If you don't write me the progress of things I shall clear out from here for my position here is intolerable. I was brought up to be very particular with whom I associated and every young man wanting in refinement soon understood that he was not welcome to our house.
I am now here living on terms of equality with a common servant man and I am getting indignant. If I had a long table at meals and he sat at a distance I might endure it, if he preserved a servant's silence. But this side-by-side business equality, his rough hair and muddy coat, then evenings his company again, is more than I can endure.
When you are here you are my companion but I don't like the looks of your being gone all winter and leaving me, your wife and

a lady, such companionship. I have commenced tonight sitting in my own room.

That you should be willing to leave me in this situation and that you should see nothing derogatory in it, hurts me. It is not as if I had grown children.

He is waiting for you to find him a place and you could have easily written or spoken to Richard about seeing if he was needed on your mother's place and if not you could have told him distinctly that your mother and brother did not need him and that you must tell him frankly that you gave up all hopes of finding him a place. You don't consider that poverty and work don't make me any less naturally a woman of refinement."

On February 4th 1871, David apologizes for Ellen's situation, and says he is still planning to raise some cash by selling his filly to his brother:

"Robert has offered me $300 for that Filly of mine, and I am going to accept it tomorrow."

David is beset with frustrating situations to do with the Connolly case, all of which he details to Ellen. He hopes to come home soon, but fears that if he doesn't poke and prod all the actors in the case that nothing will progress. He wants to "stay (at home) until the case comes into court." On Feb. 5th he writes,

"I was until two o'clock decided to run up home tomorrow, but at that hour Boyne told me he should make a motion in court on Monday morning to compel Race to proceed, so decided to stay and see the matter out. Unless I do stay, Boyne will do nothing. What a tiresome business this is -- nothing but putting off from day to day -- with now over one months delay!

... I have the blues terribly now -- all on account of this external delay in the Connolly suit."

On February 8th 1871 David responds to Ellen about their debt (Capt. Francis is one of the players in the Connolly case):

"That we are in debt is undoubtedly true, but I have only borrowed that $41 to pay Capt. Francis...The $41 was borrowed from Foley, Conger & Co. That $300 for the Filly will go upon account of my debt to Robert. I hope I shall need no more money for the suit."

David is in New Orleans in March, and he and Ellen write each other nearly every day. In mid-March of 1871, David thinks of dividing his portion of Energy into two pieces and selling half of it. David has the blues about the Connolly case, and is tortured about what decision to make regarding accepting a compromise from the defense, which would net them less money, versus pushing the case through court, which would take longer, potentially incur legal fees, but possibly result in getting more money. He seems unable or unwilling to make a decision by himself, without constantly deferring to Ellen's father and/or uncle, or appealing to relatives and friends for advice.

March 13th, David writes Ellen about dividing Energy and keeping half:
> "...we are to have Mr. Thibodeau come next week and survey the property, to then run a line of division -- giving the respective areas of the two tracts -- with a description of the buildings etc. Now this will take some weeks to perfect. And then will come the question of which party taking the house and sugar House -- the cabins will necessarily go with the other tract. Now some arrangement must be made with the consolidated bank, about dividing the mortgage. And after all this, if there is a compromise in the Connolly matter, we must try to work out our half of the place, from the Connolly money. I see no other way. Have been thinking of this for several days, and have concluded that it might be done -- of course only in a small way, but still it can be done."

March 15th 1871, Ellen writes David,
> "...I think you had better telegraph father for I feel pretty sure he will compromise after that awful blue letter of Boyne's. I was for compromising myself. How like a humbug he has acted-
> I hope you will decide to put this place up and sell it. The more I think about it the more convinced I am that it will be perfectly ruinous to divide it. When once divided, if you take house and sugar house you have a terrible outlay to make for cabins etc. with three or four years work besides, before you make a sign of the crop. If you take the other part it will be no manner of use to you and if you want to sell either half, you will never get for the divided parts, anything, I am convinced.
> On the other hand if the whole place should be sold for $20,000 you have then to go and buy a small working place and make a crop this year. If this place sells for no more than $20,000 you can buy a small place with the first year's cash payment less than $10,000. Do think well on this subject."

March 16th, David writes that Ellen's father has telegraphed:
> "Today at two o'clock, his dispatch came in, as follows 'proposed compromise insufficient. Prosecute suit. Explanation per mail today'".

But by the morning of March 23rd 1871, David's letter to Ellen says he has written Ellen's father and her uncle to say that he will be forced to accept the compromise unless Ellen's father and uncle are willing and able to put up the additional monies needed to continue the case. From what David says, letters have been lost (letters of his, to Ellen's father, and letters referenced by Ellen's uncle and Ellen's father, that David never received). David writes a second letter March 23rd, in the evening: he has heard from both Ellen's uncle and father. Ellen's father has stepped back and reiterated that his interest was given over to Ellen and he wants nothing further to do with the Connolly case: Ellen's uncle wants a greater amount than the compromise offered.

March 24th 1871, Ellen tells David that she doesn't understand his confusion, and that she has been clear about the arrangements in the case from the beginning:

"My dearest husband,
About five o'clock this afternoon I received your letter by a gentleman who drove by in a buggy. Everything is so clear to me that I wonder you do not see the whole case as I do, in short as I told you it stood. Father's letter is very natural and in fact relieves my mind.
...I see now the whole case stands yet as Father first represented it. I am put down for $15,000 (he told you this distinctly, be the bargain made by you, what it might), the case stands between, you, me and uncle and you are the acting person. You were to pay costs and engage your own lawyer. You have done so, the lawyer has acted in bad faith to us, and now we must share the brunt of this.
If we chose to get an unreliable man that is our loss and we have no business to bother uncle about this.
...Father said simply he would like to hear how the suit progressed as I am his child and you must remember he takes consequently a lively interest in my interests. You have asked his advice and he has given it, I told you this was unnecessary unless you preferred it, and your answer was, you preferred to do so.
...All that is now to be resolved is this. Will you be satisfied with the compromise for you and me. We have the largest share and if we can raise the money, can prosecute the suit even if Uncle prefers the compromise...You do not want to write, telegraph, or wait for letters, my interests are in your hands. Decide at once. If you prosecute, take the money or go ahead. If you did not choose to make a binding bargain with your lawyer in the beginning that is our loss and our fault. Nobody to blame but ourselves."

The very next day, Ellen writes on the same subject:

"Dear David,
The more I think of this business the more I think I would not take such a miserable compromise without reflection. Fix the sum (I am not enough of an arithmetician to know what this is) which after paying you and uncle will leave me $15,000, then costs besides... Tell them you will take no less than this or you will prosecute suit and then await their answer. I think this the best thing we can do. If we have to prosecute, drive the easiest bargain you can with that old Boyne... then we must rake and scrape and poke another year."

Again Ellen writes on the 26th, saying that it is clear that David has not received her previous letters.

> "...I cannot see why you should say that you don't like fathers giving up the case at this point. I have read and reread all of father's letters carefully and I can but arrive at the same and my first conclusion. Father will not dictate to us, it comes now to compromise or not.
>
> ...You are the one to act for your own wife in this case, if you want, he wishes to show you that he must not act for me but that I must be the person consulted. He is right in this, considering the claim as it stands. He would be behaving very wrong I think to say, do this or that, he places all the claim with us, you and me and uncle, and he can only suggest and answer your letters.
>
> ...No, I think fathers action now perfectly clear and gentlemanly, he will suggest or advise but not dictate.
>
> ...All this of course I write my dear husband as I talk I do not wish to influence you either. I agree with Father, you are the responsible person and you must decide. I should write nothing further to New York..."

In this same letter, Ellen expresses frustration and bias at not finding the same caliber of people along the Bayou as she did in New York:

> "There were but few real ladies and gentlemen around or with whom it is agreeable to associate. I long for a little intellectual society and some persons who I consider an equality with myself -I hold myself immeasurably superior to these people."

In a letter written the next day, March 27th 1871 from Fanny to Ellen, the divergence in lifestyle is apparent:

> "...The port man has just been here so the incident of the day is over.
>
> I had no letters, only a card for a bonnet opening from Mrs. Breadon. I believe round hats are going out of fashion.
>
> I am going to Aug's [Augusta's] for my (almost) daily visit, then dress Mother's hair and have dinner. The afternoon will probably be spent in reading and sewing with Mother, unless it clears and I go for a walk."

Despite Ellen's repeated counsel that David not only is free to act on his own, but that she wishes he would take a firm stand one way or the other in the case, David waits for further word from New York. On March 30th, David writes,

> "Yesterday my telegram came in from your father -- as follows 'yours of 23rd to Woodward received. He will ratify any settlement you make' [signed] J A Haven"

But David is wracked with indecision and says, about the lawyer:

"I have shown him the telegram, but have come to no conclusion. He advises me strongly to take the compromise, and if I had any confidence in him, might think his advice sincere. But as it is, scarcely know what to do."

From this letter of the 30th, it is seems that David goes from one person to another seeking advice rather than making a decision.

"...It is a great responsibility to decide for you, and this causes much of my hesitancy -- when I think of the possible delay of the suit. ...I have been very uneasy and uncomfortable since the receipt of the telegram -- scarcely knowing what was best...and you see my darling, I give you nothing now but doubts and hesitations...I can only give you, what I have myself, the blues -- and might as well say no more."

Ellen writes on March 31st,

"Feel as if mine, was yours, and feel no deeper responsibility than if the whole case was simply your own, and if you can decide much easier. The responsibility of deciding for me, is simply for deciding for yourself."

Ellen ends this letter with,

"Harriet wants money and I have none. Mrs. Young comes tomorrow and I have not a cent."

In fact, Ellen is carrying the duties of Energy alone, day after day, week after week.

Fanny writes, on April 4, 1871,

"I am very glad David was able to run up to see you if only for a day. It made a little change for you."

Finally, on April 15th, David writes Ellen that the case is over, and he has accepted the compromise: "At last I am -- one might say -- through with the settlement... You don't know what a relief it is not to feel the constant strain and worry about that Connolly business. But how nice it would be had we only gained the suit!"

The Daily Picayune carried the notice of the settlement of the case:

"The Daily Picayune Saturday, April 15, 1871: The Courts. Haven & Co. versus Connolly et al. -- The report this day filed by M. M. Cohen, United States commissioner and umpire appointed in this case, being now by written consent of counsel submitted upon all the records, documents, writings and evidence before the auditors and umpire in their reports.

... judgment in favor of the plaintiffs and against the defendants for $28,998.72, with 8% interest on $39,332.35 from June 1, 1861, till April 1, 1863, and from the latter date on $28,998.92 till paid, with special mortgage and privilege upon the plantation and property described in the act of sale and mortgage annexed."

Fanny has heard the news, and writes on April 28th,

"I am glad the Connolly case is settled at last and I hope it is satisfactory to you. I have not inquired particulars, only understood generally that it was settled. I hope David got from Uncle Woodward, or will get, just as much money as he possibly could."

Also in this letter, Fanny comments on "Miss Alcott". Louisa May Alcott's father knew Ralph Waldo Emerson (Emerson's brother married Fanny's aunt). Fanny may have heard about the loss of Alcott's manuscript from her friendship with the Adamses. The Adamses, friend of the Havens and particularly Fanny, were connected to publishers Ticknor and Fields (Annie Adams married James T. Fields). Fanny recommends getting Alice Miss Alcott's new book.

"If you don't think of anything else please get her Miss Alcott's "Little Women" in 2 vol. It is a sweetly pretty story and if she has not read it she will like it, but I don't care about it if there is any trifle she would prefer.

...Miss Alcott is a New England girl, lives in Concord. She went as nurse in the war and her "Hospital Sketches" was, I believe, her first book. "Moods" is very interesting and I like it, Aug. thinks it an improper book and perhaps it is demoralizing in its tendency. "Little Women" made her fame and fortune and she is abroad now enjoying the well earned money. I think it was $40 or $50000 she realized. I heard the other day that the manuscript copy of her last book was sent to Mr Fields and he most unfortunately lost it out of his pocket. Of course he will have to pay her for it and lose by it."

By May, Ellen's father has received hurtful letters from both Ellen and David (Mr. Haven refers to David as "Mr. Pugh"). On May 22nd 1871, he summarizes the amounts she has recognized by virtue of his efforts:

"My dear Ellen,

I have your letter of the 12th, and one from Mr. Pugh of the 9th. I am much surprised at their contents, and cannot conceive why he and you have stirred up such a mess?

I have replied to your husband per this mail.

In answer to your letter I have only to say that my motives, or my letters, have been entirely misconstrued, but I have never for a moment imagined you "grasping or ungrateful", nor have I ever doubted in the least your affection, I may add, though perhaps unnecessary, that I have always thought your husband was doing all in his power to secure for you the Connolly debt.

You have, as always, my love and esteem, so you must remain contented and try to be happy in possession, and prudent use, of the sums received from me. So let us terminate this matter and in future find more pleasant themes to write about.

You understand that the 16 lots was my gift to you at time of your marriage. They produced about $29,000.

The Connolly claim results in $ 9900

This last in the effect against $15,000 at which the claim was transferred to you to be deducted from your share of my estate upon final settlement of my property.

You thus realize now $9900 on which no interest is charged, in all probability is worth more to you than $15,000 would be at a future day.

Your affec father
JAH"

By Nov. 20th 1871, David is in New Orleans doing follow-up work on debts and notes related to the Connolly case, and attending to business on Energy. He describes his new livestock purchases and how he will care for them. In subsequent letters, David writes in detail about purchases he is making for the house, and clothing he is buying for the children.

Thanksgiving day, Nov. 30th 1871, Sarah writes Ellen about the items she has shipped to Ellen for Christmas. At the end of the letter she adds a little dig:

"...our post man who comes every day on a very plump black horse and hands us our letters and takes all we had to send. This last is quite a handsome man -- he wears spurs and I think he must have been a soldier in the last war.

He must have been on your side, for no such fat plump looking man ever came back here from your kind care and prisons –

You give me a nice slap in each of your letters to me, even now, this is the only one I believe I have ever given you -- I have refrained from principal and love to you my dear child –"

Later that Thanksgiving day of 1871, a little more than 16 years since the terrible fire of 1855, the Havens had another encounter with fire. Fanny describes it to Ellen:

"Thursday, the 30th of Nov, was Thanksgiving day. Mr. Carter and Woodbury dined here, no other company. It was intensely cold and a very high wind blowing.

At ½ past six in the afternoon, the old barn took fire and was burned with all its contents. I can't begin to tell you how fearful it was. Woodbury, John, and Mr C- were there at once and in ten minutes the place was covered with gentlemen, men and policemen, in 20 minutes the engine was here from the village as the report was that our house was on fire.

For a little while the house was in danger, if it had been wood would doubtless have caught. The wind was in this direction and blew the sparks and burning hay in showers on the roof (tin you know) and my balcony. John stayed some time on the roof with pails of water putting out the embers that fell on the railing and scuttle. There wasn't much danger, but there was some. Fortunately there was a very light fall of snow on the grass which checked the flames as they run on the ground. The men devoted their care to trampling out the fire as it caught the dried leaves. At one time Mr C- had fears that the bridge would take from the sparks; some of the pine trees caught and here and there parts of the fence. However in half an hour the danger was over. About nine the gentlemen came back to the house, leaving the hose playing on the fire. They had to go round to the valley and cut a hole in the ice there in the pond to get water.

Every one says it was set on fire, it is supposed some vagrant or straggler may have crept in there to sleep on the hay and perhaps had a pipe or let fall a match. Of course it is all supposition. We lost the double sleigh and the cutter, plows, harrows etc., John's rabbit hutches, the cider press and a good many odds and ends, besides hay and wood. We heard afterwards that the people in the Ingham house were much alarmed and in the house opposite that, the lady put up her jewels and silver. You can imagine what a state Mother was in for a while. Indeed neither she nor Father have got over it yet."

Dec. 9th 1871, David is back in New Orleans trying to resolve issues with the Connolly case.

David continues the pattern of going to New Orleans on some business or other, and makes purchases for Ellen, the children and their place. Ellen never gets away to do her own shopping, such as selecting fabrics and choosing her own groceries and supplies. David is looking for another place to buy, perhaps in keeping with an earlier notion of his that they could make a better living on a different place, or by leasing out one or another place.

On Feb. 6th, John Appleton Haven writes Ellen that he hopes,
"your husband will not decide on any purchase of a "place", till he has well considered all the pros and cons".
He adds,
"...I would like to know how your money is invested and what interest you are receiving from your property. It is quite important that your husband [Mr. Haven omits a word] your resources very carefully -- for you must not depend upon the future for what may be forthcoming from real estate at Fort Washington.
...I will only add that I look with hesitation and some fear upon your investing any of your funds in the purchase of a "place", you must bear in mind that it is much easier to buy a place than to sell one in Louisiana -- it is easier to put money out than to call it in."

February 18, 1872 finds David in Galveston, TX, looking at and trying to sell land, possibly on behalf of Ellen's brother John. Five days later he is in Waco, TX, and learns that the legal requirements for sale of the land have not been met; also that in order to inspect the land, he must ride 80 miles on horseback each way. He must have a map made, have the land surveyed, and a deed created. The value of the land is compromised by the presence of squatters. And, he says,

> "Traveling here is very fatiguing and rough... is attended with many annoyances. Railroads run slowly, and make bad connections, whilst the stage traveling is rough in the extreme, as well as being slow. The hotels are horribly filthy, and a really clean and good meal but once since I left Galveston and that only endurable."

Not forgetting Energy, David tells Ellen,

> "Please send for Nelson, and tell him -- that he must plank up those cut places in the levee at once, for the river is now rising. He will understand about it, and you can give him the sugar house key, to get the plank.
> I shall be gone about a week or 10 days -- in a place where there are no mails, so you must not expect to hear from me immediately."

In a letter dated March 10, 1872, David explains how the squatters complicate things.

> "A suit is required, in the New Orleans court, to oust the squatters and get possession of the land, whilst if I sell now, the purchaser takes this travail etc. upon himself.
> These squatters claim under sales from a man who bought the land under a fraudulent tax sale in 1850 -- or 55. In any other country but Texas the whole thing would be pronounced a fraud, but here, where a man has a shadow of title, and lives upon the land for five years, working and paying taxes -- no matter whether the real owner pays taxes on it or not -- he then becomes the owner.
> These squatters claim to have bought in 1859 from a party who had possession from 1855, but Coke, Herring, and Anderson assure me there was really no party in possession until 1859. Now from 1859 to 1872 would of course make more than twice five years. But fortunately these "statutes of limitation" were suspended from the time that Texas seceded January 28, 1861 until April 20 1870 -- a period of fully nine years, which saves John, if those parties did not have possession before 1859.
> ...I have written John a very long letter explaining this, and telling him that, if I cannot sell now, we must not lose a day in instituting suit against the squatters, every single day counts against him and in favor of them.

John of course knew nothing about these laws, and thinking that by paying the annual taxes, through his agent at Galveston, no possible trouble could arise. Now this agent never troubled himself to find out whether any squatters had come up on the land, or anything about this fraudulent tax sale, and the mischief really commenced about 1855, nothing but the war saving John."

David's letter of March 16th 1872, from Waco, Texas, gives the impression that he feels somewhat trapped in another family business duty whose complexity is reminiscent of the Connolly case. But the fact is that David, unable to make a living, was probably offered this work by John Haven in an effort to create a win-win situation for them both.

"I am most heartily sorry of ever getting into this trouble, but now, ought to do something for John if possible. If he (John) had only availed himself of my offer of 1866, to attend to this matter for him, all this trouble, and worry of doubt of title would have been avoided.

...Now, I cannot sell the land for anything like its value, until that question of title is settled in a New Orleans court. And this suit will cost time and money.

...Have been again humbugged by a proposal to purchase. The party proving to be of no solvency whatsoever -- this result obtained by careful inquiry today. I am now of the opinion that the land cannot be sold for the present. Wish the whole tract in bottom of the Red Sea."

March 31st, David writes from Brenham, Texas:

"Do you know they (Indians) were in Hamilton County on the morning after I left, and passed over the very ground traversed by me. One day later for me, or sooner for them, would have made something of a change in my fortunes."

From her mother, Ellen receives a newsy letter in March 1872, urging Ellen to come visit for the summer, either alone or with some of the children. With John and his (essentially invalid) wife Lydia there, as well as Fanny, Sarah must consider some constraints on the numbers.

"I wish you to bring two of the little girls with you, old enough of course not to need a nurse (I cannot have another servant in the House either mine or yours). Those who will be little, or, no care to you. Your rest, recreation and pleasure are to be the first things is to be considered, and I deem them very important things. I can accommodate three of them, if one of them can sleep with you. We would prefer that Alice should be one of them, if you bring three."

David is delighted to get letters from Ellen at Brenham, Texas April 2nd, 1872:

"I cannot describe to you, my darling, the joy with which I received, yesterday afternoon, your two letters -- 24th and 26th. What a relief to my mind! I capered about like a child, and felt almost as happy as if I had your dear arms around my neck, and that dear face close to mine.
I shall soon have this I hope, for today is my last one for business. The sale comes off this morning, and I hope to be through with all papers etc. by night.
If not then, then tomorrow noon at the latest -- when I shall take the cars[37] for Galveston, and at 2 p.m. next day, a steamer for home. So be sure and look for me on Friday."

April 27th 1872, Ellen gets a letter from her mother saying that Sarah is delighted Ellen will be coming to visit, with several of the children. On May 6th, 1872, John Appleton Haven's brother and partner in Haven & Co., as well as the partner in the Connolly case, J. Woodward Haven, died suddenly[38]. By early June, David is in New Orleans making purchases (linen, corn, cornmeal, soap) again.

By August, Ellen is in New York, having traveled this time by land rather than steamer. David writes on August 4th:
"I am picturing you now -- as just about to reach Fort Washington -- that is allowing one hour and a half from Jersey City, and glad indeed, my dearest wife, must you be to reach home once more, and to see your dear parents again -- as also your brothers and sisters."

Edith, Alice and Thomas are with David; Grace, Mary and John are with Ellen.

On August 10th 1872 David describes matters on Energy:
"I have been busy all the week seeing to the hauling of the manure into the garden, finished last night, with 40 cart loads. Next week shall start to seeding, for turnips and cabbages. Wednesday -- from half past nine to a quarter past 3 -- was devoted to sponging the cows with coal oil, for ticks. 19 cows were sponged, and a troublesome job it was for me -- in fact made me quite sick all next day. I had three men to help, and yet consumed nearly 6 hours -- to say nothing of 8 gallons of coal oil.
On Monday night our cistern fasset gave out, and Jeff could find none in town to suit, so I was obliged to go myself.

A few days later, David writes to say that the heat has been unbearable, and, in an unusual twist, there has been so little rain that he was forced to

---

[37] "take the cars" almost certainly refers to horse cars.
[38] Joseph Woodward Haven, born 6/14/1803 and John Appleton Haven's junior by 11 years, died in N.Y. at age 69 on May 6 1872.

139

haul water from the Bayou for laundering, so the crops suffered as well. And, "The weather has been so
intensely hot as to cause most of our cream to turn to whey."
On August 17th, David makes a comment that suggests his bitterness about helping his mother has softened:

> "I returned from up the Bayou yesterday morning, should have been down on the night before, but waited to see General Nichols about some land business for mother."

August 22nd 1872, David has bad news about their animals:

> "We seem to be having quite a run of bad luck around the premises. Two days since Jack [a dog] took to worrying the chickens so much as to require his shutting up. But that fine Brahma hen in the yard was bitten so that she died during the night before last.
>
> Then one of those fine large gobblers, brought from July Anne, was killed yesterday afternoon. Struck by a stake -- either by Minerva or old Ellen, I am not sure which -- and died in a few minutes. Then this morning one of our young turkeys and a capon and found dead in the hen yard.
>
> And my finest essex sow must, during the night, overlay three splendid pigs just two days old.
>
> And now, whilst I am writing, Minerva comes and reports the loss of 12 young Leghorn chickens -- hatched out a few days since. She says they were shut up in a coop -- so that not even a rat could get to them. So it must have been a snake who passed through the round holes.
>
> I am having a search. But am satisfied that with our Wood house and wood piles we are harboring rats, snakes and perhaps minks -- rather I find it is a rat."

David receives a letter from Ellen that elicits a reply on September 4th 1872:

> "My Dearest Wife,
> Upon going to P.O. yesterday, I found yours of Aug 29th. I have been looking for something ever since you left. At last it has come. Not what I expected; but better that than nothing.
> During the thirteen years of our married life where we have had differences in most cases the fault was mine. And as soon as convinced of this I have wished – cannot say that I have always succeeded – to express my sorrow and regret.
> In the present instance the case was different. Nevertheless, when on the day you left – in the carriage – I told you I was sorry you were going and that I should miss you, and when I took your hand, my feeling of anger was entirely gone, and I used those words and the action to show it to you. I was perfectly sincere – as in fact I always have been – showing irritation when angry, but never retaining anger long: and, my love for you was as strong as

at any previous time. I wished entirely to forget the fact and never to recall it. That feeling is as strong with me now.

I have loved you since I first knew you well, in 1852. And every day proves how much you contribute to my happiness. Your absence has been felt keenly: but at the same time the feeling has been different from former occasions. For now I know that you were estranged. That you had talked of a separation; and of course this last could but have its effect.

Now however that you have written, I feel better, simply because it is time that this estrangement should end by proper explanation and understanding on both sides. I have nothing but affection for you and I know that you love me strongly.

Any mention of simple friendship between us is absurd and one which I could never think of. I tender to you the same love as when we vowed together to love each other forever, 13 years ago. You say one thing you will exact: that I speak to you as a man should, to Woman. Where I have been wanting in this respect, it certainly has not been intentional...I earnestly hope never to offend in the future. "

David ends his letter on the subject of their marriage:

"Recollect I send no sham love, but the real and true to you: and there must be no talk of friendships."

Sept. 12th 1872, David tells Ellen of more livestock woes:

"I have had bad luck with my pigs. My finest sow died yesterday. She never seemed well after having her pigs, and finally got down on Sunday, I doctored and nursed her to the best of my ability, but was of no use.

Then one of my pigs from the first litter was found dead this morning. It must have been killed either by a horse, or struck by some thief. I have seen Nellie kicking at the pigs of late, or should be sure of the latter cause.

We have had some chickens stolen of late, despite my being up part of every night. I shall change my hour of watching -- from the last part, to say from 10 till one, as this seems to be their hour for coming."

On the subject of the dairy products, a mainstay of their income, David has concerning news:

"Something is defective about our milk, and this since very recently, it neither makes cheese nor butter. Up to last Sunday we had plenty of clabber for cheeses, and sold from 12 to 14 pounds of butter.

During the last weeks this has dropped down to seven or eight cheeses, and the butter account shows only 4 pounds sold. This too with about the same quantity of milk.

I cannot make out the trouble. The pasture is becoming dry and hard, owing to dry the weather, but this ought to affect the quantity of milk, rather than quality."

On Sept. 21st, David begins a letter to Ellen with an intriguing leading paragraph:
"My dearest wife
Your letter of the 15th came to me yesterday -- as also the one from John, together with his to Thomas. I had been hoping to hear from you since Monday, and now the letter has come, wish that it had not. How much it has pained me you would scarcely desire to know. And as it implies a wish that no further reference to its contents be made, of course I shall say nothing more."

What could Ellen have written him to cause this reply? Perhaps she has rejected his overture (in his letter of Sept. 4th) to restore their relationship to its former intimate status. His letter continues, recounting descriptions of the children's activities and the events at Energy. His next letter on Sept. 25th makes no allusion to whatever Ellen had written him.
On Oct. 1st David indicates in a letter to Ellen that they will be returning from New York together, which means he plans to make the trip to New York to bring them home.

On Oct. 3rd, David writes Ellen and again touches on whatever it is that Ellen has pressed him about in her letters:
"Your letter of the 27th came yesterday. It has humbled me completely my darling. I now see that I have been harsh, cruel and exacting, where I should have understood you better, and been tender. Pray forgive me my own dear one! I shall never forget this, and hope -- will try earnestly -- to do better for the future.
I feel now how often I have been cross and rude to you, and have had no sympathy at times when you needed it, and came to me for it. This too when I felt you were all and everything in the world to me. Many times too have I nursed up anger, and encouraged myself to think I was right in all things -- and that I was doing my duty by you.
Now my eyes are opened, and if you will only forgive, and trust me once again I shall do my best to deserve your love -- that love which has been so true to me all these long years. How I wish I were with you my darling to ask this in person. Then you could see how deeply I feel what I am now trying to write.
...And may you feel that you can give me back your full love."

On Oct. 6th 1872, David writes Ellen:
"The last one [letter] gives me much sorrow, and much pleasure. Sorrow that I should have so long misunderstood you, and caused you so much pain by my selfishness and obstinate determination

to bend you to my will. The Joy is that you can forgive. It shall be my work and my pleasure to try and make you forget.

It is not necessary my Darling that the Children shall be a bond of sympathy between us. I love you more – much more- than all of them put together. And I think of you ten times to once for them. My only happiness in this world comes from you."

Oct. 12th, David sends a letter describing his plantings, the activities on Energy, and the purchases he has to make. Then he adds a note revealing the gist of the economic landscape:

"The city looks dull, and everyone short of money – particularly the sugar merchants, who seem discouraged with their prospects. From what I learned of the crops elsewhere than on the Bayou -- there will probably be 250 plantations abandoned next year, from want of funds to carry them on."

October 21st, David replies to Ellen, who may have softened a bit:

"...I am so glad my own dear darling, that you can feel towards me as you did of old. There has never been a time when my love for you was not very strong, and even in my angry moments I'd never relaxed that love -- only thought I could mould you to my will, and never thinking that I was causing you such pain. I see it now however, and for the future will try earnestly to prove to you that I have profited by the past.

That beautiful passage which you quoted, has been coming up before me since yesterday, and I feel that it will make me a better husband.

The time is soon coming my dear wife, when I shall take you to my heart, and tell you this. And I hope earnestly and truly that there may never be the slightest difference, in thought or word between us from that hour."

In a letter of Oct. 29th, David responds to a suggestion Ellen has made that they stop at Niagara on their way back home:

"You ask about Niagara. Of course we can return that way, and it will only delay is two or three days at the farthest. The children might perhaps never have another opportunity of seeing it -- at any rate for a long time."

November 3rd 1872 David says he needs to finish up some work with their hay before he leaves for New York, and he mentions that he is troubled by the work he is doing for Ellen's brother John:

"Now my darling I must stop, to write a letter to Texas -- on account of John's business. I received one from John yesterday. He is not satisfied with the way things are going, and I must do the best I can. But it is a troublesome business, and I wish I was clear of that. I shall tell him so when I go on."

After a letter from Alice to Ellen November 10, 1872, there are no more letters until Dec. 3rd, when Sarah writes Ellen a birthday greeting. Sarah says she received a letter from Ellen written Nov. 27th from Niagara, and that she guesses Ellen and her family have reached St. Louis.

March 8th 1873, David writes Ellen from New Orleans. He mentions that he has just received a letter from her, and that it is the first letter he has gotten from her since the prior October before he went to New York to get her and bring her home. The rest of his letter is about purchases for their place and local news.

April 21st David writes Ellen from New Orleans. He and Ellen had been in New Orleans together for a time, but Ellen went home to take care of the children and Energy. David made some purchases for the place, but otherwise is looking for livestock and has been to the races. By May 24th David is back in New Orleans again and is about to leave for Virginia, where he is to pick up Arthur Foley and then return home. He writes again the next day from Atlanta, and in both these letters he includes instructions for Ellen about their place. Two days later, on May 27th, Anna writes to say she has heard of the death of David's Uncle Patrick Foley. David may have made the trip to Virginia to retrieve one of the Foley's, after having learned of his Uncle Patrick's sudden death. On May 30th David writes that he has picked up Arthur and will be leaving Alabama soon to return home.

Sarah writes Ellen on June 19th 1873, to say she has gotten a letter from David telling her that Ellen is suffering from a severe illness. On June 29th, Sarah writes again saying she received Ellen's letter written June 19th, and she is sorry that Ellen is feeling so sad and discouraged. Sept. 12th Sarah writes again, and from one of her comments it is possible that Ellen's severe illness and discouragement were caused by miscarriage:
> "I have been quite grieved to learn how ill you have been, you see now my dear, what serious results occur from married women straining and reaching so and working so hard -- you would never believe me telling you all this -- you have preferred to learn by experience, even to your insides being turn all out of place. I am very, very sorry and I am very angry likewise. Be sure to write to me every particular of your recovery. You know I miscarried once and came very near losing my life by reaching up to close a very high window -- it jerked me."

In October, Sarah writes again, this time referencing a fever that Ellen and the children have had:
> "I have been endeavoring to feel able to write a few lines to you to say to you how grieved I am and have been, to learn of you and the children being ill, although we are told that this fever which has attacked you is not of a dangerous character."

On Nov. 7th 1873 David writes Ellen from somewhere, probably near New Orleans, and says he has just received her letter written Oct. 30th. He speaks of issues on Energy, of Ellen's dental work, Alice's piano lessons, and problems getting help at Energy. November 20th, Sarah writes that she has received Ellen's letter of Nov. 13th, in which Ellen says she has begun to recover from the violent illness. Nov. 23rd, David is in Alabama for reasons unknown, and he refers to their effort to grow rice:

> "In case any lumber is put out on the Bayou -- don't be uneasy about it. It is intended for the rice troughs."

Two days later, David is back in the New Orleans area, and has taken Mary to the doctor and looked into several purchases for them. On the 28th, he is still making purchases:

> "I went to Lewis about your shoes. He promised to make the next pair of better leather -- said he was often deceived in his leather, and could not be sure -- that since the war in France, leather was nothing like as good as before. The same thing about French satin -- that it would not now last at all, and he much preferred using "English lasting". I took a piece of this last to show you before ordering the cloth shoes. Lewis says he can put new leather on your shoes of last spring.
>
> Have bought the starch soap and the yeast powders. They all were shipped today, with the half barrel of white sugar, tea (2 pounds of English breakfast and one black) tomatoes, one flat peas and coal oil.
>
> The flannel shirts were also sent from Levois, and in the package, Irish moss, Sapolio, lamp wicks, and letter paper. These all ought to reach home tomorrow at -- say 2 p.m., on the flat boat, together with 20 sacks of corn."

On November 29th, 1873 David is still in the city, shopping. Some of the items are far from qualifying as "necessaries": a pop-gun for Thomas, a real gun for John, a croquet set and some candies. He responds to a question Ellen has asked, "You ask about our money matters, they are, I believe all right." David is still away from home on December 1st, but comes home soon thereafter. His next letter is written January 24th, 1874, when he is in and around New Orleans, again making purchases for Ellen and their place.

Ellen's brother John Haven writes her from Fort Washington on January 28th, apprising her of her investments, commenting on David's involvement with land in Texas, and telling her about her parents. Ellen's mother, Sarah Sherburne Langdon Haven, is now 77 years old, and John Appleton Haven is 82: for the times, they are very advanced in age. John tells Ellen,

> "I suppose Fanny and Anna have kept you advised of mother's condition -- she has gained strength I think rapidly -- she is, of course, feeble and delicate, but so much better than she was a month ago that we ought to feel much encouraged -- the recovery

from such an attack as hers, at this season of the year, and in a person of her age, must necessarily be very slow.

Father has been under a heavy cold -- but he is better. He and mother have kept each other company in their room -- not that father was of necessity confined to that chamber -- but, not feeling well and the weather being disagreeable, and mother keeping her room, he thought he would stay there -- should we have two or three real pleasant days he would think it beneficial to move out."

In this letter, John responds to a comment Ellen has written, and infers that he believes people have a measure of control over their condition:

"So you have turned philosopher and are satisfied to take the good and ill which the gods send to you in just such doses as they measure them out to you.

I can't say that I believe in this doctrine. We make, and can make, much of both good and ill ourselves. Can increase our happiness by making the best of every thing, and can easily work ourselves into the most painful and pitiable condition by nursing and brooding over our trials, and sorrows.

I quite agree with you that it is not well to set our hopes too high -- "Blessed are those who expect nothing, for they shall not be disappointed" -- nevertheless if we did not look onward and upward there would be no progress."

On the subject of David's planned trip to Texas, John says,

"You speak of David having some plans about going to Texas -- and in a letter to one of the family since I received yours of the 12th you say that he will probably be absent a month -- perhaps two -- I do not see what he can possibly find to occupy so much of his time there, unless he proposes "running a place" -- I have heard nothing about Texas affairs for several weeks.

Perhaps he wishes to stay there until he sells out all the land and can bring back a pocketful of money -- I shall be very sorry to have him find it necessary to make any such sojourn there. I suppose I shall hear from him something about his plans as soon as he has matured them."

Meanwhile, David is still in New Orleans, as he writes January 29 1874:

"You are doubtless surprised at neither seeing me nor hearing from me for so long. The fact is I have been hoping from day to day, to go home since Tuesday. But have stayed to arrange for the getting end of our funds, and to see about investing them for another year.

In 1874, times are still bad for planters. David says they cannot get the types of advances they used to (before the war, Haven & Company's business involved, in part, making advances for seed):

"Times are awfully dull here in money matters, and sugar planters have no showing at all for advances."

January 31st, David writes again, and his sense of frustration at not having work is evident:

"For a new investment, I am as yet undecided. If put out on mortgage, another year like the last might, and certainly would ruin the planter, and me perhaps lose the whole if not, a part at least...
Have half a mind to leave it in the house, bearing interest at 8% -- at least for awhile, until things look a little different.
And again, am almost tempted to look about for small sugar plantation. This because I ought to, and must go to work some way, have been idling quite long enough, and I'm not sure whether I could not make something at sugar -- since the prospect for a crop seems good. Have been thinking it all over in every way all day, but as yet with no conclusion...This keeps me here, otherwise I have nothing in the world to do."

David sounds busy with purchases, despite his complaint of having little to do. Included in his purchases are sheeting, gauntlets and kid gloves, belts, flannel shirts, pillowcase linens, some re-worked shoes for Ellen, and

"a barrel of flour, one of meal, one of Bass's ale for you, and a case of coal oil. The grid iron I shall probably bring up with me."

March 5th 1874, Ellen receives a kind letter from her mother, in which Sarah says she is feeling somewhat better. March 19th, Ellen gets another letter from David, who is in the city getting provisions:

"I have shipped today, per Henry Tete, the barrel of grits, 20 sacks corn, three barrels of flour, two barrels of cornmeal, one cake containing five dozen yeast powders, 1 gallon Demi John whiskey and one cask bacon shoulders. All this freight ought to be landed on Saturday morning, and I wish John to be on hand to see about it."

He also gives instructions as to how John is to distribute the freight, since some of it goes to other people. David says he is also looking into another plantation.

May 22nd 1874 brings a letter to Ellen from David, who is on his way to Texas; he writes again twice on May 24th from Galveston and Houston:

"Am growing very tired however of being away from you -- don't this appear strange to you, when I went to New Orleans for nearly a week without writing?"

Ellen writes David on May 24th, about John Pugh and school matters, and May 26th David writes Ellen that,

"...from failure of crops and low prices last year, there is but little money in the country, and no demand for wood lands just now... now no sales to be made at anything short of ruinous prices."

May 31st 1874, David writes a letter filled with details about his efforts to resolve the Texas land matters for Ellen's brother. Typically (typical of David, or typical of the times, or both) it is complex and the principals are difficult to untangle. Nor is it clear what David's stake is: presumably John has offered some percentage to David, if David is able to sell John's land at a profit to John:

> "I shall perhaps offer to sell to Remnick for $7,000. This will give John -- provided Remnick accepts -- a very handsome profit on his investment, and relieve both him and myself from much vexation and worry. Besides, when the matter will be finally closed out, if we go on as up to now, it is impossible to say."

Also on May 31st, Sarah writes Ellen urging Ellen to come visit over the summer. In this letter written about a year and a half before her death, Sarah says she would like Ellen to bring Alice and Grace with her. She says she would have written Ellen sooner, but she needed to see how her own health progressed.

> "I have taken my pen to invite you to come and pass this summer with us, we likewise wish you to bring Alice and Grace with you: I mention these children, not only because your father and I wish them to come, but, to please Frances as she wishes a visit from them particularly."

Sarah adds that if Ellen can't come, she should consider sending the girls with a safe escort.

June 5th 1874, David writes from Waco, TX,

> "...after a tedious trip – just 175 miles altogether, and with a horse traveling at best only about 4 mph."

The Texas land matters are a mess, and David is disgusted, seeing scant hope of selling. He is afraid there is much work involved to get things straightened out. And, he has learned that John Haven has not received the letters David sent him:

> "Now, the nonreceipt by John of my letters is inexplicable. My last was from New Orleans, mailed May 16, if you recollect I read you a copy of it. I have that copy here with me. Then he has not received your letter acknowledging receipt of check. I mailed that letter in Thibodaux myself.
>
> I have not written John from here, because I hoped to add a large amount in the sum received from Gentry and send all from here. Besides I hoped to be able to announce a final settlement of this worrisome business with Remnick.
>
> Now I wish you would take my letter from Brenhorn, the one sent you from here last Sunday and this one, do them all up in a big envelope and mail them to him. It will at least give him some idea of how matters stand.
>
> ...As soon as I find out what I can do with Remnick -- for sale or settlement -- shall write John a detailed statement of everything, and forward in the money."

By June 11th, David writes that he has painstakingly gone through the accounts for one of John's land investments, both for payments made on it and interest due. He has,

"...written John a long letter -- 3 1/2 sheets -- giving a full statement of everything," and hopes to sell the land to the man who seems to have been a partner in John's land purchase before leaving but the man has thus far been unable to come up with the necessary cash."

On June 19th 1874 David is back in New Orleans making purchases, bringing Alice to the dentist and to visit family, and finishing up the Texas land business:

"I have been so busy yesterday and today in writing up and sending off the money and papers to John, as not to give me any time."

Because Alice needed extensive dental work, David is still waiting for the dental sessions to finish on the 22nd. He says, in a letter of the 22nd, that he thinks Alice and Grace can go to New York by steamer around mid-July, so it seems Ellen will not be going to visit her family after all.

Then on June 25th, Sarah, having received word that the two girls will come without Ellen, writes to say,

"I write now to beg you will think again about your coming on with Alice and Grace, we wish very much to have you do so if you can make any arrangement to that effect. Your father bids me say that he wishes you to, and the two children also. That he will pay for your passage coming on and returning also for the two girls passages coming and returning.

Enquires have been made and it has been ascertained that there are two splendid steamers belonging to the Cromwell line, one, the "Knickerbocker", the other I do not remember the name...

Having full authority from your father to thus write to you, I have caught up my pen to tell you as I have written also, of his wish that you should come. You know my dear child how glad we shall be to receive you.

...If we are to be disappointed about you, which we will not think of -- your father will pay the passages of the girls, if you find an opportunity to send them by."

John Appleton Haven writes Ellen July 10th to say,

"Your letter of the second just received by your mother, shows many and sufficient reasons why you should hesitate, and perhaps decline, visiting us this season. It would, you know, afford us great pleasure to see and have you with us. But upon careful consideration of the lateness of the season, and the many objections that interfere and would mar the comforts of your visit, we think you had better defer it till another season - you must act as you deem best, and let us know, as soon as you can, what you decide upon.

Your mother continues quite an invalid, and endures much pain and exercises much patience under her afflictions, she walks about the premises and rides out occasionally."

There is no indication of what problem prevented Ellen from making the trip, until a letter from her father of July 20th 1874 makes clear that it was a lack of help:

"I have just seen your letter of the 15th to your mother, and we are all delighted that your good angel, Miss Ann, has descended and visits you just at the happy moment, to enable you and Alice and Grace to make us the visit we have been so fondly anticipating."

Ellen's father says he is writing in great haste, so as to get the letter in the next mail, and he says he sees no reason "for altering or revoking my promise to pay the passage of you and the children coming and going." He adds a postscript in jest:

"PS I shall not send money for your passage - but pay when I see you here. I give no credit in my business matter but pay in cash on receipt of the articles."

Ellen, Alice and Grace came to Fort Washington and stayed until November. On November 8th, Sarah writes Ellen,

"I thought you would like to receive a line from us on your arrival at home, have therefore taken my pen to say that we are thinking or speaking of you all the time."

Sarah is not able to get down the stairs, and says,

"I wish you would tell Alice and Grace that I crawled to my south window, with my cane and saw you pass from down the hill through the entrance gate."

On Nov. 20th 1874, David is on the road again, and says, "I go to Mobile, Atlanta and Lynchburg." But he writes again on the 21st, and is apparently doing some shopping for them in New Orleans. He gets matting, binding, oilcloth rug for the hearth, material for pantaloons, a vest and coat, and shoes. He mentions that he has a check that he is having trouble cashing, and that this is holding him up.

From a letter of November 23rd from Ellen's father, it is apparent that something has gone very wrong with David's handling of some funds. John Appleton Haven writes Ellen that he has received her letter of Nov. 16th. Conger is the man with whom David kept his money, from whom he borrowed, and with whom he spent a significant amount of time:

"I am not surprised at its contents. I shall now make no comments. No one, but your mother and Fanny, will know anything from me about it till Mr. Pugh has made his visit to John which probably be at the end of this week.
I wish you at once to see Mr. Conger, if you cannot see him then write at once, so that you may get his answer before your husband returns, ask him to send you at once any balance however small,

even if it be not over a dollar - and request him to send to you an exact statement of the sum that was deposited in his house, and any particular statement of the dates and sums drawn out by Mr. Pugh. Whether all drawn at one time, or at different times, and be very exact in his statements and to send you any sum remaining in his house, if it be but $25.

It is very important that you have this at once and before your husband returns.

When you next write let me know about your city railroad stock and what money reserves you have in hand.

You have our pity, that is from consideration under your dreadful affliction."

At the bottom of this letter are notes, as if Ellen was making a draft of what her father had suggested above, that is, that she ask Conger about her money:

"I wish you would send me word whether you have any balance of money belonging to me in your hands remaining from money which was put in my name in the firm before Uncle Patrick's death. If there is none remaining to my account will you send me an exact statement of the sum that was deposited in your house and a particular statement of the dates, and sums drawn out and whether all were drawn at one time or at different times. Also how long the principal was drawing interest."

The very next day, Nov. 24th, John Appleton Haven writes again. The reference to "Mr. Pugh" is David.

"My dear Child,

I wrote to you yesterday, wishing you to get immediately from Mr. Conger a statement of his account of the monies deposited with him and of the particulars for the disposal of the same and an order for him to send to you any balance remaining in his hands - I write now to urge you not to let an hour pass till this is done and I wish the accounts sent to you and not directed to Mr. Pugh.

There has been great mystery and immorality somewhere and we must try to find out all its particulars and to know all about the speculation in the land and other transactions in which your uncle's funds have been lost as Mr. Pugh tells you - take nothing in trust of what he says and have no confidence nor faith in anything he tells you. I write this for your eye only - destroy this letter. I have my doubts if I can see him here and should he come on I will advise more fully after I learn the results of his intentions with John."

On Wednesday, November 25th 1874, David writes Ellen on the way to Lynchburg saying he expects to arrive in New York by Friday the 27th, and he signs his letter,

"Goodbye my angel wife
shall write you again tomorrow

> kiss our dear children for me
> your husband"

He writes again Thursday the 26th, saying he expects to arrive in New York at about 5 p.m. friday. He signs his letter,

> "With love to our dear children, and a loving kiss to you my angel wife,
> ever your own
> DBP"

He writes Ellen again Friday the 27th, from the Grand Central Hotel Broadway[39], in New York City, saying that he expects to see her brother in the morning, or, at the latest, by Sunday.

On Saturday Nov. 28th at 2 p.m., David writes Ellen to say he visited his Aunt Elizabeth Foley, who lives in the city, and,

> "Am just out of bed, having had fever and terrible headache all night, just able to crawl about the house, so shall not go out today."

Sunday and Monday he does not write, but on Tues. Dec. 1st, he writes,

> "I have not written you since Saturday. Have been quite unwell -- with fever -- until now. Went today down to John's office, but did not find him in. The clerk said he generally -- when in town -- comes at about 12 o'clock. This was at half past 11. I passed back about one, but did not see him. Left the note -- the first time -- asking him to call here to see me between three and 5 -- when I thought he would be through with his business for the day.
> In case he did not go downtown, or has not seen my note, after five o'clock I shall write him and send a message up to the Brunting house -- to know when he can see me. If the answer comes before the last mail closes -- 7 p.m. -- I shall write you.
> It is terribly lonely here. I have not seen a soul except Aunt Elizabeth and two of her sons -- one was at home when I went, and the other, John, called to see me.
> ...As soon as I see John, will write you everything in detail.
> With love to our dear children
> Ever your own
> DBP

Why David does not simply go out to the Fort is not clear. His fondness for whiskey and staying in hotels may have played a part, or he may have been avoiding the Haven family.

Sarah writes Ellen on December 7th, about David and the (apparently) missing money. There is no indication that she has seen David at the Fort.

---

[39] Also known as the Broadway Central Hotel, it was opened in 1870 and was said to be the largest hotel in the U.S., with 400 rooms, all of which would be steam-heated.

"This terrible business of yours has almost made me ill, I am thinking of it continually: I commenced writing a few lines to you, but, had to give it up, my hands are so swollen and lame.
You must now keep any sum of money, if ever so small, you may have on hand and any sum, or sums you may receive of your interest money here, or, may receive from any other source in your own hands, do not give to anyone any money for any purpose, or, alleged purpose (necessary) household purpose -- even your right to pay for everything you purchase, and you ought to keep an account of everything your money is spent for -- remember, my dear, darling child, that you are trying an experiment and give no delegated power to anyone, but, know that everything is paid for -- keep all and everything in your own hands.
It is my present intention to make no mention of this sad subject to you again and I think you are bound to attend to what I have now written to you."

There are no letters the remainder of December 1874 or January 1875. It is possible that there were some, but that they were destroyed.

Sarah, with some effort, writes Ellen February 4th 1875.
"Waldenfield
February 4th 1875
My dear Daughter,
Yesterday (3rd) -- I received a letter from you of the 29th of January. I wish you would give my love to each of your children and thank them each for the many pleasant letters they have written to me -- say that I am not well enough, oh no, to write to them..."
At the bottom of this letter is written in John Appleton Haven's hand, "Your father's love to you. Keep up and do your duty and have patience under all trials – J.A.H"

February 26th, 1875 (less than a year before her death), Sarah writes, mostly in pencil and in a very shaky hand, to advise Ellen. The Mr. Conger she refers to is a long-time friend and advisor of David's. Ellen has long taken a dim view of Conger and all the time David has spent with him, and she may also feel David has either chosen to rely too much on him, or, that Conger has taken advantage of David.
"Go to your own room by yourself to read this
You know, my dear Ellen as I have cause to know myself, that we cannot afford to throw away kind offices received from anyone, or to throw away friends who have been kind friends to us.
I have been thinking a great deal of you and made up my mind to tell you what I believe would be my course were I you; I have placed myself in your place and I have placed myself in Mr. Conger's place with regard to you.

I presume he knows nothing of your dreadful trouble -- he has no reason to have an unpleasant feeling then why do you turn him adrift? What right have you so to do?

He knows that he has done nothing to offend you, he sees your domestic relations go on as usual and I should yet in his place believe that you blamed <u>him</u> for money hereto for placed in his hands.

Had you not better as a matter of justice to him write a handsome note to him asking him to attend to your business as he formerly did?

I believe that he will consent if your note to him is written in a very kind, courteous spirit, he certainly has no reason for declining, unless you <u>are</u> <u>employing</u> someone else -- I am sure you will be doing right, if he declines that will make an end of him, do not fire up my dear Ellen. There are cares where we must not allow our pride to decide for us.

I do not expect you to allow any eye but your own to read this - - you must shut yourself in your own room to read this – when you have it by heart, burn it --

Mother

26th of February

A little more than five months later, Ellen is in New York with her son John, to visit her mother Sarah. On July 15th, David writes,

My dearest wife

Yesterday's mail brought a letter from Anna to Alice, telling of your safe arrival at her house on Friday last, also that your mother was no worse, I trust most fervently you found her much better than you expected, and, If it is her desire, she may yet be spared for some time to you.

Anna said she was not now suffering much pain, but was prostrated more by nervous excitement, if this last can be relieved, and the pain does not return, I see no reason why she may not live for months yet.

Anna bids us expect a letter from you or John by today's mail, so I am going down. She says you looked fatigued from the journey. I hope you have not suffered much in this way, or that you had no trouble like last year. The weather here was intensely hot, and if it was so on the cars the inconvenience must have been terrible.

...Have just opened letter of ninth with your penciled addition. How I feel for you my dear wife in this terrible affliction. Until now I have not been able to realize that all was so hopeless with your dear mother. But now I know what it is. May god comfort you my darling, and all in this terrible trial.

Ever your own husband

On July 23rd, 1875, Ellen writes Thomas (her youngest child, 7 years old).
"Master Thomas Pugh

Thibodeaux
Friday, July 23, 1875
My dear Thomas, I have written to all of the children and now it is time to write to you as it is your turn -- I am glad to hear that you are busy studying your lessons and hunting up the turkey's nests. John stays at his Aunt Augusta's and I don't see much of him. He comes down once a day to see how his grandmother is, and how I am.

He has already worn out his shoes on the rocks here and yesterday he went in swimming for the first time. He is amusing himself principally just now with shooting with Frank[40] at a mark with Frank's rifle. I see boats passing on the river here all of the time.

Large steam boats with flags flying, on pleasure excursions, barges with music on board carrying parties of pleasure, ships pass, rowboats, sailboats, yachts, canal boats towed down, ice barges with windmills on each barge and all the barges fastened together with a small tug pulling them along, and also immense rafts pass, one of these had a three-story house on it. So the river is beautiful night and day.

Everything is lovely here, so much more beautiful than in Louisiana. But poor grandmother lies sick and suffering in her rooms upstairs and wishing that God would open his heavenly gates and take her home to meet her own mother and her children who are waiting for her in heaven. When she calls for her mother and calls to go home, Uncle John says some beautiful comforting words out of the Bible to her and reads her some hymns or a beautiful prayer and then she gets quiet and peaceful.

Do you think one of these days when I am sick that you will give up all your pleasures for me as Uncle John does for his mother? Never mind how sleepy or tired you are night or day, forget yourself and fan your mother hour after hour, turn her with such very kind and gentle hands such as only love for your mother, can give you, makes her drops and never get tired of taking care of her? Will you learn some hymns to comfort me with one of these days? Many times when I have been sick way off in Louisiana I have had no one to read a hymn or a verse to me and I have had to shut my eyes and say hymns to myself.

Lou has just come in with rosy cheeks and a message. Appleton has a bottle with little sugar plums in it and I must bring you home some like them if I can -- Appleton gave me a few –

You must study as hard as you can so as to be ready for Mrs. Young's school next October --

Give Edith a sweet kiss for me and take a nice large kiss yourself from your dear mother. My love to Miss Ann and your sisters.

---

[40] Frank is Frank Hopkins, Augusta's son. The references to Lou and Appleton are to Louise, Augusta's daughter and to her son John Appleton Haven Hopkins.

On August 4th, 1875, David writes Ellen and speaks of Sarah, then gives news about the children and their clothing, and talks about having sent some documents to Ellen for which she apparently asked. He ends with information about their place, and issues with some of the help.

"It is nearly a week since I have written you, and since then two letters came from you -- of July 23 and 28. Both give cheering accounts of your mother's condition -- the last particularly so. I am truly glad of this, and hope she may be spared for some time longer. There seems to me no reason why her mind should not become clear again, for with returning strength of the body, the brain ought certainly to be strengthened as well -- at least I think and hope so...

I send you by today's mail, an envelope containing those papers from the US court, showing about the transfer of claim to McCollum and amount paid by him, also Clark and Boyne's statement -- when I asked Boyne to make out one for me, he said, a copy from one on his letter book would suffice, he hunted this book up and copied the statement.

Then I recollected where -- and amongst the Connolly papers -- I must have placed the original, and hunting it up, now enclose both to you. I send also the agreement between McCollum and myself, about selling the plantation. And Dr. Oliphant's receipt for $75.00 gold -- $100 currency -- all that I ever paid Oliphant for his last testimony -- I had previously sent him an amount of his charges for testimony given under previous commissions.

The amount which ought to have come to you was 66/100 of $15,000.

My interview with Mr. Conger was not a pleasant one, and I do not wish to speak of it. Just now at any rate..."

David writes again on August 30th 1875, describing how Alice and Grace have been visiting at his cousin Eliza's, and he has taken Thomas, Edith and Mary with him to Eliza's for a visit. From there he proceeded to his mother's at Madewood with Thomas, Edith and Mary. He left Edith and Mary with his mother for over ten days, and he and Thomas went back to Energy, then got the girls from Madewood and made another visit to Alice and Grace at Eliza's.

David asks how Anna is, and whether she ever has pain where the tumor was: this marks the beginning of Anna's bouts with recurrent cancer tumors and operations to remove them.

He describes how the high waters have impacted the health of both the rice crop and the people:

"Our rice crop is just ripening, and one tenant, Michael Guillot, started this morning to cut -- in a small way as yet. I hope we shall have better weather than other rice men, whose crops were more forward, have had. Some have been cutting for upwards of a fortnight, and there has been heavy loss from rains -- rice lying in the water and sprouting badly. It cannot be stacked up when even damp, for fear of heating, so Planters must leave it just where they cut, until dry weather.

The present high water carried out on the rice fields has brought every amount of sickness -- chills and, what is worse, bilious fever, and our doctors are on the go all the time. I don't recollect as much sickness since the high water of 1865 -- when you were in New York. Almost every household has someone down -- either white or black. And I am very glad to get our children away for awhile. Am giving Thomas bitters every day, to keep him well if possible."

David advises Ellen not to come home before October due to the risk of illness.

September 15th David writes that he has had trouble with the help being sick, Thomas has the fever, and he (David) is running late in picking up the girls (who are still with Eliza, and at Madewood).

Ellen has heard from others that David's mother, Eliza Pugh, has been ill. David says,

"When I took up the children, I found she had been sick, but was then much better. She had given up the housekeeping to this, and also her seat at the head of the table, but was looking pretty well. In fact, nearly as well as usual. In fact she was just as talkative, and as fond of scolding as ever, so I concluded there was nothing serious."

Ellen writes that she plans to return home to Energy soon, to which David replies,

"I think it too sickly for you to come so soon.
And besides, there are strong rumors of considerable yellow fever in New Orleans, with how much foundation I cannot say, but Mr. Williams told me on Sunday last, that there was fever in the lower part of the town. And Dr. Fleetwood told me on Monday, his letters told him of a good deal, and the doctors were trying to hush it up."

Two days later David writes about the fear of yellow fever:

"I went to Thibodaux yesterday, and found the community pretty well excited and scared. It seems there have been one or two deaths from bilious fever, where the bodies have turned yellow immediately after death, and the whole parish is under alarm. One of the cases is reported to have died with black vomit, but whether this is true I cannot say.

To give you an idea of the alarm, Dick, who came over here yesterday afternoon to learn about Thomas, told me -- the reason why Mary [Pugh, Richard's wife] had not let Tony come over was, she was afraid until something more could be learned about Thomas's illness.

Dr. Dancereau...says it is not yellow fever, but a malignant type of bilious, which is generally fatal, and which in time of yellow fever epidemics would be called yellow fever, it is not contagious, but comes from malaria in the air. So much for what Dr. Dancereau thinks.

Now I think you had better stay away until all this is over. I do not wish to have you undergo such risk, or even to be sick at all. You are too precious to me -- although you do not think I believe so."

David writes on September 19th that Thomas is still battling the fever. Alice and Grace have been brought down to Energy by Eliza, on instructions sent by Ellen. Ellen and John returned home, most likely in early October, and the next letter is a note from Fanny to Ellen of November 6th.

"Mother has been very rational lately, quite right some days. She says "Give my love to Ellen over and over and over again, she did perfectly right to go home if she thought it her duty and I hope she will be very happy with her children, I send my love to them too. I think she did quite right to go, but I wish she could have stayed with me.""

Illustration 39: Alice, 1874 (photo courtesy of Alyce Rossow).

Illustration 40: John Haven Pugh's christening
dress, currently restored and made available for
family use (photo by John J. McInerney, Jr).

Partings (1875-1880); David's Alarming Behavior

In November, Anna writes Ellen about the death of her much beloved husband, Dr. William Sweetser, who died October 14th 1875. Anna was utterly devoted to "the Dr.", and although he was not very active as a member of the Haven family, he was notable in his field. Anna, born in 1819, was about 22 years younger than the Doctor (Sweetser was born the same year as Anna's mother Sarah).

Her letter telling of the Doctor's final day and death is long, and is very moving. She says, in part,

> "...it seems as if my heart would break, it is very sore, every inch of the house is sacred, every hour I miss him more and more, I feel so homesick. Father came in, was with me and you don't know what a comfort that was. I seemed to be sustained, and the reason was I could not realize it, I seemed to do things mechanically, as though walking through a dream. He seemed to be with me and comfort me. Miss Oakley said he had a most noble head, and after his death it seemed as if I could not look at him enough. He had such a quiet placid expression. I think his expression was very (intensely if I may say so) patient and beautiful for the past few years. I loved to look at him. When he was reading and was not conscious I was. I think he always tried to do his duty consciously, and if he had met with many sure trials, that he is at rest now."

By early December, Ellen's father is taken ill. Born in 1792, he was 83. On December 7th, Fanny writes Ellen,

> "Dearest Nell
> There is no change in Father since yesterday, Last evening Dr F. said his situation was critical and there must be a change for the better soon or he would not rally.
> He takes very little nourishment but has retained what he took since yesterday …
> Dr. Metcalfe is to see him this afternoon.
> John has sat up for three nights and Anna and I most of the time. Augusta is here during the day.
> Will write each day
> Yrs
> Fanny"

December 8th 1875, Fanny sends another note to Ellen:

> "Wednesday
> Dec 8th 8.20 A.M.
> Dear Nell

161

I see no improvement in Father this morning, not the least change
for the better. He is very feeble.
Dr Metcalfe saw him yesterday afternoon and said unless he
changed for the better before night he should consider it hopeless.
No disease but failing of all the vital powers.
Will write again after Dr F- has been today
Fanny"

Fanny writes twice the next day, December 9th 1875. In the morning she
writes that Mr. Haven seems better. Mr. Carter is there with them, and
they are getting a male nurse. But that afternoon, she writes,

"Dear Nell
The Dr said this morning that Father was not quite as well, had a
little fever and was weaker than yesterday. Still he was not in
immediate danger and as long as there was life there was hope.
I think him very ill, but still do not give him up.
Yrs
Fanny
Thursday 2.40 P.M."

The situation appears grim by December 11th, when Fanny writes,

"I wish I had an encouraging word dear Nell to send you, but I
cannot. When the Dr saw Father yesterday morning, he said his
pulse was feeble and he much changed. His case was hopeless and
he thought he could not live two days. Then I sent you a telegram.
In the evening Dr F- said there had been no change since morning
and he might linger some days.
He lies in a quiet way, takes very little notice of any one but when
he does rouse expresses a wish to have John and me with him
constantly and as soon as I come, puts his hand out for me to take
and hold, so I stay with him all I can.
We fan him day and night.
I asked him just now if I should give his love you and he bowed his
head.
Yesterday we spoke of you to him and he said "good child".
Just as soon as I can I will write you everything.
Yrs
Fanny
Saturday 11th 9 A.M.

John Appleton Haven died December 13th, 1875, age 83; Sarah Sherburne
Langdon Haven died within about a month of her husband, passing away
January 17th 1876, age 79. There are no letters from David, nor any from
Fanny, between December 11th 1875 and late February 1876. Based on a
comment in a letter written from James C. Carter to Ellen, Ellen probably
came for her father's funeral, then left for Louisiana, and shortly thereafter
her mother died.
Carter's letter to Ellen is dated February 11th 1876:

"New York City
Feb 11th
My dear Mrs. Pugh,
I have supposed I would have had a draft of your will prepared
and ready to be sent to you ere this; but I could not draw it until I
had examined your father's will and could not see that until last
Sunday...
Do not think you are causing me any trouble. It is a friendly office
which it is a pleasure for me to attend to.
In the meantime it will perhaps relieve you to know your father's
will leaves your share in trust for you and, should you die without
making a will, in trust for your children until they reach the age of
21 years. And as to your own property you already have a will.
I most sincerely and deeply sympathize with you in your
afflictions. To be absent from the bedside of your dear father and
mother when they were passing away- to feel that your old home
around which so many fond recollections cluster was to be broken
up - and all this to come upon other cares and troubles must have
overwhelmed you.
You must however remember that in the course of nature your
dear parents could not much longer be with us; that your father
passed away with so little suffering, and then your poor mother's
death must have been an infinite relief. Could you but have seen
her countenance after death, serene and lovely as it was, with
every trace of suffering effaced, it would have been a great
consolation to you.
Your allusion to my long intimacy with your family and
participation in so many of its joys and sorrows and your noble and
generous expressions of friendship, so characteristic of you, fill at
the same time my heart and eyes. I can scarcely see to write
these lines.
I feel as if I had myself lost all I would call home; and, but for the
relief which is found in the incessant occupation, should be
overwhelmed with the sense of loneliness.
You must not surrender yourself to grief. This is one of the
inevitable vicissitudes of life. It is the common lot.
You must accept it as such; and, remembering how much you
have in your children, move cheerfully along.
Ever affectionately and truly
James C. Carter"

February 26th 1876, Fanny writes Ellen detailing how the silver might be
divided so as to please everyone. March 2nd she writes again, and talks
about how very different life is for her now that caring for her parents is
no longer the focus of her existence.
"Dearest Nell

> Even now it seems so strange to think that I have plenty of time to
> write to you, could write all day without any one needing me for
> anything."

Fanny goes on about family matters, and ends with a discussion about
what clothes to get for mourning during the warm summer months:

> "I don't know about mourning for summer as yet. I am making
> inquiries and sending for patterns and if I learn anything
> satisfactory will let you know.
> ...As Lizzie is in deep mourning, Mrs Green and Mrs Griswold Gray,
> I am pretty sure to learn what is best and suitable.
> ...I hate cheap looking mourning and handsome mourning is very
> expensive.
> ...I was glad to come back here, where I seem to be nearer the two
> dear ones who are gone. I am homesick for them when away."

March 3rd, Fanny writes Ellen and says she has received two letters from
Ellen. Fanny has given Ellen some money toward the children's school,
either a loan or a mix of a gift and loan. Fanny feels that Anna and John
are too sensitive:

> "Sometimes it seems to me as if you and Aug. and I were the
> three who would hang together the longest, A- and J- seem to
> exact so much in some ways and are so quick to take offense.
> Perhaps they feel the same about me, who knows?

On the 13th, Fanny resumes the same letter to Ellen, saying that one of
the Haven's servants has left for good, and her leave-taking upsets Fanny
terribly.

> "Talking with her and parting from her upset me entirely and I
> could do nothing else all day but sit and cry. John was in town so I
> had no one to interrupt me.
> ...My friends are and have been so kind to me that I feel that I
> have no right to impose my grief and sadness upon them any
> longer. So now when I have to see anyone, I always try to put my
> own feelings aside and enter into theirs, but life is one long heart
> ache, day after day.
> Whenever I sit in the front parlor with any one, I see Father in his
> arm chair and Mother in her low chair close by his side, with her
> knitting and I listen and talk like a machine with my heart full of
> memories and struggling to keep up an outward composure.
> You know how the least thing brings back everything, Gussie
> [Hopkins] came in brightly the other day and said there were two
> yellow crocuses in bloom under the parlor window, the first ones
> out.
> She no doubt wondered (poor child) what she had said to make
> me throw down my sewing and walk up and down my room, but
> all I could think of was how Father always brought in those first
> crocuses to Mother, every Spring. So every day brings up
> something.

Physically, I am very well, but there is no spring inside to keep the works in play, any little trifling thing upsets me completely and I do not seem to be my own self at all."

March 25th, Fanny mentions the money she has given Ellen:

"Also, I want to say now, what I have had in my mind for some time, that if you prefer, or think best to use the money I give the children, in any other way than schooling or music for their benefit, of course you must do so, you being the best judge what they need."

Again Fanny describes her loneliness:

"Augusta is lovely to me, so kind and tender and seems to be thinking of and for me all the time. The girls too – for instance, Gussie always tries to be here when I come out from the city, to open the front door and welcome me and little things like that. But no one, with all the kindness, can take away the heart ache and the loneliness of living. It grows more intense day after day. While I do not wish really to have them back, I find it more and more hard to live without them."

Toward the end of this letter, Fanny makes the case for Ellen to come North: Fanny's pain is palpable:

"Is there not any possible chance of your coming on this summer or fall with one of the girls? Then perhaps you could leave her to keep me company till Jan or Feb. and then I could come out with her to you for three or four months. Then perhaps coming back I should be drowned and then I need not make any further plans. I suppose I shall have a room or rooms somewhere next winter. I do not think John will stay here after the fall. I should not mind being here alone if Aug. and family were here, but if they go in for the winter, as they are desirous of doing, I should not care to stay. In that case should want to have some hole in the city to stay in till I came to you.

You be thinking it over. We are all exceedingly desirous to have you here again before the house is given up. If we could be all together, so many things could be settled far better than by letter. Indeed it seems almost necessary, apart from the pleasure of being together here once more. I want you to think of it seriously. The expense we can easily manage.

We would be very glad to advance the money to you and some far off day you could repay it when the property is sold. Aug. and I have spoken of it many times and Anna too. The expense between us you know would be very trifling and either of us could well do it. I think Father would have been so pleased to have it so. You know one of his last messages to Mother by John was "Tell her to live as long as she can and keep you all together."

I do not want to make any plans without talking everything over with you and this it is almost impossible to do by letter, so many

pros and cons come up. Then such an important thing as a family giving up a homestead, which it was a strong wish of Father's could be kept as such, certainly ought not to be done lightly or without serious debate and consideration.
So do think of this for several months most seriously."

There are no letters in 1876 other than one written the end of August, by Anna. By March 25th, 1877, Ellen has gone to New York. David writes Ellen, March 25th:
"...the House is lonely, and we are wobegone."
He writes about the weather and vegetables, and the children. On March 30th David writes again, with news of the place and the children. He signs his letters lovingly, "my angel wife", "my dear angel". In his letter to Ellen of April 2nd, he mentions Anna's illness, which suggests that Ellen may have made the trip to be with Anna:

> "Poor Anna must have suffered terribly from this worst form of a disease of which our experience must be slight. I am truly glad of her now great improvement, and hope she may soon be well again. Please give her my love and sympathy, as well as best wishes for her rapid recovery."

David and the children are excited that Fanny is coming to Energy with Ellen:

> "The children are all perfectly delighted at the prospect of Aunt Fanny's return, and are flying around the house with so much joy and life as almost to upset my equilibrium...And not one of them (the children) will be more rejoiced to see Fanny's sweet smile again than myself."

April 4th, 1877, David writes Ellen again, although he is not sure she will get the letter before she leaves New York for Louisiana. They have learned that Aunt Fanny won't be making the trip to Energy with Ellen after all:

> "Children all well and looking forward to your coming. Grace much cut down today at the prospect of not seeing Aunt Fanny -- this from your letters to the children."

It is possible that Fanny didn't want to leave Anna. David writes Ellen again April 6th:

> "Friday night April 6
> My dearest wife
> This afternoon John brought me yours of last Sunday -- just four days from the time it was dropped in the post office, and faster work than your previous ones.
> How pained and grieved I am to read of your poor sick dear sister, and to think of such a sad and painful future.
> Had hoped that this last operation might have eradicated the disease, and nothing more would come of it.

But now your letter leads me to think of the worst, and that there can be but one thing to dread and look forward to."

David is busy with the garden, and the children are often visiting one or another family member along the Bayou:

"My garden looks a little better, have worked my peas and snap beans -- or rather some of the latter, have scratched the coco around the beets and the rows where carrots are supposed to grow, and am about to plant musk melons.

Radishes, a little lettuce, some Swiss chard, perhaps parsley, more snaps, tomatoes, lima beans, cucumbers and squash are up.

Have only the melons to plant just now, when I shall wait for rain to set out eggplants and a little more okra, and all the ground will be taken up, until the turnips are off -- then shall prepare that ground for radishes, beets, carrots and lettuce, have a good second planting of corn, and plenty of okra, and have more ground for a third planting of corn. The potatoes must be worked next week."

April 8th David writes Ellen, and again talks about Anna. He has a letter Ellen sent on March 25th:

"At any rate I was glad indeed to receive it, not only as coming from you, but because it gave me a clear idea of how much poor Anna must have suffered, and how dangerous her case must have been - up to now yours to Alice being the only channel of information -- about even the effect of the attack. I don't wonder John was alarmed and sent for Fanny. The danger was certainly great, and your poor sister's suffering must have been intense. Let us thank God the attack is over now! But still she will require time to recover her strength. Please give her my best love, and hearty rejoicing that all is well now."

On April 11th, 1877, David says he has just received Ellen's letter of the 5th. It seems that John Pugh (age 17) is going to New York to get Ellen and travel home with her.

"How sorry I am to hear such accounts of your poor sister Anna. I cannot understand how this extreme prostration and apparent breaking down comes. She is still comparatively young, has never suffered from severe illness, nor showed weakness of constitution, and this sudden giving way is inexplicable to me, let us earnestly hope your fears may be exaggerated, and that she may yet grow strong and hearty again.

As for you, my darling, I have no fears, shall rest perfectly easy in regard to what the doctor shall say to you.

I wrote Mr. Conger yesterday, asking him to purchase a ticket on the steamer New Orleans for John, and to give John $20 in cash.

...John ought to reach New York next Wednesday night, and be out at the Fort on next morning. I don't think the voyage will do the boy good, besides gratifying his desire for the sea."

He speaks about their place, and adds,

"Our butter making improves a little, but still does not come up to what the quantity of milk should furnish -- so much (milk) that I shall be compelled to purchase a half-dozen more pans.
Our young turkeys have done very badly, and most of them died from diarrhea..."

David writes Ellen on April 17th, 1877, about "household troubles and worries", as well as the garden and housekeeping. He ends with,

"I trust you have had no more returns of those faint feelings. You must stay a little longer in New York and be sure to get well, before coming back into this land of hot weather and mosquitoes. We miss you very much, but I want to see you perfectly well, in the meanwhile we shall do the best we can to get along. So don't hesitate about staying longer."

Ellen and John Pugh apparently made it home without incident, and the next letter is from December 1877. David is writing from New Orleans, Dec. 28th, having just put John Pugh on a boat for New York. John is almost 18, and ready to start out on his own.

"The boy promised me he would faithfully try to carry out all the good precepts instilled into him by you, to try hard always to do right and, if possible, to act in every way according to our wishes, and I hope most fervently he will always carry out these promises. I told him, that in case of trouble he must let us know at once, and we would befriend him in every way."

On December 30th, David sends a note to John Pugh enclosing a note to David's Aunt Elizabeth Foley, who lives in N.Y.C.:

"My dear boy
Enclosed is a short note to your aunt Elizabeth, which you can read and show to your uncle John. And if he thinks it necessary to present it, you can take it around. Even if you do not present it you will of course call upon your aunt, and make the acquaintance of your cousins. You must also give her my best love..."

Also on December 30th, 1877, Fanny writes Ellen. Alice Pugh (age 16) is in New York at the Fort with Fanny, so perhaps Alice went with Ellen to New York in March and stayed on. Alice is taking piano lessons, and Fanny has learned of some boarding house rooms for John Pugh:

"Miss Stone (where Mr Carter boards) will let John have a small room with breakfast, six oclock dinner and tea, for $8 per week."

Fanny says she hopes to take Alice to hear Theodore Thomas, the German conductor who directed the NY Philharmonic.

On January 1st, 1878, Fanny writes Ellen to say that John Pugh arrived on December 31st. She says,

"He speaks with great affection of you and seems to be thinking of you all the time.

Just as we were going to tea last evening at 7 he said "I wish I
knew what Mother is doing just now." And then again he burst out
"Oh what a splendid plum pudding Mother made for us."
So you see you are not forgotten."

On January 11th, 1878, Fanny says she has received a wonderful long
letter from Ellen. Fanny reminds Ellen that John Haven said John Pugh
would be welcome to stay at the Haven house at the Fort:

"I presume you had well considered the matter when you told him
to board in town rather than stay out here."

January 14th Fanny writes again, thanking Ellen for her letter of the 5th and
saying she is,

"...very glad to hear that Mrs. Pugh has made David such a
handsome present again, she is indeed most kind."

Fanny writes about the relative merits of schools for Alice, and asks,

"Would it meet yours and David's views (if it could be managed) to
have Alice go to a day school in New York and be with me the rest
of the time?
The terms at Miss Haines, Miss Green's etc are $250 per year. Miss
Charbonnier's $215 which includes the hot mid-day dinner and
German. Lulu says it is worth the difference the way you are
taught and have to study.
This could be compassed only by my boarding in town with her till
June when the term ended. Of course her board I should pay, as I
should not desire to be alone. Then she could be with me
somewhere, probably at the sea shore and return to you if you
chose during the summer or early fall when people are going
South, or if thought best then, remain and begin another year.
I do not know if this is practicable, I only say would it in any way
meet your views?
If it would, if it seems at all advantageous, I will take it seriously
into consideration which I have not as yet done. Of course it
involves giving up my visit to you now which would be a
disappointment to me and perhaps to you too, but I do not think
we ought either of us to consider what we would like best, but
what is most for the advantage of the children."

Fanny speculates on how it could play out for her own plans, about which
she professes to care little:

"As far as I had any, and it was very unformed, it was to go to La.
in Feb. and remain till May – then return, either with or without
Grace as might be judged best and wisest, board in N.Y. till June
and then locate at the sea shore for the summer.
In the fall come to N.Y. and hire a small house or flat for a year,
keeping house in the most economical manner of course and trying
whether I could like or interest myself in a city life.
Then after a year's trial, I could decide if I wished to locate
permanently in city or country. It seems to me now as if I should
never want to live in the city. To be sure boarding is not the same

as keeping house, but I suppose I could get an idea of how I would like the city, by being there now from Feb. to June.

You will understand that I have not thought seriously of this, I only want to know how it strikes and in regard to Alice."

About John Pugh, Fanny says,

"John has had his first day's experience of business and seems quite bright this evening, eat a good supper and has been reading since. Nothing especial to tell you about his doings. He has pretty much decided to take a room in 38th St. from the 1st of Feb. From what we hear it seems to be a nice house."

In another note, Fanny expresses her intent to come to Ellen's:

"The time draws near for Alice and me to be turning our faces towards Louisiana. I propose the first of Feb – Alice begs me to say the middle. I shall find out about the steamers and then decide...

If you and David don't want me you must warn me off, otherwise I shall come sailing down on you."

Fanny refers to family tensions between David and his brother Richard, and about a recent spat she had with John Haven about his wife Lydia (about whom Fanny feels John is too "touchy"). She then says that John Pugh has secured a position with Woodbury Langdon's company, Joy, Langdon.

In early February 1878, Alice writes her mother from the Fort to say that she is greatly enjoying the New York winter and has been out on a sleigh ride with her cousin Louise, Augusta's daughter:

"This is the second snowstorm this year and over six inches fell and the first sleighing this winter commenced Friday. I was wild with delight when Loulou sent down to come up and take a sleigh ride at half past eleven. It was delightful to get into the sleigh and wrap up in the warm robes and start off and hear the little bells tinkling.

Alice writes about the exciting world of sleighing:

"The first one I saw was Uncle John's cutter which was at the door to take John to the train that morning.

Then the postman came in one; then I took another yesterday morning and saw some stylish turnouts[41] with the long red tassels on harness and fancy gilt gongs for bells.

Last evening at six o'clock the door bell rang and who was it but Cousin Woodbury who had driven out in a sleigh and brought John with him. Was it not splendid in him for it gave John a beautiful sleigh ride which I was afraid he would not get this winter and he came through the park and saw all the beautiful turnouts and everything.

---

[41]Turnout: a carriage with its horses and equipment.

The snow drifts have been quite deep and going up to Aunt Augusta's I several times sank up to my knees almost in some places.

Yesterday Loulou and Sarah and I took a ride and the boys fastened Cupid to Eustis' bob[42] and drove behind us; we went to the park and created a great commotion with the bob and Fritz ran along by it all the way.

We nearly died with laughing and had lots of fun. Whenever Frank wished the pony to hasten he would make up a snowball and throw it at him and sometimes, accidentally of course, he would throw them too hard and they would come flying into our sleigh and produce a commotion.

Once they started to race with a fellow with a fast horse and as the pony goes very fast they beat him and would have kept ahead had not the pony got his foot over the traces."

Alice is engaged in preparations to come home, and says her trunk is ready; she has selected clothing that will be practical for seasickness; and she anticipates not having another opportunity to write her mother as they will be leaving soon.

On February 14th 1878, David writes John Pugh, who has begun work at Woodbury's business. David sounds as though he is the model of financial responsibility, saying that John should:

"learn the true value of money when first starting out in life -- this was instilled into me in early life by your grandfather...-- that you learn to live within whatever income you may possess, and know exactly what balance you have at your command."

David says they are battling the fever (probably malaria):

"Grace has been sick for over 10 days, and only today able to go freely about the house whilst Edith shows signs of perhaps an attack of fever also.

Your mother has been so hard at work, for the last three weeks, cleaning house and preparing for Aunt Fanny, that I am much afraid she will be down next."

By February 20th, Alice and Fanny have arrived at Energy. Alice writes her brother John, saying,

"We are all busy today, mother and Aunt Fanny are busy making curtains for the parlor and are having hard work to make them out as the Muslin is short."

Alice says they have a new coachman, and says her parents have invested in a mortgage on a plantation with David's cousin Alexander Franklin Pugh[43]. A.F. Pugh's planter's diaries (held at LSU and U. of Texas at

---

[42] Another type of sled.

[43] The son of Thomas Pugh's half-brother Augustin, A.F. Pugh was part owner and manager of Augustin, Bellevue, Boatner, New Hope, and Whitmell plantations on Bayou Lafourche in Assumption and Lafourche parishes. He married Ellen Mary Boatner (1832-1909) in 1851. They lived on Boatner Plantation.

171

Austin) paint a picture of a very busy and hard-working planter who oversaw to one extent or another about five plantations. Whether investing in a sugar plantation made sense for David and Ellen is a valid question: but having A.F. Pugh involved would seem to recommend itself.

> "He and mother went up the Bayou you know to sign that mortgage with cousin Franklin Pugh. I wonder if Uncle John thinks it is a good investment. I should think a mortgage, though a first on a sugar plantation, and having such a man for its owner, is about as shaky an investment I as would like to make."

Next is a letter of April 5th from Alice in Louisiana to John Pugh in New York. She makes an astute observation about her father's spending habits:

> "Father's Rockaway is expected soon. I think it was an unwise expenditure for at the highest there will be no more of us going to school and no man to drive us."

Alice also says that Eliza, her grandmother, has been unwell, so David, Ellen and Fanny went up to Madewood to visit.

April 14th, Alice writes John again and says she is sad that Aunt Fanny will be leaving soon, and that Fanny will be taking Grace back to New York.

> "April 14th 1878
> My dear brother,
> I have time only for a few lines for so soon as aunt Fanny appears I want to be with her.
> I feel dreadfully at having her go for I will have no one at all to talk to -- or understand me as she does, besides I don't see what I will do without the Nation and with nothing but the Picayune to read.
> Then I will miss Grace so, and I will have no companion at all except on taking up Mary and Edith, and you being gone to makes me feel very isolated."

Also on April 14th, Mary writes her brother John, and Mary's letter clarifies the reason for Fanny's leaving:

> "Grace and Aunt Fanny will most probably go to the city Friday and start for New York Wednesday or Thursday by rail, as Aunt Fanny heard that Aunt Anna was quite sick. I feel awfully about it for Aunt Fanny was going to stay till the middle of May."

May 15th, David writes to his son John Pugh from New Orleans. It is curious that he feels able to give himself a holiday:

> "I have been down here for nearly a week, partly engaged in seeing about some advances to one of my rice tenants -- Mr. Pan, who is in trouble, and the rest of the time taking a holiday."

David refers to Fanny's visit (Fanny has returned to New York, where John now lives).

"Besides, your Aunt Fanny and Grace comfort you about everything. We miss your Aunt Fanny very much -- to say nothing of Grace, and have had a dull household since they left."

Edith too writes John, and says money is tight:
"Father expects if he possibly can to send us off to school after the crop is sold."
Ellen's restriction on the frequency of the family's letters to John may be a means of conserving money:
"Mother says we can only write one letter a week so I can only write you one every two weeks."

By January 4th, 1879, Fanny writes Ellen about the son of Fanny's best friend Lizzie Morris. The boy, Lizzie's only child, has a life-threatening illness, and Fanny has been devoted to Lizzie and the boy. Fanny received a Christmas package from Ellen after learning "the joyful news that the Drs had hopes for our darling little boy", by which she means Lizzie's son, Gray Morris.
Fanny goes on to describe some of the trials of the boy's illness and its outcome and the level of her involvement with Lizzie. Based on her reference to Anna, Anna may be struggling with her cancer again.
"Then very soon I undressed and went to bed, the first time for three nights.
...All went well till about two in the morning when Dr. Morris noticed a great change in the child's breathing. Dr Draper was at once sent for, then Dr Lands, who did the only and last thing possible to save life; opening the throat and inserting a tube to breathe through. They gave him ether and the operation was soon over – in one case in ten it is successful and anyhow saves great suffering.
As soon as he recovered consciousness Lizzie was back again at his side, said she can never, never forget how his parched, hot lips formed the words which he could not utter and how pleadingly his eyes sought hers to tell him what it meant. They brought him his slate and he wrote now and then a word on that – just some little loving word for his Mother and asking for a prayer – His Father said the Lord's prayer and his own little evening prayer and he tried to follow it.
He suffered dreadfully and after a while lost consciousness – now and then he would revive and know them and put up his lips to be kissed. At a quarter before twelve it was all over. In the night just before Dr Lands came he said "Mama I cannot bear this any more – tomorrow there will be black crape on the door with a white knot in the middle for a little child[44]." Then once he roused a little and with the sweetest of smiles on his face kissed his hand twice.
Lizzie said, "What is it my darling". He said, "Why Mama don't you

---

[44] The use of a white item amongst the black crape (as in the white knot in the door decoration) meant the death was of a child or infant.

see Grandma? I am kissing my hand to her, but I don't think she sees me very plain yet."

I believe when he died, he went right to her arms.

No words of mine can describe to you Lizzie's agony. I never in all my life saw anything so heart-rending. The Drs feared her mind would give way – I never did. I knew she would have to live and have to retain her reason and have to bear it.

Tuesday night I stayed though I slept now and then. Each morning I came up at seven to breakfast with Grace and Willie and part of each day I passed with Anna. The day he died and Sunday, the funeral, are the only two days I have not been with her (Anna). Now I divide the days between her and Lizzie."

Fanny says Anna is doing better, and "– lies on the sofa now part of each day."

As for herself, Fanny says,

"A dark cloud has come over everything for me – perhaps by and by I shall see some light. I see no mercy nor love in God's providence in taking that dear little loving pure child out of the world and out of his Mother's heart, her one ewe lamb.

She (Lizzie) asked me today if I had not word of comfort for her and I told her no, I saw none for her anywhere."

Fanny ends this letter saying that she still has some concern about Grace (Grace has been staying with Fanny in New York):

"I felt very anxious about Grace fearing she might take the fever, even now she may have it, the time is not up yet. I did not go in the room, but was in the room that opened out of it and with Lizzie and Jim constantly."

On January 16th, 1879, Fanny writes Ellen,

"...I went down to sit with poor Lizzie, there is nothing anyone can do for her, but I cannot bear to be away from her long, so divide my days pretty much between her and Anna...Lizzie sits day after day in the same place, in the same chair, almost like a statue of utter woe. I don't know what can ever rouse or stir her into life again."

Fanny wonders how the rice crop will be this year (David has two or three tenants growing rice, and possibly his own crop), and asks whether Eliza Pugh continues to give David a generous sum of money at Christmas:

"What are the prospects from the rice crop this year and did Mrs. Pugh send any present?"

On January 17th 1879, Alice writes an interesting letter to her brother John. Alice, about a year younger than John, is about 18. She has learned that John has been sick, and that he is thinking of giving up his job with Woodbury Langdon's company and coming back home.

"Mother received a letter from you yesterday, I have not heard the letter but this part of it, that you consider your health broken and you want to come home. I don't know what is mother's idea on the subject, but I want to ask you a few questions.

...Do you realize what a very important step you are about to take, you are throwing up a career that we most carefully have struggled to get for you, and it is cruel of you now to throw away an opening where energy and industry might have made so much of you."

Alice goes on to say that if John is seriously considering coming home, he must "come in the right spirit", and she has analyzed his possibilities in regard to a career back home.

"As far as I can see there are two careers for you to choose between -- one is to start as an under-overseer with a salary of between $30.00 or $40.00 a month, this position has become very difficult to attain and can only be held by strong perseverance and energy, it keeps you very confined as you can never leave the place except on Sundays.

Now the other career possesses many attractions for me, but it requires firm determination to work and to shape it for yourself. It is of my own planning, this- you come home, take this place with Henry Crozier (I think he would like it extremely and he is hard-working, energetic, honest, upright and free from all bad habits, surely no young man could suit your purpose better). Besides, you want one of these smart, hard-working young Creole. All three working together with a zest can make a fine rice crop, which is not a difficult thing you know, with father's good judgment to assist you.

This place makes at a moderate estimate 35,000 sacks of rice which at the very low estimate of $4.00 a sack gives $14,000. This, subtracting $1000 for rent and $126 dollars for taxes, gives a fine profit, of course, there are other expenses. Besides this when the rice crop is laid up, you have plenty of leisure to go into rolling [45] and as an engineer say or as learning to be a sugar maker, this would pay you well, besides giving you the experience so that you could turn the plantation into sugar by degrees, if it is too unhealthy in rice, then you would have little expense also for you could get the crop taken off at Mr. Williams sugarhouse.

In cultivating the rice, you have plenty of leisure, which could be turned to good account in improving and cultivating your mind, time for employment, time besides to grow us a garden, which we shall be denied this year. In time we could buy in the place and build ourselves a comfortable home besides employing many luxuries.

There I have done. Perhaps you will call this very visionary but it seems to me perfectly practicable and probable, all depends on you, your industry, your determination."

Mary, who is about 15, writes her brother, also on January 17th:

---

[45] By rolling, Alice means rolling sugarcane.

"I think it would be very silly in you to come home when you have just started in life and will not probably get such a chance again when you have regained your health again but however I will not talk any more about it, for in truth it is none of my business and I don't think Mother would like what I have already said."

In a letter from Ellen of January 19th, Ellen tells Fanny that although Lizzie's loss was a tragedy, Ellen has experienced great trials. Fanny tries to explain that the nature of Lizzie's loss is different.

"But you must forgive me for saying that having never lost a child you cannot measure the depth of grief that a Mother must feel who has lost her only one. You say you have been through more desperate torture, but you write of something you do not understand. Suppose your John were taken from you? Even then you would have five left – suppose them all taken, one by one. Then and then alone could you measure the depth of a Mother's agony who has had her all taken. There is no tie on earth so tender and so strong as that of a loving Mother for a child. No other love lasts or is never replaced. A man or a woman loses a wife, or a husband and marries again but a Mother has no new child to fill the place of one taken."

Based on Fanny's letters to Ellen, Grace is enjoying her stay in New York. Grace visits Fort Washington, goes skating, has sleigh rides in the city, and is taking both painting and drawing classes.

In 1879, then, Alice is away at school in New Orleans, Grace and John are in New York (John in a rooming house or at Augusta's), Grace is living with Fanny in Fanny's apartment at 74 West 45th St., Mary and Edith are day students at the Catholic convent in Thibodaux, and Thomas is with Ellen and David.

On January 25th 1879, Fanny gives Ellen an update on Lizzie and Anna:

"I spend every Sunday morning now with Lizzie while Jim goes to church, then I go in the afternoon. There is very little change in her condition, last week we thought she would have brain fever[46], but the symptoms passed off. She only leaves her room to go down to dinner and sees scarcely any one. Anna sits up nearly all day, her nurse will leave on the 30th. She is neither strong nor in good spirits but perhaps both will come by and by."

On January 28th David explains to Ellen that he has decided to continue renting the plantation and leasing out portions of it, for the coming year. Because he is dealing with the bank, it is possible he rents acreage that was formerly his, but was lost to the bank. His need to consult his mother may mean that she has been helping him or is a partner in his business with the land.

---

[46] Meningitis

"I called today upon the Canal Bank president, and agreed with him to take the place for another year. I am to pay him $50.00 more -- making $900 for his share of the rent.
So that matter is settled -- except consulting mother, but as Robert thinks there will be no trouble there, I think I can venture to lease out the land until I see her -- which ought to be as soon as I come home."

In a letter of March 16th 1879, Fanny responds to a comment Ellen made about Mary and Edith having to take their schooling at the convent:

"I think you have every reason to be satisfied with your arrangements for Mary and Edith. I do not see it as you could do any better for them. One great advantage is that you can take them away any time without losing money by it. I hope they will be able to learn sewing and embroidery, it will be a great advantage for them."

Fanny says she hopes Anna will be able to go to Rye, N.H. for the summer:

"... she might as well have what little pleasure she can."

As for her best friend, Lizzie, Fanny says,

"Lizzie Morris continues to be utterly heartbroken, despairing and hopeless. My heart aches for her more and more. The only change I see is that for the last few weeks she has seemed to cling to me, asks me not to leave her, or to promise when I will come again.
I pass several hours each day with her, seldom miss a day. Before then, though I was with her, she scarcely seemed to know it. Though Jim of course is everything to her, I am the only woman she has to cling to."

Whereas Ellen may have been forced by circumstance to be more directly involved with putting food on the table, Fanny, from her flat in the city, is challenged by having to do her own shopping:

"The worst part of housekeeping to me is the marketing. I hate it. After I had been to the market and seen all the animals turned inside out and hanging up by their heels, I never want to eat a piece of one of them. Then I know nothing of turkeys or chickens and if I do rap one on the breast bone, I am none the wiser for it. So the consequence is the butcher sends me anything he pleases."

Three days later, Fanny begins another letter to Ellen by saying, "having received a letter from you written only three days ago I cannot resist sending you a few lines, for it seems to bring us so near."
Fanny writes on April 20th, 1879 that Anna seems to be doing a bit better, but Lizzie is still a wreck and Fanny is spending a great deal of time on her:

"I try to see Anna every day or two...

As for poor Lizzie, I feel the care of her all the time for she is in such an excited nervous state now that she absolutely needs me and I feel it a duty to go to her every spare minute I have. I really don't know what will become of her. What would affect the bodily health or strength of anyone else, with her, goes to her nervous system. She walks five or 6 miles at a time then starts on a drive of two or three hours and then another walk-it seems as if she could not keep still and nothing tires her. I have to do her shopping and plan to see to her spring and summer clothes in which she does not take the least concern or interest."

On May 11th, Fanny says,
"I was at the Fort a day or two ago with Anna. It was just lovely there, the trees just budding out and the cherry trees white and feathery with blossoms, for the season is late."
She says she may stay at the Haven house for a couple of weeks when she leaves her flat for the summer, before going to Rye, N.H. for the summer. Her brother John is in the house, so she would require his permission. Meantime Fanny is getting a break from her vigilance with Lizzie, because Lizzie has gone away for a while:
"She has been such a care and source of so deep anxiety for the last six weeks that it is a sort of relief not to have her in 36th St for a while."

In her next letter, of May 26th 1879, Fanny relates the unfortunate outcome of her effort to work out an arrangement with her brother John:
"I thought of going to the Fort the last of May and staying till Anna wanted to go, but proposing it to John by letter, I had such an unkind, disagreeable one in reply, that I gave it up it once. But this is quite private, I have not mentioned it to a soul and don't want you to.
I wrote him that I was sorry I had made a mistake in proposing it, as I saw I had done and I would give it up entirely. Perhaps then he felt sorry for the first note (but I don't know) for the second was quite friendly and I answered that in the same way."

Fanny's letter of June 8th, says she and Grace are going to Fort Washington for ten days after all, but they will stay with Augusta rather than John Haven.

David writes Ellen June 27th, 1879 from New Orleans to say that Alice's graduation from school has gone well. Ellen is apparently coming in a few days to meet David in New Orleans, and they will bring Alice home. On June 29th, David writes a note to John Pugh telling him that Ellen is recovering from an illness:
"Your mother is much better -- able to be about the house -- but is still far from well. She suffers now principally from a terrible cold in the chest -- an epidemic in these parts, and a serious one too."

Fanny writes Ellen a couple of letters from Rye that are full of business about clothes and fabrics for Ellen and the girls, about John Pugh, Lizzie and some Haven relations.

Alice writes her brother John Pugh July 16th 1879, to tell him of her return home after graduating from school.

> "What a dissipated week I have passed. In the first place I have called on everyone, gone up the Bayou to see everyone, been to Aunt Mary's[47] party Thursday night where we had a most enjoyable time reaching home at three, entertaining Henry Foley and his little sisters who spent two days here for the party.
> We went up there the next night to dance staying till midnight and walking home with Uncle Richard and Mr. Charlie. Aunt Mary had a beautiful supper, everything made at home too, we had five sorts of ice cream and sherbet."

Alice has enjoyed herself, visiting others and receiving visitors at Energy. She says,

> "Father says if anyone else comes he is going to hang out a yellow flag."

Alice says they gave a little party at Energy, too:

> "We had a real charming evening, playing croquet and archery, eating watermelon till dark. Then came parlor croquet which everyone enjoyed, games, music, singing, ice cream and cake. They left at midnight."

On July 19th 1879, Fanny begins a letter to Ellen from Rye admitting she has been remiss in writing and she feels guilty:

> "I have a letter commenced to you in my portfolio, but that does not do you any good and I'm really ashamed to think how long it is since I have written. Then you heaped coals of fire on my head by writing me a great long letter and saying you reproached yourself for not having written before.
> It is always a wonder to me, how you find time to write at all to anyone and yet you always find time to write to everyone."

Fanny goes on to describe what sounds like a wonderful time she and Grace are having, with visits from family and friends:

> "About nine I went to the beach for a walk as the morning was cool and the surf fine. I went about a mile up the beach and returning met William Treadwell and Frank Langdon coming to look for me. We stayed there for an hour or more watching the bathers and then came to the house. Gussie had come down with them, but Nellie and Grace had gone to the bowling alley at the Farragut with Willie Gray and Annie McCrae so Gussie and Anna went over to meet them. Unfortunately they just missed them so we all strolled about the country in different groups till one o'clock.

---

[47] Alice most likely means her Aunt Mary Pugh, wife of David's younger brother Richard Pugh (Mary Williams Pugh). Henry Foley is a cousin, from Eliza Foley Pugh's side.

They concluded to stay to dinner, so we had quite a party. Grace came to me in a very mournful state to tell me that she had torn Willies coat all to pieces, they were playing (or what I call wrestling) and she caught him by the coat and tore down all the front on one side.

She retired to her room to weep in seclusion, but her spirits are like an India rubber ball and she soon emerged in most brilliant condition again, ready for some new scrape."

Fanny feels obliged to look in on Lizzie. Lizzie and Jim Morris have come to Rye and taken a house right next to Fanny's, most likely because Lizzie wanted to be near Fanny.

"The Portsmouth party left about four, Anna and Nellie retired to their rooms, Grace Willie and Annie played croquet and I hastened over to Lizzie's.

We have tea at seven and in the evening some play cards, some knit and some just sit around and talk.

I usually escape about nine and sit for an hour with Lizzie and Jim in their lonely little room, where they sit so sadly side-by-side talking, or thinking, about their boy."

In several of Fanny's letters to Ellen, there are hints that Grace's behavior is odd at times. In one letter, she says that Grace enjoys playing with two children who happen to be 4 years her junior, but, Fanny says, Grace acts so young sometimes that perhaps this is all right. On July 19th 1879, Fanny writes,

"If you are all amused at Grace's account of her adventure on the ledge, I suspect she omitted to mention that she entirely ruined a nice pair of cloth boots and her pretty blue flannel dress over which I had just expended so much work and time, besides several dollars of money-trimming it with a white and letting it down by pulling in a broad band of white flannel. It was a very useful dress besides being most becoming.

I told her to change it before she went which she neglected to do and thus it was ruined.

An ordinary amount of caution would have kept them from being caught by the tide in the first place and then if she'd come in carefully she might have saved her clothes as Willie did who was not even wet, whereas Grace plunged along pell-mell rather enjoying the fun of it and was completely drenched. I was anything but amused.

Their feet were badly cut and they were limping around for some days.

They took off their shoes and stockings, but Grace kept dropping hers in the water as she floundered over the stones.

Don't read this aloud as I do not want her to know that I spoke of it to anyone."

Anna Haven Sweetser, who is with Fanny in Rye, writes Ellen July 25th 1879, to say that people have highly complimented Grace (her intelligence, looks and manners). Anna says that Grace's cousins Nellie and Gussie (Augusta's daughters) were invited by Mrs. George Wallis Haven to go to a big fete on Isle of Shoals, the home of Celia Thaxter, where 150 people gathered. Mrs. Haven "introduced them to Mrs. Thaxter [48]." Anna relates her perception of Celia Laighton Thaxter to Ellen:

> "She lives in a cottage over there. Nellie was quite charmed with it, it is fitted up so prettily, she has made a beautiful collection of sea mosses that she has pressed, and they are so delicate and lovely. She says February is the right time to collect them, the choicest ones. They all came from there, perhaps you have heard she was a Miss Laighton, a sister of the man who owned the island and now keeps the hotel, Mr. Thaxter was much older and a very odd man, who went over the board there, fell in love with this girl, had her educated, then they were married. She has quite a natural gift at painting, decorating China, one article has some beautiful wild roses, and a vase, some exquisite seaweed, she painted on it..."

On August 10th, Alice writes her brother John with local news and says,

> "Mother said the other day that if she could afford it she would write to you to have your picture taken, so now the best birthday present you can make her will be to have your photograph taken and sent to her."

On August 17th 1879, Fanny writes Ellen from Rye Beach, saying she has refused permission for Grace to take part in a play. Her comment offers a window into the times:

> "Mrs. Chauncey asked me if I was willing to have Grace take a small part in a play here next week. She said she thought it very likely that I would refuse, as she knew how very particular I was about Grace, but she was so pretty, so dainty and effective that she could not help asking for her.
> I declined to let Grace take the part, but I was quite flattered at her being invited. Mrs. Latrobe and one or two other ladies spoke to me about it and said how pleased they were to see that I was so careful with Grace and would not let her take part in the play, that it was not the thing for young girl to do, anyone could buy a ticket and go in and comment upon her and criticize her from head to foot. Others would laugh and joke with her and compliment her and Grace had too much freshness and innocence to have it spoiled.

---

[48] Celia Thaxter (1835-1894) achieved recognition for her poetry and other writing and was published in literary magazines. She was also known for her beautiful gardens, and some credit her with making the Isle of Shoals and Appledore Island a tourist attraction.

I told them I had my own ideas of what a girl might be and do and I usually liked to carry them out unless I was convinced to the contrary by some very good reason that I did not see in this case.

On September 8th 1879, Fanny writes Ellen a last letter from Rye Beach. Fanny and Grace expect to leave in several days. Fanny writes of Grace,

"Grace has changed and matured in every way and emerged from childhood to girlhood.

Her head is full of a girls imaginings and fancies and too of a girl's willfulness. It is now "I will" where it used to be"May I?".

But she has a very sweet disposition and usually excellent sense, so that I think she will be amenable to authority. I have a vivid remembrance of what I was at her age and so try to be patient with her. She has a more intense nature than Alice and so is a little more difficult to manage."

Fanny is very concerned about Lizzie:

"Lizzies's health is very poor, she has a bad cough and is not at all strong. She clings to me more and more and it seems very strange to me how entirely she and Jim depend upon me in many ways-she used to be so strong and self-reliant."

On September 14th, Fanny writes Ellen from New York. She is glad she and Grace are back, particularly because she worried that John Pugh might have missed them. He came to see them the first night they were back:

"He and Grace are very queer together-they never seem to have anything to say to each other. Grace always entertains him as if he were an acquaintance she had just met-you would never think they were brother and sister."

The rest of her letter is about Grace, Grace's schooling, and clothing matters.

On the 21st, Fanny writes again, and answers Ellen's question about how Anna is doing.

"You ask about Anna, but I scarcely know what to say. She has very little strength, that is she becomes tired very easily, but I do not see that she is more weak than she has been for some time. As yet she does not speak of any return of the trouble, but it may be coming on, indeed may have formed already, without her knowing it. It seems to me as if it must be there for it is nine months since the last operations. She is usually cheerful, always tries to be and of course with exceptions, was kind and pleasant during the summer. You know we always have to be on the watch for fear of hurting her feelings."

Fanny goes on about her brother and Woodbury:

"Of John I know very little except through occasional letters. He did not come to see me to say goodbye before he went away for the summer, though he went to Woodbury's office to see him, but I have entirely given up thinking or caring or worrying about him and if he is not fond of me anymore it is not my fault and though I regret it I cannot help it.

He has been up from Long Branch several times since my return and sent word through Anna that he should come and see me when he had a chance.

Mr. Carter has been at the seashore all summer and I presume is off gunning just now. He wrote me that he had suffered much from rheumatism in his leg and could hardly hobble about.

Woodbury came in the first night of our return and I have seen him frequently since and been out driving with him. He has a spirited pair of young horses and I should not wonder if his neck (and perhaps mine too) was broken before long, for I do not consider him a first-class "whip"".

Fanny is interrupted:

"The bell has just rung! I flew to light the gas and Grace opened the door expecting some very distinguished visitor when we heard a familiar whistle and John appeared. It was a sign we agreed upon so that we should know when John came and not light of extra gas. He is now reading Kenelm Chillingly[49] while Grace and I write."

Fanny warns Ellen about Grace's manners:

"Her manners, I am sorry to say, have not improved this summer, she is very brusque and pert and sometimes even rude."

On October 16th 1879, Fanny writes that she wishes Ellen will come visit in the spring. She says also that she wants Ellen to consider whether to take Grace back to Louisiana and leave Mary or Edith with Fanny, but Fanny says she would need Alice's help if she was to take on one of the younger girls. Her long letter is full of ideas and news, talk of clothes and people. She says,

"Our dear Mother must have had infinite patience with us all and such excellent judgment and humor in all our peculiar ways and feelings."

Fanny is still put-out by her brother John's behavior:

"I don't care now if John does not come to see me. His letters to me this spring about staying at the Fort hurt me very much and since then I have cared very little. I went to see him at the house the last time I was out.

...If John would live in the house like a gentleman and let us come and go, it would be a different thing and I should not want to take anything out, but as it is, I think it makes no difference-the house is shut up to all intents and purposes. John evidently wanted it to himself and now he has it. No one is ever asked to the house or even allowed on the place."

On Oct. 26th 1879, Fanny pokes a little fun at Ellen:

---

[49] Kenelm Chillingly is a book by Edward Bulwer Lytton, a popular author of the time.

> "It appears to me that whenever you do not feel in good humor
> with David or are a little "blue" generally that you retire to your
> room and with closed doors proceed to make your will."

Fanny allows that she misses her parents still:

> "I have just had the Rosewood desk from the front parlor brought
> in here and you don't know what a pleasure I take in having it, or
> rather what comfort, for the pleasure if it is one, is a very, very
> sad one.
>
> I have just put away in it all her precious letters to me and every
> scrap of paper with the writing on it and all my little memorials of
> her.
>
> I just long to see her and Father again and am impatient for the
> time to come.
>
> Life is very long and very empty of happiness to my thinking."

She adds that,

> "Mr. Carter has aged very much the last two years-his hair is very
> gray, has changed all at once. He was here two nights ago..."

On November 2nd 1879, Fanny talks about fabric and dresses and a box of
things she is sending to Ellen. She says she is happy to hear that Ellen is
going to New Orleans, but she is devastated to hear that Ellen will not be
coming to New York to visit in the spring.

> "I am dreadfully disappointed that you cannot come on this spring.
> I know you have not much inducement to come except to see
> John, but I want to see you so much and I wanted so much to
> show you my abode and have the visit from you.
>
> If it would be any pleasure to you, I advise your taking $150.00
> and coming on. You might as well have the use of your money, it
> will be all the same 20 years hence."

Fanny ends her letter with,

> "How thankful you and Augusta ought to be that year after year
> your families are untouched. It is very remarkable, I think, and
> cause for great gratitude."

On November 9th, 1879, Fanny tries to sympathize with Ellen over
something that has happened at Energy. Her talk of Ellen leaving David is
quite shocking, given the times; and David's relationship with money and
debt are puzzling.

> "Such a scene as you tell me of is very distressing and hard to
> bear and I do not wonder you felt miserable and heartbroken. But
> I surely would not, or would try not, to worry so much over the
> household matters. I know very well that when the mind (and
> body too) is constantly full of the household affairs they assume an
> importance which sometimes is beyond their worth.
>
> ...I suppose David like most people when he is angry says five
> times more than he really means and probably the servants
> attached far less importance to the angry words than you
> imagined.

I often have wished and been on the point of urging you to leave David and try in some way to make a home with me for yourself and the children, but second thought has always told me that it would never do. Chiefly on the children's account-it might reflect on you and through you on them. And then I do not think you would be happy separated from him, but in this of course no one could judge for you, your own heart alone would answer the question.

If it is done, it ought to be it seems to me, by mutual consent, no satisfactory arrangement could otherwise be made.

If you both agreed that you would be better off and happier apart, then I should most certainly advise and even urge it's being done for your lives might be peaceful and no blame could come on you.

I have no patience with him, I must confess, about the Texas business. I cannot comprehend how any man can owe a debt to another and such a debt, and not strain every method to pay it off and be free from it. How he can calmly sit down under it year after year I cannot conceive.

Still I do not know his side of it. Perhaps he may have done all he could.

I should think he would feel as if he wanted to pay it off at any sacrifice.

But you have nothing to do with this. I do not see as you can do anything more than you have in asking John again and again to pay himself from your money.

As you say, I cannot see any use in your pinching and saving, if the money goes on all sorts of things about the place - and it certainly is very trying not to know if there is any money to fall back on."

Fanny says John Pugh seems to lack motivation at work, but he greatly enjoys spending his weekends at Augusta's, and, when not at Augusta's, at Fanny's. Woodbury tells Fanny that John isn't engaged at work, and just plods along.

On November 18th, 1879, Fanny tells Ellen about clothing and Anna:

"I wonder if you have changed as much in two years as I have. I look old and haggard and my hair is quite grey.

Anna is not feeling well and I suppose will have to undergo the operation before long. She has not seen the doctor yet and intends to put it off as long as possible."

Fanny is reluctant to lose things that recall her parents to her:

"John wanted this fall to sell the Coupé. I felt awfully about it-I have such tender associations with it-remembrances of so many, many rides and then Father's pride in it when Campbell would drive it up with the black horses.

Scene after scene came to my mind, but there was no help for it.

I spoke of it here one evening and Woodbury said he should buy it for his mother to drive in it this winter. Entré nous strictly, I think it was partly to please me, or he thought so, so the next day he went out and bought it with the harness. He meant it for kindness, but I would really have preferred some stranger had bought it and I never see it again.

Now I shall see it all winter going through 45th St., with Mrs. Bassett [Woodbury's step-mother] in it and perhaps be asked to drive in it myself. Isn't it a strange world?"

November 30th Fanny says she has received a letter from Mary saying that Ellen has been ill, and on December 14th, it is clear that Ellen is having more trouble with David. He has overdrawn their account, and he is away somewhere (probably a hotel in New Orleans):

"You don't know how grieved I am that you are having renewed anxiety about money matters. It is very trying and hard.

Perhaps though you may be a little unjust in the matter for he may not have known he was overdrawing. You know yourself how easy it is to go on spending and spending and all at once find you've gone too far. It may have been his case, though of course he must have known if the rent was not paid. Possibly it may have been and not entered on the account.

I do not think it is strange his not writing for he never does write or is not apt to and in such a case as this would be pretty sure not to. I do not suppose he will refer to it till he comes back which will probably not be for some weeks."

Fanny's letter is filled with information about Christmas presents to and from Ellen's children for each other, and descriptions of boxes she has sent to Louisiana containing various gifts[50]. Her friend

---

[50] I was about giving it up [a dress for Edith] when by good luck I found at Johnston's this piece of 4 1/4 yards extra wide and being a remnant and late in the season I got it for $4.75. You said 5 yards of double width, but this is very wide and it took 4 yards camel's hair width for Grace's overdress and jacket. The light shades are much worn here now and I hope you and Edith especially, will be pleased. Grace and I think the combined colors lovely. The velvet was $1. per yard.

On the 13th I sent three pairs of stockings in a box with sponge back and also my presents for Alice and Mary. Another little box directed to Mary contained some of the things she wanted me to buy and Graces and my presents for Thomas. Mary will open this. A pair of old gloves and a pina half- handkerchief for anyone who wants them.

The present I send Alice was my summer's work at Rye. It took me months to make it and is trimming for a white dress. At Lenox the young ladies had navy blue dresses trimmed with it but I think it prettier on white, Alice will do as she likes. The narrow is put in as insertion, the wide on the overskirt.

The box I sent several weeks ago is your present and I hope and trust in good order, but I have my doubts. Be sure and tell me what I owe on it for I was not able to prepay it, I suppose from $2.00 to 2.50, but if you have Mr. Conger's account you can easily tell. It reached New Orleans about the 25th of Nov. ...Mary's necktie came direct from Paris.

Tomorrow I send two more boxes containing the rest of our presents and I hope and trust they will reach you. One I am anxious about as it contains a valuable lace fan which Mrs. Morris gave me some months ago saying-"perhaps Alice Pugh would like that fan." It was one of her wedding presents. I kept it till now but I would not have Alice think Mrs. Morris meant it as a

---

Lizzie has decided to sell her jewelry and establish a charity in her son Gray's honor, and Fanny is helping.

> "Lizzie Morris has sold her diamonds and I have promised to try what I can do with her laces, jewelry, shawls etc. etc. The money will be put in a memorial charity."

Fanny writes again on Dec. 16th, and on the 20th, she sends a Christmas greeting to Ellen and the children:

> "Dearest Nell and also dear Alice, dear Mary dear Edith and dear Thomas, I wish you each and all a very merry and happy Christmas.
> I send this line for you to receive Christmas Eve or in the morning. I shall be thinking of you all and hoping you are having a pleasant, merry time.
> Grace is going to Fort Washington to see the tree and to pass Christmas Day. I may go out for the tree, but shall return in the morning..."

She ends with,

> "It is Saturday night-John and Grace are having a very animated discussion about pictures, in the parlor and I write in my room. I hear Grace accusing John of not having refined tastes and John retaliated by saying that she is only guided by what other people think in forming her opinions. John dined here and will be here tomorrow to as he is not going to Fort Washington.
> Now I will leave you all to look at your presents.
> "Merry Christmas to All and to all a Good Night"
> F.A.L.H."

By the next day, Fanny has received items and a letter from Ellen and the children, to which she responds.

> "Dearest Nell
> This afternoon I received the pen holders for John and Grace. How pretty they are! Grace had a line from Alice. I will order the flowers for Anna Christmas Day. Will you thank Alice and Mary for letters received within a day or two.
> ...I am thankful to say that Anna was quite comfortable when I left her at noon today and the doctor said she was doing better than she did last year. On Tuesday the 24th he should take out the stitches.
> Instead of using the spray of Thyrmoil as they did last year, he substituted spray of carbolic acid, this is played on the wound during the entire operation to cleanse and heal.

Christmas present or indeed as a present at all.
Christmas will always mean to her agony and sorrow.
The necklace I had painted to order for Edith and hope it will please her. Entre nous I do not think it is neatly made, it is prettily painted however and perhaps she will not be critical. I can only find cloth gloves for Edith at the price you name. I got a pair yesterday for $.50, but they are too large and I must change them, will send them later.

I like the doctor and nurse is excellent so far, a thoroughly trained, capable nurse, doing something or suggesting something all the time. I believe I have told you all you would like to know, if not you must ask me.

I remained in the room during the operation and <u>part</u> of the time by her side, John <u>all</u> the time, also the nurse who gave the ether...

I set up the first night to test and watch the nurse.

Fanny ends with more about Anna:

"Anna has asked several times if I had written you and today told me to give her dear love to you and tell you she was comfortable and you must have a nice Christmas.

I believe I told you that Dr. J. said that it was best to have the lumps removed for if allowed to increase, the pressure as they increased in size could cause intolerable pain.

I said today that I did not see what the end would be, how often would this thing have to be done and John said "why as long as the strength holds out-as long as the bodily or physical condition will allow." So I suppose the doctors have told him this at some time.

I have several letters to write for Anna, so must say good night."

On Christmas day, 1879, Fanny writes again to say she has received a note from Alice indicating that there is even more trouble for Ellen:

"Dearest Nell

I had a postal from Alice yesterday which occasions me much anxiety and I suppose I cannot hear for several days what has occurred to trouble you so much more than I already know. Alice intimates something special.

Until I hear I will only write you on one or two subjects which seem to call for immediate answer."

Near the end of her letter Fanny adds comments about David that suggest he has established a pattern (overspending, running away from his debt, spending more by staying in a hotel, buying food and alcohol). David's mother, Eliza Foley Pugh, may help bail them out.

"It seems to me, though not being on the spot and knowing little circumstances I may be wrong, that I should wait till David came back before I did anything. After you have been to Mrs. Pugh it is too late to draw back and you may be sorry for it. David must come home sooner or later and probably has some plan.

He always stays four or five weeks, therefore there is nothing unusual in that part. I am afraid you will take some step that you will afterwards repent.

Perhaps Mrs. Pugh will help you out as she has done before. I think about you all the time and wish I could devise some means of helping you or even advising."

Fanny's letter of December 31st 1879 brings the news that Grace has come down with the measles at Augusta's in Fort Washington, and may miss the last month of school as a result. Fanny says she hopes David has returned home by now.

In Fanny's letter of January 8th, 1880, it is clear that Ellen's problems persist:

> "I was just going to write to you this evening when your letter of the fourth (Sunday) was brought in. I have been thinking of you constantly for the last few days, trying in vain to think of some way to propose to you out of all your difficulties."

Fanny talks about when and how Grace will return to Louisiana, and then touches upon the subject of coming down herself:

> "I thought I would wait and see how affairs went when David came home, before I decided whether I would come out or not. I don't know whether it would be best or not. For some time past I had thought that I would come, but lately (I mean just lately) I have rather changed my mind."

Then Fanny goes on about David:

> "I think your affairs are just about as desperate as they can be and I don't see any way out of it. I think about it all the time and it does seem as hard as it can be. I suppose David stays, just as he has stayed before often and often, just because he has not the strength of mind to come back and face debt and no money.
> I don't know as it is craziness, but it is a weakness at least. I think that Richard [David's younger brother] is right in some things, but I don't think he likes David, or that they ever got on very well together and perhaps what he says and thinks as to David's estimation by outsiders may be wrong.
> I don't think I should send after David at all, but I do not pretend to offer any advice. I do not suppose his staying at the hotel makes any difference for he probably does not intend to pay his bill.
> Perhaps, knowing all we know now, it would have been better if you had not gone back in 1874, but you must remember that we did not know all then-you knew nothing, you had to go to find out and if you had not gone you would always have reproached yourself for not going. I know this would have been so.
> ...I suppose David will come back and things will settle down and go on as before for probably Mrs. Pugh will advance or give money to start on.
> Probably Richard is right in saying that you will have to put up with it as he says on the children's account-I say because there is nothing else to do under the sun, I don't see as the children make any difference at all. It is a most miserable, wretched life."

January 23rd 1880, Fanny responds to letters she has received from Ellen on the 11th, and 17th. Most of this letter is about David and the misery he is causing Ellen. His behavior has had a significant impact on the children's opinion of him.

"I have not written for some time, indeed I believe it is two weeks, but ever since I received yours of the 11th I have waited from day to day thinking I should hear that David had come home or that he never was coming and I really almost hoped it would be the latter. However I might have known it would be the same old story that it has been for the last six years with the exception I believe of one winter. As long as he has any money to spend or in Mr. Conger's hands to draw, he is all right and stays at home and spends it. As soon as it is gone he goes to the city and stays till someone goes after him, pays his board bill and brings him home.

I believe there has been no variation in this programme except as to the length of time he stays. I don't see any mania, hallucination, lunacy or craziness in this. It appears to be an easy-going systematic and perfectly irresponsible way of throwing off all money affairs.

I make out that his board bill has been about $130.00, that is if he returned by the 25th of January. This makes 53 days at $2.50 per day. This sum would have paid another term for Grace at school, not to speak of all his debts at home.

I think his physical condition, his extreme nervousness etc. etc. is owing either to his drinking whiskey all the time or to that thing which is the matter with him inside.

You see I am neither his wife nor his brother, so I can only judge him as an outsider. I am very sorry for him. I dare say if he had always had an easy life and plenty of money he might have lived along like other people, but then he did have at one time a goodly sum in your money and he wrecked that, so perhaps if he had more he would have done the same. But after all my opinion of him, nor Richards, nor yours, nor anyone's, does not alter the fact that he is your husband and that you have to bear and put up with whatever he does.

No one, on our side of the family nor on his, has ever once suffered or entertained the idea that you could leave him. I suspect I am the only one however who thinks your happiness would be affected by it. Apart from the inexpediency etc. etc., I think you would be very miserable apart from him. In many ways I think you would be better off, but you would not be happy without him. After all some women have much worse to bear, though this is cold comfort.

...There is one thing that I do not think is right, though to be sure it is not in the least any of my business. I refer to the way the younger ones speak of their father, such speeches as Thomas made for instance, I am sure we never would have been allowed to say such things about either of our parents or pass any judgment, or upon anything they did with the way they spent their money. I have not heard any disrespectful words from John nor Alice, though I can judge pretty well what their feelings are and they are old enough and mature enough in judgment to take serious views on the subject and see the right and wrong.

Grace is old enough to, but she is very queer; she reminds me very much of her father in her way of throwing off all responsibilities and cares, or rather in never taking them on. She has never asked when I have letters, if her father has returned or how things are getting on home or any of the family matters.

...I am delighted that Mrs. Pugh can give her children such a handsome present, only I hope you will insist on having the money put in your hands and that David won't see one cent of it.

...After writing such a fierce letter and expressing my opinion so freely about everyone and everything, I don't know as you will be particularly pleased to have me say that it is now my intention to come out with Grace in February, from the middle to the last of the month. I will decide positively the first of February and let you know for certain, how and when we come and all about it.

...I can't think of any more dismal news to tell you so I will close this cheerful letter with much love and a heart full of most affectionate sympathy for you my dear sister."

In her letter of February 3rd to Ellen, we learn from Fanny that Anna had another operation several days earlier. Both John Haven and Fanny have been with Anna and, says Fanny,

"There is really nothing for me to do but sit with her now. Dr. Janorin performed the operation on Saturday at two. It was not as severe, nor as long as the last one and she rallied sooner and easier from it, but the lump he removed was very large and very deep, one point was attached to the bone. He says the wound will be longer in healing but not so painful as the last. She seems better and stronger in every way than last year and they do not feel the slightest anxiety about her."

Fanny says that between the unexpected operation and various unanticipated costs she has incurred, she is less sure of coming to visit Ellen in February and may need to wait until fall. Fanny's rent has gone up, and some of her bonds are up for renewal at a lower interest rate.

On February 8th 1880, Fanny writes,

"...We cannot alter facts and I keep thinking that David will come back and things go on as before. He cannot stay in New Orleans forever, he must return sooner or later.

I think you are quite right in not going down to him or writing to him, in one sense, but on the other hand I would not take the care of that place and if he can be made in any way to return and do his share of the work, and take care of his family I would put pride, affection, feeling, everything aside and make him do it. I think his conduct in staying in the city and making you do all the work and have all the care of that place is perfectly outrageous and cannot be defended on any grounds whatever. I should not want to come out this spring and <u>meet</u> him if I were to hear tomorrow that he was at home again.

...I don't see what you are living on, money I mean. Mrs. Pugh's is swallowed right up."

Four days later Fanny responds to two letters she has gotten from Ellen. Ellen has talked to David's brother Richard, and then Ellen decided to go into New Orleans to try to find David.

"I suppose you went to the city Tuesday and returned perhaps today or will tomorrow.

I do not feel the slightest uneasiness about David-it is the same old story over again. If I am not mistaken Richard has had (almost) similar interviews with him before. I don't think he is crazy, I don't think he has committed any crime and I don't think he will blow his brains out.

When he says he is afraid he simply means that he is afraid or ashamed to meet you, knowing how he has treated you. It may be too, that he does not like to face unpaid bills in Thibodaux. I have no idea there is anything more in it than just that. He will probably return with you and as long as he does return and attend to the place I don't much care what or who takes him home.

I have not and do not expect to have any sympathy with him at all, unless I hear something vastly different from what I expect to hear.

As to your leaving him I do not believe you will decide to and I have not spoken and shall not speak on the subject to any one till I hear something definite from you.

If done it would be much easier to have it done by mutual agreement and then there would be no blame attached and some terms could be made with him. I don't think there would be much talk and I do not think it would be much worse than the talk there probably is now.

I should not decide about it till I had learned from your trustees what arrangements they could make for you."

On February 19th 1880, Fanny writes again, and says she has received Ellen's letter of the 14th.

"I received yesterday your letter of the 14th which of course I was most anxious to have. The contents were pretty much what I expected. I thought he would go home with you and was probably only waiting for someone to rouse him up to go.

His condition must have been very pitiable and meeting him and all you had to do, very trying for you. Of course all my sympathy and feeling are for you. I do not pretend to have much for him, though in a certain way I am sorry for him.

I did not believe your idea of leaving him could be or would be carried out and did not speak of it to anyone but John (Haven) to whom I mentioned it as a possible contingency which might be

necessary and with a view to consulting him as to ways and means. I thought he seemed rather in favor of it.
Of course now, having heard that he had returned home, he knows the idea is given out.
I am very thankful he is home again and I hope now you will be able to have a little rest, bodily and mentally and look forward to seeing not only one, but both your children, the first of April.
Then the fall will soon come when I hope to be with you."

Fanny describes Anna,

"Anna is pleased with yours and the children's letters. She is very weak, wan and languid and suffers much, but the doctor seems satisfied with her progress."

Near the end of her letter she expresses hope that Ellen is doing better now that David is home, and Fanny also says they must find some way to afford schooling for Edith and Mary:

"I will say goodnight now dear sister hoping that you're easier and happier in your mind than you have been for weeks. It is an unspeakable comfort to me to think that this it is so.
My best love to the girls.
We must plan now, how Mary and Edith are to get school."

On March 3rd, Fanny describes Grace's fun, leaving no doubt that Grace has seen the best of New York. Thibodaux, to which Grace soon returns, is no comparison.

"Grace has just gone out and told me, if I wrote you, to tell you that she had gone to the opera with the young gentleman and carried an opera glass set with opals-also that she drove in the park this afternoon behind a pair of spirited horses belonging to a rich gentleman, well known in New York society."

Somehow Fanny has arranged for John Pugh to bring Grace home, with his round trip fare paid (whether by John Haven or some other way is not stated).

"John will bring Grace out on the third of April, make you a little visit and be back by the first of May. You will be glad to see him I'm sure and with the expense you have nothing to do.
It is a little treat with which you have nothing to do, but enjoy it."

Fanny has taken it upon herself to check with John Pugh's boss, her cousin Woodbury Langdon, about John taking the time off to go down to Louisiana:

"I have spoken to Woodbury about it and he thinks as we do that he ought to go out and see you, says he can take his two weeks vacation now and the other two weeks he will spare him.
I do not think he is in the least losing his interest in you or the family but he might if he did not see you for four years.
You may in years to come have to depend upon him and it is much better that he should realize that he may have to be of importance to you and his sisters as well as take care of himself.

193

He certainly now has the warmest affections for you and it had
better be kept up by seeing you now and then."

Fanny addresses the issue of David's coming home. Fanny's support and
pragmatic perspective may have been welcome, particularly if Ellen was
feeling embarrassed and ashamed (if not humiliated).

"I knew it would be very hard to have David come home and after
little while, go on just as if nothing had happened. That was what I
said before that irritated me so, that he neither realizes, nor cares
for all that you went through, all the work and care and anxiety
about the place as well as the anxiety about him. He takes it as a
matter of course that you will stay there and look after things.
However as it apparently can't be helped, there is no use in
dwelling on the subject or making it any worse than it is. We might
as well make the best of that as of everything else, that is, get
what good there is out of his coming home and let the rest go as
talking about it and thinking about it cannot alter it."

On March 10th 1880, Fanny writes with general news, including news of
Mr. Carter and Anna. Carter, who had begun showing his age after having
a medical event (perhaps heart-related), has come back to the city to
work, but Fanny says,

"I have no idea it will amount to anything. I doubt if he ever takes
it up as he did before. He has abundant means to live without
practicing his profession, though he still keeps up his partnership.
He goes from place to place gunning and fishing and enjoys it very
much."

Meantime, she says "Anna is doing pretty well, her nurse is still with her."

On March 31st Fanny says she has gotten Grace (who has been in New
York for about two years and is now 18 years old) ready to go home.

"Tomorrow Grace will go to the Clarendon to say goodbye to Mrs.
Morris and in the afternoon make a farewell call at Fort
Washington. On Friday I shall pack her trunks."

In the same letter there is troubling news about Anna:

"Poor Anna is in a very sad condition. About a month after the
operation, a small lump began to form and grew to be the size of a
pea. This was taken out yesterday. It was small and movable
under the skin and removed very easily. The doctor did not even
give her ether, he sprinkled the spot with a fine spray of ether till
it was entirely frozen and then removed it in about a minute
without any pain, she did not feel it in the least, only the nausea
that the odor of the ether causes her.
It is not the operation itself that causes anxiety, but the necessity
of it so soon after the last operation. I suppose these spots are
offshoots of the growth under the arm which cannot be removed at
all. It is so near a nerve that it cannot be touched. The doctor says
it will be a very slow growth in itself but I presume its presence

there poisons the blood and it manifests itself in this way, by the small lumps coming in the surrounding parts.

It does not give her continuous and actual pain but every now and then a darting pain, great soreness when touched and occasional pain all down the nerve of the arm to the wrist. Considering this I do not see much hope of her even recovering such health as she has had before.

The least change in the weather gives her severe neuralgia pains all through the side, she has very little appetite and passes restless nights. I think she is exceedingly discouraged about herself and sees no prospect of even regaining a few months health.

I am by no means sure that she will be able to go to Rye in June. It does not look like it now –"

On April 9th 1880, Fanny writes Ellen saying that Grace and John should have arrived by now. She offers a sobering projection about Anna:

"Anna has been better for the last week, seems to be gaining strength and sits up most all day. But I do not believe she will ever have another operation performed. When the next growth comes it will probably be the last. I do not think the doctor expects ever to do it again."

Fanny says she misses Grace very much, and,

"Since Grace left school the first of February we have been together all the time and she has been quite a companion for me. She has developed very much during the last six months and changed from a child into a young girl. I think she has many very fine qualities and will make a very noble woman if she fulfills the good that is in her and does justice to herself. I do not know any serious fault that she has except her extreme thoughtlessness and in this respect she has improved much and will still more as she grows older and realizes the responsibilities of life.

She has refined and delicate instincts and a high ideal of life and is ambitious for her own improvement. I think during the last year she has acquired and cultivated tastes which will be a lasting benefit and pleasure to her."

Fanny is puzzled that Grace never developed any girlfriends:

"I was in hopes that at school she would make acquaintances and friends who would supply the girl element that she needed but it has not been so.

None of the girls called on her nor invited her to their houses. I am sure I don't know why. Now she will enjoy the companionship and society of girls of her own age."

Apparently Ellen has learned that Fanny paid John Pugh's fare down to Louisiana and back:

"As to his passage money I don't want you to speak of it or think of it again. It is not worth it. I never meant you to know anything about it. If I ever need the money I will come to you for it."

By May 3rd 1880, Fanny has moved out of her flat and into the Clarendon Hotel where she will stay until June. Ellen must have described Mrs. Pugh as being angry with David, to elicit Fanny's comment:

"I don't wonder Mrs. Pugh "pitched into" David when he went up. I should think it strange if she did not."

On June 6th Fanny writes from Rye Beach and describes busy times.

"I went to Fort W- once each week to see Augusta who was sick, and to see Anna at least every other day. I had a few errands to do for her and Aunt S- and a great many for Lizzie especially her supply of fancy work for the summer to plan, procure and usually exchange or alter each piece.

I had six or seven calls of ceremony and condolence to make and two days were occupied by my trip to East Hampton."

Fanny and Anna's trip to Rye was by boats, train and carriage. Fanny is encouraged to hear that Ellen is going away:

"I am perfectly delighted to hear that you are going away... I don't know anything about the place and you probably will not be as comfortable as you are at home, but the change of scene and air and diet, if the latter even is not as good as your own, will be of benefit to you."

She urges Ellen to accept John Haven's kind offer to pay for Thomas' schooling:

"Do not deprive him of the pleasure of feeling that he himself was able to send Thomas away. He could not make a better use of his money nor derive more pleasure from it if spent for his own gratification."

On June 16th 1880 Anna writes Ellen (possibly the last letter Anna wrote to Ellen). Ellen has asked Anna about a family relationship, and Anna, who is a storehouse of family information, obliges her.

Several days later Fanny writes Ellen, who is leaving for Alabama on the 28th with some of the children. This is the first time Ellen has ever gotten away for a holiday on her own. Her destination is over 350 miles away.

On July 8th, 1880, Ellen writes David from Alabama to say that Thomas is quite ill with malaria. The doctor there wants to know how much quinine Thomas has been accustomed to taking when he gets the malarial fever, and Ellen says,

"...I told him (the doctor) I could not tell and did not remember the various kinds of quinine he had taken but 10 grains generally divided in three doses (and now I write it I think it was in two doses) but I would write you.

He said "I should give him 20 grains of quinine, if the fever returns, quinine must be given" -- after some talk he decided not to give anything today but if the fever returned then he would start with the quinine. Meanwhile, he said "write and get me an

answer as quickly as possible of how much quinine he is used to
taking, in what forms the doctor gave it and how it affected him.""

The holiday sounds as though it is off to a terrible start in terms of Ellen's
and the children's health: adding insult to injury, their cottage leaks.

"...He (the doctor) told Thomas he was a little weak dishrag...The
water made all of us feel badly. It took all Mary's appetite away
and took the color out of her cheeks. It constipated the others and
grew me a terrible headache which I still have. The cold baths of
sulfur weakened the children this morning so I shall let them take
freestone water baths again.

...Yesterday we had our leaks in the cottage stopped and our
things fixed up generally. Today I feel badly and weak but I shall
fix up the remainder of our things and attend Thomas.

There are some pluses about the place, but overall it sounds less like a
vacation than another trial for Ellen:

"...The place is very romantic and pretty as far as scenery is
concerned. The night pleasant and cool -- I made the Carpenter
put a few wooden slats across the windows so I feel safer.

The fare poor, I say all in all -- horrible tea and coffee, table cloths
very dirty, and the doctor told me in no account to let the children
eat the cornbread, that they did not know how to make it and it
was very bad and unhealthy. The rolls at night are good and the
cake nice and the vegetables are smothered in the bitterest lard
imaginable. The potatoes, bullets --

We all like being in the cottage although things are rough. We are
shady, private and with little galleries front and back. The children
see everything but the waters, colour de rose, and find even the
fare, good - I, with little romance, see things as you and I would
see them..."

Meanwhile Fanny writes on July 14th 1880 from Rye Beach and says she
has learned of Ellen's arrival at the cottage in Alabama:

"Letters from Grace to her Aunt [Anna] and from Alice and Mary to
me announce your arrival and settlement...The girls seem to be
very happy and I'm sure I hope that you will have a pleasant
summer."

Fanny says, with more accuracy than she probably knew,

"I am very glad you decided to go, but you probably will not be in
many respects as comfortable as you are at home."

On July 22nd, Fanny writes again:

"I'm very much grieved to hear of your illness, it not only spoils all
your pleasure, but it must be very dismal to be sick away from
home.

I cannot do anything for you and can only hope that you may
speedily recover and that none of the children will be taken sick,
for their own sakes and because it will make so much care for you.

Anna and I are just so sorry as we can be and think and talk about you all the time.

...I can't put any secrets in this letter because I presume one of the girls will have to read it to you.

Fanny's summer at Rye Beach sounds very different from Ellen's holiday:

"It is very pleasant here and I'm really quite fond of the place. The best part of the year is the three months I am here.

The Sawyer's like us and will do anything for our comfort and the table is excellent, even better than last year.

There are no disagreeable people in the house and most of them are pleasant. We take breakfast at eight, then sit in the parlors or on the piazza with our work till the mail arrives at 11. We always have a circle of pleasant ladies around us. At 11 some go to bathe and others to their rooms to write.

...I do not bathe every day, only when I feel like it. After dinner at one, I change my dress and go in to Lizzie's where I pass the afternoon unless we dine, which is pretty often. Anna is always in her room at that time unless driving. About nine in the evening I go to Lizzie's and stay till bedtime, between 10 and 11. When I write it is either just after dinner or at bathing time.

...Alice and Grace will like to know that Lucy Freylinghusen and Mrs. Griswold Gray were invited to the reception given by Mr. and Mrs. Morton at Newport in honor of Prince Leopold..."

On July 31st 1880, Ellen writes David about clothing and family, and says,

"All four of the girls are great belles, the belles of the place --Their praises come back to me continually and young men arrive and request to be introduced saying they have heard from other gentlemen of the charming Miss Pugh's and stop on purpose to see them. They are all four considered beautiful dancers and Edith is besieged by gentlemen as such a beautiful dancer.

Dr. Bassett informed me during my illness that they had been great belles who had received more attention than any ladies here and there had been great emulation among the gentlemen while the military were here, to secure them as partners and for the bowling alley, walks etc.

...You may be proud of your daughters.

...When your letter came to Edith today telling of the rain and mud there was a more general clapping of hands to think that they were here and far away from such a dull and fearful picture. Alice, in fact, declared she believed she would never go back.

I think of you a great deal and wish you were here.

Yours with much love

Ellen"

On August 6th 1880, Fanny writes Ellen again from Rye Beach, and says she wonders how David is getting on without Ellen. She asks how the girls are and says,

"Mary and Edith are too young to be at a watering place, for they will want to have a share in all that goes on but there seems to be no help for it. I do hope you will all be benefited as to health. Have you any plans as to school for Mary and Edith?
I suppose it would be quite impossible for them to come north and perhaps it would not do for them even if they could, or be best for them.
Does Grace fall into their ways easily or have they been separated too long to have much in common? I hope not.
...Entres nous, Grace writes the best letters of the family, they are more like yours in style, appearance and clearness of writing.
John (Haven) says your letters are models of neatness and fluency."

By August 20th 1880, Fanny has gotten positive reports in letters from Ellen and Grace:

"Letters from you and Grace received yesterday tell us how much pleasure the girls are enjoying and how much admired they are. I have no words to tell you how delighted I am to have both these accounts.
I do not know when I have heard anything that pleased me so much. I do so want them to have a good time while they are young and have the capacity of enjoyment."
...We were so glad to see your handwriting again dear Nell, but you really ought not to write and I hope you will not write to me till you can do so without trying your eyes in the <u>least</u>.
Anna has failed within the past few weeks and I think by the first of September she will be glad to go back to her home. She is very feeble and suffers very much from want of breath.
...want of breath is the chief difficulty. I do not know if this is caused by failing strength or by some pressure, caused by the disease.
I have been thinking lately that I may not be able to come to Louisiana, but I do not suppose there will be any serious change by that time. I cannot tell till I see what the doctor thinks of her condition, but I mention it as one of the possibilities."

On August 27th, Ellen writes David that Alice, Grace and Mary have gone to Huntsville, but Edith and Thomas are quite ill with malaria. Both children are taking frequent doses of quinine. Ellen's big news is that Alice has taken up with a young man, the son of the governor of Alabama.

"The great anxiety which is weighing upon my mind is in regard to our dear Alice. The night before they all left for Huntsville Governor Chapman's son asked for a private interview with me and formally asked for Alice.
...Then I saw Mr. Chapman and told him he and Alice could correspond but he must come to our home and house in Louisiana and there you and I would give him an answer.

> I had had a talk with Alice and found the dear child loved him and he was to bring her a gold ring and send to New York for a handsome engagement ring.
> …He said he had inquired about us more than we knew anything of and her want of money was nothing if he could have her."

Fanny has heard about Alice and writes on September 1st, 1880 of her concerns, not least of which is the idea of Alice marrying a Southerner:

> "The contents of your letter were not altogether a surprise to me for from what Grace wrote I imagined that Mr. Chapman and Alice were quite devoted to each other, but it does seem so strange that Alice should be old enough to take her life in her own hands.
> …what can she know of his true character. Does she realize what she is doing or is she only thinking of the fun and excitement of being engaged and of having an engagement ring.
> …It seems to me that I should want to know a man for three years rather than three weeks before she became engaged to him.
> …It will be very hard for us to give up Alice and to me it will have an added weight of disappointment to have her marry a Southerner. I have always hoped the girls would marry Northern men and live at the north."

Fanny ends with a note of sympathy that Ellen has been so sick and tells of her own plans for the end of the summer:

> "I am very, very sorry that you have been ill so much of the time. You might have enjoyed the summer so much, if you had not been sick. When do you return home? Send me word in season so that I may direct my letters to Thibodaux.
> Anna will return home on the seventh. John will meet her in Boston and take her on. I shall stay on for a while and probably go to the White Mountains with Lulu before I return to New York."

The next letter is from Ellen to David on September 4th 1880, and talks about Ellen's and the children's misery while ill.

> "Sept 4th
> My dearest Husband,
> Edith's fever has left her but she is very languid and weak. I do not think she will be fit to travel on Monday so I will say decidedly that we will not leave until Tuesday and even then she may not be strong enough. But if she is able to leave on Tuesday I will telegraph you on Monday…
> Thomas is up, got out of bed yesterday. The weather is very bad, very damp and rainy, so much so, that the doctor is anxious to get Edith carried up today, that is, if the sun should come out.
> There are several causes for this sickness and various opinions. Thomas had begun his hot baths again when he was taken down so I think the baths did not agree with him. I am better."

The bright spot in their trip has been making the acquaintance of a Mr. Gordon.

"...Mr. Gordon returned on Tuesday last according to his promise and brought the children home.

He has taken a perfect passion for me and the children and I believe we reciprocate it. The children perfectly worshiped him and I never have fancied anyone out of my own family as I do him. He was taken in our cottage with one of his attacks and his brother and I helped him to his room where he had one of those fearful turns.

The next day he was too weak to rise but left yesterday for home. He is to sail for Europe on the 13th. His departure threw a gloom over us all.

...Mr. G. and I are firm and fast friends and he says if he recovers and returns from Europe, his first visit will be to New Orleans to see us."

Ellen gets a lift from the reaction her children elicit:

"...It is strange the fascination which our children seem to exert. They were just overrun with attention, each one, from young men, middle-aged men, literary men, men of the world, also the ladies. All Huntsville fell in love and lost their hearts over the whole Pugh family.

...They take all the partners at a dance at once, their cards being filled for every dance to the close of the evening.

Are you not proud, I am."

Mary, Anna; Carrying On (1880-1883)

Sad news arrives from Fanny in a letter written September 23rd, 1880 (she is writing from Anna's house, at 252 W. 21st St.):

"Dearest Nell

I am writing on my lap by Anna's bed side, this Thursday morning. Tuesday evening I had a telegram saying the Dr thought Anna was failing fast. I was then at Bethlehem and we had just returned from a drive of 32 miles, besides climbing about on the rocks etc etc. We left B- at eleven that night but were obliged to wait five hours for the Montreal Express, so we sat from 1 A.M. till 6 in a little station up in the mountains. You can imagine what I felt, waiting there for the train.

We reached N.Y. at 8 P.M. the next day, yesterday and found Anna living, indeed, she has rallied a little. John, Aunt S. and Augusta have been with her constantly for the past three days.

Last night for three hours we thought she was dying and she thought so too. She sent her dearest love to you and I thought they would be the last words she would ever speak. When she came to, she spoke of you, sent her love again and said to tell you she knew she could not see you again, but she had been thinking so much about you.

Letters from you and Grace are waiting here for me to read to her when she can hear it. She would not let the others read them, thinking you might speak of Alice.

Strange to say she suffers no pain in her side, which is so merciful. The disease has gone inwards and though there is a very large lump on her breast, there is no pain at all. She suffers dreadfully at times for want of breath and will have spasms of gasping for half an hour or an hour at a time.

No one can tell how long she may live, days or weeks – she may die at any time. She rouses now to send her love to you and to your children."

In late September 1880, Ellen must have come to New York to visit Anna, who was almost certainly dying. Ellen left for Louisiana Saturday, Oct. 2nd, with her son John Pugh, as we learn from a letter of Fanny's. Most likely Ellen's daughter Mary was dangerously ill (perhaps with scarlet fever) such that David sent a telegram for her to come home as soon as possible. Fanny writes that David's letter of Oct. 2nd has just arrived in New York followed by another letter of his, written Sunday Oct 3rd. The letter of the 3rd says that Mary is better. Per Fanny's letter to Ellen,

"About half an hour after you had gone came a long letter fr. David of the 2nd: you ought to have received it earlier in the day. I glanced it over and finding it full of particulars of Mary's illness, I read parts to Anna, who wanted to hear all she could.

It proves to be very much as we supposed.

If you want the letter, I will send it to you.

My waking thoughts were of you this morning and I imagined you and John taking your breakfast when I took mine. I wish I had thought to put in the basket some hard boiled eggs. John at least would have liked them and perhaps you too.

Not hearing any bad news fr. Thibodaux I am feeling very hopeful about our dear Mary and cannot but believe that a telegram will reach you on the way which will relieve your intense anxiety.

Tell Alice and Grace that I am constantly thinking of them and sharing their anxiety and misery.

...I shall tell John that your John left a good bye for him as I know he would have done if he had had time to think.

I said good bye to Aunt Sophia for him.

Another letter fr. David has just come, dated Sunday and saying Mary was better, the fever being the only bad symptom."

The next letter, from Fanny, is dated October 16th, 1880 and is written from Anna's house. This letter is mostly about crape, which is a fabric used for mourning clothes. Fanny has purchased and sent the crape and black stockings to Ellen. Mary Haven Pugh probably died on October 7th[51], (her gravestone says simply "1880, Fifteen Summers").

"I sent yesterday to Mr. Conger's care a box containing crape and stockings. Arnold would not risk sending the crape by mail. I wrote a postal to Mr. Conger and asked him to forward the package at once to you.

I send you 4-1/4 yds of crape at $5 per yard. I give $8 for mine but thought this would answer very well. As soon as you receive it, it ought to be rolled so as to avoid a seam down the middle. I allowed 18 inches for hem and Grace's veil 2 yards (with hem) Alice's 2-1/4. Perhaps she will need a little more and Grace a little less.

I have found by experience that it is very hard to get good black stockings, they so soon turn grey. I got six pairs for Alice Grace and Edith..."

Fanny ends with a note about Anna:

"Anna sends you ever, ever so much love and says to tell you she thinks of you all the time."

---

[51] The 7th is the probable date of Mary's death based on these facts: David's letter of Oct. 3rd says she was improving; she had passed by the second week of October; there was a telegram of David's of Oct. 8th that Fanny references, which was probably a telegram announcing Mary's death. Further, Fanny later states that Thursday was a sad day of the week for Ellen, and the 7th was a Thursday in 1880.

Illustration 41: Mary Haven Pugh's gravestone, Madewood: "Fifteen Summers". Photo by John J. McInerney, Jr.

Fanny writes again on October 24th from Anna's. Anna's situation sounds very grim:

> "It is Sunday morning and I am writing on my lap by Anna's side, the nurse sits up every night and so rests from nine till one during the day, but even then is often called down or comes up of her own accord. Dr. J- says she is much weaker than she was 10 days ago and thinks she cannot last more than two weeks, but I really see very little change since I first came a month ago.
>
> It is very hard for her to have to linger hoping and longing for death, which certainly for her will be the crowning gift of life, but she, as we all, has to just bear God's will.
>
> She takes very little interest in anyone or anything, indeed scarcely knows who is in the room. I am not in the room at night, only the nurse, who holds out wonderfully."

Fanny refers to two letters she has gotten from Alice, and implies that Alice has begun recovering from the blow of losing Mary.

> "Their young lives will all blossom out again, but yours is shadowed for life, for time brings little healing for a mother's heart, indeed as days and weeks and months go on you will miss your child more and more as you have to live without her. The only comfort that I find and feel for you, is the way that heaven is made more real for us, as one by one those we love are gathered there."

> "...But I do not think I can ever be quite, quite reckoned to the death of Mary or Gray Morris."

She asks,

> "Did your dear child know that she was dying and could they pray with her? How kind and good everyone has been to you and the children, Grace wrote me almost everything that I wanted to know and I am much impressed by what your relations and friends have been to you and done for you.
>
> I am afraid it will be hard for you to go to Mrs. Pugh's[52], but it is probably for the best for you all. I suppose you and the children have some comfort in having John with you.
>
> I hope Alice and Grace will be more drawn to each other now. Grace writes me that Mary was lovely to her from the first day she was at home till the last.
>
> Shall I send you the last letter I had from her and the one she wrote Anna?
>
> I cannot express to you how I mourn her (selfishly), how much has gone out of my life with her as it did with dear little Gray, an element of joyousness from a life that is mostly in shadow."

---

[52] Subsequent letters clarify that the reason Ellen and the girls are going to Madewood is because David has to do major work on their house. Whether there was a precipitating event is not known, but the timing, so close to Mary's death, seems odd and so it may have been a major and critical repair job.

Three days later, on October 27th 1880, Fanny writes with more sad news:
> "Dear Nell
> Our dear sister passed away this morning at half past seven, just breathing very quietly.
> I was called at 5:30 but she did not recognize anyone then and we just sat by her till the last, Aunt Sophia, I, nurse and Bridget. I think from what I can learn, that she did not speak after four or perhaps earlier. She began to sink on Friday last and we knew she could not live long, but I thought it might be a week.
> She took very little notice of any one the last few days, and it is a great comfort to me not to hear her short pants for breath which have been incessant night and day.
> I cannot tell till John comes whether the funeral will be Friday or Saturday.
> I have your long letter and will write to you all when I can.
> I sent David a telegram this morning.
> Yours
> Fanny
> October 27th 3 p.m."

On October 30th, David writes Ellen to say that he has gotten the news about Anna's passing. Ellen, Alice, Edith and Grace have gone to Madewood to stay with Eliza Pugh while David works on the house, with John and Thomas. They have undertaken major work along the lines of leveling the house, replacing joists and floors, etc. David says,
> "I am so glad that your sister escaped that terrible suffering in her last moments. She is now with your dear father, mother and sisters, and with our beautiful Mary. And where you will eventually join them, and be eternally happy."

Fanny writes on November 1, 1880,
> "Dear Nell
> We took Anna to Woodlawn[53] Saturday the 30th 12:30. It was a very stormy day and very forlorn --
> John and I, Mr. Hopkins, Woodbury, Alfred Morewood and all Alfred's family except Carrie, Mr. Collier and nurse.
> I shall stay here for a little while, but I want you to write at once and let me know if you would like me to come out now or come later in the winter, if now, how soon, if the house is being altered it may not be ready.
> If Nellie wants to come now, do you want her? I must make my plans right away, but it makes no difference to me when I come. I cannot write anymore today.

---

[53] Woodlawn Cemetery, where John Appleton Haven had purchased the Haven family plot in 1870. The Havens and Woodbury Langdon are buried in the Spring Lake section of Woodlawn, near Webster Ave. and 233rd St. in the Bronx.

I have just received letters from Alice, Grace and Edith. Tell Grace
Aunt Anna had a letter from her some days before she went.
Yours
F.A.L.H."

David, from Energy, writes Ellen at Madewood in November about the
work on their house, and quashes any notion Ellen has about returning
home:

"...if you had seen the house, you would have wondered how
anybody could stay here. The parlor, your room and dressing room
and Alice's room only with floors retouched.
The hall -- from your door and parlor door all up, and every plank
in dining room. Today the floor in nursery down, but still plenty of
work there, carpenters now laying down hall and dining room floor.
An immense job in all -- very much more than carpenters counted
on -- and yet considerable work upon your room and dressing
room. My bathroom has been half up since Friday, and still not
finished. Front gallery half up, and all to be up as soon as rooms
and side galleries -- yet untouched -- finished. I moved from your
room to parlor by front gallery -- watching each step for loose
planks, and we now eat upon lower side Gallery -- I getting
through bathroom as best I can.
I simply walked off from your door into bottom of hall on Saturday
night. Hurt myself considerably, and have been suffering torments
ever since (inside).
You suggest my going up to Mrs. Williams -- I am obliged to watch
the carpenters like a hawk, and besides, can scarcely walk even to
do that, going up to Mr. Williams would upset me completely[54].
And furthermore I could not inflict my present weakly body upon
anyone -- to say nothing of being better off at home.
You speak of coming down tomorrow -- utterly impossible for you
to live here yet, and if you will insist on leaving mothers, you must
make up your mind either to select the best hotel in Labadie, or go
down to Madame Gamarre's at Thibodeaux."

David writes Ellen again in November 1880, and his resentment is ill-
concealed:

"I wish sincerely you had turned your mind to something else
besides touching the house -- which suited me well enough.
John wants you home, but just now, with your tremendous energy
and desire to turn the house upside down, I should go crazy.
So you must wait a few days longer."

He writes more letters in November, filled with frustration about the
weather, which has turned relentlessly wet and thus impedes his and the
carpenter's work on the house. Meantime John has injured himself

---

[54] David's reference to Mrs. and Mr. Williams are to John Williams and Mary Louisa Maguire
(Williams) of Leighton Plantation. Leighton was next to Energy, and the Williams' were
Mary Williams Pugh's parents.

(somewhat of a theme with John) and Thomas has some pain about his face, whether a dental issue or some other is not clear.

In his comments on the probable visit by Fanny are found a genuine appreciation of Fanny, and an interesting reference to his own moods and behaviors:

> "I am glad you wrote Fanny to come out at once, although I'm not sure the house will be ready for her.
>
> I wish most fervently she could be induced to spend the winter with us -- she makes everything so bright and pleasant around her.
>
> If she does not stay because of my cross ways, I will do my best to suppress them, or if I find I cannot, will keep out of the house when the fit comes on."

By November 14th, Fanny writes from the Clarendon Hotel that she can come see Ellen. She talks about being met at the Lafourche railroad, and it is not clear whether she doesn't want David to come because it will take him away from his work on the house, or whether she does not want to be met by David alone because she is not comfortable with the idea (although she also states "I am much obliged to David for his kind wish to have me come"):

> "There is no one to come and meet me if John is sick, for it is best that David should not and I do not on any account wish Mr. Conger asked to, as I have not the least claim on him. I am quite used to traveling now and can come up alone quite well."

Fanny recognizes how painful it must be for Ellen to return to Energy:

> "It must have been very hard to go back again to your desolate home. I have been dreading it for you all along."

Fanny writes again from the Clarendon Hotel on November 25th, Thanksgiving day, 1880. Her letter speaks about Anna's will and Anna's funeral, and she mentions Alice:

> "You spoke in a letter several weeks ago, of Alice being so lonely and missing Mary so much.
>
> I pity her with all my heart and know just what she is suffering, for I know what I suffered for years without Grace (Fanny's sister, who perished in the Haven house fire of 1855) but I never told anyone. But I do not see why she should be any more lonely than Grace, nor why she and Grace should not be more to each other, than they apparently are."

Fanny ends with a note in which she looks forward to being with Ellen:

> "I think we will have a severe cold, stormy winter here. With you it will probably be frosts and rain, but I hope we may be together and then we shall not mind it."

On November 30th, Fanny writes from the Clarendon again, expressing sympathy for Alice's grief and saying she hopes to leave for Ellen's by the end of December at the latest.

On December 9th Fanny writes again from the Clarendon. There has been yet another change in her plans: Augusta's daughter Nellie, who was to accompany her, has had to postpone her departure, but Augusta's other daughter Lulu is eager to come.

> "I suspect you are tired of hearing my plans and counter plans and moreover when you receive this letter and hear the present one, that your hair will stand on end with dismay.
>
> ...I now propose starting on the 20th of December with Lulu Hopkins, by sail, Lulu is wild to go and has coaxed a consent from her father to allow her to remain till Nellie comes. Lulu wants to have all the time she can and would like to start today, Milt's objection to her and Nellie's going, is that it will make extra care and expense for you.
>
> Augusta's is that Lulu may not be able to find a chance to come home before Nellie comes out. Mine is, that our coming now, after saying we had given it up for the present, may interfere with some of your arrangements...
>
> ... if...you do not want Lulu or do not want us just yet, will you send me a telegram (which I will pay for).
>
> If I do not hear by the night of the 15th, I shall think we can come and arrange to start on the 20th. Augusta and I both trust to you to speak out plainly. If we come, we must all be watching for a chance for Lulu to return in January.
>
> I know that you will not care to have us with you on the 25th and we could stay over in New Orleans and come up on Monday if you prefer. Lulu would be glad to see the city.
>
> If we come, I want you to promise that you'll make no difference for us in any way. Will you do this? Lulu knows exactly what life is and expects, nor wants nothing, but to see you all and pass quiet days with you.
>
> ... If no telegram comes, I shall think we can come, so if you want us, don't telegraph.

On December 15th, Fanny writes Ellen to say she is assuming the trip is a go, because she hasn't heard otherwise:

> "I have not as yet had a telegram warning us off, so I presume you intend to let us come on the 20th. Lulu is perfectly delighted at the thought of going, it is her first journey and a great event to her."

She ends with specifics of their trip:

> "We leave here at 10 p.m. of the 20th and are due in New Orleans at 9.25 a.m. the 23rd.
>
> There is no need at all of our being met, as if we are not on time for the noon train, we will go to City Hotel and come the next morning. I know just what to do."

Fanny takes the time to try to explain how it was that neither she nor John specifically wrote about Anna's will right away, and why John Haven's letter to Ellen may have seemed brusque:

> "Don't regret that you asked to be told about our dear Anna's will, it was quite natural you should. Some of us, or one of us, ought to have thought to write you. Neither of us spoke to the other, on the subject of your wanting to know, so we could not impute any motive, or misunderstand you in anyway. We just simply never spoke on the subject-except this.
>
> One morning I met John at 252 [Anna's house in the city] and he said (or words to this effect) "I found a letter from Ellen when I returned last evening, she seems to be very unhappy and despondent and I am afraid she thinks I might have written her before in regard Anna's will, I have had no time to write to anyone; however, as soon as I had got warm, I sat down and wrote to her."
>
> No other remark was made except I said, "Oh, I don't believe she cares and by this time she has received my letter, which gave her some particulars, but not all."
>
> If his letter was cross, I do not think he meant it to be and it was probably the result of being cold and tired and hungry and half sick with a wretched cold, which would have kept any other man in bed."

On December 18th 1880, David writes his son John Pugh from the City Hotel in New Orleans with news that he has renewed their lease on the land. He is also taking a few days for himself, which will put him back home two days before Fanny and Lulu's arrival, provided he sticks to his schedule:

> "Say to mother, with my love, that I have arranged with Mr. Morris -- of the bank, for a release of the place for another year. Am to give him a note for the amount -- $900 -- same as before, tomorrow. Am very glad I talked with him personally, for he wanted more money.
>
> When this is done, I shall have nothing now to keep me in here in the way of business, but find myself so much better -- from being able to walk about -- that I shall probably stay over beyond Sunday -- say until Tuesday."

There are no letters again until late March, because Fanny is with Ellen in Thibodaux at Energy.

On April 5th 1881, Fanny is back in Fort Washington, where she writes Ellen about a burglary and says that clothing taken from the Haven house was found burning on the grounds.

> "...they found clothes burning and Sarah and Gussie rushed down there, half burned, was a large quantity of John's clothing and my dresses... -pieces of mother's dresses, the ones you and I had—
> It thickens the mystery so that we don't know which way to turn.

The woods and grounds have been searched in every direction by police and by John and the girls -- they have even dug up places that seemed suspicious to look for the silver. It seems as if it must be in the neighborhood somewhere."

...Detectives out here and in the city working at it. A <u>faint</u> suspicion attached to the flagman at the end of the cut who is being closely watched. A $200 reward offered for the silver and lists of it sent to the different pawn brokers and jewelers.

I have been interrupted in my letter and now hasten to finish, not to lose the mail. I have been down to the house and you will be glad to hear that I found my <u>box of jewelry</u> in my closet. <u>All</u> my silver is gone."

Fanny ends by saying she misses them all:

"My dearest love to all. I will write a proper letter very soon. It is bitterly cold today, thermometer 18 and high wind. The house, when I went down, felt like a tomb.
All send love.
Goodbye dear for the present.
I miss you all so much
Yours affec
F.A.L.H."

On April 8th 1881, Fanny writes with general news and alludes to a communion service that Ellen has asked her to get at Tiffany's, as a memorial to Mary.

"I have made inquiries about the Communion Service but cannot get it for you by Easter.
Will attend to it as soon as possible, but it is not a thing to be bought in a hurry."

On April 17th Ellen writes her cousin Charlotte Haven. Her grief for Mary is deep:

"Dear Charlotte,
Early this Easter morning, quite unable to bear the memories of other Easter mornings, I take out those verses you sent me with the lovely Easter cross, the cross filled in with the forget me nots, the great burden and sorrow of my life sacred with never to be forgotten memories, and read and think of you."

Also on April 17th 1881, Fanny writes Ellen from Fort Washington, and makes light talk but also says she is mourning for the loss of a valise that had belonged to her mother Sarah. The valise was stolen from the Haven house when the house was broken into recently:

"The carpenter came to begin to repair the injuries done by the thieves to the doors etc.
...I find they carried off a little valise of mine, probably put the forks and spoons in it. It belonged to Mother and was the one she brought up here the night of the fire in 1855. I valued it so much

and would never use it. There is no use in talking anymore about it."

After some talk about fabrics and friends, Fanny mentions James Carter:

> "My letter was interrupted by Mr. Carter, who passed two or three hours with me. We walked down by the river, but there was a cold wind and it was not very pleasant. Mr. Carter said he could hardly realize that 30 years and more had passed since he first saw the rocks and the woods. He is looking remarkably well and handsome and feels better than he has for years."

Fanny is lonely, with Anna gone and Aunt Sophia choosing to leave New York City. Fanny is probably going to stay at Fort Washington or a hotel until it is time to leave for the summer.

> "It is painful for me to stay out here anyhow, I do not like it-but it will be better to be on the spot for the work to be done at the house."

On April 20th Fanny says she has been to Tiffany's for a Communion Service per Ellen's request. The service is for Ellen to donate in Mary's memory.

> "I ordered today at Tiffany's a design sketch of a Communion Service which I am to inspect on Monday and then have sent to you...
> When you let me know which you prefer, the service can be made in about two weeks. I think the inscription you propose quite appropriate. Do you want any date put on? You ought to receive the designs about the 30th."

On April 29th Fanny writes from 31 Washington Square, where she is staying with Lizzie.

> "It was a great treat to have your delightful long letter yesterday, almost as good as having a talk with you."

Fanny says she hopes that Alice will be able to come to New York and go away with Fanny for the summer holiday. She also reports that James T. Fields, of the publisher's Ticknor and Fields, has passed away. James T. Fields had married Annie Adams, of the Adams family who were close friends of the Havens. As history would show, Annie Adams Fields didn't let the loss of her husband slow her down[55].

> "Perhaps you have seen by the papers that poor Annie Fields has lost her husband. It will be a crushing sorrow to her, for they lived for and in each other. He had heart disease and while she was reading to him one evening, he passed away."

Again Fanny dwells on the valise of her mother's:

---

[55] From Wikipedia: After Fields' husband died in 1881, she continued to occupy the center of Boston literary life…(she and Sarah Orne Jewett were) friends with many of the main literary figures of their time, including Willa Cather, Mary Ellen Chase, William Dean Howells, Henry James, Rudyard Kipling, Harriet Beecher Stowe, Alfred Tennyson, Oliver Wendell Holmes, Mark Twain, Sarah Wyman Whitman, Henry Wadsworth Longfellow, Nathaniel Hawthorne, Lydia Maria Child and John Greenleaf Whittier.

"That dear, most precious valise that was Mothers, was inside the trunk the robbers opened. I...put it in the trunk, for fear it would be scratched or injured if sent by express. I never used it, except once and then kept it with me, not giving it to any express or baggage master. I try not to think about that or the other things."

Fanny ends the letter with a comment about Woodlawn Cemetery:

"I was at Woodlawn yesterday, where the grass was vividly green and all seemed so restful and full of peace. I wondered how long it would be before I could be put away there too and be ended with life, which really has so little to give or promise now, everything lies beyond and seems so far off."

On May 6th 1881, Fanny writes Ellen from the Haven house in Fort Washington. She delves into Ellen's painful situation:

"Old House Fort Washington

6th May 1881

Dearest Nell

... I have been down here all day, just going up for dinner and am now writing at my own desk in my own room. It seems very strange to be here again, but I have kept busy all the time.

I need not say how entirely I sympathize in the trouble and anxiety you have had to go through. It is the same old story, for which there seems to be no remedy and which must always be a source of care and constant trial to you.

But I am sure you make one great and fatal mistake in undertaking to pay any one of David debts, nevermind how incurred. I feel sure you ought not to do this, nor feel bound to, under any circumstances.

I suppose I am very obtuse and wanting in proper pride that I don't see as calling it "a debt of honor" makes any difference. I don't think I know exactly what "honor" means. One debt to me is the same as another and I can see no difference between borrowing a sum of money of a man out and out or taking goods from him which you can't pay for.

...I am sure Robert [David's brother] once told you that you were not bound for David's debts and if you undertake to pay them, you will find your hands full. If people lend money, they do it at their own risk.

But enough of an unpleasant subject."

Fanny says she is delighted that Alice will be coming to her soon, and that the two of them will go to Rye Beach, N.H. for the summer. Meantime, due probably to David's debts, Ellen no longer feels she can afford the communion service from Tiffany's, but Fanny says it would be awkward to back out of it now, so Fanny will loan her the money.

"But though it is not ordered in so many words it was quite understood that they were to make it as soon as you had chosen the design. I do not see any reason I can give for countermanding

it for if I said you could not afford it, they would think you would
have known this 10 days ago as well as now.
...I have several hundred dollars which I intend to put in the
Savings Bank next month, so that it will draw interest from first of
July. It will be probably six months before I shall need it to use
and you can pay me the interest on it for that time if you choose
and have the use of it, till your mortgage is paid off."
In her gracious way, Fanny makes it easy for Ellen to accept her offer:
"...it will be conferring a favor to allow me to feel that, however
indirectly, I am contributing towards the carrying out of your
darling wish and desire."
Fanny touches upon the estates that must be settled: it seems that their
brother John is handling several at once:
"John is almost distracted and says everything seems to be against
him. The doctor's [Sweetser] estate is closed, but he still has
Anna's, Fathers and Mr. Reillets on his hands, the latter gives
infinite trouble."
Fanny says she will begin going through Anna's belongings in 21st St. the
following week.

On May 15th, 1881, Fanny says she is about to leave for Anna's house
where she will meet Augusta and begin going through everything.
Meantime they are still working out how to divide some of the things from
the Fort Washington house.
On the 16th, Fanny writes from 31 Washington Sq., Lizzie's house, to say
that she has agreed to pay a higher price for the communion service, due
to a misunderstanding:
"I am just so sorry about it, as you will be, but there seemed no
help for it. I hope you will forgive me."
Furthermore, it sounds as though Fanny is burdened by the fallout from
some of the wills:
"It is so very provoking about the legacies, everything seems to
have gone wrong."

By Fanny's next letter of May 23rd, Alice has arrived safely. By her letter of
the 29th, Fanny has gathered all the furniture and carpets from Anna's
house and the Haven house to send to Ellen by steamer. Ellen has asked
about the disposition of the Haven house, and Fanny says,
"In regard to having the place at Fort Washington offered for sale
which you spoke of sometime ago. I had already spoken on the
subject to John before your letter came and he said that for some
little time it had been in the hands of a broker, or more correctly
speaking, he had told the broker that any offer for the place would
be considered and that he must see what he could do with it.
There has been no offer of any kind, nor as far as I can see any
chance of any.
Nearly all the houses out there are for rent or for sale."

Fanny explains that John Haven wants to be out of the house, but with all the work he has to do with the estates and legacies,

> "We cannot take up carpets and clear out the house till he leaves and week after week he has had to put us off, so that I have been put back in all my plans and lost much time.
> Unfortunately he was called to serve on the jury for two weeks, just when he had his hands more than full."

Fanny is so busy that she doesn't think she and Alice will leave for Rye until mid-June.

On June 1st, 1881, St. John's Episcopal Church sent a letter of thanks for the silver communion service. The Greek-Revival style church and communion service can be seen today on Jackson St, Thibodaux.

On June 2nd 1881, Fanny writes Ellen all about items from the houses, including furniture and silver. She then alludes to Ellen's ongoing difficulties due to David:

> "I am sure I wish you and John (Pugh) could manage the place entirely and have the good of your money. It is all very discouraging and heartsickening. But I suppose if you do the best you can then take it as your cross to bear it bravely and patiently, it is part of the battle of life which everyone has to fight in one form or another. Of course it does not make any the less hard to endure, only a puts it in different light and makes the daily cares become less petty and wearisome.
> It seems to me that in the fall when your mortgage is paid off, I should appropriate a small sum, even $1000, to pay for the service, the picture, the lot and removal etc.[56] -- thus feeling the pressure of them off your mind and in a certain sense have the comfort of them.
> The whole sum would not be more than the expenses the dear child would have been, if she had been spared to you. Her clothing, her pleasures and her education, would soon have covered the sum.
> I should not pay out of my money one cent of any debts contracted anywhere.
> I think if David looks ahead at all, or makes any plan, it is that he counts on his mother's annual present to cover his expenses and debts.
> I do hope the rice crop will prove a success this year."

On June 16th Fanny writes Ellen from Boston, on her way to Rye with Alice. She again details many items she has shipped:

---

[56] By "the service, the picture, the lot and removal", Fanny means the communion service that Ellen has donated to St. John's Episcopal Church in Thibodaux, and the lot and removal means that Mary Pugh will be reburied at St. John's (she was originally buried at the Madewood Cemetery).

"From Jackson, a Morgan line, will come sofa, arm chair and six chairs, also four carpets, instead of three, as I first said. By Cromwell's line, Doctors book case, arm chair and three chairs, glass top table, commode, Fathers washstand from home, oil painting, two boxes of books, a barrel of glass and China, hat case into which I put everything I could."

Three days later Fanny writes a lengthy letter from Rye, and says she is happy to be done with her duties:

"Rye Beach 19th June 1881
Dearest Nell
It is a great relief to feel that I am justified in writing about something other than boxes and barrels and furniture and dollars and cents. I do not intend even to remember that these are such things to be thought about or talked about."

She writes again on the 29th, and both letters are filled with family talk and business. Fanny ends this letter with,

"It is afternoon and the house quite still. Alice is asleep in her room. I am sitting at my window looking out on the sea which is a beautiful dark, deep blue with here and there a tiny white sail against the horizon. The Comet[57] is most beautiful, we admire it every evening."

On July 11th 1881, Fanny writes that she and Alice have received letters telling of the removal of Mary's body to St. John's Episcopal Church:

"I had a sweet letter from Grace a few days since and Alice has just now received one telling about the removal. How very very trying and sad dearest sister this has all been to you, sad beyond expression, bringing back all the agony and grief and seeming as if you have lost our dear Mary again.
I knew when it was to be and was thinking of you all the time. As it had to be done, I am very thankful it is over and hope it was made as easy to you as possible and your feelings consulted in every way.
How carefully and faithfully David has attended to the making of the vault. How nice he can be when he chooses."

In the same letter Fanny expresses distaste for David's recent behavior:

"I think the whole affair about General Martin's[58] funeral, was perfectly disgraceful, I am afraid Mrs. Pugh will be very much put out with David, will she not, and Robert probably will at least challenge him! I never heard of such goings-on, to think of quarreling about a man when he is dead!"

---

[57] The Tebbutt Comet of 1881.

[58] R.C. Martin married W.W. Pugh's sister, Mary Winifred Hill Pugh, in 1835. Martin owned Albemarle plantation (located about 2 miles from W.W. Pugh's Woodlawn).

On July 26th, Fanny says she hopes Alice will stay with her through the winter, and she also hopes there will be some way for Edith to come for the winter and go to school in New York. But Fanny imagines that Ellen will not be able to afford it, what with her ongoing money struggles that seem due largely to David.

> "I often think about Edith's school in which some satisfactory plan could be devised for sending her. I have long had it in my mind to tell you that if it could be managed in any way I should be very glad to have her come on this fall, pass the winter with me and go to day school.
>
> ...I fear your money affairs will not allow you to do anything for the poor child this year, beyond sending her to Miss Sothern.
>
> I am very fond of Edith, very much interested in her and very desirous she should have all possible advantages. I wish I could really do something for her."

On August 17th 1881, Fanny says that when she and Alice return to the city, Fanny will suggest that Alice wear less deep mourning (for Mary):

> "When we return to New York I shall suggest that in a month or two, she should take off her long veil (as I shall do) and lighten her mourning generally."

Fanny passes along the information from Augusta that their brother John Haven is being worn down by his duties related to probating estates for various family relations. Despite having had occasional fallings-out with John (in part over his wife, Lydia), Fanny sympathizes with him and respects him.

> "He has had a wretched summer, no rest at all...when he goes up to the city for a day's business and has to climb up and down steep stairs to business offices and walk about in the heat, he goes back perfectly used up and is literally good for nothing for several days.
>
> ...It is a great pity he has to be bothered by other people's affairs so much, it is a most thankless task and he does it in such a conscientious way, that it is double the trouble that it would be to any other man."

Fanny wonders what John Pugh will do.

> "I am sorry to hear John has been sick and hope he is well again soon. Is he making any plan to do anything? He has had almost a year to "rest"?"

On Sept. 25th 1881, Fanny writes from Fort Washington about the burglary, and John Haven's health. She is in transit, having returned from Rye but not yet in her apartment.

> "I am told that among the silver recovered there is nothing of mine, but still am going to look it over. I had no hope of getting anything.
>
> John has been here some days and is still quite sick with dysentery... Augusta and I wanted to go over to see him, but he begged us not to."

On the topic of the burglary, Fanny suggests that because she Is a woman, she can't get any information:

> "If John could have seen the police...he might have found out something, but they would not tell us anything."

Tellingly, Fanny remembers what this day in 1880 represents to them. It is probably the day that Ellen set out from Louisiana to come and visit her dying sister, and while she was away her daughter Mary died.

> "This time is inexpressibly sad to me and I do not dare to think what it must be to you. I keep recalling each day as it comes. Yesterday it was the day you started on your ill starred journey. And yet we ought not to feel so, for you thought you were doing what was right and best."

By October 18th 1881, Fanny is installed in her apartment at 14 5th Ave. She still worries about John Haven.

> "Dearest Nell
> It is very long since I have written you and it seems ever longer than it is. I have been, as you know, very busy and I have been anxious about John.
> I have seldom seen anyone more sick than he has been and now Lydia seems at death's door.
> ...I think it will be a fortnight yet before John will be able to be about again and I do not know when Lydia can be moved to Philadelphia even if she lives to be taken there. Before she is moved I think I had better take Alice to see her."

From a comment Fanny makes about Alice and the theater, we learn that Fanny, Ellen and Augusta heard Charlotte Cushman read in 1874:

> "If necessary I shall go with her, but I have not been to the theater for seven years, the last time I went was with you and Augusta in 1874 to see Miss Cushman.[59]"

Apparently Ellen has returned the letters Fanny had written to Mary, to Fanny:

> "Thank you so much for sending me those letters.
> I could not bear to look at them, but just put them away. The last present I had from her, I keep, with the last I had from Gray in the little black cabinet Anna gave me. Hers was a little blue pitcher and his a little glass one."

The day before Thanksgiving 1881, Fanny writes more sad news to Ellen:

> "14 Fifth Av
> Dearest Nell
> John's telegram of the 19th has announced to you that his poor suffering wife breathed her last after days and even weeks of almost incredible suffering, so that her death was a blessed release and John now seems to dwell more on that than on his own loss. Indeed I think he hardly realized what had happened till

---

[59] Charlotte Cushman, American actress (1816-1876), performed in New York in 1874 as part of her farewell tour.

219

Tuesday morning, when the body was taken to Philadelphia for the funeral and interment.

It was most unfortunate and great trial to him, that he could not go on[60], but it was physically impossible."

Fanny talks about her mourning clothes and about her feelings toward John Haven.

"I make no change in my dress being already in mourning. I had just left off my veil and shall not resume it.

It is pleasant to me that I have lately the opportunity given to me to show how entirely I had forgiven John and Lydia for their neglect of and kindness to me in former times. I do not think they took that view of that, or thought I had anything to forgive, what I mean is, the satisfaction was for my own self, I knew in my heart I had entirely forgiven them, but God was good in giving me the chance to prove it to myself.

I think you will understand what I mean."

She also tells Ellen that she dressed Lydia's body before it was placed in the casket, for John's sake and for his viewing, and she describes the sad transformation effected by Lydia's illness.

"I dressed the poor, thin, wasted form in a nightdress, brushed her hair as she used to wear it, (the pretty, bright -- brown hair, now matted and a little gray), put on a dainty, tied with a strand of silk, the wedding ring on the wasted figure from which it fell, put a few white flowers around her and then called John to say goodbye to the pretty, bright winsome wife, whom he had been so fascinated by and so proud of in her prime of youth and beauty.

...I only dressed her for her husband to see and part from."

On January 4th 1882, Fanny explains to Ellen that she doesn't want Christmas presents anymore because of the association with Gray, Lizzie's boy, who died around Christmas.

"I never want to keep Christmas now-since I lost dear Gray, the day has been one of peculiar sadness and I never want to have it bring gaiety or presents to me again. It is hallowed for me as the last day he was on Earth."

On January 26th Fanny expresses more loss. In addition to the memory of Mary Pugh, whose birthday just passed, Fanny has lost a friend who passed not during childbirth but from a related infection.

"Yesterday was our dear Mary's birthday and I was thinking of her all day. I do not think she was out of my mind for an hour, going over and over her brief young life and trying to picture to myself what her life would have been if she had been spared to us.

...Saddest of all to me, for I was very fond of her, I have lost my dear young friend May Cole, who died day before yesterday, leaving a beautiful little baby, three weeks old.

When I saw her last she was so full of happiness and hope, looking forward with such innocent longing to the coming of her baby and

---

[60] John Haven was too ill to "go on" to the funeral services for his wife.

yet so full also of sweet affection for me, as she always was. Today I saw her in her coffin, very beautiful, as beautiful as a marble statue.

The third day after her baby came I was there and Emma told May she was not quite as well she had been, nothing much, only little fever-her words went to my heart like a knife for I had all along felt very anxious about her.

Then she grew worse and then better, fluctuating between life and death, then came chills, fever, delirium, unconsciousness and now death. Her poor husband, who adored her, is almost distracted and her loss is a very keen grief to me."

Fanny also faces losing Alice's company because Alice wants to go home to Louisiana.

"She has not spoken to me on the subject, that is not her way, but she has expressed to others her intention of returning home this winter and latterly to my amazement I have heard her say in answer to casual inquiries that she intended to return in February."

Fanny would like to have Alice stay through the summer and go to Rye with Fanny, or at least stay until spring, but Fanny wants to honor Alice's and Ellen's wishes. She wants to know what Ellen desires for Alice. After lengthy discussion, Fanny says,

"I think, or at least hope, that I have made my meaning plain to you. We usually manage to understand each other, but I want to make it especially clear to you and to our dear Alice, and I shall not be in the least hurt or even surprised, if she decides to return soon to her home, on the contrary only grateful to you for having spared her so long and to her for having stayed. I think we have been very happy together, at least I have been in having her."

David is not so much as mentioned in these letters from Fanny. Ellen has asked Fanny to come visit, and Fanny replies,

"I thank you very much for wishing me to come out to Louisiana but I cannot think of it this year. Next winter, if I am alive, we will consider it. I wish that I could see you all."

On Feb. 16th 1882, Fanny is getting ready to leave one flat while looking for another. While looking at flats, she is shocked to see how some people live:

"To give you an idea of how some people manage, we went in one first-class house just off Fifth Avenue to see a flat. The servants room opened off the kitchen (which I especially dislike) and there in the sink where the dishes are washed was a certain article from the bedroom waiting its turn to be washed. What do you think of this?"

Fanny has also talked to Alice about staying with her until fall, and Fanny explains to Ellen the reasoning she used with Alice:

"...that I knew it gave you great satisfaction to have any one of your girls happy and enjoining innocent pleasures such as belonged to girl life, pleasures which, as you were circumstanced and from the fact of your home being in the country, could only be compassed by their leaving that home for a time."

Fanny talks about how to handle mourning clothes if Alice stays on and Grace comes to join them:

"If Grace comes on I should let her wear colors, unless my dear sister, this would be painful to you. I suppose in the fall or early winter they would wear colors anyhow and a few months more or less would make but little difference especially if they were here away from home. Colors are much more becoming to both than black."

Fanny closes on a note of sadness about her brother:

"John seemed very lonely and sad and unhappy when I was out. I wish I could do something for him and perhaps I ought to make some plan to live with him. I don't know."

On March 9th 1882, Fanny unabashedly expresses relief that Alice has not found a way home yet:

"I am happy to say that no chance has as yet presented itself for Alice to return to Louisiana and I hope it will be made a matter of necessity for her to remain here till late summer or early fall and that Grace can come on in June...It seems a pity that for the sake of a comparatively small sum either of them should be deprived of any innocent pleasures they can enjoy now while they are young. I certainly want to give them all I can."

Fanny relates a funny story about an embarrassing situation she and Alice got into, when a man they knew from Rye Beach contacted them in the city.

"Yesterday I had a note from our artist friend Mr. Waller asking me to come to his studio with Miss Pugh to see a picture he had painted of Rye Beach...To make sure of going, we started off then reaching his studio soon after three, but alas! surprising him at work with a "model".

From the glimpse I had of her as she swiftly and gracefully disappeared behind a screen she was quite pretty and in "Demi toilette", very "Demi".

I was much more embarrassed than he was and I think Alice enjoyed it. I thought it was very improper. While we were looking at his picture, there came a knock at the door and when Mr. W. -- opened it, a woman's voice asked if he was busy with his models, so I presume she knew that was the time (of day) he had them. She came in and...Alice declares she took us for "models" and I daresay she did. I go off into fits of laughter whenever I think of the scene, which was very ludicrous, though it does not seem so, when written out. Alice has the faculty of always finding something to say and I leave it entirely to her to get us out of scrapes, so we made our retreat as best we might."

On March 18th 1882, Fanny says Alice has been invited to Marblehead, MA, to stay part of the summer with Lizzie Morris, so Fanny hopes that both girls will be able to stay at Rye Beach with Fanny for most of the summer. She is willing to help pay for it:

"My wish is to have one of the girls with me at Rye and to pay her fares on and back and her board while there."

On April 1st, Fanny writes that Alice has been downtown to see a novelty:

"The first thing she did was to go with Mr. Morris to see a great big whale, 70 feet long, which was at the foot of Wall Street[61], she seemed to think it very wonderful."

Fanny recalls a sad memory triggered by the passing of a much-loved pastor who supported the family after the tragic fire of 1855:

"The first thought that came to my mind when I read of his death, was how he came to us at Fort Washington after the fire and how he sat so long in perfect silence, just mourning with us, not trying to comfort a sorrow for which there was none to be given-the silence which was at length broken by his repeating from the Gospel of St. John -- "let not your hearts be troubled" et cetera. I can recall the whole scene so perfectly, the darkened room, Father's bowed head, Mother's silent weeping-everything came back to me in a rush of memory."

At the end of April, Fanny writes that she and Alice have packed everything to move out of Fanny's flat. Alice will be staying through the summer, for which Fanny is grateful: Fanny still hopes that Grace will be able to come. Fanny is concerned about Ellen's health:

"And how is your general health-do you still get so very tired? Please answer these questions, for it is very long since I have heard anything about yourself you always write and speak and think of others."

She gives Ellen their itinerary for the coming months:

"We are going to stay at Lizzie's till about the 10th, after then please direct to Fort Washington. The present plan is for us to stay there till about middle of June, then if I hear of anyone going on (as is most likely) I shall go to Rye and Alice will stay with Lizzie and go with them to Marblehead about the 20th, joining me at Rye the early part of July."

On May 9th 1882, Fanny writes that she and Alice are exhausted from moving out of the flat. She realizes that she doesn't see how Grace will be able to join them due to the expense:

"I will say very plainly, as I did in writing to Grace last week, that I do not see how you can manage to have two of them here at the

---

[61] According to the New York Times archive, in March 1882, an 80-foot long right whale was captured near Sag Harbor. The captain hired two tug boats, hauled it to N.Y.C., and placed it at the foot of Wall St. on exhibit.
The whale was embalmed and was to be taken on a tour through the major cities of the US after leaving N.Y.C.

North this summer, but then it is a matter entirely for you to decide on."

On May 21st, Fanny writes from Fort Washington that they have had visits from Woodbury Langdon and James Carter, amongst others. Woodbury took Alice to the horse races at Jerome Park[62], and,

"Alice was just wild with delight over the beautiful dresses and the gay scene altogether.

Alice looked very pretty when dressed for the races, wearing her Surah and broad hat with feathers, her Spanish lace fichie set off her dress fastened with a pretty pin Mrs. Morris [Lizzie] gave her.

She looked so like a lady as indeed she always does."

Fanny hints that there are several suitors for Alice, including a Dr. Poore and Woodbury Langdon.

Letters from Fanny to Ellen on May 21st and 22nd 1882, indicate that David's mother Eliza (age 76) is ill. Ellen has been up to Madewood to stay with Eliza, and is now back home, but Fanny says,

"I am very sorry to hear such sad news of Mrs Pugh. I do not see what can be the matter with her, for it seems to me very unusual for a woman as old as she is to have severe headaches.

Perhaps she may rally from this attack. If not, we could not regret death for her, she has lived a long, useful life, has been a faithful wife and mother and doubtless will be glad to join her husband to whom I believe she was much attached.

To her family, I think she will be a great loss."

Fanny says she understands that Grace will not be coming this summer. She describes how John Haven is faring with his grief:

"John seems pleased to have us here and is kind and anxious to please me. He says he does not intend to stay here after July, but I do not think he has a plan about going to any place.

He seems quite interested in the place and is usually in good spirits, then at times depressed and sad. He keeps a pretty picture of Lydia always before him on his writing table, a glass of fresh delicate flowers always stands beside it."

On May 27th, David writes Ellen from New Orleans saying he has visited with Edith and they had a wonderful time. Edith has been ill, and her eyes have bothered her. David says he should be able to sell his rice and start for home. But he writes again on the 30th, having again spent time with Edith, and says he hasn't been able to sell the rice.

---

[62] From the N.Y.C. Parks and Recreation web site: Leonard W. Jerome (1817-1891), a prominent and wealthy Brooklyn citizen. He was a successful stock speculator, making and losing several fortunes and, in the process, earning the nickname "King of Wall Street." He was also the principal owner of The New York Times for several years, the founder of the American Academy of Music, and the maternal grandfather of Sir Winston Churchill. Jerome built the Jerome Park Racetrack in the Bronx...The track opened on September 25, 1866, and it marked the return of thoroughbred racing to the metropolitan area after a hiatus during the Civil War.

On June 12th, Fanny replies to a letter from Ellen with two interesting comments. One may be a reference to a perceived slight on the part of a suitor for Alice, and the other is a self-reference:

> "I think you will find that every family has a skeleton in the closet and that our lives are more equal than we would think.
> Miss Haven has no visitors for her hand and does not want any."

She also says that while the people Alice saw at the horse races may have appeared to have no cares,

> "Most of the people who looked so gay and happy at the races most probably had "atra cura" ["black cares"] sitting behind them as they drove home."

By June 22nd 1882, Fanny has heard that Ellen is in pain:

> "A letter from Grace of the 17th tells me how painfully you are suffering from rheumatism, which I am very much grieved to hear...I can only make suggestions, I cannot help you to bear the pain, nor do anything to alleviate it. I am so very, very sorry about it."

Edith is due home from school, and apparently David is away again:

> "I presume Edith will return this week. Give my love to her and tell her I am glad she is home and I hope she will be a great help and comfort to her Mother.
> Has David returned?"

Fanny laughs about how she frustrated a suitor who'd come to visit Alice:

> "I came downstairs the first of the afternoon and sat in the room with them for some time, laughing to myself all the time as I thought how he probably wished me in Guinea."

Fanny reiterates her concern for her brother John Haven:

> "I am very sorry to leave John. I think he will be lonely. He has been kind and nice to us both, more like his old self to me than he has been for years. He has softened I think in various ways.
> I suppose we all do as we grow older."

She ends her letter wishing Ellen could be with her:

> "I will write you when I get to Rye. How much I wish you were to be there too."

On June 27th Fanny writes from Rye Beach:

> "Grace's letter of the 21st says you are still suffering dreadfully. All I can do is to tell you how deeply I am sympathizing with you, thinking of you so often and just longing to be able to help you. The intense heat must be so hard to bear added to the pain. Perhaps a few lines about what is going on here, may divert your thoughts for half an hour from your pain, though it seems so selfish to write of one's own affairs to anyone who is suffering so keenly."

She describes her journey from New York to Rye Beach:

> "I left New York at 11 a.m. on the 24th. Mr. Carter came with me and John and Alice were at the depot to see us off..."

We reached Boston just after six and Mr. Carter took me over to the eastern depot and put me on the seven train. It was the Mount Desert express train and only stopped at Northampton to leave Boston passengers, or passenger in this case, I being the only one. It was half past eight, but I feel so at home here that I did not mind it at all. I was driven over in a buggy, trunks behind in a wagon and as it was moonlight, it was a pleasant drive."

On June 28th 1882, David writes Ellen. He indicates that he knows he is a burden.

"My dearest wife
I am truly pained to learn of your having suffered so much, and never heard of it till yesterday -- and again last night, from Edith. Although neglecting to write you, it has not been because I did not think of you, in fact you -- and only you, have been in spirit with me all the time -- night as well as day. And I always rejoice when I think of such a wife that God has given me -- One so far above me in every way, but I often feel -- as if it would be a blessing to her if I could be taken away, and no longer stand as a trouble and worry to her.
I had no idea that you were even sick at all, or should have abandoned everything and gone home to you."

He says he is still trying to get money to pay his debts in Thibodaux, and he ends his letter with,

"Now may God bless you my angel life. Be sure of one thing -- that I always worship you
Your husband"

On June 30th he writes again to say that he and Edith should be home on the next day's train.

On July 26th Fanny writes from Rye Beach to say that it is terribly hot, in the 90's with a land breeze that is stifling, but Alice,

"...is tearing along the road in the blazing sun in an open wagon with Daisy, Tom and Nannie. Young people do not mind anything."

Fanny discusses the division of family furniture and other things, then says,

"Would it not be possible for you to come on with Grace in November and make me a nice visit? I do so wish you would. Just think! You have never made me a visit-never even seen my flats. We are both getting old and may not have many years more to see each other. I want you to consider this seriously-all the pros and cons."

On August 20th 1882, Fanny says,

"I suppose you can hardly believe that Alice and I are sitting in the clubhouse-Mr. Savage is playing airs from "Lucia" and "Trovatore" for our benefit. Dr. Poore has a photographing instrument down

here and we have been amusing ourselves watching him print off
his plates.

…John (Haven) came down to Portsmouth and stayed two or three
days … then he went to Star Island for a week and I presume left
there today. I wish he would stay there a month, it would be of so
much benefit to him-he seemed weak and listless and in low
spirits. I know the next two months will be very trying to him and
it is a pity he should stay alone at Fort Washington and brood over
his sad thoughts."

Fanny muses about Alice's return to Ellen's, and says that if Alice's escorts
fall through,

"…there is still the chance of my coming out for a month-then we
would come by steamer in October. I can hardly make up my mind
to this, it seems such a great undertaking and yet I do long to see
you and the children.

I suppose Edith will be at school by that time. Do you think Grace
will want to return with me if I came, or will she want to stay on
for a while with Alice? Perhaps she will not want to come at all.

…I am delighted that you have been on a visit to Eliza B -it will do
you good to be away for a while from home cares.

I cannot help hoping that you will decide to bring Grace out by and
by and make me the visit I so long to have. That would indeed
solve the question of my going -- would give a gist and interest to
my moving in to 27 (which I must confess is now altogether
lacking) some object to work for -- would give me Alice's most
efficient aid in settling and take her out a little later.

Of the delight of having a visit from you I need not enlarge -- you
know what it would be -- nothing else that I can think of that gives
me so keen pleasure and you see, all told, though I have so many
comforts and blessings I really have not very much of interest in
life."

By the time she writes Ellen on September 2 1882, Fanny has decided to
come to Ellen's:

"…I have decided (D.V.) to come out with Alice in October and
pass a few weeks with you.

…What quite decided me was knowing that Grace could return with
me, for if she stays on for a couple of years or even less, it would
prevent me from coming out for so long a time."

Fanny's letter of September 18th reveals that Ellen had planned to go away
with Edith and Grace for a week or so at Grand Isle, La., but she has had
to cancel her plans. Fanny suggests that Ellen consider coming to New
York instead, in which case Fanny will defer her visit:

"Best of all would be decidedly, for you to bring Grace on and take
Alice out. As I have said before, this covers everything. There
seems to be no doubt but what you need a change, very likely you
will break down altogether without it and the $100 it would cost
you could not be better spent.

I can quite afford and will most cordially contribute $25 towards it...This is not just talk, I want you to consider it most seriously. I am not at all bent on coming out just now-if Grace could get here and Alice taken out, I should be quite inclined to defer it. Your coming on will more than accomplish what I am coming for, to see you.[63]"

Fanny comments at the end of this letter about John Pugh:

"Of John's affair, of which you wrote me, I have no comments to make -- it is best I should not."

The affair she refers to was a duel in which John (who was about 22) engaged on August 31st 1882:

"In view of the meetings to take place tomorrow morning August 31st between Mr. John H. Pugh and Walter J. Sullivan, it is agreed as follows:

1. That both parties leave New Iberia not later than six and a half o'clock a.m. and proceed at once to the ground already selected; it is on the Wilson place about five miles below New Iberia.

2. Immediately on meeting in the field the distance shall be measured and the stations marked.

3. Choice of positions shall then be tossed for.

4. The right to give the word shall then be tossed for.

5. The principles shall then take their stations as already marked, but without weapons in their hands, facing each other.

6. The party who is to give the word shall then proceed to explain how the word is to be given, it is the "Gentlemen are you ready" and if there is no response, he continues "Fire one- two- three" with about a second's interval between each word from "fire" to "three".

7. The principles shall not fire before the word "one" nor after the word "three".

8. The weapons shall then be handed the principles, and they shall be held with the muzzles pointed to the ground until after the word "fire".

Signed in duplicate at New Iberia, Louisiana this 30th of August, 1882

(The document is signed by S. Williams H. Collins for John H. Pugh and two signatures for Walter J. Sullivan.)

---

[63] Ellen did not come to New York; Fanny went to Ellen's instead.

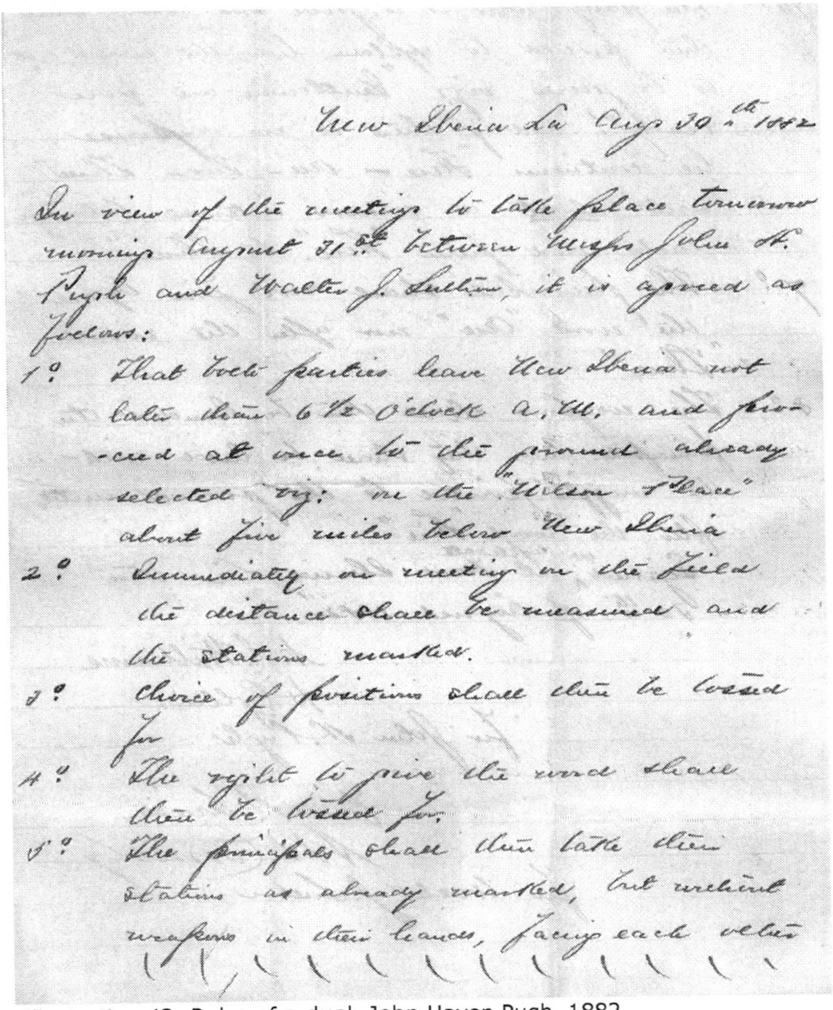

New Iberia La Aug 30th 1882

In view of the meeting to take place tomorrow morning August 31st between Messrs John H. Pugh and Walter J. Sutton, it is agreed as follows:

1º That both parties leave New Iberia not later than 6½ O'clock a.m., and proceed at once to the ground already selected viz: on the "Wilson Place" about five miles below New Iberia

2º Immediately on meeting on the field the distance shall be measured and the stations marked.

3º Choice of positions shall then be tossed for

4º The right to give the word shall then be tossed for.

5º The principals shall then take their stations as already marked, but without weapons in their hands, facing each other

Illustration 42: Rules of a duel, John Haven Pugh, 1882.

On October 4th 1882, Fanny writes Ellen from Fort Washington. Woodbury Langdon has taken Alice "to drive, dine and go to the theater", with him, his brother Frank and others, then to spend the night at Woodbury and Frank's house. Woodbury, born in 1836, was about 46, whereas Alice was about 21. Perhaps there was some special attraction on the part of these Langdon relations for the Havens, because Woodbury showed interest in Ellen, Alice and Edith, and Frank married a cousin (Helen Bell Haven). Fanny still plans to come to Ellen's by steamer in November.

On November 28th, David writes Ellen from New Orleans: Ellen has been there with him but has gone home, and he has stayed on. He has seen Edith; the rice has not sold, and he is waiting to hear a court decision before he renews the lease on their place. November 30th he writes again to say the rice has sold, and he is taking care of various chores.

On December 3rd 1882, Fanny writes from New York, having returned from Ellen's with Grace.

> "I was thinking especially this morning how very, very good and kind you were to me last month-always making me the first object in the house and constantly thinking of something that would conduce to my pleasure and comfort.
> I appreciate it most keenly when with you and miss your tender solicitude very much. It is very nice to be taken care of sometimes instead of having constantly to be looking out for yourself. I knew my visit would be an oasis of pleasure and of home affection and I look back upon it as such now."

On December 6th, David writes Ellen from New Orleans, and it seems that the reason David and Ellen had been to see Edith at the end of November is that she was ill.

> "Edith was in bed, from a similar attack as when you were here.
> She had no fever, but considerable trouble about the stomach."

David says he is sorry to hear that Thomas has the fever again (malaria), and he speaks of business on their place as well as of provisions he is purchasing.

Fanny writes from her new flat at 27 Waverly Place, N.Y.C. on December 10th. She has talked to Mr. Carter about Ellen's will.

> "I spoke to Mr. Carter about your will. He said that leaving David a life interest in $8,000 was creating a trust-the executors being the trustees, unless others were especially named.
> He thought that paying it might be a cause of embarrassment as matters now stood, because he would have it in his power to call for sale of the property, so that he might receive his interest. Leaving the $8,000 to him out and out, would involve the same difficulty. I told him you only desired that David should have the interest on that sum during his life. He said he preferred to think

about it and decide in what form it had better be put, as to render the payment as easy as might be.

He advises no change in the age specified as the time when the property should be paid to the girls as they come of age. "A woman (he said) has no more sense nor any better judgment at 25, than at 21, in fact a woman's property never should be left to her outright, always as a trust-it is never safe otherwise, I never advise leaving it to her-. In this case some chap will come along and marry Alice and the probability is, squander or lose her money for her-the proper way is to leave it to trustees." (I quote his language because it amused me so much).

...There is one clause in your will, which is not clear. In case of one of your children should marry, have children and die, before you do, the will does not clearly state that such issue as that child may leave, shall inherit that child's share. I told him perhaps you intended that if one child died his or her share, should belong to the brothers and sisters, but he inferred not from another statement in the will.

He has written a clause in regard to this, which you must insert when you re-write the will.

It seems to me, I should not provide for grandchildren but if one child died, let his or her share go to the rest, but of course this is as you please. Mr. Carter did not say so.

I will wait till Mr. Carter tells me what to say about David's $8,000 and then write again and return the will.

Mr. Carter will attend to it as soon as possible, as he thinks a will like yours is invalid if opened. It must be found sealed after your death-so this one would not hold. I hope I have made it clear."

Fanny's friend Lizzie, who lost her little boy, has become quite thoughtful toward Fanny:

"Here my letter was interrupted by the arrival of a dish of ice cream from Lizzie. She is all the time sending me something- has given me several jars of tomato sauce, three or four of grated quince and a pot of mangoes. I do not believe anyone ever had so many presents as I do.

One day came a pot of white hyacinths, four or five, which perfume my parlor."

On January 15th, 1883, Ellen writes her Aunt Eliza a note that is part reminiscence and partly about the loss of Mary. Eliza Wentworth Haven married a cousin, Nathaniel Appleton Haven; Eliza was born in 1794 and died in December 1883.

"It is many years since I have seen you. I think it must be twenty two years and yet to me it does not seem long ago, not so many years as dates really show. The little baby which I took to you is now a rice planter, or essaying to be one. You have seen my two oldest daughters and I am very happy with them and my two youngest children added –

One lovely girl has been transplanted to her other home. She was
perfect in face, form, mind and soul, a pearl of rare price, and
worshiped by us all in this home.

I can never be reconciled to this separation and I look over the few
intervening years which will soon pass and carry me over to her."

In March, Ellen writes Eliza's daughter Charlotte (Charlotte was Ellen's first
cousin). Again she remembers the past:

"...tell her that I often go back to those days when I was ten years
old and visited grandmother with Anna – Cousin Eliza I was with a
great deal. Helen Haven was a little girl then and at grandmother's
part of the time. Eliza was so gay and bright with me and I
remember so well going with you two to your Sunday school and
singing out of a little hymnbook which I have now.

How vivid are our youthful memories.

Grandfather read prayers every morning. It is pleasant to me to
recall all these old remembrances.

My children cannot know anything of those days or Fanny, my
sister, and so many have passed away who took part in those
days. Only a few of us are left."

April 10th, 1883, James C. Carter writes Ellen.

"My dear Ellen,

I ought to have heaps of excuses for delaying so long to answer
your more than kind, your delightful letters. I say this, because it
reproduced to me so freshly yourself, as I used to know you and
still love to remember you."

He says he has been struggling to regain his former health and he
apologizes for not having replied to Ellen's letters sooner. He compliments
her children:

"I have had the greatest pleasure in seeing and knowing your
children.

Poor...bachelor that I am with no pets of my own. I have to borrow
the children of any friends and I take a double satisfaction in
yours.

I should flatter both you and them too much if I should say all I
think of them. I miss Alice very much, so do many others; but
Grace has no mean attractions. The picture you draw of Edith
makes me wish very much to see her and I hope she may appear
under our skies ere long.

John does indeed seem to have tough experiences. I see him often
and I wonder that he is so cheerful."

Carter thinks his old friend John Haven would be happier in a small house,
but he understands that John prefers to stay in the family home in Fort
Washington.

"...he cherishes so much the memories of the past and the spot
around which they cluster, that he seems to cling to Fort

Washington, in spite of the present cheerlessness of an empty
house."

A large section of the rest of Carter's letter has been intentionally torn off:
it is possible it contained advice about Ellen's will.

Alice Meets Ralph; David Declines (1883-1885)

By October, Ellen has asked Carter for another favor. October 23rd, Carter says he has, per Ellen's request, done a check on a young man who is pursuing Alice. The young man's name is Ralph Stone, and he is from Buffalo, NY. In several letters about Ralph, the opinions are similar: his character and social standing are fine, but he seems to lack the drive to become a top-dog:

> "not possessing the talents or the dispositions which gave promise of success in life. He did not think he would be likely to make much of a figure."

On November 3rd, 1883, Ralph Stone[64] writes Ellen about Alice. Alice had written a letter to "The Nation"; Ralph saw the letter, was impressed, and wrote Alice. The two began a correspondence, whose nature Ellen did not fully understand. He now writes Ellen to assure her of his love for Alice and of his honorable intentions: he says that even though Alice and Ralph have not yet met in person, he knows that he loves her.

On November 9th 1883, Mr. Carter writes Ellen with more references about Ralph's character. Again the reports come back saying Ralph is of excellent character, very likeable and so on, but lacking in drive:

> "He is, in a word, a refined gentleman. Whether he has the push to make a distinguished lawyer remains to be proved."

Ellen writes Ralph a long letter (her copy does not have the exact date, but is probably written between the 8th and the 16th of November). Her characterization of David is very revealing.

> "Dear Sir,
> I am glad that you have written to me, for since my dear child came to me so innocently and told me, to my utter astonishment, of the culmination of what I supposed to be a purely literary correspondence, I have felt very much worried and aggrieved. Do not think but what I blame myself supremely.
> I have never allowed my daughters to correspond with even their most intimate friends although frequently solicited, by the gentlemen. But in this instance my sympathies were especially appealed to. My daughter had been in New York for 18 months

---

[64] Ralph Stone was born in Calais, Me., 27 Apr. 1849, went to Phillips Exeter Academy and graduated from Harvard College in 1872. In 1876, Ralph was admitted to the bar in Buffalo, N. Y. From 1888 to 1892 he was clerk of the Superior Court at Buffalo, and in 1899 he was appointed librarian of the Law Library at Buffalo of the New York Eighth Judicial District. He died in Buffalo on March 25th, 1910.

---

where she had enjoyed the society of so many cultivated and pleasant friends. She had left me in terrible grief and distress occasioned by the loss of her dearest sister. Upon her return old associations were revived, her sister went north and I sought any distractions to make her happy.

She answered a little political piece in the Nation and she received notes from the Nation in regard to it. In asking me if she could write and answer one, I demurred. She urged me, pleading it would only be a literary correspondence about books and leading events.

I consented, thinking it would serve to pass time and trusting in her good judgment and her knowledge of my dislike to any intercourse with strangers as regarded my daughters. I thought it would serve to interest her for awhile.

When she came to me I felt very much to blame, knowing I had transgressed all my rules and had, in indulging a whim of my child's, placed myself and her in a very perplexing position. I forbade her to correspond any longer with you and she obeyed me with a pathetic look which went straight to my heart.

Then you wrote her again and asked her if she was not acting a little whimsically and I scarcely blamed you for your conclusion. But surely seeing the innocent heart in my child, you, a man of the world, should scarcely have overstepped the conventionalities.

Your manly and straightforward letter, however, has disarmed me and since we have all been to blame, I can only wish now that we may meet and become acquainted.

My daughter will be perfectly honest and true and if you win her, you will have won a Pearl of rare price. Her father and I idolize her and the happiness of my children is my first thought and wish.

A high principled man, refined and good who dearly loves my daughter, cannot but find a friend in me, her mother. This is her secret. She has come lovingly to me and asked me to keep her secret and I shall do so. It weighs heavily upon me and causes me great uneasiness of heart, but if you are noble and true as your letter persuades me you are, I will wait patiently and we will meet. I do not feel that it is necessary for me to tell you of ourselves as you entered upon this path blindfold.

But as you have frankly stated to me your position as regards wealth or poverty, I shall as frankly tell you that our daughter has been cherished in her home life as daintily as a pet, but when she leaves our loving shelter and care, she will have to depend upon the industry of the man who promises to cherish her in sickness and in health. She will have no dowry.

My husband is an invalid and has always been one. His father was very wealthy, the best sugar planter in Louisiana, Mr. Thomas Pugh. My husband lost his money when he lost his slaves and plantation.

The following is crossed out:

~~He makes a living but has nothing laid aside. It takes all of his income to live. If you still desire to win my child I am too loving a mother to sacrifice my child's heart to worldly advantages I have been too happy in poverty myself to think wealth is the first consideration but it is natural for me not to wish to expose a child to all the cares which poverty brings to a wife, unless her heart loves irretrievably.~~

~~If you do not really mean what you have said when you have to weigh this consideration, then write at once to my darling child or to me and do not hesitate to retrieve the past. I feel however you are in truly in earnest. Very sincerely yours Ellen E. Pugh~~

The following begins after the crossed out section above:

You are right, there are many things which money can never buy and you appeal to me at once when you say you would rather die than do a mean action.

With such sentiments life is worth living.

My children have been brought up with the greatest care and while we have cultivated their intellect and their hearts, they are very innocent in the ways of the world.

Very sincerely yours

Ellen E. Pugh"

On November 24th, Ralph writes another letter to Ellen to thank her for treating him kindly in her letter to him, and to say that he had not known Ellen had forbidden Alice to write him, else he would have minded the order.

"I have already confessed my fault in speaking plainly before I could go south and you have been so good as to overlook it and forgive me. It shall ever be my ambition to be that which you are pleased to say my letter persuades you that I am. That your child is a pearl beyond all price I am very sure. If I had ever had any doubt but that she has been gently nurtured in all that may become a woman, her mother's letter would certainly have dispelled it."

Another letter comes from Mr. Carter on November 28th to report the receipt of a reference that corroborates the previous ones: Ralph is well-liked, bright, has honor, integrity and social standing, but is not likely to be a big success at the bar because of his retiring personality and a lack of drive.

On January 1st 1884, Fanny writes Ellen and mentions that Eustis Hopkins[65], Augusta's son, is visiting Ellen. Fanny urges Ellen to share her concerns:

---

[65] Eustis became a partner in Joy, Langdon Co.; then Chairman of the Board and a director of Bliss, Fabyan & Co. in New York; and was director of the Bank of New York & Trust Co., and five other companies.

"As there is but little chance of ever seeing each other, you had better let me share your anxieties and worries by telling me of them.

How are David's business affairs with Mr. Conger and have you been able to find any good and safe investment for your money?"

Aunt Eliza Haven, whom Ellen recently wrote, has passed away:

"We have heard no particulars of aunt Eliza's death, indeed I suppose there are no particulars to hear -- she has been lingering for so long on the borderland between this life and the next. She just passed away, very quietly."

On January 18th 1884, Fanny writes Ellen, and talks a little bit about Grace, who is now about 22.

"...Grace does not appear to be attractive to gentlemen, or to strangers generally, but I think those who know her well, like her. ...G- has appeared much better this winter than she did last – she looks like a different girl, so much more healthy, and seems to try to make herself more acceptable to people.

She has fine traits of character which all who know her must respect. I cannot gain the influence over her, or win the affection from her, which I would like to do. Very likely I am to blame in not approaching her in the right way – she resents very sharply my advice, criticisms or suggestions from me, tells me she knows quite well how to conduct herself and what is proper and gets very angry with me. I find the best way, is just to leave her to herself, only watching to plan what is best and happiest for her. She has to work out her own life problems, as we all do.

Sometimes she comes and says how sorry she is that she has been rude, or that she has hurt my feelings and I think this is a very noble thing to do."

And on Jan. 24th 1884, Fanny expresses how much she will miss Grace:

"I shall miss Grace very much, feel perfectly lost without her, but I must make the best of it."

Thomas, now 15, has gone away to school at the Culleoka Institute in Tennessee, and Fanny says,

"I am very sorry that you are not satisfied with the way Thomas is to live. Could not David have arranged to have things made more comfortable for him before he left, I thought that was what he went for."

Next Fanny responds to Ellen, who said she wishes she could do as much for Fanny as Fanny has done for her:

"The idea of your imagining that I could under any circumstances, ever think you selfish about anyone, surely not about me, when everyone who knows you, knows that you have the most generous heart in the world and could not do a selfish thing if you tried. Truly and really, I do not know what you mean, or when you say that it troubles you that "I cannot do towards you, as you have done towards me in mine.""

I am sure I do not know what it is I have done, or that you have failed to do.

You know I have always said that having one of the children with me, was no favor on my part. Your sparing one of them and their being willing to come, made it quite equal. Indeed for some time, it has involved sacrifices on your part in regard to money, which you could ill afford to manage and which have worried me very much. It is not just the actual expenses which you can count up, but the incidental ones which come up every day which cannot be calculated upon."

Although eight years have passed since her parents died, Fanny continues to struggle to find meaning.

"Every year the burden of life becomes more heavy to bear and the years to come stretch out with more and more of dreariness and utter emptiness.

As you say, I learned years ago, the only way is to live from day to day.

I have absolutely nothing to look forward to and all the time find myself more and more indifferent.

Grace often says in a despairing way "Oh, Aunt Fanny, why are you so indifferent about everything, isn't there anythlng you care about"? I do not want to discourage her by saying "no, Grace, nothing" and try to turn it off with a jest."

Also on January 24th 1884, Grace writes Thomas, in Culleoka, from Fanny's. Grace is preparing to go home to Louisiana via Huntsville.

"My dear Thomas

I have eaten an orange and prepared myself for a good long letter.

I had a nice letter from mother today enclosing one from you.

I am awfully glad you are gone and that you like it. I feared you would be so lonely.

Eustis has been telling me all about you, he says you are already taller than Edith so you must be growing.

… I hate to think of really going and leaving so much behind me although I want to go more and it is my own wish to go so soon."

On January 27th 1884, Ellen writes her cousin Charlotte Haven, who has sent her some family pictures.

My dear cousin,

I cannot tell you how much I thank you for your beautiful letter. The photographs are invaluable to me. I remember Grandmother and Grandfather perfectly. Your dear mother's photograph is not as round in the face as when I last saw her, so this likeness gives her a more aged look. But it has been years since I saw her and I think her face in this photograph is wonderfully young for her years and very like her too. I thank you so very much for both pictures. I have one of grandfather Haven copied from Stuart's portrait, also one of Dr. Samuel Haven, my great grandfather.

By February 3rd, Fanny is alone, Grace having left for Louisiana:

> "She took her two trunks with her, the rest of her belongings I had to pack in a box and send by the steamer of the ninth.
>
> ...I felt dreadfully to have Grace go away, but I would not let her know that, for I wanted her to go off cheerfully and not feel uncomfortable about leaving me.
>
> For the last three years I have had one of the girls with me and I ought to be contented."

Fanny ends with an oddly prescient statement about Grace:

> "If Grace is sometimes rude, or sharp-I am often cross, and perhaps unreasonable, so we are quits. At her best, she is charming.
>
> Anyhow I do not want to find fault with her. I fear she will meet with disappointments and have horrid things to bear."

After several letters of general talk and news, Fanny writes on Feb. 13th to thank Ellen for having sent a cake. Fanny's description serves as a reminder of what it used to take to make a cake:

> "I should think it would have taken you a week of steady work to stone the raisins, wash and dry the currants and strip the citron."

On February 15th 1884, Grace writes Thomas in Culleoka, and describes David's brother Richard's[66] situation.

> "I think it is dreadful about Uncle Richard and I am very sorry for him and for cousin Frank [Williams]. Mother wrote me that he could make no arrangement to manage the place, cousin Frank I mean.
>
> It is particularly hard because the family is penniless, Mrs. Williams has not a cent nor Mr. Winder.
>
> Sugar planting seems to have been the ruin of them for if Mr. Winder had not bought a plantation he would be well off to this day and Uncle Dick can manage his coal business better I think. If they go away we shall miss them dreadfully."

On March 3rd Fanny writes Ellen about packages and general news of friends and family, and sounds as if she is lonely:

---

[66] Richard Lloyd Pugh, the youngest son of Eliza and Thomas Pugh, married Mary Louise Williams, the daughter of John Williams and Mary Louisa Maguire of Leighton Plantation. They had nine children: Ellen Kavanaugh Pugh, Lou Maguire Pugh, Tony, John Williams Pugh, Eliza Catherine Pugh, Peter, Edward Foley Pugh, Guy Preston Pugh, and Henry Allen Pugh.

Richard Pugh served as a private in the Confederate Army, Louisiana 5th Company Battalion of the Washington Artillery, March 1862-June 1863. Upon the Federal invasion of Lafourche Parish in 1862, Mary relocated with her father, children, and their slaves to Rusk, Texas. Richard met them in Texas after he left the service, and together they returned to Dixie Plantation in Thibodaux, Louisiana. Richard died in July, 1885.

"Lulu [Augusta's daughter Louise] will leave me on the 10th. Then I will be quite alone. I do not mind the days so much, the evenings and nights are the worst."

Grace writes Thomas on March 11th 1884 with news of several crevasses on the bayou (breaks in the levees) and says,
"We had a splendid time at Mardi Gras, went to all the balls. You know I had never seen it before...Edith had her program so full that she had to refuse any masker."

Fanny writes on March 19th 1884, lamenting that Ellen's trip to New Orleans was marred by feeling ill:
"I fear you did not enjoy the Mardi Gras trip as much as the girls did, Alice said you felt sick all the time."
On April 2nd, Fanny says she has enjoyed a long letter from Ellen, and she jokes,
"I was delighted to receive your four sheets of letter paper, well filled-which you refer to as "just having a few words with you". What do you call a letter?"
Fanny describes her solitary life:
"I have been nowhere and seen no one for the last ten days. Even Mr. Carter did not come to dinner last week, which was my sole dissipation. I had a large piece of roast beef and one of fine boiled shad and had made a tipsy cake for dessert and then an hour or two before dinner he sent word he could not come. So I sat at my feast all alone and felt very silly."

On April 29th Fanny writes about the Williams':
"You will miss Mrs. Williams sadly and I am so very sorry that she will be gone so long and then how hard it is for a woman at her age, not to have a home[67]. Have Richard Pugh and his family moved from the old house and where have they gone and who has taken the house. How I wish you could have it!"

On May 16th 1884, Fanny sends Ellen a letter about their letters:
"My dear Nell
I have lately been devoting my evenings to reading over the letters I have had from you since your marriage. I have always intended to do this before I destroyed them.
I find among them quite a number which I think will be interesting to you and the children and I shall send them out to you in detachments.
Some will be interesting to the girls as relating to your early married life, others have war episodes which they will like. You will take pleasure in reading and recalling many incidents which you have probably forgotten, or of which the memory will at least be

---

[67] Possibly referring to Leighton Plantation, Thibodaux.

dim and then the descriptions of the children at various stages of their lives, are irresistible.
I have had many a laugh over them. I would advise you to read them to yourself first.
I have destroyed three times as many as I shall send."

On May 22nd Fanny writes to say that she may have said something that resulted in Thomas being invited to Portsmouth, N.H. by Woodbury Langdon for the summer:

"I spoke of Thomas being at school and how hard it would be for him to stay so far from home during the vacation, about his improved health etc. Frank [Langdon] said "He had better come and pass the summer at Woodbury's new place." This was all he said and I never gave it a thought.
I do not know what the plan is to be about the place. It is five or 6 miles from Portsmouth on the river, at Fox's point. Some 30 acres I believe; with an old house which is being renovated. W- said he should have a man and his wife there to take care of it and he should come when he had time and felt like it."

And on May 25th, 1884 Grace writes Thomas that she has heard the news that he is going North for a summer vacation:

"I am perfectly delighted that you are going to Portsmouth, Thomas, I am just as glad as I can be. Mother has not yet decided whether you will stop in New York..."

Grace is full of advice for Thomas about what type of clothes to wear, and says,

"Keep your nails pushed back and clean for that is a sure sign of the gentleman and remember you are a high bred little Southern man and do show those northern men some manners for they haven't any and I was all boasting about you at Rye and saying that my little brother had more the manner of a gentleman than all their men put together. You mustn't go back on me now."

On June 9th, Fanny writes that Thomas has arrived safely in New York. She refers to the package of letters of Ellen's:

"I have sent a box to Grace and in it are the letters I promised to send you. I think the children will value them. Letters of my mother's early married life would have been a priceless gift to me. I do not want them returned except one little package of letters written from home before you were married. Those I do want to keep to look at in years to come. Please send that little package back to me some time."

On June 19th, 1884 Fanny writes Ellen from Fort Washington. Fanny will leave for Marblehead on June 25th, and then for Rye on July 1st.

> "I wish you were all here with me this morning, it is so lovely, I am
> on the Piazza just after breakfast and the trees have grown up so
> that the river is entirely shut out.
> ...Thomas is as lively and gay as possible, it would do your heart
> good to see him so well. I can hardly believe he is the same sickly,
> feeble looking boy I left in Louisiana eighteen months ago.
> He and Appleton took lunch with Eustis yesterday in the city,
> bought his suit of clothes etc., inspected the Brooklyn Bridge and
> returned by the elevated in a very hilarious state of mind.
> Tomorrow, Augusta is to take him to Woodlawn.
> I am afraid he will miss the boys when he goes to Portsmouth.
> He revels in the strawberries and cherries, beef steaks and roast
> beef..."

Fanny has enjoyed being at Augusta's after being alone for months in her
flat. She speaks fondly of Augusta's children.

Grace writes Thomas at Portsmouth July 4th. John Pugh seems to struggle
with one problem after another.

> "Edith is coming up someday next week and we want John to go to
> Huntsville as soon as he can get off. He has a bad cough and can't
> go out in the field anymore, then has fever all the time, off and on
> and the only thing to cure him is a change. He can't finish his crop
> and is trying to hire a Creole at a dollar per day to "boss" it for him
> but he has a great deal of trouble."

Grace corrects Thomas regarding their relationship to certain relatives, and
proves that she too has visited with the Portsmouth families. She refers to
the house in which John Appleton Haven grew up:

> "We have stayed in the house a good deal, it is grandfathers old
> home, where he was born. And Uncle George is the youngest son,
> he kept the house, in the parlor are two portraits of great
> grandfather and grandmother painted by Stuart, our great
> American portrait painter, they are almost worth their weight in
> gold - and are to hang in the house so long as it is occupied by any
> member of the Haven family.[68]"

On July 7th 1884, James Carter writes Ellen in response to her request for
his advice about whether to let Alice marry Ralph. She seems to lean
heavily on Mr. Carter on this point, which begs the question about David's
role, if any, in deciding about his daughter's suitor and marriage. Carter
lays out some guidelines for Ellen and encourages her to write again if she
needs to, saying he can be reached care of the Morrises at Marblehead.

---

[68] The Gilbert Stuart paintings of John Haven and Ann Woodward were done in 1824, and
stayed in the Haven family for the next hundred years. In 1924, Fanny gave them to the New
York Public Library: sadly, the Library sold them in 2005.

On July 10th Fanny writes Ellen to acknowledge receipt of Ellen's letter as well as a letter from Alice, with the important new about Alice. Fanny is clearly hurt that Alice didn't confide in her.

> "As you may imagine her letter took my breath away and yet I cannot say that it was an absolute surprise. Somehow I knew all along what was coming; as soon as I heard that he was staying there and that he was a friend of Alice's, I said to myself "she means to engage herself to him". I must confess that it hurt me deeply that I had never even heard his name till two weeks before.
> … You can understand how I felt to hear she had engaged herself to someone, who was to me, an absolute stranger. Of course you could not say a word; her confidence was inviolate for you.
> … The only question now that is of any importance in the affair, is the dear child's happiness and I hope and pray with all my heart that it is to be secured, as indeed seems most probable as far as we can tell."

Fanny is happy that Ralph Stone is not from the South, however:

> "I have always so much dreaded that she would marry a
> Southerner and be buried alive in some hole of a plantation."

Fanny is impressed with the positive reports about Ralph's character and standing, but, ever the pragmatist, she is concerned about his ability to provide for Alice. She doesn't want Alice to know that she was hurt:

> "Do not even tell her that I felt hurt that I have never been told about Mr. Stone. I do not want her to have a cloud, however slight, come over her happiness."

Fanny goes on to talk about John Pugh and David:

> "I have felt uneasy about John for some time, from what the girls wrote me, indeed when I was last in Louisiana I thought he looked badly. I share your unhappiness about him, but am thankful he is to go away, for I feel as if the change would do wonders for him. I do not think it is possible for anyone to remain in that climate for any length of time and not feel it's bad effect, certainly none of your children can. I shall be most anxious to hear where he is to go, will he stay with the Gordon's at Huntsville?
> As to David's conduct it is simply outrageous and seems to me without excuse. Still, as you say, I feel pity for him, though I do not wonder that the children do not. I am very sorry that he has alienated their affections from him.
> I really do not think he is right in his mind. I do not think a man in his senses would talk as he does.
> Grace has always taken his part, in a certain way, and stood by him and he loses a good friend in losing her. Alice and he had never agreed. In reading over those letters it quite touched me to see how fond he was of the children when they were little and how happy you and he were in each other.
> I truly think that for some years his mind has been weakening.
> Oh! Dear me, how hard life is to almost everyone.

... I fear your silver wedding day was not a very happy one. I hoped we might have been able to make it a little fete for you, but I don't wonder that the children had no heart to. I thought of you often on that day."

On August 4th 1884, Fanny writes Ellen, after having gotten a long letter from Ellen. Fanny's is the voice of reason regarding Ralph's prospects for Alice:

"I had formed a very favorable opinion of R. S. from all I could gather from your letters and what Mr. Carter said, though I inferred at once from what the latter said, that he, R.S., was never going to make his way in the world. I supposed though when he talked of a "small income", that it meant two or three thousand, but when you wrote that he talked of supporting Alice on $1200 a year, my heart died within me.

Do you realize, Nell, what this means for your child? It is not just "living comfortably" or "saving and being economical", it means nothing but abject, grinding poverty. A man has no right to ask any girl to marry him on such a pittance, I don't see how he could dare to do it. For a hotheaded boy of twenty there would be some excuse but for a man of his age, there is absolutely none and when you talk of spending $500 on her house linen, I wanted to say, "Buy her some unbleached cotton sheets and save the rest to put bread in her mouth."

Don't let your daughter leave you for a life like that, if he is so deficient in common sense, or so selfish as to want to sacrifice her, you ought to see and act for them and say "When you have an income to support my daughter and give her just the ordinary comforts of life, then I will give my consent", it is what any Father would have said and you have to act as a Father for her."

Fanny then lists their probable living expenses[69] after which she says,

---

[69] "Just to take the figures. He says he can have his house for $500; we will skip the question of buying furniture etc., perhaps he already has it or has set aside a sum for it-and come to the actual cost of living. We will presume they will keep one servant, her wages will be at least $12 per month (I have no idea it would be less than $14 or $15), that is $144 a year-- then three people could not be fed for less than $1.00 a day-I mean enough to keep mind and body together-this is $365 a year-thus $191 a year is left for fuel, lights, clothes and incidental expenses for two people, not counting dentists or doctors bills.

...You know how Dr. Sweetser lived on $2000, and that was 30 years ago and he had a house and garden. Of course the cost of living in New York is no criterion for Buffalo, but food and clothes have an actual market value anywhere.

Any social life would be out of the question and I think the silk dresses and piano would be superfluous.

Alice is very romantic and very much in love, but she has excellent sense and I do not see how she can be so blind. Either the man is wanting in common sense or else narrow and mean beyond belief. If he has it in his power to increase his income he had better set about it as fast as he can and then come and ask her to marry him. Perhaps they could board at some common boarding house for $7 or $800 a year-this is possible."

"You see this is a sheer folly and you know the figures I have put down will not cover the cost of their living.

You see I have written very plainly and I daresay you will be very angry with me. I can only say, that every word I have written is inspired by a love for Alice and the keenest interest in her happiness.

... Please do not begin a trousseau till all this question of living is clearly understood."

Fanny says Thomas has now been in Portsmouth for about 6 weeks, and,
"I have no doubt he has been enjoying the excitement over the Arctic expedition[70]. I saw the arrival of the fleet and the naval reception, a sight I would not have missed for anything."

On August 8th 1884, Fanny writes Ellen,
"Dear Nell,

I have yours of the first and write to say that if you want to keep Thomas at school and the money is not forthcoming in time, that I can lend it to you quite well and you must not hesitate about it. It would be a pity for him to go home and then two months hence to wish that he had stayed at school."

She adds a note about her previous commentary regarding Ralph and Alice:
"I cannot say that I regret or retract anything I said about Alice's prospect, but I recognize the fact that it is quite useless to remonstrate or make any objections."

And about Thomas' schooling,
"Now don't hesitate to let me advance a quarters schooling (at least) for Thomas if you want him to stay and David does not furnish the means.

I would not offer if I could not do it."

On August 13th 1884, Fanny writes to say that Frank Langdon has complimented Thomas in the very highest terms. Then she says,
"My especial object in writing today is to extend an invitation to Alice and make a proposition to you, so that you will have time to think it all out before you have to decide.

If Alice intends to be married in the spring, I would like so much to have another visit from her-a parting one. So I propose to pay her fares on here and back again if she would like to come. I think the trip might do her good and build up her health. Perhaps she would like to make some of her purchases in New York. Having a trousseau is quite an incident in a girl's life.

---

[70] The arctic expedition was probably Greely's scientific expedition, which consisted of a group of about 19 army officers traveling 1000 miles north of the arctic circle to gather data. They were to meet a steamer ship to take them home after several years of study, but the ship sank and the men had to survive a winter on an island. All but 8 died over the 8-month period before they were finally rescued.

... I send the invitation to Alice and through you. Will you give it to her with my love."

On August 18th James Carter replies to a letter Ellen sent him. He writes from Marblehead,

"...You can not do this work for Alice; she must do it for herself, and therefore I think with you that if she has made a choice deliberately, you ought not to say no unless you see clearly that the man she has accepted cannot support her. You do not see that. You have your doubts and anxieties, but I suppose you would have those upon some point on the care of anyone."

Fanny writes Ellen from Rye Beach August 21st 1884 about various matters. She has heard from John that Thomas (who is at Fort Washington as of Fanny's letter) has received a check from David ostensibly for the next school term. She says she is willing to loan Ellen money in order to get Alice's trousseau ready:

"I don't wish Mr. Stone, either, to know that it was deferred because we could not between us, muster money enough to give her some clothes. I want him fully to realize that he is taking her from affluence to poverty! (Perhaps you think this is mean in me)."

On October 5th 1884, Fanny writes Ellen from Augusta's in Fort Washington. Fanny left Rye Beach and spent about a month in Marblehead with the Morrises before returning to New York. She will leave Augusta's for the city and her flat soon, for, as she says,

"If I were in my own home I should like to stay in the country till November, but I am not fond of visiting. I am too old for it."
She mentions that Augusta's daughter Nellie was in Portsmouth the day the Rockingham Hotel burned. Fanny does not mention it, and may not have known it, but the Rockingham was where her (and Nellie's) ancestor Woodbury Langdon lived.[71]

"I hear the Rockingham is to be rebuilt at once, the contracts are out now. The owner, Mr. Jones, is fabulously rich, has ever so many millions per annum, all made from beer. Nellie stood two or three hours watching it burn."
Fanny's comments about David leave no doubt about Ellen's painful situation:

"It is very hateful to have David stay on in New Orleans, it is such a senseless thing to do. I do not see how you can stand such a life.

---

[71] From the history of the Library Restaurant at the Rockingham: The Rockingham House, on State St. in Portsmouth, occupies the site of the home once owned by Judge Woodbury Langdon. When this mansion was built in 1785, it was one of the most handsome brick houses in New England. Frank Jones became the owner of the Rockingham in 1870 and greatly enlarged it. In 1884, there was a disastrous fire which destroyed all but the octagonal dining room (the Langdon Suite and the four golden lions). Mr. Jones rebuilt the hotel around this room, sparing no expense. His payroll for the project was more than the entire Portsmouth Naval Shipyard.

> Would it not be possible for you to make a home elsewhere, you are killing yourself with hard work and anxiety and the climate is doing the same for you and the children."

On October 15th, Fanny thanks Ellen for a telegram and adds a note from which we learn that Ellen had gone to New Orleans to try and bring David back home:

> "I suppose too that you had just got back from your most trying and anxious visit to New Orleans and were almost distracted and perfectly worn out, body and soul.
>
> ...I wish I had not written, as I know it put you all in a state of agitation, which you are in <u>no</u> condition to bear.
>
> Grace's letter today, tells me all the trouble and worry you are having. How I wish I could help you and how thankful I am that your children are now old enough and capable to help you, as I am sure they do. I shall most anxiously await the results of your visit to New Orleans. I suppose something will be patched up, but confess I do not see how. I hope you will write me when you have the heart and the time."

After talk about getting sheets, tablecloths, napkins and other components for Alice's trousseau, Fanny again raises the subject of Ellen's difficulties due to David:

> "I am grieved to hear that Thomas is to leave school this winter. Can you not make up your mind to take the Texas money for his schooling? Why do not you go to Columbia?
>
> Or to New Orleans? I think you overestimate the cost of moving. I wish John [Pugh] could be in some good business and all of you out of that beastly climate."

Fanny replies to a letter from Ellen on October 21st 1884, and it seems that the situation with David has grown much worse:

> "Dearest Nell
>
> Of course I was very anxious for your letter after your return from New Orleans. I did not expect any new phase of the old story, but what you tell me is very sad and I cannot but feel much pity. It is very disheartening and very hopeless, yet I cannot but hope that his condition will improve rapidly now that he is at home and above all with you.
>
> His wife has always been a tower of strength and refuge. I know the home life etc. will do much to restore him. What can I say dear sister but to assure you of my heartfelt sympathy. Could you make any plan with the bank or with Mr. Conger and what is the outlook? I am thankful that John will be able to take the care and responsibility, in a measure from you, or at least act for you."

The rest of her letter involves Alice's trousseau: linens, cambric, cotton, muslin, bands and waists, edgings, sheets, dresses, skirts and patterns.

On November 18th 1884, Fanny describes Ellen's sad situation. It sounds as though David has descended into some form of mental illness and/or dementia.

> "I am so very sorry that Grace has that horrid fever; it makes me almost wild to have you all staying in that poisoned hole of a place. If any chance ever presents itself to get out of it, snatch at it, never mind what it is.
>
> You ask me what I should do about using that money for Thomas' schooling. I must frankly say that in your place I should not want to, at least for the present.
>
> With David in this sad condition, I should feel as if I were taking advantage of it, to use money which he has always been firm in not touching. It seems as if you ought to more than ever respect his wishes about it, when in every way, he is so dependent upon you.
>
> It may be a matter of feeling and sentiment, but everyone in that state has a peculiar claim, I think, upon anyone who loves them, for their very helplessness.
>
> If he continues so, or becomes worse, then you would necessarily have to manage everything and then would be time enough for you to decide what use to make of any money he might have.
>
> I am extremely sorry to hear Thomas is to be taken from school. I wish he might have ambition or energy enough to start out in the world and make his own way -- but this is not probable and I am sure I do not know where he could go or what he could do. I am glad he has had this year's experience at any rate. I know it has done him good in every way."

Fanny writes on many topics on December 7th. She mentions that she went to see "Twelfth Night", performed by the English Lyceum Theatre group (with the English actor Henry Irving) who was touring in America. She also saw the Republican nominee for president, Blaine:

> "I regret to say he was enthusiastically cheered and clapped and the House resonated with cries of " Blaine, Blaine".
>
> He behaved very well, merely bowing slightly. He has an imposing presence and a foxy face - eyes which look sideways."

On December 22nd, Fanny says Ralph Stone (Alice's fiancé) and Thomas will be with Ellen over Christmas:

> "I hope you will all pass a pleasant Christmas and I daresay you will with Mr. Stone there and Thomas coming home and I am very glad to have you say that you like Mr. Stone."

About David she says,

> "I suppose there cannot be much change in poor David's condition from week to week. Does he seem to like Mr. Stone or not take any notice of him?"

Both Fanny and John Haven are deeply concerned about Thomas' schooling, and something seems to be in the offing from John in the way of help. Fanny has spoken in a previous letter about Lehigh University as a place where Thomas could go for free provided he passed some rigorous examinations.

> "I will get a circular of Lehigh University from Mrs. Wilmerding- it is situated in the Lehigh Valley, Penn. The preparatory school is at Bethlehem, Penn."

All along, Fanny has had one plan and another to come see Ellen, but her plans have changed multiple times due to her reliance on escorts whose plans change. On December 29th 1884, she writes,

> "Dearest Nell
> I should think you would be so tired of hearing that I am coming and then that I am not coming and then a plan for one train and then for another. I imagine you saying "oh, gracious, I wish Fanny would know her mind and not tell me first one thing and then another. It does seem absurd."

She closes with,

> "How glad you must be to see Thomas again. Does David seem glad to have him, or does not he care?"

On January 11th 1885, Fanny admits in her letter to Ellen that she knew about a plan that John Haven has now proposed to Ellen. John's plan is for Ellen and the children to move to a farm in Pennsylvania and live with him.

> "I knew John's letter about Pennsylvania would burst like a bombshell in your family. I had known for some time that it was coming.
> As it is not necessary to give an immediate decision we can discuss it when I come out, though as I have told John I feel quite incompetent to give any advice-my opinions on the subject you will both probably hear quite often!
> It has seemed to me a vague sort of scheme on his part, with so many objections, rather obstacles as to be next to impossible to be realized, but he seems to have now toned it down to rather a definite plan.
> Then on your part, you well know what I think of the climate in Louisiana and that I would as soon think of living in a coal mine as in a rice swamp. Grace and John and Thomas are martyrs to it and have been for a long time. It seems to me anything would be preferable to staying there an hour longer than was necessary. Naturally, you will not take this view of it. It will be a momentous decision for you to make and will require long and anxious consideration and neither you nor John are very young to start a new life in a new country and together.
> But, as I told him the other day, the subject can never be decided by letter-you will have to talk it over face to face.
> There will be constant misunderstanding. I do not mean quarrels by any means, but simply failure on both sides to comprehend the others meaning. Written words have an entirely different

significance from spoken ones, always seem to mean much more or much less than is intended. For instance he does not mean that you must all "pitch in and work for a living," he means he offers you a home and land rent free; if your income suffices to maintain you there, well and good, if not you can, if you choose, eke it out by raising fruit, flowers, vegetables, eggs, milk, butter, cows, eggs, anything that can be got out of the land- there it is at your disposal, simply he cannot offer to support you. He does not want John to be an overseer, or work under him or anything of the kind, only to make his living off the place if he wants to, and in any way he wants to.

He simply wants for himself a home without the trouble of housekeeping which he hates; to have his own rooms and his own ways and only take his meals with you. He says he will not mind having young people about him, on the contrary it will please him; says he likes Grace and always thought from what he had heard of Edith that he should like her, though he is not sure from her pictures, but what she may be a little fast, he is evidently undecided on this point and is turning it over in his mind."

In the same letter, Fanny talks about several gifts she has sent Alice, as well as a sum of money she has given her:

"I would prefer that no one outside of your immediate family should know that I sent her a sum of money; will you mention this to her?"

Fanny is due to leave for Ellen's on January 31st, arriving at Energy February 8th 1885.

There is one letter from Fanny to Ellen written during Fanny's visit. Eliza, David's mother, was seriously ill and Ellen and John Pugh went up to be with her (in fact, she died April 11th, 1885, age 79, at Madewood). This letter does not indicate the day, but it may have been written the 10th (April 11th was a Saturday, and Fanny's letter is written Friday). Fanny makes some cryptic comments, and she describes David as if he is no longer rational. Meantime, Alice's wedding was due to occur April 27th.

"Friday 10.30 A.M.
My dear Nell
When Bob was in Thibodaux early this morning, he saw Mr. Robert Pugh's man who told him you and John reached your destination safely last evening. He added that Mrs. Pugh was still breathing this morning.
I felt very anxious about you, for after eight it was very dark. All goes on well here.
David is incessantly telling everyone he can get hold of this morning to go to Thibodaux for your telephone and as there is no one to go, it is a little embarrassing. Alice is sewing busily with Miss C., Mrs. Dick Pugh sent her such a pretty present this morning.
Yrs

251

Fanny

All send love.

I am writing at Fathers edification, He says "tell Mother I have the messages brought by Guity – I am too sick to come up myself but the children will go up."

We will wait for your telegram and go up as you say. It will be only Edith and me unless aunt goes and I think not. Grandmother will not understand messages and this is why Father does not send any."

There are no letters until April 21st 1885.

On April 21st, Fanny writes from New Orleans that she, Edith and Grace have arrived. They are doing some last-minute shopping in preparation for Alice's wedding, and they are going to the New Orleans Universal Exposition and World's Fair. Then Fanny leaves for New York, the girls go back home, and Alice gets married.

Illustration 43: Alice as a young lady (photo courtesy of Alyce Rossow).

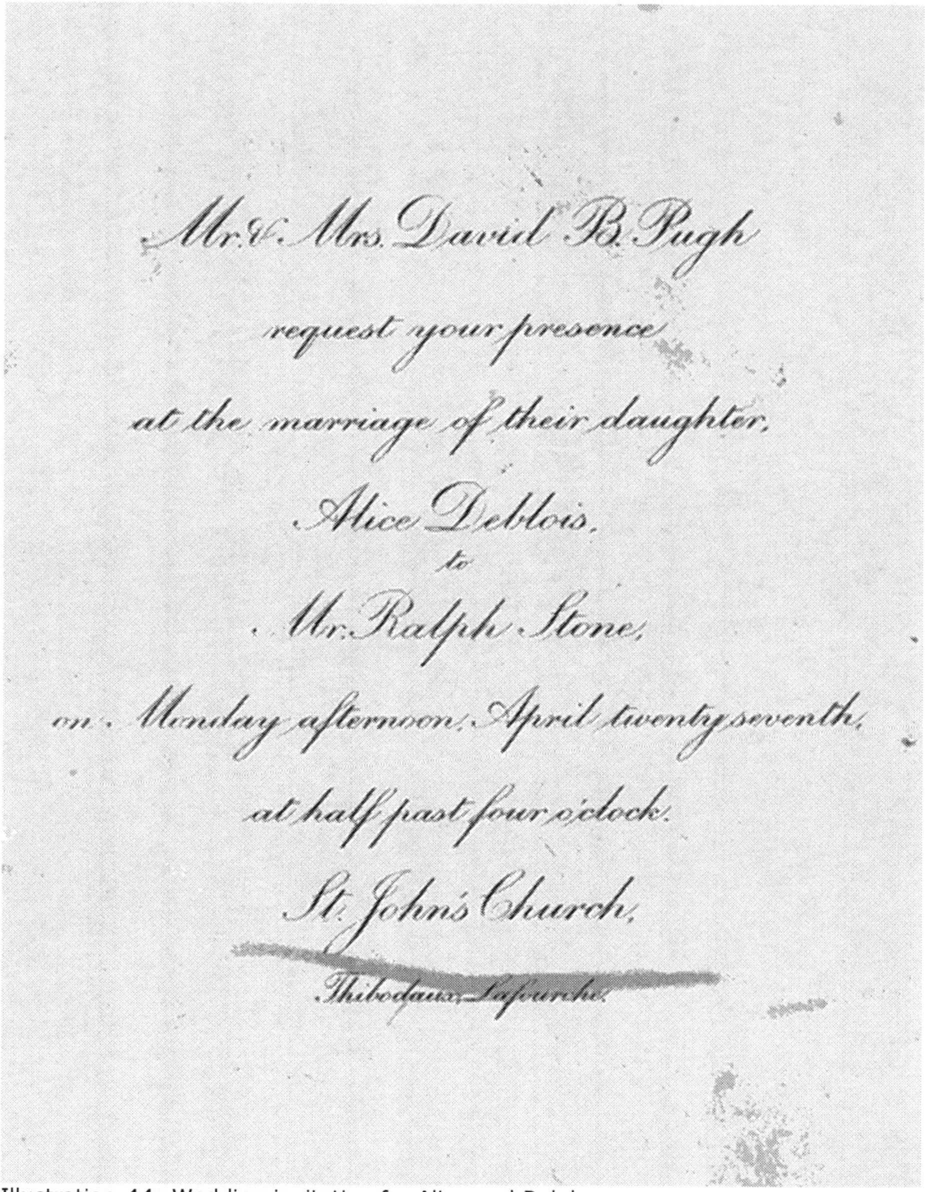

Mr. & Mrs. David B. Pugh

request your presence

at the marriage of their daughter,

Alice Deblois,

to

Mr. Ralph Stone,

on Monday afternoon, April twenty-seventh,

at half past four o'clock.

St. John's Church,

Thibodaux, Lafourche.

Illustration 44: Wedding invitation for Alice and Ralph.

The Times-Democrat

Thibodaux, La.

A NOTABLE WEDDING.

Special to The Times-Democrat.

THIBODAUX, April 27.—A brilliant gathering of the elite of three parishes assembled to-day at St. John's Church, Thibodaux, to witness the nuptials of Miss Alice D. Pugh, of Lafourche, and Mr. Ralph Stone, of Buffalo, N. Y. The bride is the eldest daughter of that well-known citizen, Mr. David B. Pugh, of this parish, and the groom a prominent young attorney of Buffalo. The service was that of the Episcopal Church, which there is none more beautiful, and was impressively read by the Rev. Alford S. Clark.

The fair hands of the lady friends of the bride had busied themselves in the most lovely ornamentations with flowers, and every portion of the church edifice was beautifully decorated. Over the altar a light, graceful arch of enterwined vines, relieved by roses, supported a floral ornament; massive pedestals, crowned with pyramids, flanked the chancel rail, while the pulpit and lecturn were embowered in flowers of every variety, and garlands of roses festooned the capitals of the columns. From the seclusion of one peered forth a dove.

The bride was attended by her sisters, Misses Grace and Edith Pugh; the groom by Mr. Lee Conger, of New Orleans. The ushers were Messrs. ▩▩ Shaffer, Alfred Tete and John ▩ Pugh. The happy couple left on the evening train and propose sojourning for awhile at Pass Christian on their way North. The congratulations were numerous and hearty from a host of friends.

Illustration 45 Alice and Ralph: a notable wedding.

Illustration 46: Wedding photo: Ralph, Ellen, David, Alice.

On April 28th Fanny writes Ellen from New York to say she has received the telegram saying Alice is married. On May 1st she writes again to say she has settled in, has heard from Alice, and is happy that Alice will be arriving at Fanny's within a week (they will be traveling to Buffalo, Ralph's home town). Fanny says that Carter has been to visit her, and,

> "Mr. Carter had been at Mr. Pendleton's dinner the evening before and said it was quite a remarkable one, in as much as it included men of both sides in politics, all writing in the course of civil service reform. What a fool James Eustis has made of himself! I suppose John has read the sharp criticisms of him in the "Evening Post". I wish he would change his name.[72]"

On May 10th, Fanny writes with news of Alice and Ralph.

> "May 10th 1885
> My dear Nell
> I think you will like to hear that I have Mr. and Mrs. Stone with me; we have been to church and they have gone to 31 to call on Mrs. Morris; then will come lunch, then church again, (for Alice and me) then dinner at 6.30 and probably a very quiet evening.
> It seems very queer to have this strange man walking about the flat, but we get on very nicely, he is very quiet and never seems to be in the way."

Fanny describes the hectic pace at which Alice has been receiving society:

> "After breakfast the first day, Alice went over to 31- Lulu came in and Mr. Stone and I entertained her; then Helen Wright came on to see me and call on Alice and she stayed to lunch. In the afternoon Miss Lindsay and her brother called and Sen. Wyeth, and Mrs. Emerson and Augusta and Willie and Daisy Jones, so that

---

[72] The political patronage system, also called the spoils system, had come under attack and been reformed by Senator Pendleton (the Pendleton Bill). Members of both political parties gave a dinner at Delmonico's to honor Senator Pendleton for his work in civil service reform and the removal of public offices and officials from the realm of party politics. Meanwhile, Senator James Biddle Eustis (part of the Eustis branch of Fanny and Ellen's family) distinguished himself by crying out against the reform because he relied upon the spoils system. For his efforts he was roundly criticized by his own party and the press. Biddle's political history in Louisiana was deep: from Dictionary of American Biography, http://bioguide.congress.gov, Biddle was born in New Orleans, La., August 27, 1834; pursued classical studies; graduated from the Harvard Law School in 1854; admitted to the bar in 1856 and practiced in New Orleans; served as judge advocate during the Civil War in the Confederate Army; resumed the practice of law in New Orleans; elected a member of the State house of representatives prior to the reconstruction acts; one of the committee sent to Washington to confer with President Andrew Johnson on Louisiana affairs; member, State house of representatives 1872; member, State senate 1874-1878; elected as a Democrat to the United States Senate, served from January 12, 1876, to March 3, 1879; professor of civil law at the University of Louisiana 1877-1884; again elected as a Democrat to the United States Senate and served from March 4, 1885, to March 3, 1891; practiced law in Washington, D.C., in 1891; Ambassador Extraordinary and Plenipotentiary to France 1893-1897; settled in New York City; died in Newport, R.I., on September 9, 1899.

Alice had barely time to don her black silk with jetted front, for dinner.

Mr. Morris dined here and Lewis M- came, self invited, but most welcome. He and Alice carried on like everything and it amused me to see Mr. Stone watch them.

Alice is very thin, but looks better than when I left her on the 19th of April. I am quite delighted that I am to have a week's visit. Mr. Stone says he need not be back in Buffalo until the 19th, so they will stay with me till the 16th, I believe.

Tuesday, they are going to Fort Washington."

There had been talk of Grace coming to New York, and now it is decided that she will come to Fanny's in early summer, then to Marblehead to visit the Morrises, then to Buffalo to visit Alice and Ralph:

"I am glad for Grace's sake or rather for the sake of her health, that you decide to let her come on this summer. I hope she can find a chance by steamer for the last of May or first of June.

I cannot bear to have her leave you and feel so badly about it, that I cannot take much pleasure in expecting her here. Perhaps if she were really sick now, I should feel differently, but she seems to be well and very likely would be well all summer.

She will have a very quiet time until she gets to Buffalo, then perhaps she may have some fun. I hope so. Marblehead will be stagnation for her."

Fanny writes again on the 14th, full of news about Alice's busy schedule: they are inundated with visits and they are shopping for articles for Alice's new home in Buffalo. Despite the sea of visitors (Fanny's "parlor was quite gay and quite festive"), they made some visits themselves:

"Wednesday morning, Woodbury sent his open carriage to drive them to Fort Washington where they were invited to take luncheon. They persuaded me to go with them; Augusta had a handsome table and everything as nice as possible.

John (Haven) came up and took them down to the place and showed Ralph everything and everywhere, what he thought you would like him to see."

Of the visit, Fanny says,

"I have enjoyed their visit extremely, every minute of it; Alice has been lovely to me, and considerate and thoughtful as always. They both have been so nice to me, consulting and talking over their plans in a way that has gratified and pleased me very much."

Then Fanny assesses Ralph:

"I think Ralph will make her a kind husband.

I like him on the whole and I think the more you see of him, the better you like him; he is very considerate of me, very unobtrusive in his ways and never offends.

He is slow, but I do not think I mind it as much as you might. I wish he would exert himself more to talk, for when people call, he really never opens his lips and it is very hard to entertain him. He ought to try to make some conversation, for it seems awkward and makes them appear at great disadvantage.

I do not think he is at all handsome, but he has a good face; his figure is poor I think and his clothes have what I call a slouchy look and he has an awkward way of sitting, but these are external trifles which after all are not of much consequence. It must be very hard for him to come in among strangers and no doubt he thinks it a great bore.

I think he likes John better than anyone he has met."

Fanny writes on June 7th 1885, that Grace, who is in N.Y. with her, has been very busy.

"She is very well and as bright as a lark, full of engagements and going all the time. She has had five young men to see her already and Daisy has been twice and her Aunt and Uncle John and cousins. We were going to Fort Washington yesterday, but had so tempting an invitation, that we deferred it. Mr. Carter sent me tickets to attend the unveiling and presentation to Central Park, of a statue of a "Pilgrim Father", by the New England Society of New York[73], of which he is a member and an Ex-President.

He sent an open carriage for us in which we drove to the park and took our seats on the audience stand; we heard the speeches of Mr. Curtis's address and fine music and so many celebrities.

When the affair was over, Mr. Carter joined us; then we had a delightful drive through the park and ended off with a dinner at Delmonico's, reaching home finally about eight.

The day was perfect and the whole affair very enjoyable. Grace especially gloried over the dinner at Delmonico's. She wore her red silk and looked very pretty.

About Ralph's Aunt Townsend, who is staying with Alice and Ralph in Buffalo, Fanny says,

"Ralph's letter was very nice; he amused me by saying that "the relations between his Aunt and Alice had been a little strained at times." Is an elegant mode of expressing that they fought like cat and dog, which is probably the fact.

Poor Alice has many lessons to learn and your advice to her seems to me to have been most excellent.

I hope the old thing will clear out before Grace gets there."

On June 28th, Fanny writes about being in Fort Washington, and how she has enjoyed John Haven:

"I have enjoyed exceedingly being with John for the past week. I never care to stay out here, for the place and House are full of

---

[73] The Pilgrim Statue was given to New York City by the New England Society of New York to memorialize the landing of the Pilgrims. The unveiling of the statue was preceded by a parade to Central Park, with the Seventh Regiment Veterans, and the procession stopped in front of General Grant's house to pay their respects to him (Grant died less than two months later).

memories and associations with all my young life with its joys and sorrows and I never want them recalled, only I like to be with John and therefore I come."

At the end of July, Fanny writes that Mr. Carter has made a visit to Alice and Ralph in Buffalo:

"I told Grace to forward to you a nice letter from Alice telling about Mr. Carter's visit, which was quite an event for her, or rather she made it so. Mr. Carter wrote me "Alice lives very nicely and I met her at her house in the evening, several of as nice people as there are in Buffalo"."

Fanny mentions Richard Pugh's illness: by the time her letter reaches Ellen, he has died (Fanny's letter was dated July 25th; Richard died July 20th 1885, age 47).

"I am sorry that Dick Pugh is so sick, if he has Bight's disease all the springs in the world will not do him any good. I daresay it was brought on by drinking too much whiskey."

She asks about David, and mentions Grant's passing:

"And is David any better during the warm weather?
I am so thankful that poor General Grant's sufferings are ended at last."

On July 30th Fanny has heard about Richard's death and writes about Richard's support of Ellen during her trials with David:

"A line from Alice told me of Richard Pugh's death, a day or two before your letter came; it is all very, very sad and I feel the deepest sympathy for his wife, for they always seemed devotedly attached to each other and he was also a kind and loving father. It is a dreadful blow to them all and he is a loss to you too; from the time of your marriage, you have been fond of him and of late years he has been a good friend to you. How often it happens that one death follows another in a family."

Fanny knows Richard's family from her visits to Louisiana, and says,

"I wish sometime you would give my love to Mrs. Richard Pugh and tell her how deeply I feel for her, not mere words, but a heartfelt sympathy; she is very, very often in my thoughts, and Pinksie and Lou too, give my love to them."

Fanny says Ellen must find another home somewhere, and concedes that the options are significantly narrowed if Ellen feels obliged to find a location where her sons John and Thomas can make some kind of living. Her comments suggest that Ellen may have rejected John Haven's offer to live together in Pennsylvania and that Ellen will be leaving for another home by or about January 1886.

On August 12th, Fanny writes from Rye Beach, having come there by way of Cooperstown and Albany, N.Y. She again mentions Ellen's having to leave Energy by next winter: it may be that they can't afford to renew the lease. Fanny says Grace is welcome to stay with her in N.Y.C. Grace is now in Buffalo visiting Alice:

> "She and Alice seem to be very happy together, Alice says they talk all day long, which I can readily believe."

About Mr. Carter's visit to Buffalo[74], Fanny relates,

> "Mr. Carter gave me a very laughable account of Miss Townsend [Ralph's aunt]; he said "she and Alice did not appear to career along together very well." I think this expression will please John. He spoke in high terms of Mr. Stone, said he liked him extremely."

Fanny writes again from Rye Beach on August 25th 1885, having heard that John Pugh had some kind of accident, and about Alice being pregnant.

> "You have had a very anxious time with John and I have shared the anxiety, only I did not hear of the accident until the worst was over; it was a satisfaction to have postals from you every few days, but it is sad to know that John is still sick with fever. Give him my love and tell him I hope he will not try anymore such experiments.
>
> I have no doubt Alice and Grace write you constantly of their gay doings in Buffalo. Grace has been having a delightful time, indeed all her summer has been pleasant.
>
> I am dreadfully sorry to have you confirm my fears about Alice's condition. I say "fears" because I am so very sorry that it should be so. Even now she has too much work to do and what will it be a few months hence! You must be preparing your mind to include in your plans for next winter or spring a trip to Buffalo. It will never, never do to have Miss Townsend go there again."

Fanny mentions that she has met General Armstrong[75], who was about Fanny's age, and who founded Hampton University in Virginia:

> "General Armstrong, who has the Indian School at Hampton, was here for a day or two and I found him very intelligent and interesting, a handsome man too."

September 9th, Fanny says she is happy that Grace will come back to New York in October. John Pugh's career as a planter seems to have failed:

> "If there is to be no sale for this year's crop, I should think it would be hardly worthwhile for John to stay on a year longer and plant another, he would probably be only deeper and deeper in debt. I think the sooner he can get out of it the better."

Fanny talks about various plans for Ellen's future home: Baltimore, Washington, New York, Pennsylvania. From what Fanny writes about old

---

[74] Mr. Carter was able to visit Alice and Ralph because he had been invited to give a speech commemorating the establishment of the opening of the Adirondack Forest Preserve and the New York State Reservation at Niagara (considered to be landmark conservation legislation, made possible in part by the efforts of Frederick Law Olmsted).
Fanny wrote, "His oration at Niagara is very highly praised by everyone, Mr. Carter's I mean."
[75] A Williams College graduate (1862) and Major General in the Union army, Samuel Chapman Armstrong (1839-1893) founded a college for African-Americans in the deep South during Reconstruction in 1868; in 1878 he added a program for American Indians.

Ellen (a valued servant), it sounds as if Ellen plans to try to take old Ellen with her when she relocates. David's care is a problem:

> "Then as soon as you leave Louisiana who is to take care of David, take old Ellen's place with him? I puzzle over this more than anything else.
> Fortunately there are still several months before it must be decided and I am in hopes some of us may be inspired before then.
> I hope that John and Thomas may be able to keep together at any rate.
> In making your plans, I certainly hope you will be able to go to Alice in the spring, or whenever she will need you. I think you ought to, if you possibly can manage it and can leave David. If he continues the same as when I was there, I do not see why you should not leave him for six weeks, but no one can tell what his condition may be at that time."

On September 26th 1885, Grace writes Ellen from Alice's in Buffalo. She too mentions Ellen's coming relocation, possibly to Texas:

> "The sooner we all get away I am convinced the better. Next year at this time I hope we will be writing Alice of the superb oysters and crabs at Pass Christian."

Grace, now about 23, advises her mother about Alice, and sounds very much like Fanny.

> "...you need not worry your self and plan to spend more money that you have not, when Ralph and Alice are both better off than you are at this minute. They get along very well, now and have every comfort and some luxuries. It is for the future that I fear. However he is a grown man, certainly old enough to know how to take care of his wife. And you let him do it. Don't give her any clothes, let him understand that he must buy her clothes, the sooner the better. If she lives too long on her relations, he will begin to think she needs no clothes."

Grace writes Ellen several letters in October 1885 from Fanny's, having returned from Buffalo. Alice is feeling a little bereft with Grace gone, and she too comes to New York City and the Fort. Grace says,

> "Aunt Augusta has taken no end of trouble for Alice, found out all about a nice nurse and sent her lists of the modern outfits. It is particularly sweet of her as they were never very fond of one another. Alice asked her advice while here and it seemed to please her so much."

On October 16th, Fanny writes Ellen that she is happy to have Grace back with her.

> "It is very pleasant to have Grace here again and I am glad to see her looking so well; she seems to have enjoyed her visit in Buffalo

exceedingly and I have been much interested in hearing all sorts of details about Alice's home and life and housekeeping.

One thing she told me and in the most innocent and unconscious way too, which I will repeat for your private ear.

She said Alice told her that she had told Ralph she wished to have five children, three girls and two boys, but that Ralph said he did not believe he could afford to have more than three, but she told him she chose to have five."

Alice is at Fanny's by October 29th:

"I think you will like to hear a word about Alice, who took us by surprise Sunday evening and much to our delight marched in, looking very smiling and pretty and also very well. I have enjoyed so much having her with me, I can hardly realize she is married. I think she looks much better than she did last May and she says she feels perfectly well."

Along with Grace and now Alice, Fanny has another surprise visitor:

"I was interrupted here by the appearance of Dr. George Haven[76] from Portsmouth, he has been in Europe for two years and has wonderfully improved, is very good-looking and has acquired an ease of manner he lacked before."

In Grace's letter of November 4th 1885 to her mother, she says,

"We were delighted to have letters from you and from Edith and so sorry to hear about father. Give my best love and a kiss and tell him he must be well when I get home.

I am glad the family mustered and came to see him."

Grace writes again November 12th, and apparently David is still sick but Thomas has gotten a job.

"It is too bad father should have had a chill and gone back up on all the good he has had done him.

It is splendid about Thomas - just think of five dollars a week."

Augusta and Fanny have been doing everything they can to help Alice prepare for her baby, and to get Alice adequate clothing. Fanny writes November 16th 1885 and says Grace was delighted by a concert she went to:

"I suppose Grace wrote you about going to the symphony concert with Bertie Wilmerding, you do not know how delighted Grace was and how thoroughly she enjoyed it. The music was delicious and I was wishing all the time that you could hear it."

---

[76] Son of George Wallis Haven, Dr. George Haven (1861-1903) was the same age as Alice but was Fanny and Ellen's first cousin. He graduated from Harvard Medical School in 1882, and had been abroad for two years studying obstetrics and gynecology. He worked at Boston City Hospital and taught at Harvard Medical School.

About Alice, who has secured both a doctor and nurse along with baby provisions, Fanny says,

> "I think she is very much frightened and is just beginning to realize what it all means."

About David Fanny writes,

> "I felt very much worried about David when you wrote what the doctor said and how all the family started out to come and see him, it seemed as if there must have been a report about that he was very ill. Since then he appears to have been about as usual, no better, no worse and I suppose when the doctor said that the decline would be gradual, he said no more than we have known for the past year or more.
>
> If he means anything more than this, I think Grace ought to come home as soon the she can, but I do not think he does. It is very, very sad for him to be conscious himself of loss of memory and failing brainpower. I wish I could do something for him, I think about him so often and find that the harsh feelings vanish and only kind memories remain.
>
> I am sure it is the greatest, and only comfort he can have, that you can be with him so constantly, doing so much for him and though the work and care are so incessant, I am quite sure you would not want anyone to take your place with him.
>
> But still, all the same, it makes no end of work for you."

Finally, Fanny is angry that a relative of David's, "Bee" Pugh[77], has not paid Ellen the interest he owes on a note she holds.

> "It makes me very angry to think that Bee Pugh has not paid you the $160 he owes you and I do not believe he ever will. More than that, he is not going to have the money to pay his interest this coming winter or spring. If he cannot pay you $160 now, how is he to pay you $660 in February? I should sell his note without waiting another day, what do you gain by it? You cannot afford to fool with him any longer and you know perfectly well, how it will be when the time for payment comes.
>
> I cannot speak of it with any patience."

Grace writes Ellen a lengthy letter on November 21st 1885 and says,

> "We must move so soon as we can and it will be best for all parties concerned. On no account do you want to spend another summer there and have a $300 drug bill in addition to wretched health. As to cousin Eliza I have no patience with her or with Cousin Bee. Did they offer to pay you your money and have they any plans about it. She ought to have offered you the pecan money and everything until you were paid. It is not high principled. This year you will have to sell the note. As to Mr. Conger's affairs, he may not be going to fail of course but I take Uncle Robert's advice against all of theirs in a bunch, on a business matter.

---

[77] William Whitmell Hill Pugh, Jr.

Is it not hard on Thomas to have to pay out of all he earned, poor, unlucky boy."

Grace goes on at length about Alice and her situation and says,

"You can't reason with Alice. She ought to have known before just what it would be. That you could no more afford to come to her than she to you. But for this same reason you can't help feeling sorry for her. If the time were only near I would stay, but everyone here has been more than kind offering for her and advising her."

Fanny writes Ellen on November 29th to wish Ellen a happy birthday (Ellen is 53), and weighs in about Alice's situation:

"Now in regard to Alice, fond of her as I am and anxious as I feel that everything should be done for her comfort and well-being, I do not think the whole family should be sacrificed to her.

Grace does not want to stay and go to her in February; it is not a pleasant thing for her to do and I see no reason why she should. It would be very nice if you could go to her, but I do not see either the least necessity for it. I do not apprehend any danger for her and I think the chance of anything going wrong to be very small. She has a good nurse engaged and a doctor and her husband and will get along just as well as hundreds of women have gone before her. If she should be desperately ill or anything go wrong, time enough for you to go to her, as you would to any child who was very ill away from you.

Leaving David, taking all the money it would cost and going to Buffalo at that season of the year, are all great and serious obstacles to your going. I wanted to tell you that I decided soon after her visit here, to go to her myself as soon as her baby was born and pass several weeks with her; I do not myself see any use in having any one with her just at that time (unless it could be you)-but I am quite willing to go down and be in the house, if she feels as if she would like to have me.

I shall write to her pretty soon and tell her so and I want you to consider it as settled in making your plans. Then when February comes, if Grace is at home, David continues the same, money is forthcoming and you feel equal to it, you can carry out your plan of coming by steamer with Edith, have her with me and you go to Buffalo.

Or if Alice should not be as well then, as she now promises to be, it is time enough for you to start, but in the meantime consider it a settled thing that I am to make my visit then instead of earlier or later. This is decidedly the best way to arrange the whole thing. I disapprove entirely of Grace or Edith going to her and though it would be very nice if you could go, do not consider it at all necessary."

Fanny bluntly sums up Alice's ways:

"Any other young woman would have commenced her preparations
months ago, but she is going to dawdle along and have everything
done for her just as she did when she was married and in my
opinion will be no more ready for her baby at the end of the nine
months than she was at the beginning.
But that is Alice and you cannot make her over."

Grace writes, on December 6th 1885, that she plans to be home by
Christmas at the latest. She writes again on both December 17th and 18th,
saying her Aunt Fanny has been extremely generous to her. She says she
is very disappointed that she will not make it home by Christmas. On
December 22nd, Grace still isn't certain how she will get home (there are
several options), and says,

"I feel very blue as Christmas approaches that I am not home."

Christmas Eve day, Fanny writes Ellen and says,

"Tomorrow we are going to hear the music at Trinity in the
morning and in the evening will dine with the Morewoods. We are
also invited to Miss Bassett's and to Fort Washington.
Grace is much disappointed at not being at home for Christmas,
but she makes the best of it. I think she will have to go on the
"Hudson" on January 2nd, that is if I can find any lady going out, if
there are only men of course she could not go."

December 31st 1885, Grace's trip is still up in the air. Grace writes,

"I meant to write you this morning, asking you if I could come out
by myself. Aunt Fanny would not let me without your permission."
Grace wants to be home with Ellen, and feels Ellen should have her there
since Edith is away for the winter. If Ellen consents, Grace will leave on a
steamer January 16th 1886. About their overall situation, Grace says,

"I am very sorry for both Thomas and John. I have thought a great
deal about their hard work all going for nothing so I hope you have
not thought of staying another summer, throwing away your
health and time."
She says she is sure her mother has heard about Uncle Alfred Haven's
death, and says John Haven has gone to the funeral. Alfred Woodward
Haven (born 14 March 1801, died 31 December 1885) was Ellen's uncle.
Grace is excited that they may have Italian royalty call at Fanny's, and
makes a joke:

"We are in daily expectations of a visit from Count Francesco
Veltri, second son of the Duchess of Poggiardo- An Italian and a
friend of Mrs. Wright's who has asked Aunt Fan's permission to
have him call. I expect to be countess Veltri, poison off my
brother-in-law and be the Duchess elect."

Losing David; Grace Returns (1886)

On January 5th 1886, Fanny writes Ellen to say they are still uncertain about Grace's travel plans and departure date, and that they are working on every possibility. She says Uncle Alfred Haven's passing was a blessing, and says,

> "Now, Uncle Wallis [George Wallis Haven] is the only member left of Father's family and only Aunts Elizabeth and Sophia on the other side."

Apparently David rallied enough to send Fanny a message in Ellen's recent letter:

> "Give my love to David and tell him I was very much pleased to receive such a cheerful little message from him the first day of the year, it was quite inspiriting, also, that I was just wondering the same thing about myself, if I should be above the sod, I have not yet made up my mind."

On January 24th, Fanny writes to say that Grace's travel plans have not come to fruition:

> "Grace has again been disappointed in getting off. She was all ready to come by the Hudson on the 23rd when just the day before we were told that not one lady, or woman was going out, only one solitary man for passenger. Of course it was impossible for her to go that way. Now we are perfectly desperate and Grace declares she is going alone by rail. I tell her she must wait patiently for Jenny Gordon or for the next trip of the Louisiana two weeks hence. Every chance we have heard of falls through.
> I shall miss her more than I can express, but I try to think how grateful I ought to be that she has been with me since October. So I try to dwell only on all the pleasure she has afforded me and how bright she has made the winter by her companionship.
> She has enjoyed herself thoroughly I think and for the last month had really quite a gay time in the sense of going out to the opera, theater and to dinner and having company at home."

On January 27th Fanny says that by the time this letter reaches Ellen, Grace will have arrived. It is uncertain whether Grace reached home before her father died. David Bryan Pugh died, on January 29th 1886, aged 58.

> "January 27, 1886
> Dearest Nell
> When this letter reaches you Grace will doubtless be with you and have told you all the story of her journey home, how opposed I was to her going alone and thought she ought to wait for some chance of escort and how I would never really gave my consent,

though I could not but confess that it really seemed the only thing to do.

The thought of her taking that journey all alone made me almost sick, and I could not, at the last moment, have allowed her to start, if it had not been that Eustis could go with her and put her in the sleeper at Washington. Now I feel more reconciled to it and saw her off this afternoon with less anxiety than I had yesterday, but still with an aching heart.

I think she was very brave to decide to go off alone and was thankful to have her so cheerful. I only hope she will hold out as bravely till she gets to New Orleans. As soon as she had started, I sent a telegram to Edith so that she could be sure to meet her."

By January 31st, Fanny has heard the news about David's death and writes Ellen:

"Sunday, 27 Waverly Place

Dearest Nell-I cannot say anything that can really help you to bear your cross of bereavement and sorrow, never are we so utterly alone as in the keen grief we all have sometimes to suffer of having our loved ones taken from us.

You are surrounded by your devoted children who are sorrowing with you and trying to help and comfort you, but they are all young and can hardly realize who you mourn for; they have lost their Father and must stand aside in the presence of a grief that mourns for husband, friend and lover.

I have been with you all day in my thoughts and now I am sitting with you in the house that is so empty and desolate.

I have gone back many, many years and am weeping with you for all that is passed and gone, but which can never be forgotten-memories which will be dearer and sweeter to you as the years go on.

Someone whom your children never knew, but whom you and I remember well, you have today laid by the side of your darling child in the churchyard.

By and by you will find comfort and many soothing thoughts in the recalling all that you have been to him during the past year, how he has rested on you, lived in you, loved you, but now it can only be the one thought, what he used to be to you and what you have lost."

Fanny closes saying she wishes she could be there with Ellen:

"My dearest love to John and Grace and Edith and Thomas. I need not say how I long to be with you in bodily presence.

I have had but that one thought since the first message came."

DIED,

On Friday, Jan. 29th., 1886, at 5 o'clock P. M.,

DAVID BRYAN PUGH,

in his 58th year.

The funeral will leave his late residence on Sunday, Jan. 31st. at 10 o'clock A. M.

Interment will take place at St. John's Episcopal Church, Thibodaux, at 10:30 o'clock A. M. same day.

The friends and acquaintances of the family are invited to attend.

Thibodaux, La., January 30th., 1886.

Illustration 47: David's death notice, January 1886.

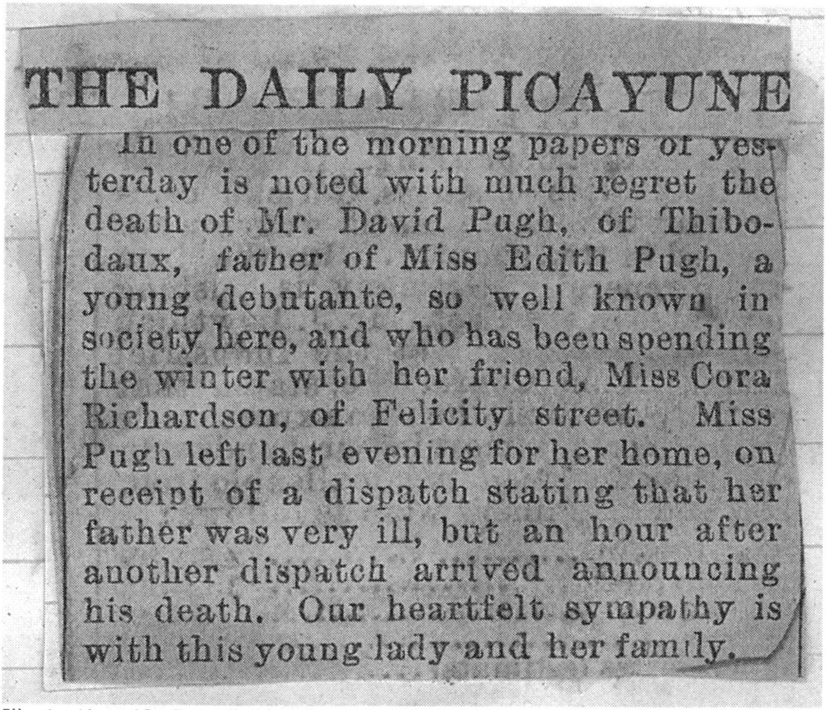

THE DAILY PICAYUNE

In one of the morning papers of yesterday is noted with much regret the death of Mr. David Pugh, of Thibodaux, father of Miss Edith Pugh, a young debutante, so well known in society here, and who has been spending the winter with her friend, Miss Cora Richardson, of Felicity street. Miss Pugh left last evening for her home, on receipt of a dispatch stating that her father was very ill, but an hour after another dispatch arrived announcing his death. Our heartfelt sympathy is with this young lady and her family.

Illustration 48: David's death announced in the newspaper.

On February 13th 1886, Fanny writes Ellen about John Haven's offer for Ellen and her family to come to back to Fort Washington and live with him in the old Haven family home. She also has kind words for David.

"Dearest Nell

Before you receive this letter, you will have had one from John, proposing that you should come to Fort Washington, for the present at least.

I have delayed writing, as I did not want to speak on the subject until he had done so and I knew that it was his intention to.

If it is his wish that you should come, I see no objection to it. I told him that if the boys were to be with you I did not think it would answer at all and I do not know him so well that I do not think he would be contented; his ways and their ways are so entirely different and it would be very uncomfortable for you to be trying all the time to make things run smoothly.

He did not altogether agree with me.

I told him I was not sure anyhow that he would like to have his entire household and all his ways of life changed, but he seemed to think he would not mind, that he would like to have companionship and did not mind at all the introduction of a young element.

I feel as if we owed a great deal to John, everything, for his judicious and generous way of managing the estate during the last two years; what we should have done without him I am sure I do not know, everything would have gone to rack and ruin and we would have been obliged to pay thousands of dollars which have been saved to us. He persistently refuses to accept one cent in compensation for all the services he has performed.

My desire is that he shall always have a home at Fort Washington and the absolute control of everything there as long as he may live or may desire it.

He would not be happy anywhere else, although he may think he would be.

Feeling this as strongly as I do, I could not consent to, nor advise any arrangements that could interfere with his comfort and happiness.

To have you and the girls there, I think would conduce greatly to his pleasure and I feel sure that you would make his comfort in every way, your first object. I should not say so, if I did not think that he felt so too; minor discomforts and annoyances to him, will be compensated for by companionship and the cheerfulness of home.

...I think you and Grace and Edith could be very comfortable there, though it would be very dull for the girls; for the summer though, they would not want any gaiety. I should think they personally would rather be at Pass Christian.

I am very much annoyed that David's property does not come to you. I quite understand how it is, but regret it extremely. I supposed of course, you would have the control of it.

I was deeply interested in all the particulars you wrote me about your dear husband's illness and death.

Of course I should wish to wear black, not only as a tribute to his memory but in respect to the sorrow and loss it brings to you and the children. I share this sorrow and loss with you all. I have only now the kindest thoughts about him and feel very strongly, as I have always felt in a measure, that no one knows how far he was really accountable for his ways and deeds. I think for years, there has been something wrong about his mind and no one can say where responsibility ended and disease began.

Years ago he was very kind and sweet to me and personally, I have always had great consideration and kindness from him and now I have only kind and charitable thoughts for his memory. I think he had naturally a very sweet nature."

By February 16th 1886, Fanny has received a package from Ellen containing preserves, nuts and mementos of David, and says,

"I thank you so much for sending me the little cork screw which I shall prize very highly; that and the pocket handkerchief brought him so vividly before me, that it made me feel heartsick.

I recall him so plainly as I last saw him, on the gallery that Sunday afternoon last April, when I said goodbye. I felt then that I might never see him again and yet I did not realize it."

Responding to Ellen's feeling that she (Ellen) must pay Fanny for Eustis' fare to Washington and back (to help get Grace home), Fanny says,

"...of course I cannot think of your paying Eustis's fare to Washington, cannot listen to it for one minute. I never spent a small sum of money with more satisfaction than I spent that and when I consider now all that the journey meant for Grace, I would gladly have spent twice the amount to get her there."

Fanny is going to Fort Washington to see John Haven, then to Buffalo to help Alice with her baby:

"I am going to Fort Washington tomorrow and expect to talk over your plans with John, perhaps can offer some suggestions to him about what household arrangements to make. I am impatient to know whether you will decide to come.

It must be dreadfully hard to break up your home and have to part with so many things you have associations with."

By February 28th, Fanny is in Buffalo with Alice and they await the birth of Alice's baby.

"Dearest Nell

I hope my next letter will announce to you the arrival of your grandchild, but just at present there seems no immediate prospect of it. Alice is very well, very cheerful and brave, very beaming and

smiling; she is delighted at the idea of having a baby and is
planning to have five, or rather, four more.

...Perhaps a week hence she will take a different view of the
matter."

Ellen says she will not take John Haven up on his offer, because Ellen feels
she must take care of John and Thomas too. But Fanny presents
alternatives in an effort to make the plan work.

"...you feel desirous to provide a home for him as well as the girls,
and for Thomas too.

...I wish so much that you could stay at Fort Washington for a
while, have rest, comparative freedom from cares and anxieties,
have the benefit of John's advice and opinion and decide on your
home after due deliberation.

If this is at all practicable I would be delighted to have John and
one of the girls stay with me until I go out of town the first of July.
Will you tell him so with my love?

If Thomas should go on a farm, then you and one daughter could
be at the Fort; if not, he could take turns in making visits at
John's, Augusta's and 27 [27 Waverly Place, i.e., Fanny's].

Could not Frank Williams look after your stock etc. until the fall? I
know that John would not mind in the least having a visit from
both John and Thomas, though a permanent stay might not be
practicable for either side. In fact, I know he would like it.

It seems to me this could be easily arranged for the summer and
at very little expense for you. Of course when with me, the two
would be at no expense, except washing for one."

Fanny offers Ellen money to help with her move:

"If you need money to help you move, or to complete any
arrangements about taking the new house, let me send it to you
for an indefinite period; $500 or less, just as it may be necessary.
Count on this in making your plans.

It must be very, very hard for you to part with your belongings
and sell everything, right and left. And then the packing is a
stupendous undertaking. Not a day passes that I am not thinking it
over in my own mind and realizing what it must be for all of you."

On March 10th Fanny writes again to say that her 2-week visit to Alice
appears to be wasted, because Alice still hasn't given birth. In fact, Ralph
Townsend Stone was born March 13, 1886.

Ellen Comes Home; Grace Afflicted (1886-1893)

On April 24th 1886, Fanny tells Ellen she is very happy that Ellen is coming to Fort Washington.

> "We are all delighted that we are to have you all here and I am so afraid you will not get here before I go away for the summer; do come as soon as you can."

Apparently Ellen feels that if she is going to live at Fort Washington, she should compensate Fanny in some way. Her reasoning is that the four of them (Augusta, Fanny, Ellen and John) effectively share ownership of their parent's house. Fanny dispenses with her suggestion with humor:

> "I do not want any rent for my share of the house and when I want to live in my quarter of it, I will come out with my yard measure and measure it off."

Mrs. David B. Pugh and family have permanently removed from the Lafourche to New York City. An announcement so simple can give no idea of the great loss sustained by the Church and community in their departure. Identified for so many years with our people, on the bayou, their circle of friends and acquaintances was exceedingly large, and seemed to increase with the on-coming years. Not content merely with the society of those who showed their tastes and sympathies, the poor, the suffering and the distressed were made partakers of their cheer in the sympathetic word and the delicate remembrance. Thus their lives became linked with many others, until it was felt that for life itself they were part and parcel of our community. In the Church itself they had their memorial, not only in the costly Communion Service of solid silver which was their gift, but in their attendance on the services and devotion to every good work. It was at St. John's altar that the younger members of this family renewed their Christian vows, and there they seldom failed to kneel in the Church's highest act of worship. To say that we shall miss them is not enough; to say that we wish them well where'er they go is not enough; but we must say, though it seems selfish on the very face of it, we wish them back again, for the Lafourche has too few of such tried and trusted friends and. St. John's cannot afford to lose the membership of such as these.

Illustration 49: Ellen leaves Louisiana to return to New York after David's death.

On August 25th 1886, Fanny writes Ellen in Fort Washington from Rye Beach. There are no intervening letters, so there is no way of knowing when Ellen reached Fort Washington, but it may have been in May (otherwise there would probably be a letter from Fanny written in May). Ellen has received another blow: her dear friend Mr. Gordon has also passed:

> "The news of Mr. Gordon's death must have been a great shock to you, it was even to me when I opened Grace's letter. It seems as if you had nothing but death and sorrow among your friends and relations, one blow follows another. All your intercourse with the Gordon family is so associated with dear Mary, that you have very tender feelings and memories connected with them, but then besides that, you were fond of Mr. Gordon for himself and I grieve that you have to part from so dear a friend."

She ends her letter with a humorous anecdote about her companions at Rye Beach:

> "My boon companion at this house, is old Mr. Higginson, age 82, we talk all day long and he considers me as a contemporary, he says "I suppose you remember Miss Haven, it happened in '27" and I always assent."

There is another lapse in letters, indicating that Ellen and her family have been in New York and living at Fort Washington with John Haven. Grace writes Thomas (from Fanny's flat at 27 Waverly Place) an undated letter, across the top of which Ellen has written "1/1887". Her reference to "home" is probably the Haven house at Fort Washington.

> "It has been two weeks today since I came in to stay with Aunt Fanny.
> ...Edith is making Cousin Woodbury[78] a visit, she went last Thursday and seems to be having a pretty good time. Helen Langdon is there with Mrs. Bassett.
> ... I went out Saturday to spend the day with mother and found them all very well. It is beautiful out there, the snow is so deep - but nice paths shoveled in every direction. The house as warm as toast."

In March of 1887, Grace writes her aunt Mary Williams Pugh, and refers to her engagement. No other letters mention Grace getting engaged, or speak of an engagement breaking off.

> "I beg your pardon for not writing you of my engagement. Oh far from meaning any discourtesy I should have written you first among one or other first ones had I written at all but mother mentioned it in answering a letter to Mrs. Williams and did not speak of it afterwards in writing you as she thought you would

---

[78] Woodbury Langdon, a cousin of Ellen's, was born in 1836 (Ellen was born in 1832 and Fanny in 1838), and was 30 years Edith's senior.

have heard it by that time. Then she mentioned it in answering a letter to uncle Robert but did not think of writing anyone for that special purpose. You know Aunt Mary that girls do not like to talk of such things and I thought it would leak out in every direction as it is no secret. Mr. Morewood arrived from Europe on Saturday and we were only engaged ten days before his departure. For plans I have none as yet but think we will be engaged at least a year. That is my desire.

Your letter is a very sweet one – and I shall certainly tell Mr. Morewood of it -- most of his relations are abroad and I have his congratulatory letters to read -- he has very pretty tastes, ?? in pen and ink very delicately and has promised to carve a box for these letters. So that it may have the honor of holding yours between its covers.

We are all at home again for a wonder. Generally either Edith or I are with aunt Fanny and Edith has been in for two weeks or more with her. I keep busy all the time never wasting a minute to spare. ...John is very happy studying the stenography and very much interested -- he spends all the afternoon writing for dictation when he comes home from his classes. At night he cannot use his eyes. Thomas is going with a cheese making factory. Thomas' picture I meant to have sent you. Lovingly, Grace

In May of 1887, Lizzie Pugh's husband, W.B. Ratliff, writes Ellen in response to a letter she sent to him and Robert Pugh. She has heard sad news about the demise of David's close friend Mr. Conger. Ratliff says that Robert's business is now principally in livestock, and that Robert endures his "long, continued illness". About Mr. Conger Ratliff says,

"...from all I hear his family affairs, and monetary matters were in such a condition that he could stand it no longer, and the general impression is that he has destroyed himself."

June 28th 1887, Grace writes (from Fort Washington) to Thomas in Gilbertsville, NY (in Oneonta county). She speaks of her mother having an old friend out to visit, and about her Uncle John Haven trying to keep unwanted picnickers off the Fort Washington property. Grace says she accompanied her uncle to see the police, and saw artifacts from the days when Fort Washington was a battleground between the British and Americans during the Revolutionary War (the Americans were defeated at the Battle of Fort Washington):

"We went down with Uncle John to the captain's office not long ago. He is very nice and showed us a large collection of old relics dug up at different times round here from the old forts, buttons and shoe buckles and flint's and old pistols and all sorts of shot and bullets."

Grace says that Edith has gone to spend time with Mrs. Bassett, who is Woodbury Langdon's step-mother. Otherwise, Grace describes what sounds like an exciting time:

"Oh! The other day cousin Woodbury took us to Coney Island to the races. They were very pretty and we had dinner and saw the fireworks, then we came home by boat so as to see the Staten Island fireworks in honor of the Queen's Jubilee[79] and the Statue of Liberty lit up."

On July 28th 1887, Fanny writes Ellen from Northeast Harbor, Maine, where she is staying until she leaves for Newport, R.I. Ellen has been visiting with Carter at one of his summer places, and may have gone to Gardiner's Island with Carter.

"I am delighted that you went to Good Ground [known today as Hampton Bays, L.I., N.Y.] and wish that you had stayed a day or two longer to make up for the day you lost.

I do not think I should have recognized that Mr. Gardiner, I remember the man and that his name was Gardiner, but do not recall him in the least. I have heard a good deal of him from Mr. Carter."

Fanny expresses sorrow about Robert Pugh's illness, and is shocked that David and Ellen's portion of Energy, in the end, was not worth much. Fanny indicated in an earlier letter that whatever property David had did not go to Ellen.

"What you write of Robert Pugh's condition is very sad and it seems hopeless.

Is it possible that all your plantation is worth only $10,000? I can scarcely believe it. But I am pleased to think that the children have received something on their shares, will they ever have any more coming to them?"

Robert Pugh died at age 54 on August 14th 1887. On August 15th Fanny writes Ellen in New York from Northeast Harbor. She has heard that John Pugh and Grace have gone to Gilbertsville, N.Y. to see Thomas. Edith is in Portsmouth visiting with the Langdon family and Mrs. Bassett. Fanny says she is bored with hotel life, but her summer sounds entertaining:

"I am getting very tired of hotel life as I always do about this time every summer. I am tired of all the people and tired of being polite to them.

...as I left the dining room, an old lady, Mrs. Allyn from Cambridge, asked me to come to her room and take coffee with two or three other ladies; she makes wretched coffee, boils it over a lamp and I have been victimized several times, but there was no escape from it so off I went.

Then when I left her room I was pounced upon by a very tiresome, uninteresting lady and asked to go to walk with her; this I got out of by saying I thought it was going to rain and then I started for my room; on the way there a lady put her head out from behind her door curtain and asked me to come in and make her a call...

---

[79] Celebrating Queen Victoria's 50th year of reign. The fireworks were said by the New York Times to "surpass anything of the kind ever seen in New York."

Last Saturday Mrs. Story invited me to join a sailing party which, as it was composed of very pleasant people, I was very glad to do. We had a delightful sail to one of the islands where we landed and spent the day, taking our dinner under the trees.

We bought freshly picked wild raspberries from a child, bought eggs and milk and butter at a cottage-the gentleman carried up the baskets from the landing, Mrs. Bowditch made drip coffee over the lamp and Mrs. Story scrambled the eggs, then we had sandwiches, doughnuts etc.

... he and I roamed all over the island while the others were content to sit under the trees.

When we had cleared up the remains of our feast, we started off in the boat and sailed about the rest of the afternoon.

Altogether it was one of the pleasantest days I have had here."

There is a long period with no letters, indicating that Fanny and Ellen were together in New York (Fanny in her flat, Ellen at Fort Washington). In addition to the death of yet another Pugh brother, Walter (Feb. 8, 1888), something terrible has happened to Grace. Somehow, in the space of a year, Grace has gone from being healthy, bright, accomplished and articulate to being acutely mentally ill, requiring institutionalization. Grace almost certainly succumbed to schizophrenia, whose average age of onset in females is about 25 (Grace was 26 in 1888).

On top of the unimaginable heartbreak is the crushing cost of caring for Grace. July 15th, 1888, Ellen writes the superintendent of Bloomingdale Asylum[80] in New York, from Fort Washington.

"Dr. Nichols
Dear Sir,
Since my return from the asylum I have been reviewing our conversation and I would like to consider a few questions before deciding finally the question of my future payments. Will you therefore instruct Dr. Lyons to consider my indebtedness $40[81] per week and allow me a few days until I fully understand my position. My whole income for myself and children is less than what I am now paying a year for the comfortable maintenance of my daughter in the asylum. You are therefore not mistaken in regard to my pecuniary affairs.

[80] Bloomingdale Asylum was one of the first mental hospitals in the United States. Located in what is now Morningside Heights, N.Y. in the early 1800's, it was moved to Westchester in the 1890's in order to free up the valuable city real estate for other uses. Columbia University now occupies the original site of the hospital, and one of the few original asylum buildings remaining is Buell Hall, which was probably named after Dr. Buell, one of the doctors who treated Grace.

[81] According to measuringworth.com, $40.00 in 1888 would have the same purchasing power of at least $900.00 in 2009, and some worth calculator indexes place the figure at $5,000 or more.

You will therefore understand why I asked the question which follows.

Will you write and tell me what the $40 a week gives which the $10 does not ensure.

Do I understand correctly when I say it provides for Miss Pugh a special attendant. Does it also provide private drives for her if she does not want to go out with the other ladies? If so, how many private drives a week are allowed if she is in a condition to take them?

If I decide to ensure her these two comforts I must aside $2080 out of my principle.

Of course this is for me alone to decide.

Perhaps I may believe the ray of light these comforts may throw upon her sad and clouded life worth the sacrifice.

I would also like to know whether you consider her case a hopeless one, or if not entirely hopeless, about how many years does a case like hers usually take before a cure is effected.

I do not ask from curiosity but because your answer will have its bearings in determining perhaps my ability to meet the future demands upon my property.

Hoping you will give me an early answer.

I am yours respectfully

Ellen E Pugh

I must also state to you that inasmuch as you deem only one visit a week to her advisable on my part, this visit will have to be on Saturday as my son can only leave his business on that afternoon to see her – unless you wish me to see her on Wednesdays and you will admit him alone on Saturdays.

If you prefer to have only one visiting day and that [the word "alone" is stricken through], will you tell her that you have told me not to come but once a week and that on Saturday.

Otherwise she will think I do not care to see her and she is expecting me on Wednesday next."

Ellen wrote Fanny at Northeast Harbor about the situation with Grace and the Asylum. Fanny writes back on July 17th 1888, and it is clear based on what she says that she has been to the Asylum with Ellen; also that she is willing to help pay for Grace.

"My advice would be to tell Dr. Nichols that you have considered the subject and talked it over with your sister who takes the greatest interest in Miss Pugh -- that she is very averse to having any change made in Miss Pugh's arrangements as she had observed that she appeared to like to have Miss Gleeson with her- she wishes her to have every possible amelioration that her condition allows and proposes to advance the money to pay for her remaining in just the position she has had since she first entered the asylum, that is $40 per week and begs that Dr. Nichols will allow her to continue to have the services of Miss Gleeson just as long as he deems it conducive to her improvement-in other words not to withdraw them until absolutely necessary.

... Let me know the exact amount of the quarters payment at the rate of $40 per week and I will send the check."

On July 19th 1888, Fanny writes again from Northeast Harbor about the services of the attendant for Grace, which was apparently undertaken initially because Grace was suicidal.

"If he really thinks it better to do without her, he must think there is no further danger of Grace attempting to take her life for it was to guard against and prevent this, that the attendant was given when she first went there..."

Fanny seems committed to paying for much of Grace's care:

"...so long as the greatest amount of comfort possible is secured for her it seems to me of so little consequence who pays the money. I expected to pay $2080 a year for two years..."

And Fanny agrees with Ellen about visiting Grace:

"I have no doubt it excites her more or less to see the family, but how could you give up going to see her, at least once a week and not know how she was treated, or what they were doing with her, or perhaps have her miss us and think we did not care."

Ellen has sent Fanny a copy of the letter that Ellen wrote to Dr. Nichols, and Fanny says, in her understated way,

"I think your letter to the doctor was just to the point (except that I never sign myself "yrs respectfully" to any man-"yrs truly" is quite enough for anyone)..."

On July 29th 1888, Fanny writes from Northeast Harbor, Maine, after going to Isle Au Haut for a few days. Edith will be coming up and staying at Northeast Harbor with Fanny; meantime Alice has written to say she is again pregnant.

About Grace, Fanny says,

"It seems so dreadful to me that the poor child should have to be forced to do anything, dragged about and carried in and out -it is so horrible that she should be subjected to it, she, so fastidious, dainty and proud, oh! It is just heartbreaking to think of.

... Is there anything I can send Grace? I write to her every few days. Do you suppose the doctor objects to this."

A letter from Dr. Nichols to Ellen in Fort Washington tells Ellen how often she can see Grace:

"I am willing that you should come three times weekly, for the present, to read to your respected daughter, Miss Grace. I think this will be often enough, and I will designate Monday, Wednesday, and Saturday afternoons as the time to come."

There are no letters again until 1890, so Fanny and Ellen were probably together in New York. Their sister Augusta died February 15, 1890; Thomas and John were both in some kind of business and working hard by 1890. On March 22nd 1891 there is a letter from Jefferson Davis' wife Varina (whom Ellen and Fanny's mother, Sarah Sherburne Langdon, had met). Ellen had written Varina in New York, in hopes Varina might provide an escort for Edith's trip to Louisiana.

> "To Mrs. David Pugh
> Fort Washington
> New York City
> Dear Mrs. Pugh,
> Yours of the 21st has just been received and I grieve for your sake and my own, not to be able to respond that I will take your daughter to New Orleans with great pleasure, but I am not able to travel and cannot foresee a time when I shall be, as I have been ill with heart failure for four months and seem to have gotten into the habit of relapsing, so the doctor forbids me going south for some time.
> However, if you will allow me, I will make inquiries of my acquaintances and at the hotel office, and perhaps may find some desirable chaperone for Miss Pugh, it should not be a difficult undertaking. A gentleman sent me word this evening that he was going up to Atlanta, now there is no change from there to New Orleans on the Piedmont XXX line south, and if Mrs. Blanc would meet your daughter at the train, there is no risk, or inconvenience involved in her going from there alone.
> My poor child came here alone on that route [?] When she needs must during my illness without any trouble, and was astonished to find how little a thing it was to come alone -- of course she was met in Washington and in Jersey City.
> Of course I am very familiar with your last name, as my cousin, Miss Frances Sprague, married Mr. Thomas Pugh, and as she left several children, it has been a continuing connection of memories and one of my fathers grandnieces married another Pugh -- her maiden name was Lydia Carter, but I do not know her husband's Christian name. He left her a widow and she is now I think a Mrs. Purnell and lives at Fort Adams, Mississippi. We should be most happy to welcome any of your family here, and believe me we would not fail to serve you if it were in our power.
> Yours faithfully,
> Varina Jefferson Davis
> Room 128 New York Hotel
> Sunday the 22nd 1891

An undated letter from the then-current Superintendent of Bloomingdale Asylum, Samuel Lyons, says Grace feels the family has conspired against her, and that this necessarily impedes their ability to visit with her.

"I think it is evident that she chafes under the constant supervision of her movements which her family has exercised, almost from necessity, and she may be more difficult to bring into proper and ordinary methods of life on account of the constant irritation which she feels against her family and if some separation exists she may become more normal in her feelings and actions."

On May 22nd 1891, Ellen receives a reply to two letters she has written to W.W. Pugh, a cousin of David's. W.W. writes from his home at Woodlawn Plantation. Edith apparently found an escort and got to Louisiana, because W.W. Pugh has heard she was in New Orleans. W.W. Pugh tells Ellen about the current situation at Madewood,

"Lew Pugh is spending a large sum for improvements on Madewood, some 60 or $70,000[82]. His wife and child spent much of their time there."

Ellen receives a letter written on September 24 1891, from Thomas' employer, at 68 Wall St.:

"...I may tell you that I have been watching him closely, and I am more than pleased thus far with his work. This should delight a mother's heart, and I can assure you that you have in him a son to be proud of.

He came to us with the sole introduction of being Appleton's cousin, which went a great way with me, because the stock from which they both came was so favorably known to me, and ever since he joined our force I have regretted giving him a trial.

He is always most faithful industrious and willing, which traits if persisted in are sure make him a successful man..."

Ellen gets a letter from her cousin Eliza Appleton Haven written October 17 1893. Ellen had visited Eliza in Portsmouth, N.H. and consulted her about moving Grace to another facility or residence.

"Since your call here, on Sunday, Charlotte and I have longed to be able to assist you in finding a suitable place for your dear Grace."

---

[82] According to measuringworth.com, $60,000.00 would have the purchasing power of about $1.5 million in 2009.

Edith and Woodbury (1894)

By early 1894, Edith, about 28, and Woodbury Langdon, about 58, have gotten married. Ellen gets a letter from her Aunt Elizabeth Langdon Porter, age 80, written on April 4th, 1894 about the marriage.

> "My dear Niece
> I am much interested in the marriage of your daughter Edith. Woodbury is the son of my dearly loved brother, whose death almost broke my heart.
> From all I have heard of Mrs. Langdon I feel sure that she is as good as her mother was when I knew her..."

W.W. Pugh writes Ellen again on May 13th 1894.

> "Dear cousin Ellen
> I am in receipt of two of your kind letters, and I will answer each in its turn --
> I congratulate both you and Edith on her marriage, and wish her many years of happiness."

It sounds as if Ellen has considered moving in with Alice or, more likely, Edith and Woodbury, although nothing has been decided:

> "...I note that you speak of your movements in the future as being somewhat unsettled. Do you not think that after being the head of a house for so many years that you will miss the cares and responsibilities attending it, and feel out of place even in a daughter's home, the habits, and thoughts of years (though often wearisome) will maintain their hold on us despite of our wishes to the contrary."

Based on W.W. Pugh's letter, Ellen has asked him about interest payments he owes her.

> "I note what you say as to business, and again with you as to future arrangements. At this time it is difficult to foresee what may be in store for us, but so far as present aspects are concerned I fancy I will be able to meet your wishes without any serious inconvenience. When this crop is made.
> ...At present our crops of plant and stubble are about a good as they ever get to be, and to date our prospects for a crop of sugar are flattering."

In the spring of 1894, Fanny travels to Europe. She writes Ellen on May 18th 1894, from Granada, and says she has previously written from Seville. Fanny goes to the Alhambra (built in the 1300's), which she enjoys greatly.

> "Now we are at Granada under the walls of the Alhambra where we go every day... I do not attempt to describe the Alhambra because no word or brush can do justice to it, or give much idea of its exquisite beauty."

Fanny says they will leave on the 21st for Madrid, and she wonders how Ellen is doing. She assumes Ellen is with Alice, and mentions Dr. Buell (Dr. Buell is one of the doctors involved with Grace):

"I suppose you are in Buffalo, I wonder if you saw Dr. Buell and if he would give you any encouragement, probably not."

Fanny offers a succinct summary of the Spaniards:

"The Spaniards are never without cigarettes, they light them in the cars with ladies, driving and at the table d'hote. The women are pretty when young but have no intelligence in their faces and have nothing to fall back upon when older to supply the place of youth; they are all covered with powder and use toothpicks freely."

Ellen gets a letter from Dr. Buell, written from Litchfield, CT. on May 29th 1894, so Ellen may have moved Grace to another institution.

"May 29, 1894

My dear Mrs. Pugh

In the letter of Miss Pugh's which you enclosed for me to read she exaggerates the treatment of her exceedingly and I presume it was written when she was still excited from the disturbance of feeding. She is not thrown about on the floor or abused by the doctor and nurses although that night it was necessary to hold her arms and head in order to feed her. The whole disturbance grew from the fact that Dr. Bolton would not obey her...

The winter coat that she has she wishes washed in soap suds, fur silk and all. Then dried and ironed but I am not willing to do this without direct instructions from you...

Miss Pugh objected to all form of wire screen for the windows so we have compromised by having the windows opened wider at both top and bottom. I am sure she cannot crawl through the lower opening and do not believe she can climb over the top without making enough disturbance to attract attention. The nurse does not stay in the room constantly for this disturbs Miss Pugh exceedingly..."

On June 3rd 1894, James Carter writes Ellen. She has written him the news that Edith and Woodbury are getting married.

"My dear Ellen,

Your letter reached me and I was indeed surprised to learn of the engagement - a surprise however occasioned wholly by the difference in ages.

I quite agree with you that this is a matter which only concerns the parties themselves.

The great point is whether they have the affection and respect for each other which will make them happy together. That Mr. Langdon will be a good and fond husband I have no doubt, and these qualities will make Edith attached to him. I can easily understand that it must have been hard for you to give your assent; but I suppose it was your duty to give it if you thought it would promote Edith's happiness.

My dear Ellen I reciprocate most cordially the constant friendship which breathes in your kind note. I am growing old and less active in making friends than I once was; but I am glad to perceive that you feel that my sentiments are unchanged, and my interest in everything which affects your happiness is the same as of old.
Ever truly yours
James C. Carter"

Also on June 3rd 1894, Fanny writes again from abroad.
"Dear Nell
This will be my last letter from Spain, tomorrow we expect to go to Biarritz, Pace, Milan, Genoa.
We are stopping here over Sunday for rest and a quiet day. It is lovely here, a summer's day, the first for two weeks. San Sebastian is a watering place on the Bay of Biscay, high hills all around and thickly wooded, a rare feature in Spain, where there are so few trees. Miss Kobbe suggests that all the trees have been chopped into toothpicks to supply the inhabitants, for you can see one in the mouth of every man and woman."

Fanny says tickets to a box seat at a bull fight were presented to her co-travelers, so the group felt obliged to attend. Upon their return, Fanny says,
"You never saw so depressed a party-they said it was a most brutal, disgusting sight without one redeeming feature. Mrs. W.-says she can never forgive herself for going-she kept her fans before her eyes all the time but could not help seeing a little and hearing all. Eliza was deadly pale and crying and Daisy trembling with anger and excitement."
After stopping at Toledo and Avila, they came to Burgos, home of a spectacular Gothic cathedral begun in 1221:
"We arrived at Burgos at midnight and devoted the next day entirely to the Cathedral -you can't imagine anything more grand and beautiful, it is a poem carved in stone, interior and exterior seem equally fine."
Fanny expects to continue to Pace, Biarritz and Monaco.

Woodbury Langdon writes Ellen June 12th 1894. Woodbury, Ellen's cousin, was born in 1836 and thus was about four years younger than Ellen and 2 years older than Fanny.
"My dear Ellen I have been intending to write you every day for a week but have had so much to attend to I have positively had no time. I returned to New York last night after taking Edith to Portsmouth.
I believe Helen has condescended to go to Europe with us on the America that sails on July 3.

Edith drove out to see her Aunt Sofia and seemed to have enjoyed her call. We went out to the home Sunday and they will all go to stay a week or so Thursday of this week, it is delightful there now. I hope you are feeling better and not suffering from the heat.
With love to Alice
Your affectionate son
Woodbury"

John Pugh receives a letter from Dr. Buell dated June 18th 1894 about Grace, describing her behavior.

"Probably you have heard numerous complaints of late as the rooms have been cleaned and a change in attendants has been made. The result is about what I expected. The new nurse is no more acceptable than the others have been although I see no point in which her work on the care of Miss Pugh is neglected.
… she requested to be tied to the chair, I presume in order to have some grounds for complaining of ill-treatment…"

On July 5th Dr. Buell writes John Pugh again and says Grace escaped for a short time.

"…(she) opened the window at night and was gone some six hours before we found her again. She must have used a shoehorn to remove the screws with during the day when the nurse was out of the room and then having these loose it was not difficult with her nurse at the farthest end of the room having the high head of the bedstead and a folding door between them, to get up upon the sofa and go out."

Apparently John asked for additional details, because Buell writes again on July 7th:

"Miss Pugh got out of the window at some unknown hour and her escape was not discovered until 5:45 a.m. She was found near Watertown 10 miles south of here in the neighborhood of the railroad station.
The weather was warm and clear but there was a light shower about 6 a.m. lasting perhaps half an hour. She was found at eight o'clock and was walking quietly. The first trace we found was 5 miles from the house. A man met her on the road as he was coming to Litchfield about half past five and noticing that her actions were strange made enquiry as to whether we were looking for such a person. She objected to returning but made no resistance.
The only precautions that can be taken under the circumstances I suppose is to have the nurses bed near the front of the room as it is now and to secure the windows more thoroughly."

On July 18th, Dr. Buell writes John Pugh, showing his frustration in dealing with Grace.

"…For several days past she has several bundles tied up to send away and is very much provoked because I will not consent to their being forwarded until I receive personal directions about them from either yourself or Mrs. Pugh. This seems the only way to do considering my past experience in the matter.

She also tells me that Mrs. Pugh has written to her that if it is annoying and unpleasant to go out of doors in her chair she does not desire this so I wish you would state just what either you or Mrs. Pugh wish on this point and who I am to be covered by in my actions.

If I am to understand one thing and Miss Pugh is given a different idea it only makes confusion and a cause for argument which is in Miss Pugh's mental state is certainly injurious.

If her life here is to consist in living in her room and being fed three times a day I shall not expect to see much improvement and if, when we require any reasonable and just action on her part, we are not to look for consent until after she has corresponded and received the approval of Mrs. Pugh or yourself, it would be better to have her where you could use more direct supervision.

Miss Pugh's complaints about her attendant are both unjust and exaggerated, not to use a stronger term, so having made three changes and each time with the same amount of dissatisfaction on Miss Pugh's part I do not feel called up to experiment further. If the attendant ill treats or abuses Miss Pugh or does not treat her in a simple and proper manner I shall discharge her at once but until this happens I can see no gain in going over in the same ground a fourth time."

On July 20th 1894, Woodbury writes Ellen, who is in Buffalo with Alice. Woodbury and Edith are probably in Narragansett, R.I.

"My dear Ellen
I was glad to hear from you that Alice is so comfortable.
The sea air I think agrees with Edith…her appetite is good and seems contented and happy by the sea where she has everything to make her comfortable.
Her brother John was in early this morning and we saw John at noon as well but complaining of the intense heat particularly… I expect Eustis and Helen on for a week also the horses and carriages as the drives are lovely at Narragansett.
With love to Alice
Your affectionate son
Woodbury"

Ellen gets a letter from Fanny, from St. Moritz, Switzerland dated August 2nd, 1894. She has heard of the birth of Alice's fifth and last child, a girl, Frances Haven Stone (born June 30th)[83].

---

[83] Alice and Ralph's children: Ralph Townsend Stone b. 3/13/1886, John Haven Pugh Stone (aka Jack), b. 3/5/1889, Woodbury Langdon Stone b. 11/8/1890, d. 1893, Lawrence Pugh

---

"Engadin
August 2
Dear Nell

It is more than two weeks, I think, since I wrote to you from Cortina, just after mailing a letter I received yours, telling of the birth of Alice's baby.

It was such a comfort to know that she was safely through her confinement. I felt a little anxious as she had not been strong. I was so glad too that the long wished for daughter had at last arrived and of course am much gratified that she should have my name; it is very kind in both Alice and Ralph...

...what an unspeakable comfort that you are with Alice at this time and can take care of the boys and relieve her of anxiety! It must have made all the difference in the world for her recovery. I wrote to her as soon as I heard of the birth of the little girl."

Fanny comments on Edith's canceled trip to Europe: the implication is that Edith is pregnant.

"I am very sorry indeed that Edith had to give up her trip abroad and even more sorry for what I presume is the reason for the change of plan."

Fanny addresses the problem of Grace's placement and behavior, and acknowledges that she doesn't have all the facts:

"As to poor dear Grace her condition is pitiable beyond all words and almost past bearing for us all. What can be done? Nothing, so far as I can judge.

She must be kept somewhere and I daresay all private places are alike, more or less, at the same time it seems to me absolutely inexcusable that twice she should have been able to wander away and not missed, nor traced until she had wandered ten miles. I can scarcely believe it; my impulse would have been to remove her at once from Dr. Buell's asylum but I probably should have regretted it as soon as done.

I think it would be very injudicious for John to assume the care of her and I hope he will not carry out any such scheme. We all know what the result would be and if her wretched life must be endured, there is no reason why there should be another victim.

It is very dreadful that she should have such a brute of an attendant but I am not sure that Dr. Buell is altogether to blame, as we know that no woman can, or will, long or patiently endure Graces caprice's etc.

As I am so far away and do not know all particulars, it seems foolish and injudicious to offer any advice; as I feel, here and now, I should take her back to Bloomingdale. Of course you and John have to weigh everything, I am glad that he can come to you in August to talk it over."

Fanny counsels Ellen against spending a winter in Buffalo, and points out that she may be needed closer to home.

Stone b. 9/25/1892, Frances Haven Stone b. 6/30/1894.

"I hope you are planning not to be in Buffalo next winter; it is too cold, altogether for you. I imagine that Edith will insist upon your being with her, which I should think, would be an excellent plan." Fanny says she has enjoyed the travel through the mountain passes, and says that when she leaves the Alps, she may go to Paris or Vienna. She closes with a vignette,

"We saw the Crown Princess of Austria, Rudolph's widow, taking lunch at a hotel where we stopped."

On August 9th, 1894, Dr. Buell writes John Pugh more of the same: Grace is extremely difficult to work with, resists all efforts to help and misconstrues everything that is done on her behalf.

Fanny writes Ellen from Germany on September 24th, 1894. She has been to Munich, and has heard a Wagnerian opera. Now, she is in Dresden, having come by herself. She mentions a shared experience that prompted her to visit the Gallery:

"Then, finding Dresden was so near, I could not resist coming for the famous Gallery and especially to see the Sistine Madonna[84] which I have longed for ever since you and I bought our engravings from it, in Boston, years and years ago, you Pope Sixtus, and I the angels. I "screwed up" my courage and took the journey and came alone to a city where I did not know a soul and where I could not speak the language. I arrived at 10 o'clock at night, but was met by the "commissionaire" from the hotel and had no trouble whatsoever. Early the next morning I was in the Gallery and seated before that wonderful Mother and Child of which no words can give any idea. It is an immense Gallery with many lovely pictures but the Madonna is the gem of the collection."

Fanny suggests that Ellen may wind up moving Grace back to Bloomingdale.

Fanny writes Ellen again on October 7th, 1894, from Vienna. She has not received a letter from Ellen and is worried: she guesses Ellen has been busy at Fort Washington. Fanny plans to go to Paris in about a week, then to London, and she expects to sail for home by Thanksgiving.

On December 2nd 1894, Ellen writes Edith from New Orleans, where Ellen is visiting before going up the Bayou to stay with David's sisters, Lizzie Ratliff, Fanny Beattie and Mary Flower. Ellen is also looking for a nurse for Edith's baby.

"My idea was to return on the 15th of January and go to you unless you all deem it best for me to stay around here.
Let me hear all about your Aunt Fanny's arrival etc."

---

[84] Raphael's Sistine Madonna, an altar-piece painted in 1512, that is in the Royal Gallery at Dresden.

On December 4th, Ellen writes Edith to thank her for a birthday telegram. Ellen has turned 62. The letter is full of news about old friends and relations.

> "This morning as I was finishing dressing for breakfast I received yours and Woodbury's telegram which was a most pleasant remembrance and greeting so I went down stairs with a smiling face –
>
> ...Your letter and one from John and one from Aunt Fanny all written to get to me on my birthday were received on that day and were a great pleasure to me.
>
> ...Yesterday I put on my best dress and went out to make some calls. My dress looked very pretty everybody thought, my boa with it. As all were presents from you and as I told everybody this, you were quite the belle of the day. I thought of you darling, and wished you were alongside of me...
>
> ...I wrote to your Aunt Lizzie to send for me and after visiting her I shall go to Fanny Beattie for a few days, see the servants, Aunt Mary, Mrs Allen, Dr. Dansereau and shall visit the cemetery and Mrs Thilson-
>
> Then back here until the 15th when I shall start for you –"

Edith has asked Ellen to buy some hams for their former servants:

> "I shall attend to the hams for you for Harriet and Ellen –"

Ellen ends her long letter with a loving reference to her father.

> "I know I shall enjoy the package of candy dear – especially as I saved the box of Sherry's you put up for me for lunch at the expense of much self denial, too. Give my love to Woodbury and tell him I was pleased at the telegram –
>
> Father, my father, never forgot to drink my health on my birthday and it used to please me so much –
>
> With very much love dear, yours as ever
> Mother"

There are two partially burned fragments of letters from Edith to Ellen written before Christmas 1894. One of them speaks of some slight or offense committed by Fanny. The fragment below refers to Fanny's return from her trip to Europe, and therefore is written in early December.

> "...Have just heard of Aunt Fanny's safe arrival Wednesday afternoon -- John, Eustis, Uncle John all went to meet her -- I sent her a note asking her again to stay with me not that I care much as she never even answered the invitation I gave her in my letter to her in Paris.
>
> I can't forgive her the way she acted last winter to you and me.
> I don't think Woodbury will ever forgive her, at least I think it has made him take a dislike to her from what he saw himself though I have never mentioned the subject to him..."

Edith writes Ellen to tell her about the Christmas gifts she has gotten for all the family, including gifts she has gotten on Ellen's behalf.

"Ralphie I wrote you I had a suit shirt and cravat for -- Lawrence a cloak and I have for Jack a dear little blue suit braided. Ralph Stone Harper's monthly -- Thomas a lovely silver mounted umbrella from Goram's, Aunt Fanny I have a silver backhand letter blotter and a pen holder to match -- both very handsome. Uncle John a small hat brush, silver mounted "

On December 23rd, Ellen writes Edith a long letter from New Orleans after returning from visits to the Bayou. This letter may have been returned to Ellen by Woodbury. She has seen many relatives, and has visited with the family servants with whom she was particularly close, old Ellen and Harriet.

"Dearest Edith,
Here I am back in New Orleans after a delightful visit on Lafourche, a week or nine days most pleasantly spent with your Aunt Lizzie where I saw the Foleys, cousin William, Annie Pugh, Annie Flower Pugh, Robert Martin, Bee Pugh twice, and visited the church, went to Eliza Lofton's grave, took drives, eat plenty of nice cane and Cuite[85] and in fact received and returned calls. I was most pleasantly entertained by your aunt and Mr. Ratliff and warmly received by everybody.
I had a sort of ovation up and down the bayou...drove up past my old place, past Leighton....
Ellen spent the morning with me, she is well and heard it was you and she dressed herself up to see your husband -- she wore no handkerchief, her hair was combed in a knot behind and the braids in front were kept down by a band of black ribbon passing round her for head, the ribbon 1 inch wide. Mast. Thomas gave her this, Miss Fanny her jacket --
A fine handkerchief bordered with white lace Miss Alice gave her and she only wears this when she visits white folks.
Her underskirt or petticoat was bordered with a flounce which was once on a white silk party dress of Miss Edith's. Her dress was given her by Miss Edith and the scarf of lace round her neck by Mast. John.
You see what Woodbury lost --
She brought six huge sweet potatoes for you which she had raised herself, two broiling chickens, and woolen gloves made by herself. I presented her with your ham and a pretty dress from you, a handkerchief and white apron from Alice, and a dress from me. She was much pleased and promised to come the next day.
Harriet, Henrietta, Ellen and Alexander all came the next day. Harriet told me to thank you much for your present and I gave her a dollar for Alice, a dress from Eliza and one from myself -- also a dollar to pay her expenses for coming to see me -- I had them all

---

[85] Cuite, or masse-cuite, is a by-product of concentrated sugar cane juice containing crystals and viscous juice.

in my room for two hours. Fanny gave Harriet a nice breakfast and I was glad to see them --
I worried all night about Harriet. She looked sick and altogether from what I learned I wanted to see her again but I missed her and left five dollars with Fanny to give her. She says she does not expect to live long -- I kissed her goodbye, my farewell kiss. Wednesday morning Fanny sent me to Mary's -- there I found Mrs. Williams just up from New Orleans...
...Just before dark Gussie came upstairs with an express package just delivered, to her surprise, at this house. It was to me and from New York and proved to be the most beautiful alligator bag I ever saw -- I took it right down to show to all.... We all examined and admired it to our heart's content -- it is so nice, so handsome and just what I most need -- it was lovely in Woodbury to send it. I must send him a line and I have several notes to write tonight -- I shall not get to bed until most daylight --
A Merry Christmas to you and Woodbury darling and my dearest love to you both –
Mother

Alice writes her mother on Christmas day 1894 to thank her for her gifts. She says Edith has been extremely generous with her gifts to Alice, Ralph and the children. Ellen writes from Napoleonville, La. to Edith at 18 w. 56th St., on December 28th. Her letter talks about Christmas presents, Carrie Hopkins' coming wedding, her efforts to find Edith a servant, clothes, and visits on the Bayou. She is enjoying seeing David's family and her friends:

"All of them are very nice to me and I feel at home and enjoy myself with them and don't want or care for outside people. We are going to St. Rock and the cemeteries.
...I have a good deal to tell you when I get home --"

Illustration 50: Edith Eustis Pugh, who married Woodbury Langdon.

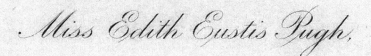

Illustration 51: Edith's calling cards, before and after marriage.

Losing Edith, Enduring Grace (1895-1898)

On January 1st 1895, Ellen writes Edith a short note from New Orleans. Across the side of this letter is written, in Ellen's hand, "My last letter to Edith".

On January 3rd, Fanny writes from the Hotel Albert in New York City to Ellen in New Orleans. Fanny's dear friend, Lizzie Morris, is not at all well.

> "Dear Nell
> I intended to write to you this evening and now your letter has just been handed to me.
> I returned from Philadelphia last week and intended to go on again today but Jim wrote to me not to come and Dr. L. -- would not allow anyone to be in Lizzie's room except Mary, Jim had not seen her for three days."

From Fanny's letter, it sounds as if Thomas and John may have undertaken to care for Grace:

> "John and Thomas have told me how Grace had bills everywhere and how they could not stop it in any way.
> It is astonishing to me that Delia, the waitress, is willing to stay on, of course she must know what the matter is."

Fanny's understanding is that Ellen is coming home to New York from Louisiana in order to be with Edith when the baby is born.

> "I am sorry you have to return so soon but I suppose you want to be with Edith. What time does she expect to be confined."

She mentions Carrie Hopkins' wedding, and John Haven:

> "I took dinner with John New Year's Day and shall be with him again on the eighth when Carrie is married."

The eighth of January 1895, the day of Carrie's wedding, was the day Edith Pugh Langdon died. Her baby also died, or may have been still-born.

> "Langdon - On Tuesday Morning, Jan 8, 1895, At Her Residence, No. 18 West Fifty-Sixth Street, New York City, Edith Eustis Pugh, Wife Of Woodbury Langdon and Daughter Of David B. Pugh Of Lafourche.
> Services Will Be Held At St. Thomas Church, Fifty-Third Street And Fifth Avenue, Thursday Morning, At 10 O'clock. Daily Picayune 1/9/1895"

On January 11th 1895, John Haven Pugh writes his Aunt Sally Pugh (wife of Walter Pugh) about Edith's death:

> You undoubtedly saw the notice of Edith's death in the New Orleans papers of the 9th or 10th, and I now write you the particulars in regard to this crushing loss. Edith was very well up to Christmas. Two days later she caught cold, getting chilled while out shopping on a very cold day. This cold caused her to cough

violently at frequent intervals, and this coughing strained the stomach so much that it became too irritable to bear food. At first she could retain Chicken Jelly, then it had to be Koumiss[86], and for three or four days before the 8th she could retain nothing whatever. This lack of nutrition produced extreme weakness, and this weakness was the immediate cause of death. Her baby was buried in its mother's arms. This is a very dreadful blow to Mother and to Mr. Langdon. Mother feels it all the more because she arrived from New Orleans too late – just as happened at the time we lost Mary in <u>1880</u>. No one was to blame, for we notified mother as soon as we ourselves suspected danger, and the end came like a thunderclap to us. Edith was buried at Woodlawn. The services were held at St. Thomas'. Edith passed away without the slightest pain or struggle, simply ceasing to breathe. She had everything to live for, and, while we all want to live, her case seems <u>particularly hard</u> for the husband.

Kate Haven, whom Ellen had met in New Orleans, writes Ellen on January 13th 1895 from South Carolina. Kate was a daughter of Alfred Haven, John Appleton Haven's brother.

"Dear Cousin Ellen,
I cannot tell you how deeply grieved and shocked I felt on hearing of your great loss. The thought of it abides with me constantly. To lose a dear daughter, your constant companion, and just when you had hoped to enjoy so much with her and the expected baby, it goes along very hard to think of it. And though I had known Edith so short a time, I was strongly drawn to her.
The thought that her summer home would be so near mine and that you and she would in future be near me, during part of the year, was so pleasant. At last, I thought, you would both be within reach for a good part of the time[87]. For Edith's husband I feel a great sympathy. This sudden blow, shattering all the happy life so recently entered upon is dreadful indeed. Please give him my kindest remembrance and assurance of my most heartfelt sympathy. And when you can do so I shall be so gratified if you will write me particulars of Edith's departure. I trust you were in time to be with her?
After writing of other things, Kate Speaks of Grace:
"I think often of your Grace. Sad indeed that she cannot make herself contented after all you have done to make her comfortable and happy. It is doubtless the effect of physical cause that she feels as she does, but it is nonetheless sad and trying. You must be greatly perplexed -- as to which it is possible to do for her."

---

[86] A fermented milk drink, thought to be a cure-all.
[87] Kate Haven may have spent part of the year in Portsmouth, N.H., and with Edith and Woodbury having a second home at Fox Point, near Portsmouth N.H., Kate could have seen them often.

On January 16th, Alice writes Ellen. Grace is acting out again, and Alice says,

> "It is dreadful about Grace and I think you had better come up here if she is to annoy you in any way. Otherwise go to Nellie Treadwell's for a couple of days and say you have left town."

Both Kate's letter and Alice's refer to a pearl cross of Edith's that Ellen would like to keep, but Grace insists she wants it. Both Kate and Alice feel that Ellen should not be deprived of the cross.

> "How you must dread it all. I am sorry she has set her heart on Edith's pearl cross, that I would not give her.
> ... Write Grace you wish to [keep] your dear child's cross yourself."

On January 29th, 1895, Ellen's good friend Eliza Williams writes Ellen from New Orleans.

> "We so often think and speak of you. I don't see how you can ever be reconciled to Edith's loss. Cousin Ellen, others have had the same trouble but yours seems harder to bear, to think you are deprived at the closing years of your life of the one daughter who could and did make your life happy. Alice is away from you and Grace an invalid, I think you have had more trouble and sorrow than anyone I know and I cannot keep you out of my thoughts. I have wondered if Edith's death did not awaken Grace and make her take some more interest in others?
> I am so glad you write to me about Edith - I wanted so much to know about her sickness and about her little baby. I had such a pleasant dream about Edith the other night. I could see her so plainly. I thought she was here, standing in the tower with all the windows open and a bright light about her. Aunt Harriet[88] and I were in the yard, she had her apron full of corn and I was standing by a crock full and running my hand through the shelled corn, and said to her, Aunt Harriet, I will help you shell it, but it is more than we want for dinner- someone came up and asked for Edith. I told them they would have to go way up in the tower and I looked up and waved my hand to her and she smiled back. I never had a more vivid dream."

While still buried in grief about Edith, Ellen gets more heartache from Grace. On February 14th 1895, Helen Haven (another cousin of Ellen's) writes her aunt Matilda and mentions that she has seen a newspaper article about Grace Pugh (it is not clear how this letter came to Ellen: perhaps Matilda sent it on).

> "This morning came the paper with a piece about Grace Pugh. It was most pathetic to read about and magnificent as well. I have to think very hard about her having had a home she could have gone to if she had chosen and even then it seems too bad that she could not have been directed to W. 56th St. Nobody could mind being

---

[88] The Williams' had a place next to David and Ellen's Energy; Aunt Harriet was a cherished servant of the Pughs.

299

mentioned in the paper in connection with a person who could behave in such trying circumstances with such wonderful dignity. I was not surprised, and my surprise has been great that things have gone on so smoothly as long as they have done. Something was sure to happen but it was hard to imagine what.

I wonder what cousin Ellen will do about her now. Please give my love to her and tell her I shall write to her very soon. She is not allowed very much peace in this world."

On March 2nd 1895, Ellen gets a letter from Dr. Lyon's office of the Bloomingdale Asylum: she has moved Grace back to Bloomingdale.

"In reply to your question concerning the visiting day, I am willing that you should come up Tuesday or Thursday, this I think once a fortnight, as often as Miss Pugh could be visited with benefit.

Our wagon meets the 1:50 train, and also takes passengers down to the 4:30 p.m. train.

On account of the fact that Miss Pugh has now commenced eating, is less depressed and is anxious to see you, I think it well for you to come up next Thursday."

On March 4th, 1895, Ellen gets a letter from Eliza Appleton Haven, most likely about Edith.

"It makes me feel very lonely, not to have received a note, nor a message, from any of the family, since your great and sudden sorrow came to you. I do not even know where you have been staying, since you returned from the South. I wrote you a short note, which is addressed, as I shall this one, to the care of your brother, John; as I presume he knows your whereabouts."

By June 1895, Ellen has moved to a flat at 102 W. 93rd St. She gets a letter from Dr. Lyons at Bloomingdale dated June 20th about Grace, who is proving difficult to manage as usual. On June 24th he writes again and describes Grace's inappropriate behavior.

"You have had so many years experience with your daughter that you should not forget how difficult it is to arrive at any understanding or compromise with her, and how her morbid state of mind warps her feelings and statements.

...We had a patient about to die, whose friends desired to be with her...Your daughter's door was closed, and ordinary kindness and humanity would have dictated a quiet and sympathetic attitude on her part, but on the contrary she became violent and denunciatory and it was necessary to remove her.

I feel that she would do better if she did not see you so often and feel that she could constantly appeal to you against our management. She has false hearing and imagines that things are said about her and to her discredit which have no other foundation than her hallucinations of hearing."

There is an undated letter in Grace's hand, in pencil, written to Kathleen Pugh[89] in Louisiana, that reveals her frame of mind.

> "Day after Thanksgiving
> My dear Kathleen
> I have received your beautiful tree. The picture is excellent. I understand from Thomas that the tree was blown over by the cyclone that swept over the South from Florida up the coast. I did not know it struck New Orleans.
> I had a beautiful apple here and wanted to send some of them to Mrs. Williams but I have no money and cannot even express you things that cost very little.
> The apples come from Levi P. Morton's farm near here on the Hudson River at Dovers Plains.
> I have tried to get John and asked him for my property. I have money and plenty of property and can get no answer. All my life I have to stay here and be robbed by my mother and my sisters and brothers.
> I wish it was possible for you all to come and rescue me. As that is not so I find it difficult to get along. I do not know today where to put your picture here it can be stolen. I have not the key of the door. I send for Thomas and he told his sister a lie. Go hang the picture up with the others on the wall you noticed here. That was to give them the picture to steal. He was a rascal Thomas and had other pictures at home and those were going to be stolen by him. I wish it was possible for me to leave here and to return home and see you all.
> I believe my mother is not good. That she means to rob me all my life and to pretend she is taking good care of me in a fashionable institution. I am not dressed or supported and the property can never be put here. I beg you all not to think unkindly of
> Cousin Grace
> because I cannot return you a present or make anything honorable"

On July 11th 1895 Lyons writes describing more trouble with Grace.

> "...saying no one had a right to detain her, that Dr. Dold is not a proper person to treat her, and that her objection to me is that my hair is not gray.
> I told her of course that I was directed by a judge to keep her and must and would, until her responsible friends relieved me of the charge...She is an unhappy woman who misconstrues everything and seems to seek for causes of discomfort where they do not exist.
> ...I hope you will realize that both Dr. Dold and I are full of sympathy for both you and Miss Pugh and will do all we can to make her life more endurable."

---

[89] Eliza Katherine "Kathleen" Pugh was the youngest child of Dick (Richard Lloyd) Pugh and Mary Louise Williams Pugh. Kathleen was born at Leighton Plantation on June 27, 1880.

Things are no better by fall: October 5th, Dr. Lyons writes from Bloomingdale,

> "...I regret to say that your daughter, Miss Grace D. H. Pugh, will not open the trunk sent to her by you, and has concealed the key. We are therefore unable to take out the articles. It may be, that she has returned the key to you, in which case, if you will send it to me, I will have the trunk unpacked.
> I supplied Miss Pugh with a portable bath tub some time ago, a very nice one, but she would not use it.
> I have had blankets taken to her, but she has persistently refused to accept them.
> I wish I could send you better news."

Ellen writes Grace on November 20th:

> "Dear Grace,
> If that blanket is dirty I will have it cleaned for you. It was on my bed only.
> Those things to eat I took you were wrapped separately and were put on the <u>bottom</u> of the valise. The blanket went under the <u>cover</u>. I shall always go to see you wherever you are and will take my chances of being knocked down and robbed. I shall never stop going to see you. I want to send some oranges. You do not like me to send by Park and Tilford, shall I do so now? Let me know at once.
> I do not lie or deceive you - I tell you the straight truth.
> It is the 20th of November today and this is Wednesday.
> With love
> Mother
> I received two letters from you Monday in one envelope and two yesterday. This morning another has come –"

On May 4th, 1896 Dr. Lyons writes Ellen,

> "I am anxious as I have ever been, of gratifying any desire of Miss Pugh's, and assure you that I will make every effort to do so; but her sickness so dominates her, that even when she is supplied with articles for which she has asked, she at times denies that they have reached her. This I saw illustrated yesterday, and have noticed often before.
> I don't think it a possible thing to satisfy her; but, so far as it is possible, I will try to grant her requests.
> As for the bruises upon Miss Pugh's body, I may say that she was so violent recently, that it was absolutely necessary to remove her for a time to another hall; and I don't see how it would have been possible to prevent the struggle that took place then, during which Miss Pugh received the bruises.
> I am glad to say that at the present time, she seems to be feeling quite cheerful."

On May 9th 1896 Ellen receives a letter from W.W. Pugh, who talks about political news in Louisiana, and then tells Ellen about a fire at Madewood. Madewood had been inherited from Robert Pugh by another Pugh, Lewellyn Pugh, who was the son of David's brother Walter Pugh.

> "Llewellyn has had another fire at Madewood (the fourth) since his accession as owner of the property. This time it was the sugarhouse, and its costly machinery. He was insured to the extent of 75,000. dolls., a sum considerably short of the value of the property.
>
> It was set on fire about three o'clock on a Sunday night, a door was broken open, and coal oil spread on the floor. The fire raged within the walls sometime before any discovery was made, when it was too late to do anything to extinguish it. The cane/cow shed was saved. I learned that he intends to rebuild as is but not to the extent of the burnt building. He will make sugar in a train and not refine as he did before this fire.
>
> Three Negroes have been arrested, but I doubt if there be any evidence against them. It is more than probable that a Negro was the active agent in this nefarious burning, but it is not in accordance with our knowledge of Negro nation to suppose that he would commit so much crime for revenge. That is not their nature, for in the antebellum days when they often had much to excite feelings of revenge they very rarely resorted to such tactics to get even with those who abused or maltreated them.
>
> I trust this scamp may be detected, and punished for his crime otherwise the effort to find the incendiary having failed someone also might be tempted to try this on some other plantation.[90]"

Fanny writes Grace on August 30th, 1896, from Northeast Harbor, Maine. Fanny's letter paints a picture in words, for Grace.

> "My dear Grace
> I thank you for your long and very interesting letter. You say you did not realize that I was ever in Spain. I assure you that I was and can never forget what I saw, the scenery was very grand and very wild, it was in May and the fields were aflame with red poppies, acres of them, swaying in the wind, like a surging red

---

[90] Over the years there were some suspicious fires on Madewood but the worst occurred the night of April 19, 1896, when the sugar house was set on fire just before the cane harvest. Llewellyn, deeply upset and discouraged by the fire, quickly sold the plantation for $30,000 to Leon Godchaux and relocated his family to New Orleans. The Madewood fires were steeped in mystery for decades: some thought that Lizzie Pugh Ratliff and her husband were behind it (they had contested Robert Pugh's will, which left Madewood to Llewellyn, and they had been forced to leave Madewood, so the thinking was that they'd set the fire in hopes that Llewellyn would sell Madewood to them). Others, as exemplified by W.W. Pugh's letter, thought it might have been local malcontents. Over the years, Pugh relatives learned that it may have been Alice Pugh McCormick's son Jimmy who set the fire. Jimmy had been present during the will contest, and years later was incarcerated after being convicted of arson in another state.

wave. There are very few trees in Spain, no pasture, no cows, no milk, no butter, goat's milk only, which is bitter and horrid. Occasionally a grove of cork trees, only before we reached Seville, for miles the air was perfumed with lemon blossoms. The first cathedral I ever saw was the magnificent one there and the first picture gallery, with gems of Murillos. That exquisite one of the Virgin, with the floating blue mantle, the Virgin in the clouds with a sweet girlish face, and attendant angels and cherubs. Then there is a wonderful old Moorish garden, with fountains, terraces, lemon and orange trees, roses, roses everywhere -- there is a magic pavement pierced with the smallest, invisible holes and by a pressure of the foot, water spurts out and sprinkles the air in every direction.

We went into Spain from Gibraltar -- a steamer took us across the bay to a little town called Algeciras -- then four hours by rail to Ronda, one of the oldest towns in Spain and oh, so clear and quaint and beautiful, such wonderful carvings on the doors of the churches, ruins of castles perched up on cliffs, watchtowers so lovely and grim and the inn where we stopped for the night was so simple and old-fashioned. All houses in Spain have an inner court called a "patio", more or less simple, or vast and beautiful. At the Hotel in Seville, the "patio" was a lovely garden with two splashing fountains and tiled walks around it -- circular they all are and the rooms open off of them and it is all open up to the roof, over which is a canvas when it rains.

The houses are almost bare, they are so scantily furnished. In Seville the side streets were narrow and awnings of bright colors were stretched across to protect from the sun. But there are numerous open squares and gardens and a fine park outside the city. It is a lovely city, gay and charming and hot.

Madrid is very different. It is large and modern and has no historic charm. The chief attraction there is the splendid picture gallery, one of the most famous in the world.

One hall, called the "Salon d Isabelle" is full of masterpieces, Murillo, Velaquay, Goya, Van Dyke, Rafael, Rubens -- all their masters are represented by their choicest works.

The next time I write I will tell you about Toledo, Burgos, and St. Sebastian.

Your affectionate
Aunt Fanny

On November 12th, 1896, Dr. Lyons replies to a question Ellen has asked about Grace's paranoia:

"In reply to your question about paranoia, I beg to say that it is a chronic disease of the brain and the chances of recovery are almost nil."

Grace sends Ellen a note. The first paragraph is followed by a lengthy list of all of Graces possessions and it is followed by another paragraph.

> "Mother. I have received this package of papers and I have exhausted the package of letter paper that I found opened. This is not legal. I have no place to keep or to put away anything of value. I notice you can dismiss some woman who annoys you. I have the same legal privilege. I want you all, here. I refuse this room. I do not want their towels beddings or spoons, neither you nor they can give me a servant. I want everything to go. I want the account closed. I want the empty trunk and key. I do not agree with you. I think this is a bad place. I consider these three men completely dishonest.
>
> …"I give you this list but I do not give them my handwriting. Is it reasonable to ask me to take care of these things. On the other hand I would not receive anything from servants. You have one dress now at home. They have torn up one."

In January 1897, Ellen corresponds with two of her brothers-in-law: W.B. Ratliff, Lizzie Pugh's husband, and Taylor Beattie, the attorney whom Fanny Pugh married, who is now a judge.

Ratliff offers to do Ellen a kindness in light of the difficulty she has had in getting timely payment on a note from Lawrence Pugh. Ratliff, who is about 70 years old, offers to take the note off Ellen's hands; in fact he effects this by mid-March of 1897.

Ellen is in touch with Beattie because she wants help protecting money that Grace has coming to her from an inheritance (Ellen had also asked Carter's advice about this). Ellen wants to avoid having to go to court where she would have to expose Grace as being mentally incompetent, yet she wants Grace's inheritance protected. Beattie counsels that this is a delicate situation, because intentions can easily be misconstrued, but he urges her to write the local judge.

On November 30th 1897, Dr. Lyons writes Ellen about Grace:

> "…you probably realize that no room will suit her long, because her delusions are part of herself, and she will attach ideas of contamination to any room or any article of furniture with which she comes into contact for any length of time.
>
> I have known Miss Pugh a very long time, as you know, and it is a satisfaction to me, and I think it ought to be to you under the circumstances, and in view of her former desperate determinations, that she is as well physically, and as little distressed mentally as she now is.
>
> There have been times when her mental pain and physical condition have been exceedingly trying, at the present time, I don't think that she really suffers. She is sustained by her pride; and her delusions are of such a general character, that they do not involve much personal suffering."

On February 12 1898, James Carter replies to a letter of Ellen's in which she has asked him a legal question to do with Grace. He ends his letter with,

> "My dear Ellen, although I have not seen you for so long a time, you are first and often in my memory and I wish I could often see you but it becomes harder and harder for me as I grow old to make visits; but I keep thinking that I must go and see you and some time shall.
>
> Be sure that I think of you always as an old, a constant, and a dear friend with whom I have the most affectionate ties which cannot, while I live be broken - Ever affectionately yours James C. Carter"

Friends and Relatives (1898-1906)

By March of 1898, Ellen's Portsmouth cousins, Eliza Appleton Haven and Charlotte Maria Haven, have both passed away. The Portsmouth Haven sisters bequeathed a substantial sum to charities and educational institutions, as well as land for a public park in Portsmouth and money for a library in Portsmouth. Included in their wills were: Harvard College, Dartmouth College, Smith College, the SPCA and various other charities.

In May of 1898, Ellen's youngest, Thomas Pugh (who has just turned 30), entered the army to serve in the Spanish American War. From his diary entry:

> "Wednesday, May 18, 1898
> New York City. I was examined at the 22nd Regiment Armory tonight with a view of enlisting in the 22nd during the present war between the United States and Spain. The 22nd has already been ordered out and is now at Camp Black, Long Island, drilling; there are a number of vacancies in the Regiment. I have passed the state physical examination and have been instructed to report at the Armory tomorrow night. The examination was strict and the doctor compelled us all to strip off all clothing to the skin.
> Adjutant Treadwell asked me if I was a single man, also, who I worked for and if they intended to hold my position open for me to which I replied that Mr. Dickson was not holding my place open for me, because I was not a national guardsman prior to the war and furthermore because he was not in sympathy with the war.
> Mother was much upset when I told her of my intention to enlist, but she said if I had determined to go she would not stand in the way."

The next day, Thomas' diary reports,

> "I reported at the 22nd Armory tonight and was given a second hand uniform which we each picked out of a big pile of secondhand uniforms dumped in the middle of the big room upstairs on the Boulevard side of the Armory."

On May 23rd, Ellen writes Thomas to say,

> "So you passed the last examination and are really off for the war! When you can get leave of absence come up to see me.
> I am tearing the flat to pieces today, taking down curtains and rods.
> I have made jelly for Grace too -- keeping busy keeps me from thinking but I miss you all the time."

She ends her note with,

> "Whenever you want money I will let you have it only tell me how to get it to you. What is the name of your captain? Shall I not bring you some money when I come down to see you."

May 28th, Fanny writes from Jaffrey, N.H. to Thomas in N.Y.:
"Thomas Pugh
Company K20 second Regiment
Camp Black
Hempstead LI

Jaffrey, New Hampshire
My dear Thomas
What a trump you are! I am very proud to have a soldier nephew and think it was splendid of you to enlist.
I am afraid you are a very wet soldier just now, your first experience of Camp Black life has been fearful.
...I may write now and then I do not expect any answers, I shall hear about you from your mother.
I never expected to write a letter to a soldier in our family and think it is fine.
Yours affectionately
F.A. L. Haven"

Ellen writes Thomas,
"June 12 Sunday
Dearest Child,
I saw by the paper that you all arrived overcrowded at Fort Schuyler and had no sleep all night from unpacking and mosquitoes.
I also read that Monday strict discipline would begin constant drilling and hard work behind the guns, the big guns. This work was very hard and very tiresome -- I mean with the guns. John was going over to see you today but the paper said no one would be admitted so he abandoned this plan until we could learn what form must be gone through to get a pass. Also would they admit a woman -- your mother.
Now the first thing is to be very careful not to strain yourself trying to lift those guns and rupture yourself. A hernia or rupture makes you crippled for life. I know all about them and how you have to wear a truss and never recover. I saw too many of them in the south.
Your father always warned me from letting either of you rupture yourselves.
I suppose you will have bathing but probably this is the only advantage that Fort Schuyler will have over Camp Black, but this is certainly an advantage.
...Probably John and I will leave on July 2 to pass a week (for John) with your aunt Fanny...I shall stay with your aunt and will go to Northeast Harbor, returning here September 1.

Meanwhile I want to see as much of you as possible, either going down myself or your coming to see me. As soon as you can find out will you write and tell me.

... I suppose you're going to be made a thorough soldier and in a month or two months, will be hustled to the front. I had a letter from Alice and she asked particularly about you.

I passed last Thursday night with your Uncle John. He raised his flag the morning I left on his tall flagpole. I go up there every week now since your aunt has left. John went to see Grace Saturday. She has malaria.

... I shall try to write you as often as I can.

... Remember if you do not have decent meat that you draw on me and get it -- mine is yours always.

With a kiss and ever so much love, Mother

... Write me whether you have a tent or a hammock -- if you retain the same cook, what your drilling and work is – and what is "handling the big guns".

I miss you more and more and wish you were here."

On July 4th 1898, W.W. Pugh speaks about Thomas' decision to join the army.

"I sympathize with you in what you write about Thomas. I think he takes a commendable, and correct view of the situation, and his duty as a patriot, and single man. Though all he says on the subject is true, that the feelings of the mother are natural. I have no doubt he will make a good soldier, and there is no reason to anticipate that he will meet with any trouble in his new career. Do not worry yourself by thoughts of what may happen. It is better to avoid the results, than to be unhappy about what may never take place."

Ellen writes Thomas on July 6 1898 from Jaffrey, N.H., where she has gone with Fanny. She writes of the war, and of Thomas' regiment, the 22nd, going to Manila, and she ends with,

"If you are to be moved be sure and let me know my dear son, and where you are going. Even if I do not go down I want to know. My thoughts are with you all of the time. I left the guava jelly in the cupboard for you if you go to 102.

With dearest love

Mother"

Ellen writes again July 12th after getting a letter from Thomas:

"Dearest child,

I was so glad to get your letter written Sunday and so glad to hear that you were going as you proposed to your Uncle John's. Hours after I had read the letter to your Aunt Fanny, she called out -- "it is splendid Thomas went to John's -- John will be perfectly delighted to have such a visit". So she had been thinking of it all the time.

Also we both think Grace would be delighted to see you. Aunt Fanny says she is sure she would consider it a great event and would be delighted. She says it would not excite her except in a pleasurable way and would do her good.

So if you can go someday, do so.

Grace wrote your aunt quite an amusing letter saying she considered it a good thing for you to be learning to brush your clothes since you have to wash in "a government pot and with government soap" -- of course she said much more. You can tell her about your duties, the Fort, and your drills and marches."

On July 30th 1898, Fanny and Ellen are in Northeast Harbor, Maine. Thomas is still at Ft. Schuyler, and his future is uncertain because peace is in the offing. Ellen says,

"I am so delighted you have been to see Grace. I am sure she enjoyed your visit.

...I am going to drive to Bar Harbor this afternoon having been invited by Mrs. Chalmers and we each pay our own fare, taking a buckboard.

I also have to return a call with your aunt this morning so I just send this line to let you know this place is lovely and quite cool and I am getting braced up and my eyes are better."

From Thomas' diary:

"Sunday, August 7, 1898

I stayed overnight at mother's apartment at 102 W. 93rd St., New York City. The sensation of sleeping in a bed once more was novel but not entirely restful. The flat seems so lonesome and dreary without mother."

Thomas notes in his diary for Monday, August 8th:

"Received a letter from Mother today. She is staying at Northeast Harbor, Maine, with Aunt Fanny and expects to remain there until September 1. She is stopping at the Kimball House, she says it is a first-class house. Mother says she has been out sailing several times and enjoyed it, she was not seasick."

On August 11th Ellen writes Thomas again, saying that she plans to stay at Northeast Harbor through August 30th, but will race home if Thomas is sent off with the troops:

"I am delighted myself that you will not have to fight but I had better not rejoice too soon."

From Thomas' diary for August 13th:

"Fort Schuyler

Today's New York Times announces that war is suspended and peace assured by the formal signing yesterday by M. Cambon (French ambassador) representing Spain and Secretary of State Day."

Monday August 15th 1898, Thomas writes,
"Fort Schuyler clear and pleasant.
I got the usual 24-hour pass this morning after coming off guard between 8:30 AM today and 8:30 AM tomorrow.
After arriving home and changing my clothes I went downtown to see John for a few minutes and then took the train up to White Plains to see Grace. She was in an unusually quiet humor and seemed glad to see me. She spoke sadly about John's health and said he seemed to be in wretched health. This worries me considerably as I had not noticed any change for the worse, except that he stoops a great deal now. I am afraid that his back will never be well. He is still boarding with Mrs. Williams out in Montclair. He goes in and out of New York City every day via the LL & W or the Erie RR."

August 19th Thomas writes about his mother about the effects of war.
"I was delighted to receive a letter from mother on the 17th or 18th, in which she says she expects to leave Northeast Harbor on August 30 by the Boston express for New York. This train is due at the Grand Central Station at 3:30 PM. I intend to try to get a special pass from Captain Hart on August 31 and go down and meet mother.
The wounded and sick soldiers who are now arriving in great numbers on transports from Santiago and other points in the Puerto Rico, have suffered terribly not only while in Cuba and Puerto Rico but also on the transports coming north. It is my opinion that this terrible state of affairs is principally due to the following causes, Viz: want of food suitable for sick men, lack of good doctors and nurses, exposure prior to being sent north and gross overcrowding of transports.
It seems as though that state of affairs show gross and criminal incompetency on the part of some one. A large numbers of deaths have been caused by the reasons above enumerated. Perhaps such things are absolutely unavoidable in warfare."

On August 20th 1898 Thomas writes,
"Mother is still at Northeast Harbor, Maine with Aunt Fanny at the Kimball House and I received a letter from her today (that day August 18) in which she says she was going on a little excursion. It's an adjacent island, she seems to be in good spirits."

On August 21st, Thomas writes that he and John met briefly at Ellen's flat.
"I secured a pass today from guard management until taps and went down to 102 W. 93rd St. to spend the day. John had stayed

there overnight. He came back about four o'clock from a bicycle ride with Mr. McClymonds and immediately changed his clothes and took the 4:56 New York and Hartam Haven for White Plains to see Grace. He said he was feeling in first grade health but he did not look well and I am afraid he is breaking himself down with overworking and care."

On Monday August 22nd Thomas reveals,
"Mother and John are the only ones in this world who care much about my welfare. Oh how I would like to see mother, however she will come back in nine days now."

On August 24th, he says,
"I came off guard this morning but did not use my pass and instead I intend to try and get a special pass from captain Hart on August 31 '98 so as to meet Mother when she returns home to New York."

Thomas writes on September 7th 1898,
"Having secured a pass today from 11 AM to 10:45 PM I went to the city to see Mother, she was looking well in spite of the heat although she had suffered from it very much. This is my sister Edith's birthday today and upon reaching home I found Mother just on the point of going up to Woodlawn Cemetery to Edith's grave. Mother had a piece of good news to tell me, namely, that Eustis Hopkins has been admitted to the firm of Joy Langdon and Company. Eustis is a fine man and certainly deserves the success. Eustis wrote Uncle John that he only wishes his mother was living as he would have taken more pride in having her know about it than anyone else."

On September 9th Thomas says,
"Mother expects cousin Eliza Foley to make her a visit about October 1 and Mother is looking forward to it with great pleasure. Mother has asked Alice and her daughter Fran to come down and spend a week before cousin Eliza leaves."

On September 20th, Dr. Lyons answers questions from Ellen about Grace's inheritance. Sadly, as he explains, she needs to be declared officially insane, and it is a costly process and can involve exposure in the newspapers.
"If, for business reasons, in the proper management of Miss Pugh and her estate, you decide to have a regular committee appointed, the commission, which will be appointed by some judge to investigate the case, and preside at the trial, which is before a sheriff's jury, will require sufficient evidence to convince them that she is insane, both from her family, in regard to her condition of

mind and estate, and from physicians who are familiar with her disease.

Such proceedings are very apt to get into the newspapers; but unless they have some peculiarly sensational features, there is no inducement to magnify them, and they attract very little attention, except from those personally interested.

I may say that the usual proceedings in such cases are to employ a lawyer, who obtains affidavits, as in this case, from you and your son, and from me as superintendent of the hospital, that Miss Pugh is insane, and needs a guardian. Upon these affidavits he makes a petition to the court, and one or more commissioners are appointed to investigate the case, and at their convenience, summon a jury, and have a trial.

By October 1898, Thomas is still at Ft. Schuyler. Ellen sends Thomas a brief note and encloses an article from the Post:

"Is expected that the 22nd Regiment will surely be mustered out of service, as Colonel Bartlett has made application to Washington to this end. The men, now that they realize that there is no actual fighting to be done, are anxious to get back to their regular occupations, and are practically unanimous in the wish to be discharged."

By February 1899, Grace's situation has not improved. Dr. Lyons writes Ellen,

"As you know, Miss Pugh embarrasses every effort to make her life more tolerable by certain impossible conditions; but on the whole, I think we tide her along in about as happy a frame of mind as she is capable of, suffering as she is from her disease of mind."

Because Dr. Lyons writes John Pugh directly at 102 W. 93rd St., John (age 39) was probably living with his mother Ellen. Dr. Lyons takes the time to write John a long letter in response to a letter John has sent. Lyons ends with,

"I have written you all this because I thoroughly sympathize with your mother and yourself in your distress regarding your sister; but I sometimes feel as though Miss Pugh's family unnecessarily blame themselves for not doing more for her, while in reality they have done all that is possible, and have not succeeded because it is not in the nature of things that they should, as Miss Pugh is suffering with a disease which has been long continued, and will probably endure throughout her life.

I may add, that there is the danger of diminishing rather than increasing Miss Pugh's comfort by encouraging her insane projects and keeping her to a certain extent stirred up.

She has never been since I have known her really more comfortable than she is today, but there have been times when she has been vastly less so; and I think the object should be to keep her on a fairly comfortable plane, and to avoid the chance of precipitating her into the miserable condition in which she was at the old Bloomingdale, and what she has sometimes approached here."

On May 5th 1899 Dr. Lyons explains why Grace has worn restraints.
"On inquiry I find that your daughter, Miss Pugh, was in the camisole (i.e., long sleeved waist) for 10 minutes to prevent her from bruising and injuring her arms by pounding the door. The sleeves (as we call them) were applied by order of the woman physician whom Miss Pugh struck forcibly in the face when the doctor tried to remonstrate with her. Miss Pugh said she would claim that the bruises she sustained by pounding the door were caused by rough handling, which was not the case. The camisole without the slightest injury to the patient had a salutary effect on her. She is becoming more comfortable.

In September of 1899, James Biddle Eustis died in Newport, R.I. (it was he whom Fanny ridiculed in April 1885, for his reluctance to accept the demise of the spoils system). Ellen saved the "special" to the Boston Herald about Eustis. The article mentions that at his death,
"he was engaged by a leading New York periodical to prepare an elaborate article on "Dreyfus and the Jewish question in France." He believed in the innocence of Dreyfus."
Eustis was to provide "a critical review of the Dreyfus case, in which was to be embodied much valuable material gathered during his official residence in France", where Eustis served as U.S. Ambassador.

By March of 1900, Ellen is still in her flat at 103 W. 93rd St., and John, who is now about 40, has a flat at 25 Park Place. Dr. Lyons writes them both about the legal papers that must be served on Grace as part of Ellen's effort to safeguard Grace's inheritance.

Fanny sends a note to Ellen answering Ellen's questions about places to stay in Maine, and says she is sorry Ellen came all the way down to see her and she (Fanny) was out. With Ellen at W. 93rd St. and Fanny at 27 Waverly, in Greenwich Village, it was nearly a 6 mile trip. Fanny invites Ellen to come for dinner and says she has seen John, and she had lunch with Gussie (Hopkins, Augusta's daughter) at Fort Washington the day before.

On July 4th 1901, Ellen writes Thomas from Buffalo, where she is visiting Alice. Thomas, now 33, has a flat at 45 Beaver St., N.Y.C.
"Dearest Thomas,
You cannot tell how glad I was to see your face Tuesday night and what a comfort it was to have you go with me to the cars. I had a successful trip, only I was buried in cinders and dust, John, Alice,

314

Jack and Lawrence met me at the depot and John had a carriage to take me and my trunks to the ferry.

Alice was so thoughtful as to remember that the next day was the Fourth of July and if I did not get my trunks yesterday I could not get them today. I was pretty tired out but the air all day over here has been delightful today and has rested me. John and Alice had to go to Buffalo today to settle up some business, and Ralph too, so Jack brought my empty trunks upstairs after bringing all their contents up in clothes baskets, made me iced lemonade all day, and helped me.

I have put all of my things away, and have scrubbed my hair and now I write this line to let you know I arrived safely and to tell you that you thought I looked well but it was because I was so glad to see you.

The children told me how you treated them, as Jack did, and how you gave Lawrence some money to go to the Pan American. Jack said "Uncle Thomas was fine".

I am awfully afraid you came down on purpose to see me off and I hope you did not much as I liked to have you.

With ever so much love

Mother

Alice sends love to you"

Ellen has quite a few letters from Eliza Foley Williams, from Louisiana, one of which mentions that Alice Pugh McCormick has died (November 27,1901). This leaves only Fanny Pugh Beattie and Lizzie Pugh Ratliff left of David's siblings. Ellen saved two wedding clippings from the newspaper: one is of Augusta's son Appleton's wedding at the end of 1901 (John Appleton Haven Hopkins) and the other is about the wedding of James Biddle Eustis' daughter Tina at the beginning of 1902. By 1902, John Haven Pugh is helping Ellen with her investments and accounting, including the disbursement of interest from a Haven trust. Ellen has helped Alice and Ralph financially (buying their place and renting it back to them and loaning them money). John, who is at least temporarily in Buffalo, sorts things out, deals with Ralph and helps Ellen understand and manage her investments, principal and interest.

On August 24th 1902, Eliza Foley Williams writes Ellen to say she has been to the Bayou and has been in touch with Mary Williams (Richard Pugh's widow) and Mr. and Mrs. Williams. Of "Cousin Mary" Williams, Eliza paints an interesting picture. Eliza writes about Old, or Aunt Ellen and Harriet, the two servants who worked for Ellen and David for years, whom Ellen's children grew up with, and whom the Pughs helped support over the years.

"I do not know what to tell you of Cousin Mary, they are all just as they used to be at Leighton. Cousin Mary works and works hard, but with no system and no results. They do not breakfast until 10 o'clock, then sit on the gallery until after 12, who does the housework I cannot tell, the colored boys who sweep the hall and gallery and set the table, wash the dishes and churn. I made my own bed... their home is very attractive and the yard beautiful. Mrs. Williams rooms are as nice as possible, she has a woman to come every day and clean up, they have a nice bathroom and closet...They have no garden and as far as I can tell see not much of a crop. They sell what milk they can in Thibodaux. At two o'clock they bring to everyone a glass of iced tea and a sandwich and have dinner anytime from six to seven, they seem to have no time for anything but I cannot see what they do. Edward is getting out some crossties for some planters in Thibodaux. Allen does nothing, tends to the turkeys.

As the roads were good I asked Asa to drive me down the broulee to see Aunt Ellen, Cousin Mary said she would go, so Tuesday morning we started about 11 o'clock, took our lunch with us, when we got to Ellen's house we found she was at Mrs. Coulons, so we drove there and found her, she did not know me, but recognized Cousin Mary, she is very little changed and she knew someone was coming, told Mrs. Coulon so, I asked her how she knew, said a "yaller bee" had come by her gate and she said "go along" to him "good luck" that was a sign of luck and strangers coming, "you must always speak to him, a black bee is bad luck."

She asked a lot of questions about all of you, she seems to be very comfortable and has a good many friends among the Creoles, said they gave her meal and lard and bread. That Fanny always gave her sugar and coffee. I brought her some head handkerchiefs from the city. Every time we would say anything she agreed with she would say "truth for God."

I would like to have had a "Kodak" to have taken her picture.

Tell Alice Mrs. Coulon gave us some "may pop" syrup and water, it was very refreshing.

...We stopped at Lagrasee's place just below the St. Claire's. Harriet is there ... she knew me and wanted to know all about you, where Grace was, urged me to tell you to bring Grace to Louisiana, she would get well. Harriet has had a fall and been suffering from her knee but she was well enough to come up next morning before six to see me. She came in my room and we had a talk before anyone was up. Jeff has sold her place at Beattieville which was in his name and she has no regular home, said she was going to try to cut cane this year. She has her children and I hope they will be kind to her.

I showed her Alice and Frances' picture and she said Frances was as large as her mother and Alice looked like you. I told her Alice was sitting down I do not think she sees very well. I brought her some check for aprons.

...I left Thursday evening on the Texas to Pacific Road "that goes through cousin Mary's Place" for cousin Lizzie's [Lizzie Pugh Ratliff] - arrived there in the course of half an hour.

I enjoyed my visit very much. Cousin Lizzie has a real country home, her house painted gray with white trims and green blinds, has galleries all around, she has a hall, with the cane settee and round table from the library at Madewood, ...her parlor is on the left, with all the photographs and the big round center table, the sofa from the back parlor, her picture, Mr. Ratliff's and Grandma Foley, it looked more like Madewood than any other room.

...Cousin Lizzie has a fine crop.

We rode by Madewood and it looks like a huge white ghost, no one living in it, the yard is changed from having so many trees cut down, Godchaux has killed the Oaks in upper lot and has it all planted in cane. Miss Annie Pugh who called one morning looking about the same, and when she rode out in the evening we met her and Mrs. Flower taking a drive. I felt just as if I was going to Madewood and would find everyone there from where I was a girl.

...When I say cousin Mary lives just as they did at Leighton I do not mean their table is kept as beautifully because I do not think she can afford it, but it is the same easy life no one feels as if they had to exert themselves."

On August 29th 1902, Ellen writes Thomas from her flat at 102 W. 93rd St., and talks about family, in particular John Haven's health, and the letter from Eliza. Eliza's letter is very special to Ellen, and she says she wants to keep it as long as she lives.

"Thanks for your letter, I am very glad you went to Uncle John's for I feel sure he is very helpless and depressed and every visit you can make him counts for a real kindness.

...I am much worried about your uncle having malaria. He escaped it last year and I hoped, as he was built up once again so well, he would never have it again. Its return shows he is run down again, for which I am very much worried.

If he should get worse, will you let me know and I shall go right down to him.

...I had a nice letter from cousin Eliza yesterday, after her return from a visit to the bayou where she has not been since Frank died. She went to see old Ellen, Harriet, visited aunt Mary and your Aunt Lizzie. I will enclose her letter if you will put it on my bureau after you have read it for I want to keep that as long as I live.

With very much love, mother

You had better keep the letter for me, or open one of my bureau drawers and put it there or when they clean my room it will be lost.

Ellen Eustis Pugh"

The following summer, 1903, Ellen goes to Richfield Springs with Alice and the children. The trip is partly an effort to relieve her rheumatism. On June 7th Alice writes Thomas to tell him that Ellen is doing fairly well.

"But she takes quite a walk, with daily increase the distance on the sidewalk and in the adjoining park. ...The baths begin Friday or Saturday and the doctor thinks they will do her much good with the massage. He wants her to spend 40 days taking the baths, that makes her stay until August 1. ...But mother worries so over expense."

On June 21st 1903, Ellen writes Thomas and says she will soon leave but will meet Helen (possibly Helen Haven Langdon) and then Fanny. They will go to Harrison, N.Y., near Westchester, where John Haven is. She adds, "I suspect you must have been tired climbing Mount Whitney." Thomas was most likely climbing Mt. Whitney near Lake Placid, N.Y. Ellen writes Thomas again a few days later, possibly from Boston or Harrison, N.Y., and asks him for details about the lake. She says she will be back in Richfield by the 29th.

"1903, June 25
Dear Thomas,
I was delighted to receive your letter this morning but you do not tell me whether the air agrees with you and whether you sleep well.
Also if you are troubled with bugs and gnats and flies.
Also if you have been trout fishing.
...John and I were asked to dine with your Aunt Fanny at your uncles yesterday. We went, and reached home at 6 p.m. and passed a pleasant day. ...John has bought the tickets today for Richfield for himself and me. We will remain overnight and return the next day."

On June 30th Ellen writes Thomas again, and mentions that her weight is down to 109 pounds, whereas her normal weight is 125 pounds. Thomas and John and two friends are going on some kind of jaunt:

"I am so glad that you and John and Adams and Newbold are going to have a little holiday. I do hope the weather will be pleasant and that neither of you or John will meet with an accident. If it is hot be very careful about sunstrokes. I do not believe John has ridden since he was here last and I do not believe you have ridden for an age on account of the rain, so do be careful for remember I cannot spare either of my dear sons."

Thomas has begun a Marine Insurance business, at which he was to prove very successful. Ellen mentions,

"I am very glad to receive all your letters - - I also received a mercantile library paper you sent me."

About Alice she says,

"We are getting along very well and Alice is a great comfort to me.
...Alice is better and I think the trip and rest has done her good."
She worries about Grace, and says,

"I hope Mrs. McNabb is standing by Grace and is caring for her and
shielding her from the others who do not want her or like her. I am
paying out a great deal of money for this and I hope the child is
reaping the benefit of it."

On July 16th, Ellen writes Thomas and urges him to consider joining them:

"They have a little music there and we could all be together so
much and have nice excursions around here, you would like it
better than this hotel -- there is music in the park and time is
flying and I will soon be turning my face homeward.
Do come to please me. Mrs. Stewart has a sweet girl, a real nice
Southern girl, from Memphis, her niece, with her. There are few
young men up here and she has a lovely time -- Alice and I like
her so much. They are both going to drive with me Saturday. She
knew Edith...
So come and we will take excursions on the open trolley to
Cooperstown and Oswego Lake –Canandaigua lake and other
places. They say there is fishing in one of the lakes here. We have
a tennis court and a golf club.
With much love
Mother"

On January 21st 1904, Ellen writes Thomas, probably from her apartment.
Alice may have been visiting or had come to visit her Uncle John, who
lived in Harrison, N.Y., in the Westchester area.

"I received your letter last evening after my return from a visit to
your Uncle John who has been very ill and still is very feeble. The
doctor has forbidden him from seeing anyone and would not
except me, said he would not take the responsibility but Aunt
Fanny magnanimously said she would take the responsibility
herself, so I went right up.
When I returned I fell in the street accidentally, although Alice was
with me, and hurt my knee and wrist.
... Dr. Morris has been here and has bound my leg and my arm up
and says I must stay quiet and keep my leg up in a chair on a
footstool for two weeks.
I am so sorry I cannot invite your friends immediately but Alice
says she will, just as soon as she can.
She has been getting a nurse for us for your Uncle John...
Until I hear how your uncle is, in a day or two, I could not proceed
with the dinner party. Tuesday afternoon he had a very bad turn
and Hilda for a minute thought he was gone. She and the Cook put
hot bottles to his feet, bathed his head and revived him and the
man went off to telephone for the doctor. If he is better with his
nurse Alice can go right on and get a nice dinner party.

Of course I am laid up but this will not matter and I will have everything handsome and just as you would like."

By May of 1904, Dr. Lyons is still corresponding with Ellen about Grace. Meantime, John Pugh writes Alice May 8th 1904, about her financial affairs and Ralph. Ralph is in bad shape. Mr. Ticknor may be Alice's lawyer.

"On receipt of this letter see Mr. Ticknor and ask him to tell you what you can do. And what you cannot. It seems to me that you might take a power of attorney from Ralph to act for him, if it is necessary. Perhaps a wife can act for her husband without becoming liable herself, but I wish you would consult Mr. Ticknor about this...

Is Ralph in condition to consult with about these matters.

Do not let him induce you to take charge of them in any way until you have consulted Mr. Ticknor.

How is it arranged that Ralph's salary is to be drawn. Does it go to him, or do you draw it?"

On May 11th 1904, John Pugh writes his mother from Philadelphia, on letterhead that indicates he has a rubber flooring and tile business. Ralph's affliction may be alcoholism:

"I had a letter from Alice telling me some of the same facts which you mentioned. I have written her as per copy enclosed, it is necessary for her to be careful, or she may become liable for some of Ralph's debts. It would suit him very well to get her in that position. His mind may be affected, as Dr. Hopkins thinks, but Dr. Putnam thinks him sane. Personally I think him so myself, but until he gets over this delirium tremens I should say it was difficult to come to a positive conclusion.

I wrote Alice that it seemed to me it would injure the children less to say he was being treated for the drink habit than that he was insane.

Yours,

John

Show Thomas this letterhead."

On July 7th 1904, Ellen gets a very long letter from Alice's son, John Haven Pugh Stone, age 15, whom the family called Jack.

"Dear Grandma

I received your letter yesterday, and believe me when I say I appreciate your writing me. I know how the mail must've piled up on you ...

...I went down to Coney Island on Uncle Thomas's invitation.

...In the afternoon I went up home and took my time about dressing, but finally was ready to go to Fort Washington[91]. When I

---

[91] Woodbury Langdon, widower of Edith Pugh, had re-married (to Elizabeth Elwyn, the daughter of a distant Langdon cousin named Alfred Langdon Elwyn) and purchased the Haven's Fort Washington home.

arrived there, I found Cousin Eustis Langdon [Hopkins] there also. We had a very nice dinner.

...All through dinner Uncle Woodbury kept saying, "Bessie had we not better have them set off the fireworks now". But she told him, or rather loudly and abruptly said, "no". This is for your private ear, I would not have it get back to her for worlds. She slighted him quite openly in front of all of us. She really paid no attention to him at all. He began speaking and without paying any attention to him she began talking to us. He asked her if she would have some more meat, at first she did not pay any attention to him, then she said no. Plain and unvarnished, too. But to do her justice she was exceedingly nice and polite to Cousin Eustis and myself. After dinner we went out on the porch. By the way they have built a handsome 60 foot porch on the side towards the Hudson, which is a decided improvement. It was just finished about two weeks ago. As soon as we went out the man sent off five rockets all at once, which so angered Uncle Woodbury at the extravagant waste, that he hollered, no bellowed at him to stop that and only send one thing off at a time. At which cousin Bessie hollered at him to "hush up, stop that noise, leave the man alone, he knows his business". For my part I think the man just sent them off as a sort of opening chord, a sort of grand flourish. This was the view cousin Eustis took in trying to restore peace.

Uncle Woodbury is the vainest man I ever saw, and I can say this much, that cousin Bessie does not gratify him in this weakness of his. He kept looking low down on the boulevard to see if there were plenty of people looking on.

...But I really ought not to say all this about them, because they were both very nice to me -- exceedingly nice.

...Finally the fireworks were over and Cousin Eustis and I left.

...While I was up at Uncle Woodbury's or rather on my way home from there Cousin Eustis asked me to dine with him Thursday. So I will go there tonight.

...One of the reasons I said I did not think I would go to Aunt Fanny's was that I thought it would be just as expensive as Buffalo, but as I will not have my vacation until September, and by that time there will be "nothing do in" in Fort Erie, which is the main reason I wanted to go...I think that I would have a nice time if I went to Aunt Fanny's, judging by past experiences, and I do not think I would have an empty minute on my hand, but it would cost me more than I can possibly afford this year. And as I said I do not think she could possibly want me in September, she would be getting ready to come to town, and she would be thinking daggers at me for accepting her invitation, which she meant for the summer.

...I hope you do not intend coming back to New York the 14th of August. You would be courting certain disaster. If you persist, I shall tell Uncle Thomas so he will not let you. I think I had better anyway. You want to take plenty of baths and "do your rheumatism up" and then you will not have a bad attack this winter.

Uncle John [Pugh] came up from Philadelphia Saturday, but only stayed a couple of hours, before he went back again. I asked him to stay all night. I told him Uncle Tom was not in his room, but he would not.

By the way when is mother coming onto Richfield? Do you know the exact date.

With love to all

John H. P. Stone"

John Pugh writes Ellen on July 15th 1904, from Philadelphia. He is doing well in his tile business, and he is working on Alice's situation. Ellen, John Pugh and Fanny are all helping Alice.

> "...I wrote her (Alice) to advertise the cottage thoroughly between now and the 31st, and if no one appeared by that time, to take what we could get for it."

Fanny has bought a piece of land from Alice, probably to take it off Alice's hands and give her the use of the cash; John is helping with the paperwork.

> "...so this shows that Alice conveyed to Aunt Fanny all the land, including what she bought originally, and what she obtained afterwards. I shall write Aunt Fanny this."

From John's letter, it seems that Ellen has Jack (John Haven) Stone living with her at least part of the year:

> "I think you decided wisely about the flat. Why not leave the pantry as it is, and give Jack the room now occupied by the stairs?"

On August 6th 1904, Jack Stone writes Ellen,

> "I am going to Long Beach today. Uncle Thomas has gone out to White Plains this morning. Uncle John is coming on this morning, and I am going to take them out to Long Beach with me, and later on Uncle Thomas will come."

> ...I do not think Uncle Thomas will spend another week at Long Beach like he has this week, because the people are too formal for him, and do not become acquainted with him. He went out there for the dancing but I do not believe he has danced once, whenever I ask him if he has he gives me some of the vilest abuse that has ever been my misfortune to listen to.

> ... Another grievance Uncle Thomas has against the place is that they do not eat dinner until seven or eight, which puts him in fits. So now he is dining in solitary state at a restaurant, where the waiter wipes the dishes with a towel before handing them to the patron. He also doesn't like to have to dress when he comes home from dinner."

On February 14th 1905, James C. Carter died, aged 78. The New York Times reported that,

> "As an extraordinary tribute to the memory of James C. Carter, the Appellate Division, Supreme Court, adjourned immediately after eulogies had been pronounced yesterday."

Funeral services were held in New York City and again in Cambridge, MA. John Haven (Fanny and Ellen's brother, and Carter's close friend) wrote a tribute to Carter. John Haven met Carter at Harvard, and as a result of their friendship Carter first became a tutor to the Haven children. Carter was like another son to Sarah and John Appleton Haven, and like a brother to John, Fanny, Ellen and the other Haven children. John wrote,

> "...Mr. Carter, coming into life with no advantage whatever but his own natural gifts, stimulated by poverty and the spur of necessity, grew with the growth of the country and by sheer force of brains and character had become at the time of his death one of her best known and most valued citizens, the acknowledged leader of the great profession of the Law, foremost among its 190,000 notaries – and exercising a wide and powerful influence for good among the people of his time – Such a career is no accident, and it is interesting to recall as briefly as possible the steps by which he rose from obscurity to national and international distinction. When I entered Harvard College in 1848, Mr Carter who had already been there for two years was a very marked man among the 300 students who then constituted the entire community of that little college."

John Haven recounts how Carter became a natural leader at Harvard, and was class orator for Commencement. But Carter, lacking money to continue his education at Harvard Law School, had to teach as a means of paying for his future law schooling. Carter was employed by the Havens during 1850-1851, after which he entered Harvard's Dane Law School. John Haven was again his classmate at Harvard Law.

John speaks of the history of the law firm founded by Carter (which as of 2009 is still a leading N.Y.C. law firm):

> "In 1854 ... the firm of Scudder and Carter was formed – with whom it was my good fortune to study the Code in the following year. This firm under its successive organizations of Scudder and Carter, Carter and Ledyard, Carter, Rollins and Ledyard, and Carter, Ledyard and Milburn has occupied a great place in the annals of the profession in New York."

Fanny and Ellen must have felt Carter's loss keenly. Ellen saved two copies of newspaper articles about Carter's will. Carter left a large estate of about $1.5 million.

"To my friends John Haven, Ellen Eustis Pugh, and Frances A. L. Haven, all the pieces of silver purchased and given to me under the will of their father, John Appleton Haven.'"
To Frances A. L. Haven also are left a silver pitcher and a gold pencil case given to the deceased under the will of the legatee's sister, Anna L. Sweetser.
Mr. Carter, when he first came to New York from Harvard, was a tutor in the Haven family, and he was a lifelong friend of all its members."

On June 16th 1905, John Pugh writes Ellen about the business details arising from helping Alice. Alice's youngest child, who was named for Fanny, must be staying with Fanny:
"I hope Frances is behaving well, every child does with Aunt Fanny, and I do not think she will prove an exception."

July 6 1905, John Pugh writes Ellen again about their affairs. He is having trouble helping Ellen understand that if she can't charge Alice rent on the flat (Ellen bought the house from Alice and Ralph to help Alice), then the flat will of necessity not appear to be carrying itself.
"I have told you over and over that as long as Alice uses the flat, and pays nothing for it, we cannot expect a cent from the flat, and it may run a little behind. You will never believe this until we make Alice pay rent, like the other tenants, and you hand her back this rent each month.
...I would start this arrangement at once, if Alice had anything to pay rent with, but she has not, so I shall hereafter send you a monthly statement of the amounts received from flat, charging Alice $35 for rent, and crediting the flat with $35, paid back to her."

October 2nd 1905, John Haven sends Ellen a brief note from Harrison, N.Y.:
"I hope that you reached home safely and without any delay? And that you feel no ill effects from your visit to me, how is your cold?
Your affectionate Brother
John Haven"

On February 20th 1906, Mary Williams, wife of David's brother Richard, died at age 64. Ellen wrote to Mary's son, Henry Allen Pugh at Live Oak. Allen Pugh was born in 1868 (the same year as Ellen's youngest, Thomas) and he died at 57 in 1925 and is buried at Madewood. Allen replied to Ellen in March:
"...and on the last night we could keep mother with us, for the next morning early we took her up to Madewood on the train and laid her to rest in the spot as dear to her heart as it was to fathers.
... I shed tears Aunt Ellen every time the picture is recalled to my mind for I know how much she loved every brick and plank at Madewood on account of father's affection for the place.

... As she rested at the front of the house for a while it was the first time I have ever been reconciled to Madewood's having been vacant for we had no feeling of her presence being an inconvenience to anyone. It seemed for a moment as if the house, so deserted looking with its huge Corinthian columns, were some mausoleum, and that we should lift her up tenderly, carry her inside and leave her within its protecting walls."

On April 11th 1906, Ellen notes another passing in her diary:
"This was the day dear Olivia died and father always remained home from business that day with mother."
Olivia Hamilton Haven was 2 years younger than Ellen, and died aged 6 in 1840, when Ellen was 8 years old.
Ellen's diary also notes that
"John Pugh left for the eight train to Harrison [where John Haven lived] to get figures on Woodbury's expenses on Fort Washington property."
On April 13th, Good Friday, Ellen wanted to buy chocolate to bring to Grace but the store was too crowded. She then went to Tiffany's and bought a breast pin for Miss Hearn, Second Superintendant at Bloomingdale Asylum (where Grace was). On April 14th, she notes,
"A cloudy day. Took the 1:08 train for White Plains, taking Lawrence -- had a fairly good visit with Grace."

In July 1906, Ellen writes Thomas in New York from Buffalo. She is worried about John Haven, who was not feeling well, and she says,
"In two weeks and three days I leave for Boston to join your Aunt Fanny and go from there to Northeast [Harbor, Maine]."

On August 4th 1906, Ellen writes Thomas from Fort Erie, N.Y. (where Alice is) about repairs to a flat, giving Thomas instructions about how best to manage it. She wishes Thomas would write to tell her how Grace is. She and Alice are both struggling:
"No servants, Alice arriving very sick with high fever and threatened with pneumonia. She is better and down today.
I am about the same -- better, however, I think than when I left home. I cannot walk longer than five to 10 minutes at a time and pretty helpless in arms and legs.
With much love
yours Mother"

John Haven, who is about 11 years Ellen's senior, sends Ellen a birthday greeting from Harrison, N.Y. on December 2nd 1906, for Ellen's 74th.
"I hope that this note will reach you tomorrow before the day is far spent, for it takes you my best wishes, that the day will prove a very happy one for you, and all belonging to you.
I believe that it was on the third of December 1832 at number 1 Bond St, that I was told, that, I had another little sister. I used to

325

think that a lady 74 years of age was a very old one, thinking that Aunt Harris and Aunt Eustis were real antiques, but now I regard you as so much my junior, that I look upon you rather as a young lady.

I suppose this is because I regard myself as so very much older than you, and perhaps I might add that I can't imagine either of the aforementioned aunt's when of your present age, so full of life and spirits, as you now are.

May you live to witness many happy returns of this day. Yesterday I received yours of November 30 telling me that you were well, and had encountered and conquered that turkey, but you made no mention of the entrées which your French cook wanted to prepare for the dinner. That piece of information I presume you will impart to me verbally the next time we meet, which I hope will be soon.

I had the pleasure of seeing John for nearly half an hour this forenoon. The shortest visit he ever made me. I thought he was looking very well, and very happy.

I hope the weather has been much pleasanter with you than it has been here for the last 24 hours. The wind blew very hard all last night, growing colder as the night advanced, until this morning at seven o'clock the thermometer on my piazza registered 20°.

Nellie Iredell[92] with her two youngest daughters made a call on me Friday. She was very well and in excellent spirits. I was quite pleased with her children, the youngest one now, four and a half years old, I had never seen. They all had a fine time at Eustis' Thanksgiving dinner.

A line received yesterday from Fanny, spoke very pleasantly of a young lady whom she had met at your dinner on Thanksgiving day.

Renewing my wishes as expressed at the beginning of this sheet, I remain,
your affectionate Brother
John Haven"

---

[92] This was John and Ellen's niece, Ellen Hopkins Iredell, whom Ellen and Fanny used to call Nellie.

Ellen (1907)

In early 1907, there are two small fragments of paper with notes from Fanny to John Pugh and Thomas Pugh.

> "Dear John
> Dr. Lyle is quite encouraging, says your mother is not failing though the gain is very slow -- wants her to be put on a bed in front room. I will send bedstead and mattress this p.m.
> Thinks she can try champagne, a very little at a time – keeping a siphon in the bottle -- if it seems to excite her, stop that.
> I will try to be here when she is moved but cannot come Wednesday from one to four –
> yours
> FALH"

Written on the outside is, "Thomas Pugh":

> "Dr. Lyle says your mother can try champagne, very little at a time and stop it if it excites her -- he says she had better be moved into front room -- I will send bedstead and mattress this afternoon -- she must be moved very quietly, I shall try to be here --
> yours
> FALH"

Ellen died February 15, 1907, aged 75. Per her wishes, she was buried with her family at Woodlawn (David is buried at the cemetery at St John's Episcopal Church, Thibodaux, La.). The New York Times noted,

> "February 16, 1907 Ellen Eustis Pugh.
> Mrs. Ellen Eustis Pugh, daughter of the late John Appleton Haven of this city, died yesterday at her home, 411 W. End Ave. Mrs. Pugh was a member of Grace Church and well known for her interest in charity and other work in connection with the church of which she was a member.
> She was the widow of David B. Pugh of Lafourche Louisiana, a planter and a member of one of the best-known families of that state. In 1886, soon after the death of her husband, Mrs. Pugh returned to this city, and she has resided here ever since. She leaves three children, John Haven Pugh, Mrs. Ralph Stone, and Thomas Pugh [omitted from the article is Grace Haven Pugh]. The funeral will be held in Grace Church on Monday at 10 a.m.
> Burial will be in Woodlawn Cemetery."

At Ellen's death, Fanny was almost 69; John Pugh was 47, Alice 46, Grace 45, Thomas 39, and John Haven 86. Within the year, John Pugh married Blanche Isobel Cudlipp. John Haven died June 27th 1908, a year and four months after Ellen. Thomas married within two years, to Regina Cahill.

We do not know how Fanny spent her remaining years: there are no letters. The few letters from their 20 years together end at Ellen's death. Fanny, who expressed a pronounced lack of enthusiasm for living after losing her parents in 1876, lived until she was 86 (she died March 4, 1924), surviving her brother John by about 16 years.

After the service for Ellen, Fanny wrote Thomas a note:
"Sunday evening
Dear Thomas
A friend of mine sits far up to the front, in Grace Church, I asked her to listen for me, to the sermon.
I enclose her letter received this afternoon as I know you will like to read it to Alice – it is so well worded and expressed, I don't see how she could remember so well.
Keep the letter carefully for me.
Affectionately
Aunt Fanny
The three ladies mentioned are
Mrs. Grosvenor Ogden -- 86
Mrs. Schermerhorn -- 83
Your Mother"

Illustration 52: Ellen Haven Pugh, her son Thomas Pugh, and Thomas' wife Regina Cahill Pugh, Woodlawn Cemetery, Webster Ave., Spring Lake plot, the Bronx.

Ellen's Account Books

Ellen kept detailed account books, and saved and reconciled every check. From her account books of 1896-97 and 1904-07 (up until about a month before she died), we can reconstruct some of her activities[93].

In 1896, Ellen sent $30.00 to Louisiana for Old Ellen to cover six months of Old Ellen's board and living expenses ($793.00 in 2008 dollars), and she sent $5.00 for Harriet. John and Thomas Pugh were living with Ellen, and John was paying Ellen rent. Ellen received some money from Fanny for Grace, and Ellen also made an interest payment on a $1,000.00 note Fanny held for Ellen.
In May, Ellen subscribed to a "Confederate paper" of some kind, which may indicate she retained an interest in or fondness for the Confederacy.

Ellen was receiving periodic interest payments from Robert Pugh's estate for the children (John, Edith's estate and Thomas). She also received interest payments from W.W. Pugh, for a loan. She paid Woodbury Langdon interest on a $1,000 loan, and received interest from the wills of John Appleton Haven and Anna Haven Sweetser. She paid for a pew in Grace Episcopal Church in N.Y.C. ($50.00, or about $1,322.00 in 2008 dollars). She paid Alice a weekly allowance ($7.00, or about $185.00 in 2008 dollars), and she paid Dr. Lyons and the Bloomingdale Asylum $261.00 quarterly (about $6,900.00 per year).

There is money for a ticket to Jaffrey, N.H. in June of 1897, which was undoubtedly for a summer holiday shared with Fanny (Jaffrey was one of several of Fanny's favorite summer places). There are miscellaneous entries for fares to visit Grace in White Plains at the Bloomingdale Asylum, and fares to Woodlawn Cemetery, where the Haven family plot is.

In 1897, she saw Nellie (Ellen Hopkins Iredell, Augusta's daughter), paid Ralph Stone $75.00 "for Alice's sickness", loaned Ralph $650.00 (all the while paying Alice a weekly allowance), and went to Harrison, N.Y. (25 miles or so north of Ellen's apartment) to see her brother John Haven.

There may have been a particular reason that Ellen was at Woodlawn in April of 1897, because she went there (with someone, probably her children) on April 13th (fares $0.50), April 15th (fares $0.70), and on April 18th (combined church and Woodlawn fare of $0.65). Jack Stone, Alice's

---

[93] For an approximation of the equivalent costs of items and services, the relative purchasing power of $1.00 was as follows in 2008 dollars:

1896: $1.00 = $26.45
1904: $1.00 = $24.95
1906: $1.00 = $24.69

331

son, visited her in 1897: Ellen paid for Jack's shoes, pants, shirt and buttons.

On May 29th 1897, Ellen paid Fanny $30.00 for "rent of cottage"; Ellen made a second entry July 1st for $30.00 to Fanny for "rent for Cottage at Fort Erie for July." The cottage at Erie was probably the land and cottage that Fanny bought from Alice, which Fanny most likely did as a means of helping Alice financially. The rent that Ellen paid on the cottage may have allowed Alice to use the cottage, because based on Ellen's account book entries, Ellen was not using the cottage herself.

Ellen paid for tickets to John Haven's in Harrison in early July, then for tickets to Worcester, MA., and Jaffrey, N.H. On July 7th, Ellen gave Alice $1,000.00 for a loan secured on Alice's flat; on July 12th, Ellen gave Alice $1,648.46 for the rest of the loan (while continuing Alice's allowance).

On August 2nd Ellen wrote a check for $60.00 to Fanny for "two months rent for Alice's cottage". Ellen went to Harrison to see John (also August 2nd), and she went to Providence, R.I. from August 13-27. On September 2nd Ellen went to Harrison again to see her brother John Haven, and brought someone with her (the entry is for "Tickets" and the amount is $1.80).

On September 8th, Ellen wrote a check for $18.00 (over $450.00 in 2008 dollars) to Fanny for "half of carriage drives". On September 12th, Ellen sent a check to Fannie Pugh Beattie for $30.00 "for Old Ellen to Jan 1, 1898".

Ellen visited her brother John Haven on November 11th and December 4th; she also visited Grace in White Plains, and she probably brought Jack Stone along with her (Jack was living with Ellen, and the entry in her account book is plural, for "Tickets").

On December 30th 1904, Ellen paid 20 cents for a "Wreath for General Lee's picture" (Lee died on October 12th 1870, so this was not an anniversary of his death; perhaps it was in honor of the new year).

On January 1 1905, Ellen and John Pugh went to Harrison, N.Y. to see John Haven. On the 19th, Fanny and Ellen took a drive in a Hansom ($0.63); on February 11th, Ellen and Fanny took a sleigh while in White Plains (to see Grace), for $0.25.

Ellen sent two dresses and a valentine to Alice's youngest daughter Frances Stone on February 11th. On February 15th, Ellen noted "Fares to Harrison and sleigh", ($0.35), and ($0.75), respectively.
Again on the 22nd, Ellen and Fanny went to White Plains to see Grace, and paid the fare and the fee for a sleigh. On February 25th, Ellen paid fares to

and from White Plains, and on the 27th, she paid for a Coupe to and from White Plains ($0.75).

In March, Ellen paid transportation to John Haven's: fares to and from, in a Hansom ($0.32), and a "Vehicle at Harrison" ($1.00). There is yet another White Plains ticket on March 15th. Beginning in March there are entries for the use of a telephone (for example, on March 20th, two 30-cent telephone calls, one to John Haven and one to John Pugh).

Ellen went to a funeral service (the person was not named) on March 21st, and the "cost of Coupe and driver from 8:20 to 9:40" was ($0.25), or the equivalent of about $6.00 in 2008 dollars. By comparison, Ellen was paying ($0.50) monthly for the Times.

On March 24th, Ellen gave Frances Stone ($0.50 "for an enlarged photo of my great grandfather" (probably the Rev. Dr. Samuel Haven). Ellen paid for fares to her brother John's in Harrison on March 26th and recorded fares to White Plains on April 1st (carriage and cars, $1.20).

On April 3rd Ellen purchased "A Family ticket to Harrison" for $16.65, and she paid carriage fare "to John Haven's" for ($0.25). On April 8th, Ellen went to White Plains to see Grace, and on the 13th she took a Surrey to see John Haven. On the 22nd Ellen bought a 50-trip commutation ticket to White Plains for $14.25, and on the same day she paid for a carriage for the rest of the trip to and from White Plains for $1.00. She went to John Haven's on May 1st, paying for both fares and a Rockaway.

On May 9th Ellen took a carriage to Larchmont, probably to visit Augusta's daughter. On the 18th she visited John Haven. On the 21st, she and Jack traveled to Plainfield, N.Y. by carriage, and then took the railroad train ($2.00) to Richfield Springs (north of Oneonta and Cooperstown), where they stayed at Cary Cottages. Ellen made visits to John Haven on May 23rd and June 8th. She went out to Fort Washington on June 10th, possibly to visit Woodbury (she had telephoned him on June 6th).

On June 14th, Ellen took a carriage to see Gussie and Sarah (Augusta's daughters) in Larchmont, N.Y. and two days later Ellen went from Larchmont to Harrison (less than ten miles, for ten cents), back to Larchmont and then to N.Y.C. On the 18th, Ellen took a carriage to and from Ft. Washington for $2.50. On June 24th, Ellen took a carriage to and from Bloomingdale Asylum to see Grace for $1.00.

She bought Parlor Seat tickets to Richfield for $3.00 on June 24th, and stopped at Harrison on the 25th (fares were $0.32, and a carriage was $1.25). Two days later, on June 27th, she bought two "through tickets" to Richfield. Then on the 30th, Ellen listed fares ($0.40), baggage ($0.55), Porter on cars ($0.25), "man for bringing trunks ($0.20)". Once in Richfield, there are multiple entries for sulphur water, baths and a bathwoman during the month of July. By August 7th, Frances Stone was with her: "ointment for Frances foot" ($0.25), "Bath for Frances (swimming pool) for $0.25". Ellen's baths cost $0.75. Based on other entries, Jack was also in Richfield. Other entries for Frances included "Washing drawers" ($0.25), "curling stick" ($0.25), "Soda and chocolates" ($0.25), "shampooed" ($1.00), "plaster for her foot" ($0.15), "Frances present for her mother" ($0.25), and $0.75 "for her doll".

On August 29th, Ellen paid $3.00 for "Seats in Parlor car", and $8.00 for tickets to N.Y. On September 1st, she paid $6.00 for "Automobile bill". Also in September she sent Frances to Long Island, went to Harrison with someone, probably Fanny (" ½ ticket $1.18"), bought tickets home from White Plains ($1.25) and paid for Jack's ticket to the theater ($1.10).

By September 6th, Alice was there ("Gave Alice for Coney Island $2.00)". Ellen went to Woodbury's and back, and paid Alice "for tickets and Expenses" $20.00 on the 13th, as well as $1.40 for groceries. On September 16th Ellen visited John Haven ("cars to and from Harrison ($0.15), Surrey ($0.50)"). On the 22nd, she paid $2.50 for a Hansom. September 30th she visited Grace, and on October 1st she went to John Haven's.

On October 4th, there is an entry for "$12.50 being the amount of French Claims awarded to me from my grandfather's Estate (John Haven) and $1.56 the award from the Woodward Estate." This money was compensation for a ship that was confiscated by the French in 1802.

Ellen went to see John Haven on October 15th, paying the driver for a surry $0.15, and $0.50 for the surry itself. On the 21st, Ellen paid $1.10 for a carriage to and from White Plains to see Grace, and on the 29th, she went to see John again. On November 3rd, Ellen paid $6.95 for a "Chiffon Boa". Both Jack and Lawrence Stone were staying with her, as shown by the constant laundry bills for them, as well as for John and Thomas.

Ellen visited John Haven on November 12th, and made an entry on the 18th for "Carriage for self to and fr. Bloomingdale" to see Grace. On the 24th, Helen Langdon visited her (Ellen loaned Helen $2.00, which was subsequently paid back). On the 30th, Ellen records a carriage fare home from John Haven's.

On December 6th there is an entry for "Vehicles for White Plains each $1.00" and 3 attendants for Grace, $6.00. On the 17th, she visited John Haven. By December 22, Ellen begins recording purchases that may be for Christmas: "Music for Nellie $1.75" (probably Ellen H. Iredell, Augusta's daughter), "Gave Jack $4 for Lawrence's suit, "Lawrence a pair of shoes", and on Christmas day Ellen gave "Lawrence a present of $1.00, Jack a present of $2.00, John $6.00".

Ellen gave a dinner on December 28th, as indicated by the following entries: "ordered flowers" ($3.45), "Veg. ($1.37), "baskets for bonbons for 28th dinner" ($1.65), grapes ($0.27), Holly ($0.15), Rolls ($0.36), Cream ($0.13), Celery ($0.18), grapefruit ($0.50), waitress ($2.50).

On December 30th Ellen paid $8.75 for "Clothes for Lawrence". New Years Eve day, Ellen visited John Haven, and on January 4th 1906, Ellen went to White Plains to visit Grace.

On January 5th 1906, Ellen recorded "Paid Alice in cash $13.50 for her January's allowance – see check book", and "Drew from bank $40.00 for Alice and house".

On January 18th, Ellen paid for a "Ticket to Philadelphia for Paul Haven pd to John Pugh" for $1.80 (Paul Haven was Ellen's oldest brother Langdon Haven's son). On January 19th, Ellen "Paid Alice for nurses breakfast for 1 week", $1.75.
The next day, Ellen records "Alice took money for the nurses breakfast as she came here to stay (given Alice on Jan 19th) to buy spray and instruments with, for Lawrence's ear."

On the 24th, Ellen went to see her brother John in Harrison, gave Alice car fares, and $30.00 for a dress Ellen gave Alice for "a xmas present", and loaned Alice $2.00. On the 27th Ellen gave Alice car fares to White Plains to see Grace, and Ellen paid $14.25 for "A ticket to White Plains".

The next day, Ellen recorded entries for a "Crochet needle, worsted for Grace", and "car fares for Alice and Jack to and fr. White Plains", $0.75.

On February 1st, Ellen "Gave Alice $5.00". On the 6th, she bought a "White Plains Ticket", and on the 10th she paid Alice's car fares for the 9th and 12th ($0.30). On the 12th Ellen bought a "Valentine for Frances", and on the 13th she gave Alice "her February allowance cash $13.50", paid Alice's telegram to Grace, Alice's storage ($2.00) and Alice's fares ($2.00). The next day Ellen "Gave Alice cash $6.00" plus another $1.40.

On February 24th Ellen went to see Grace, and on March 11th she went to see Woodbury at Fort Washington ("Fares to ft wash .25, boy at Woodbury's .25"). On March 18th Ellen visited John Haven, and on the 27th she went to White Plains to visit Grace, probably with Fanny (often the White Plains carriage was $1.00, and often the next entry is "Rec'd fr F for ticket to WP .57"). On the 31st Ellen paid Jack's carfare to White Plains ($0.10), and on the next day paid carriage and fares to Fort Washington.

On April 2nd Ellen visited Gussie (Hopkins) and on the 6th Ellen bought Helen Haven candy. On the 13th, Ellen went to see Grace, and on the 18th she went to "Gussie's at night". On April 20th Ellen hired a coupe and driver "from 87th St to Fanny's", and Ellen records the time: "12:30 to 1:10 Coupe charged .25".

On April 22 Ellen records that she "Paid Fanny the rest I owed her for 2 bibles and the mailing of one". The next day Ellen visited John Haven in Harrison, and on the 26th she paid $5.95 for a "Boa Chiffon".

In May of 1906, a dozen fresh eggs cost Ellen $0.30. Again Fanny gave Ellen $0.57 toward a White Plains ticket. Ellen gave Thomas a birthday present of $4.80. On May 7th Ellen bought a ticket to Harrison to see John. On May 8th, Ellen records she "Rec'd fr. F on 2 ? for Frances at Altman's 4.30". On the 10th, Ellen paid for a carriage and driver to the Asylum. On May 11th Ellen writes "Fanny' s birthday present 3.50- White pocket 2.25, Needlecase 1.25". On May 14th Ellen pays $1.25 for candy for Fanny.

On May 18 Ellen "gave Jack $2 to Give Grace". On the 25th, Ellen visited John Haven in Harrison (carriage $0.50, Driver $0.05) and on the same day she bought a Harrison Ticket for $16.63. On June 2nd she went to see John Haven, and the next day she went to White Plains to see Grace. She records "Clothes for Grace – about $6.00)".

On June 9th Ellen "Sent Alice in letter birthday present 5.00", and on the 13th she visited John Haven.

On June 16th Ellen's entry says, "Having paid for French Claims Ship to Tiffany $14.06 ($347 in 2008 dollars) by a check I turn over $12.50 in cash from these claims". This silver Tiffany ship is today in the hands of Alice's descendants: According to Richard Townsend Harris, the ship model is of silver made by Tiffany's, and is entitled 'French Claims John Haven 1802'. Richard says his father explained that the silver ship "is a replica of John Haven's ship which was seized by the French in 1802", and that "the family had the model made with the monies paid by the French Gov't. 100 years later to settle the claim".

By 1906, John Pugh was seeing a woman named Blanche Cudlipp, whom he was to marry after Ellen's death. On June 19th, Ellen's entry says she "Paid telephones for 2 to Cab Co and One to Blanche ($0.30)".

On June 25th, Ellen paid for tickets for her and John Pugh: "John Pugh's Tickets for going and coming to and fr. Richfield 10.65, Mrs Pugh's ticket to Richfield 5.75, Parlor Seats 3.00".

On the 25th and 26th, Ellen visited with John Haven for his 85th birthday, and she notes, "Bonbons .40, bananas .15, both for John Haven". On the 27th, Ellen went to White Plains to see Grace.

In July there are many entries for Alice, for a prescription, tennis tickets, other ticket money, laundry, baths, linen, a jewelry repair, etc. Most of these costs were probably paid at Oswego Lake, where Ellen and Alice and others went in early July ("Tickets on Trolley to Okego (sic) Lake for 5,

1.75, Tickets on Boat for 4 around the lake 3.20"). Meantime Ellen records Lawrence's board at one week for $6.00. On August 1st Ellen "Gave Alice for seats $5.00".

Again in early August there are many bills for Alice (baths, laundry bills, a $13.00 bill for a doctor for Lawrence, Alice's shoes, her allowance, $10.00 for tickets home to Buffalo). Ellen got tickets for Thomas to Jaffrey, N.H., went to Harrison to see John Haven, bought chocolates for Fanny on August 14th, and bought a ticket to New York for $5.22 on September 4th.

On the 9th Ellen went to see Grace, and the next morning at 8AM she made a "telephone" (call) to White Plains for $0.30. For some reason Ellen went up to White Plains (Bloomingdale Asylum) again on the 11th, 13th and 15th, and on the 18th she paid for a "Carriage for Grace". On the 16th, between visits to Grace, she went to Harrison to see John. On the 20th she logged telephone calls to White Plains, and on the 21st she paid her servants' fare to White Plains, presumably to bring things to Grace. On September 29th and October 1st there are multiple telephone calls to White Plains, and on the 1st Ellen went to White Plains. On the 6th Ellen made another trip to White Plains, and on the 6th she went to Harrison to see John Haven.

On October 7th Ellen paid $8.00 for theatre tickets for "my theatre party". On the 9th she went to White Plains, and paid Grace's attendant $3.00. On the 14th she went to see John Haven in Harrison, possibly with Jack (there are car fares for him the same day). Ellen's party was probably the 15th or so, because there are entries on those dates to pay servants ("Kate, Mary Brown two dollars for mailing our dinner party", 10/15 "waitress for same three dollars", 10/15 "Flowers 4.50").

On October 18th, Ellen went to White Plains to see Grace; on the way back she may have lost her watch chain, because she records, "To man at Grand Central who entered my loss of my watch chain on his books 1 dollar". On the 26th she went to John's, and on the 27th to Grace's. On the 29th, Ellen records, "Coupé for call to Mrs. Cudlipp's with one horse, from 10 minutes at 3 to 20 minutes of four- one hour $1.50". This may have been a social call to Blanche Cudlipp's mother's house (Blanche was the woman John Pugh was seeing). On November 6th Ellen visited Grace again, and on the 7th she visited Gussie Hopkins. On the 14th Ellen went to see John Haven, and on the same day she gave $3.00 to John Pugh to get her an ear trumpet[94]. On November 19th Ellen paid for a "vehicle" at White Plains, and then paid for medicines (possibly for her sinuses). There are also various bills for Jack and Thomas.

---

[94] Ear trumpets or hearing trumpets were basically cones that gathered sound and funneled it into the users ear; they were used as hearing aids. Ellen had John return the trumpet to the "apothecary".

337

On December 5th, Ellen and Fanny went to White Plains; on the 12th, Ellen went up to see Grace, and she may have gone up again on the 14th ("grapes for Grace $.85 carriage one dollar"). But also on the 14th is "Ticket to White Plains commutation $14.25", and on the 15th is another "Carriage at White Plains one dollar" entry. Also on the 14th is "received from Fanny for White Plains ticket $.57"; on the 16th is "Carriage at White Plains $1.25", and "Received from Fanny White Plains ticket $.57", which indicates that Ellen and Fanny went together to see Grace on the 14th and 16th.

On December 17th Ellen went to the doctor. Also on the 17th, she received from Thomas "this date five dollars for Harriet five dollars for Ellen sent them by a check order of Fanny P. Beattie[95] this date". On the 19th she records "telephones, one to White Plains one to Fanny, one Jack $.45", and she went to White Plains where she paid Grace's attendant $2.00. The next day she again writes a check on Thomas' behalf: "Received from Thomas $10 for a check to send to Alice's children for their Christmas dinner. I sent a check number 87 December 20 $10."

On December 22nd Ellen went to White Plains to see Grace. Then follow multiple entries for Christmas tips to various people including the postman, iceman, back and front elevator men, telephone girl, engineer, milkman, two servants. Ellen continued to give Alice money for various things ("Jack's mouth", i.e. dental work, a Dr. Lyle, money for Alice to give Grace, traveling expenses, etc.).

On Christmas day, Ellen and Fanny visited Grace ("Fares gave Fanny $.50 for White Plains carriage plus $.30). The next day Ellen went up again, having paid for six nightgowns for Grace. On January 1st 1907 Ellen went to Harrison to see John Haven, and she may have gone with Fanny to White Plains on the 2nd.

On January 11th, Ellen "gave Fanny $2.25 for Grace's plants", and paid the "butcher for four pigeons $.60". On the 13th, Ellen was well enough to go see her brother John "Carriage at Harrison one dollar"). Also on the 11th she paid for a "world's directory for Grace $.25". The final entry in Ellen's account book is made on January 14th for the "Milk Bill", for her servant Mary Brown, and for "Chlorhade of potash (.05) and Keating's Lozenges (.45)". Ellen died February 7th 1907.

---

[95] Fanny Pugh Beattie, Ellen's sister-in-law (David's youngest sibling).

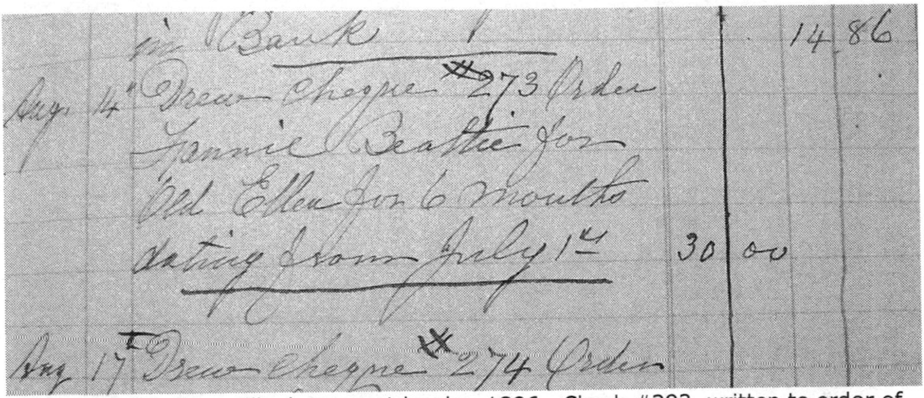

in Bank | 14 86
Aug. 4th Drew Cheque #273 Order
Fannie Beattie for
Old Ellen for 6 months
dating from July 1st | 30 00
Aug 17th Drew Cheque #274 Order

Illustration 53 From Ellen's account books, 1896. Check #293, written to order of Fanny Beattie (David's sister) for six months' support for Old Ellen, the beloved family servant.

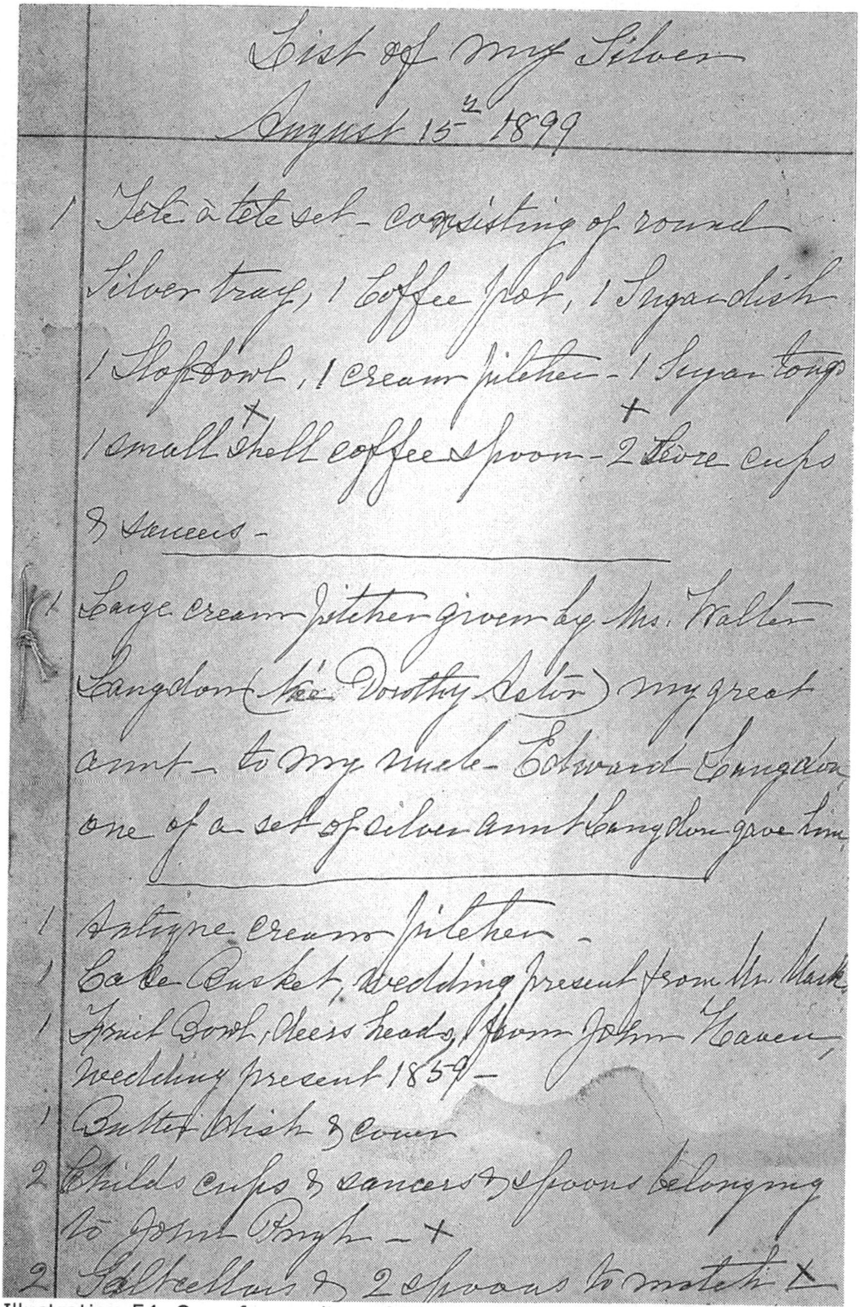

List of my Silver
August 15th 1899

1 Tête à tête set — consisting of round Silver tray, 1 Coffee Pot, 1 Sugar dish 1 Slopbowl, 1 Cream pitcher — 1 Sugar tongs 1 small shell coffee spoon — 2 Sèvre cups & Saucers —

1 Large cream pitcher given by Mrs. Walter Langdon (née Dorothy Astor) my great aunt — to my uncle Edward Langdon one of a set of silver Aunt Langdon gave him

1 Antique cream pitcher —
1 Cake Basket, wedding present from Mr. Mark
1 Fruit Bowl, Deers heads, from John Haven wedding present 1859 —
1 Butter dish & cover
2 Childs cups & saucers & spoons belonging to John Pryne — +
2 Saltcellars & 2 spoons to match +

Illustration 54: One of many lists of Ellen's silver, this one from 1899, 8 years before Ellen's passing.

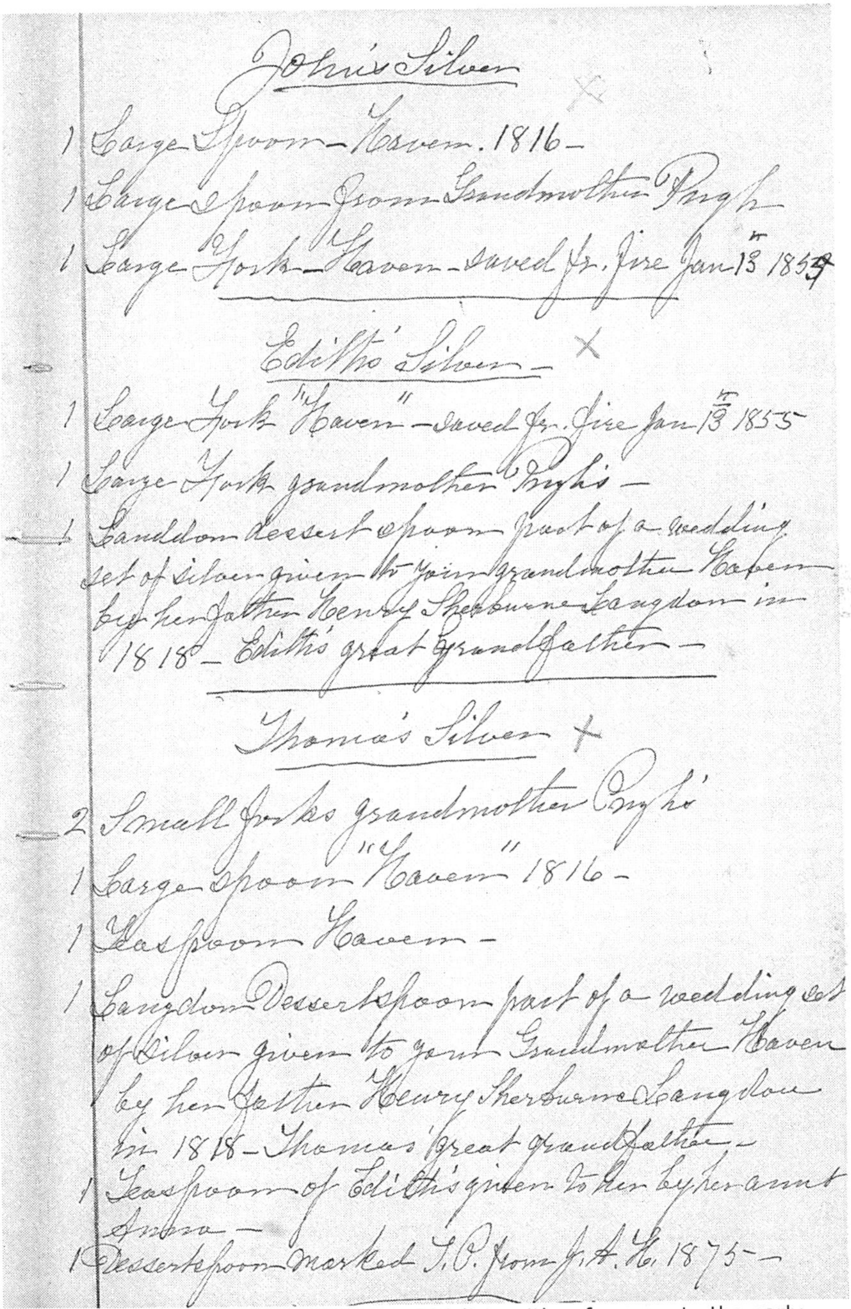

John's Silver

1 Large Spoon — Haven. 1816 —
1 Large Spoon from Grandmother Pugh
1 Large Fork — Haven — Saved fr. fire Jan 13th 1855

Edith's Silver —

1 Large Fork "Haven" — Saved fr. fire Jan 13th 1855
1 Large Fork grandmother Pugh's —
1 Langdon dessert spoon part of a wedding
set of silver given to your grandmother Haven
by her father Henry Sherburne Langdon in
1818 — Edith's great grandfather —

Thomas's Silver +

2 Small forks grandmother Pugh's
1 Large Spoon "Haven" 1816 —
1 Teaspoon Haven —
1 Langdon Dessertspoon part of a wedding set
of silver given to your Grandmother Haven
by her father Henry Sherburne Langdon
in 1818 — Thomas' great grandfather —
1 Teaspoon of Edith's given to her by her aunt
Anna —
1 Dessertspoon marked T.P. from J.A.H. 1875 —

Illustration 55: Another page of the 1899 list, with references to the early
1800's and background of some of the pieces.

Residuals (1909-1984)

In 1909, the year Thomas married, he sent money to Louisiana for Old Ellen and Harriet, the Louisiana servants. This partial letter is unsigned, but because it was written at Live Oak plantation it must have been written by one of the Mary Williams Pugh family, possibly Eliza Catherine Pugh, aka "Kathleen" or "Babe" (Mary W. Pugh bought Live Oak after Richard Pugh died).

> "Live Oak
> Jan 12 1909
> My dear Thomas
> If you could have seen the delight of Aunt Ellen and Aunt Harriet over their Christmas present from you, I know you would have been very much gratified -- I believe they were almost as much pleased that you are thinking of them as with the money.
> They are both looking wonderfully well and really seem very little changed since I first remember them.
> Aunt Harriet is living in Thibodeaux with her daughter. I went to see her first. When I told her why I had come she said, "Mr. Thomas always was a good child", she also told me that before you left here they tried to get you to join the church and you said you would not join the church until you were religious and it was now time you were getting religious and she hoped to soon hear of you joining the church.
> She said she was 108 years old -- if this is so she is certainly young looking for her age.
> Allen took me out in the broulee to see Aunt Ellen. I know she does say some of the funniest things…"

On August 3rd 1912, Thomas' first child was born. Fanny writes Thomas from Jaffrey New Hampshire August 7,

> "Mr. Thomas Pugh
> 66 Beaver St.
> New York
> NY
> Jaffrey, August 7, 1912
> Dear Thomas
> I am very much pleased that your wife has a daughter, will you tell her so, for me?
> I hope the child will be a blessing to you both, I am sure she will bring great happiness into your lives.
> You tell me to note that you have moved to Brooklyn but you have not given your address there so how can I note it?
> I should think you would be tired moving from one place to another.
> Your affectionate aunt
> Frances A. L. Haven"

In October of 1912, E. Coulon writes Alice from Louisiana. E. Coulon may have boarded Aunt Ellen.

"Pugh c/o Thomas Pugh
66 Beaver St New York
Bruly Oct 22 1912
My dear Alice
Yours of the 14th of this month was received last Saturday, how will I ever repay you for your great kindness to me, if I can't I will pray for you and ask God to bless you and yours, many thanks.
...You ask me about Aunt Ellen health good, the only thing the matter with her is her hands and feets that are cripple otherwise she's well, eat well, nothing hurt her. I wish I had as good a stomach like her, when she was all swollen sometime ago I wanted her to see a doctor, she never wanted, one day before my nephew Dr. Ags died, she was here, he came to see us, then I wanted aunt Ellen to tell him where she was suffering, she never wanted to consent, told the doctor she did not want to die taking his medicine, he laugh and laugh for I told him how she was, she said she was only hoo-doo and was going to cure herself. I painted her legs with iodine and the smelling went away but can't walk very well. I'm afraid to paint her hands because it is poison. I can't tell you how long she may live, only God knows. She may outlive all of us.
I will take care of her and board her as long as I can and she wants to stay with me. If we can sale will see that I get a room to [too] for her, where ever we would go, but I think we stand poor chance this year everybody says it is not good time to sale as the money is very scarce.
You can tell Mr. Thomas about Ellen health very good, I had answered Mr. John letter and I received a letter yesterday evening in which he send me five dollars for her board, so I let you know not to send ten in November only five he having send his share of five.
I hope Thomas wife and baby are all right give him our best regards for both of us also for aunt Ellen.
...Love to Frances. Mr. Coulon send kind regards to both also Aunt Ellen.
With luck to you I am as ever your truly friend
E. Coulon

On January 1st 1912, Alice's daughter Frances Stone writes Thomas' wife Regina from New Orleans. Frances, born in 1894, would be about 18.

"1631 Octavia St
New Orleans
Louisiana
Dear Regina,

I am tickled to death with my Christmas present. Santa was awfully good to me. I am getting up courage to have my picture taken. I have only had it taken twice in my life, and I think it is time to have some more, if it turns out all right I shall send you one.

I spent Christmas at the Malhiots and heard so many nice things about you that I am eaten up with curiosity to see you, if you are not in New York when I come home this spring I shall be terribly disappointed.

How did you celebrate Christmas? Rahula Malhiot and I went riding. It has rained so that the mud was up to the horse's knees, and we were splashed from head to foot, also it was drizzling but nothing mattered to us. ...We came home through the woods on a railroad track with swamp on each side.

...I came back Thursday night, went to a dance the next night. It was a masquerade, I went as a petite marquisee say in Louis XIV time. The powder hasn't come out of my hair yet.

Last night I went to a New Year's party, more fun than a picnic. We were supplied with horns and rattles. Then we set off fireworks.

I didn't get home till half past one. We entered the house tooting our horns, and disturbing the slumberers and the occupants. This morning I had to get up at seven. Adourny Couth would not be rejected.

Happy new year to you both and Mary Brown.

Affectionately

Frances

I do not know your address

F. S."

Woodbury Langdon, family friend, relative, husband of Edith Pugh, purchaser of the Haven home, died October 25th 1921.

"Woodbury Langdon Dead

New York financier dies at family homestead at 85 years old

Portsmouth, New Hampshire, October 24

Woodbury Langdon, formerly dry goods merchant in Boston and later director of banks, trust companies and mercantile corporations in New York, died at the Langdon Homestead in this city today. He was born here 85 years ago and divided his time recently between this city and New York.

Before he came to New York, Mr. Langdon had founded the Boston dry goods firm of Joy, Langdon & Co. During his career in this city he served as trustee of the New York Life insurance Co., New York trust Co. and title guarantee and trust Company, and as director of the national Bank of commerce. He was on the committee of 70 that fought Tammany in 1894, was twice president of the merchants club, and a member of the Union league, city and lawyers clubs."

The following article from the New York Times suggests that Woodbury's lawyers made the case that he was a resident of New Hampshire for estate tax purposes; it also details his bequests to Alice, John, Grace and Thomas Pugh.

> March 16, 1923 Woodbury Langdon legacy
> Woodbury Langdon left $2,386,820
> Former New York merchant bought home of ancestors in Portsmouth New Hampshire
> Woodbury Langdon, for many years one of the leading dry goods merchants in the city, who retired in 1909 and went to live at his birthplace at Portsmouth, New Hampshire, where the Langdon family settled in 1656, and who died there October 24, 1921, left a total estate of $2,386,820, and a New York estate of $1,218,475. Among the securities held were:
> 420 shares of American Telephone & Telegraph, $45,386; 400 American Alliance Insurance Co., $98,000; 385 Chemical National Bank, $189,612; 1195 Great American Insurance Co., $267,232; 503 General Electric, $64,791 $61,695; Guarantee Trust, $144,560; 233 New York Trust, $69,201; 673 National Bank of Commerce, $154,790; 138 Title Guarantee and Trust Co., $44,436; and 148 Realty Associates, $15,540.
> Mr. Langdon gave the residuary estate to his wife for life with power to dispose of the principal. He left $10,000 to the town of Newington New Hampshire, to buy books for the Langdon library, and left $10,000 to Langdon Lea. Gifts of $5,000 each were left to John H. Pugh, Alice D. Stone, Thomas Pugh, Charles M. Moffat and Grace Haven Pugh, and $2000 to Albert R. Ridge, an employee. Helen H. Langdon, niece, gets an income of $5000 a year and $2500 a year ago was to Frances B. Langdon, nephew.
> In offering proof that Mr. Langdon gave up his residence in New York the report states in 1911 he bought the Governor John Langdon colonial residence at Portsmouth and from that date until his death neither Mr. Langdon nor his wife was away from their home for a single night."

On June 18th, 1922, Alice's daughter Frances Stone wrote her Great-Aunt Fanny while taking a train to her honeymoon destination the day after her wedding. Fanny, in Jaffrey, New Hampshire, had once again made her summer escape from New York City. Participating in Frances' wedding were Alice's son Jack (John Haven Stone) and Thomas and Regina Pugh's children, Thomas Jr., Regina and Ellen. Present at the wedding were Alice Pugh Stone, Thomas and Regina Pugh, Augusta's children Nellie, Frank and Caroline (Carrie) and possibly Eustis among others.

> My Darling Little Aunt
> "The Bride's Version of her own Wedding".
> I began to dress at 11:15 A.M...

2:10 P.M. and they arrive, meanwhile Mother, Regina and Uncle Tom waiting for us to go up the aisle before taking their seats. I hailed an usher to take mother down and shooed Uncle Tom and Regina. Procession started at 2:12 sharp. Then when Jack and I started to turn into the main aisle after issuing instructions to the ushers to set a slow pace as my dress would not permit otherwise and hauling Thomas Jr. back into place in front of me something inside of me snapped and I felt like a mule in front of an oncoming locomotive I wanted to kick up my heels and not budge. My big brother Ralph who was more like a father to me was not there and Jack was as high strung as I and did not seem to have the soothing touch and coolness that I looked for in Ralph, the tears came but I vowed they wouldn't go further as I couldn't wipe them through the veil, then my hand beat a tattoo on Jack's arm which I could not stop. Jack said, "What's the matter, are you nervous, brace up." My bouquet rattled and my knees shook. I started with my head high but it came down lower and lower and I could not get it up until that front pew then I looked up at Mother. ...then I turned and was kissed by the groom and we cleared the church as fast as my dress would permit.
...Keep this letter with all the grim details which are fresh in my mind the day after but I may forget ten years from hence and should like to read it then. Was so glad Cousin Nellie, Cousin Frank, Caroline and Elanore were there."
I was very much touched and pleased with your letter which came on my wedding morn."

In March of 1924, Fanny Haven died.
Below are the two notices from the New York Times: Fanny's full name may have been Frances Appleton Langdon Haven, but was recorded as Amory due to a mistake in the census.

March 5, 1924 New York Times death notice. Fanny Haven -- at her residence, 43 5th Ave, on Tuesday, March 4, Frances Amory Langdon, youngest daughter of the late John Appleton Haven of New York City. Notice of funeral later.

March 7th, 1924 New York Times Haven – At her residence, 43 5th Ave, on Tuesday, March 4th, Frances Amory Langdon, youngest daughter of the late John Appleton Haven of New York City. Funeral at Grace Church Chantry, Broadway at 10th St., Friday, March 7th, at 11 AM. Interment private.

On July 4th 1924, the summer after Fanny died, Thomas writes Regina, who is probably in Maine, or in Portsmouth, N.H.
"Monday, July 4, 1924
10:30 a.m.
Dear kittens,

347

I hope you and the kids are all having a pleasant fourth today and that the sun is shining so you can all be on the beach. If you have not already done so you had better rent a bathhouse by the season right away before they are all gone. Please be sure and give the children plenty of fruit for breakfast, it pays and keeps them healthy without medicine. Peaches I think are good for this purpose also musk melons and I hope you will be able to get plenty of good fruit from Maxwell's where you buy the meat.

… With best love to all

yours affectionately

Tom"

Augusta Haven Hopkin's son, John Appleton Haven Hopkins, wrote the New York Times April 1925, about a proposed bridge (which is now the George Washington Bridge).

"Special to the New York Times

April 6 1925

Re: The Fort Washington Bridge

To the editor of the New York Times

Inasmuch as I was born in Fort Washington Park, at 178th Street and the Hudson River, the site of the proposed bridge to New Jersey, which originally belonged to my grandfather, John Appleton Haven (for whom Haven Avenue was afterward named), I am naturally very much interested in a letter which you have published from Reginald Pelham Bolton protesting against the bridge project so far as it may interfere with the park itself.

Fort Washington point, as Mr. Bolton says, is a very beautiful spot, and it was taken over by the city because it was a natural park which required nothing but ordinary care and attention.

Unfortunately, the park department has neglected the property in a most shameful manner.

This is all the more regrettable because the park includes Fort Independence, the revolutionary earthwork in almost perfect condition, and historically as well as artistically Fort Washington Park deserves every consideration.

If the proposed bridge is to interfere in any way with Fort Washington Park, Mr. Bolton's protest certainly should be regarded.

I am very familiar with the property in that vicinity, over which as a boy I used to shoot and fish, quite as if New York City did not exist, and it is quite possible to bridge the river at approximately the same place without in any way infringing upon the park itself. Furthermore, the city should see to it that the property is kept cleaned up, that the rubbish is removed, that the dead trees are removed and the others properly pruned, and that the people of New York be given every opportunity to enjoy its scenic beauty and the natural advantage which it possesses of giving everyone a

remarkably close and interesting panorama of the Hudson River and the ever-changing traffic, which is in education in itself.
JAH Hopkins
New York, April 1, 1925

In September of 1926 Regina C. Pugh passes through Portsmouth, staying at the Rockingham Hotel (the same hotel that Augusta's daughter Nellie saw burn, in 1884). The old Rockingham Hotel was the site of the original Judge Woodbury Langdon's home (built in 1785). Thomas has apparently been in touch with his Portsmouth relations to some extent, because he writes Regina,

> "Please give my love to Miss Langdon and thank her again for me as well as yourself for her invitation to the children and for her courtesy to you all."

In 1938, Alice Pugh Stone died (age 77); according to her obituary, she moved to Louisiana after her husband Ralph died. Mrs. Thomas R. Harris is "Frances", Alice's only daughter and youngest child (who described her wedding in the letter to Fanny of June 18th 1922).

> "Special to the New York Times
> Nov. 18 1938
> Mrs Ralph Stone
> Paramus New Jersey November 18
> Mrs. Alice De Blois Stone, a descendant of John Langdon, president of the first United States Senate and governor of New Hampshire, and a great-granddaughter of John Haven, who once owned the property now in Fort Washington Park, New York City, died Thursday at her home here.
> Mrs. Stone, a native of Louisiana, was the widow of Ralph Stone, former Buffalo lawyer. Mrs. Stone, who resided in New Orleans until recently, was a member of the colonial dames of Louisiana. Surviving are a daughter, Mrs. Thomas R. Harris of Paramus, three sons, Ralph T. of Philadelphia, John H. of New York and Lawrence A. of New Orleans, and two brothers, Thomas and John Pugh of New York."

On December 18, 1939 Ellen Eustis Pugh, Thomas Pugh's second daughter, became engaged to John J. McInerney.

> "New York Times
> Ellen Eustis Pugh Engaged to Marry
> Betrothal to John J. McInerney, son of former judge, is made known; at home reception
> Graduate of Wellesley
> The Bride Elect Also Studied at Packer Institute -- Fiancé Is an Alumnus of Williams
> Mr. and Mrs. Thomas Pugh of Brooklyn and announced the engagement of their daughter, Miss Ellen Eustis Pugh, to John J. McInerney, son of former special sessions Judge James J.

McInerney and Mrs. McInerney of Brooklyn and Bayport, Long Island, at a reception at their home yesterday.

The prospective bride attended the Packer collegiate Institute in Brooklyn and was graduated from Wellesley College, where she was a member of the Shakespeare society.

Mr. McInerney is a graduate of the Polytechnic Preparatory Country Day school in Brooklyn, Williams College, and St. John's University Law School. He is with Pennie Davis Marvin and Edmonds, patent attorneys in this city."

In 1945, Woodbury Langdon's second wife, whom Alice's son referred to as "Bessie", died. Woodbury may have intentionally sought out another relation to be his second wife: the Langdon Elwyns were a prominent family descended from John Langdon:

"August 23, 1945 -- Elizabeth Elwyn Langdon obituary
Lincoln – Elizabeth Elwyn, widow of the late Woodbury Langdon and daughter of the late Alfred Langdon Elwyn and Helen Dyer L Elwyn, at her residence in Portsmouth New Hampshire. Services private. Philadelphia papers please copy."

About a month later, Augusta Haven Hopkin's son Eustis died. Below is his obituary from the New York Times:

"September 7, 1945 Eustis Langdon Hopkins obituary
Eustis L. Hopkins, 81, a textile executive
Eustis Langdon Hopkins, retired chairman of the board and director of Bliss, Fabian & Co., cotton goods, died yesterday in his home, 943 Lexington Ave. His age was 81.

Mr. Hopkins was a son of John Milton and Mrs. Augusta DuBlois Haven Hopkins. He traced his ancestry to John Rogers, the Protestant martyr, who was burned at the stake as a heretic in England in 1555, and William Hopkins, an organizer of the Rhode Island colony. Another ancestor was John Rogers, president of Harvard College in 1683.

He was educated at the Wilson and Kellogg schools, and started his business career with the cotton textile commission firm of Joy, Langdon & Co., later becoming a partner.

After its dissolution in 1911 he joined the Bliss, Fabian Company. He had served as a vice president before being elected chairman.

Mr. Hopkins was a former director of the Bank of New York and Trust Company, the Great American insurance Co., the Home Life insurance Co., the Great American Indemnity Co...

He was a member of the Society of Colonial Wars, and former member of the Union, Merchants, Piping Rock and Church Clubs.

Surviving are a sister, Mrs. Edward T. Griffin of Larchmont, and a brother, John A. H. Hopkins of Baltimore. His wife, Mrs. Elizabeth Stockwell Hopkins, a granddaughter of Elias Howe, inventor of the sewing machine, died in 1936.

In 1948, Alice's son John Haven Stone died in New Jersey at 59; in 1949, John Pugh's wife Blanche died in New York City (she was buried at Trinity Cemetery); in 1950, Alice's son Ralphie died at 63 (Ralph Townsend Stone).

On January 29th 1951, Alice's son Lawrence, from New Orleans, writes Thomas Pugh's daughter Regina, in New York. Lawrence, born in 1892, was about 59; Regina Pugh, born in 1912, was 39.

"January 29, 1951
Lawrence A. Stone
1137 Nashville Ave.
New Orleans, Louisiana
Dear Regina,
I received your letter of the 22nd which was quite reassuring so I'm forwarding you under separate cover, two copies of records pertaining to New England ancestors which I'm sure you will find important. I have the books referred to as reference, so I know the references are authentic. The same ancestry as mine applies to yours except change my name to yours and instead of Alice deBlois Pugh (my mother) put Thomas Pugh (your father). This reference comment supplements the family tree which is being photostated.
Dr. Samuel Haven is mentioned too casually. He was very prominent and a president of Harvard. No mention is made of Alfred the Great who was an ancestor through the Langdon side. Francis the first of France is not mentioned but mother said we were descended from him through some English connection of the Langdon's that were connected with the House of Blois. Her middle name was given her from this descent (deBlois). However, I am a little hazy about this. Through the Langdon descent, you are entitled to the use of several coats of arms as these people came from English nobility.
You are descended from Governor Dudley of the Massachusetts Bay colony. He was a nobleman and very high ranking in the colonies. I have his biography. You are descended from Governor Wentworth of New Hampshire, prominent in Revolutionary war history. You are directly descended from Wouter Von Twiller, thru your great, great grandmother, Eliza Foley. Von Twiller was the first Dutch governor of new Amsterdam (New York).
Getting to the Pughs, I will send you more on them later. I do not know the Pugh colors in the coat of arms, but you can get it from the library from books on heraldry. You might have to look under "Appugh" instead of "Pugh" as that was the original. If you want an authoritative source on the Pughs, see Alice deBlois Pugh Stone page 435 -- volume 3, 1928 The Abridged Compendium of American Genealogy (Standard Genealogical Encyclopedia of the First Familys of America)

This book should be in the public library and confirms information shortly to be sent to you.
Sincerely,
Lawrence"

On April 20th 1964, John Foley Pugh writes John J. McInerney (who had saved, read and done peripheral research on the Haven-Pugh letters, and had reached out to those of the Louisiana Pughs whom he could locate).
"Pugh, Lanier and Pugh
Attorneys at Law
504 St. Louis St.
Thibodeaux, Louisiana

Mr. John J. McInerney
Attorney at Law
28 Park Ave.
Bay Shore, New York
Dear Mr. McInerney,
This is in reference to your letter of April 17 in which you seek information regarding the Pugh family. It is apparent that your wife and I are related, and I have quite a bit of information concerning the early generations of the Pugh family which I will get together and forward to you if you are interested.
For your information Madewood still stands and is in reasonably good repair. The other antebellum residence constructed by the Pughs named Woodlawn went to ruin some years ago.
I am the son of Dr. William Whitmell Pugh, who was the son of Dr. Thomas Bryan Pugh, who in turn was the son of Colonel W. W. Pugh, who built Woodlawn. The George W. Pugh at Louisiana State University is my brother and Nina Pugh is the wife of my brother, Thomas B. Pugh. She is an attorney and so is he, and he is presently city judge in Baton Rouge. I know that we do have relations in Shreveport, and I think that Robert G. Pugh is definitely a relation.
I am preparing to attend the Louisiana bar convention for the remainder of the week, but upon my return I will see if I could get together some of the few papers that I have and will make photostatic copies of them for you and will forward them to you if you are interested, and I hope that one of these days you and your wife will be able to visit Bayou Lafourche and meet some of her relatives.
Sincerely, John F. Pugh

In August of 1975, Ellen Eustis Pugh McInerney died at age 61. Her husband, John J. McInerney, continued his research into his wife's family.

In 1981, John J. McInerney and Ellen Eustis Pugh's son, Carl Haven McInerney, went to Louisiana.

"Monday, March 2, 1981 Baton Rouge
Dad
I haven't done anything at all in quite awhile on our ancestors, but
when I was looking around for something in the library I got
talking to some sort who work in the "Louisiana collection" and she
had a friend whose mother she thought I should meet, so she gave
me the name and address and phone number. So Saturday I called
her up and yesterday went over for Sunday lunch. Her name is
Nina and she is married to Judge Thomas B. Pugh and they are
descendents of the Woodlawn side (Dr. Whitmel and son WW
Pugh).
Judge Pugh is eccentric and Nina very sober, so between the two
of them, I felt right at home. He likes to swear and drink (Sunday
lunch is always deviled eggs and bloody Mary's), wears a leather
visor and is forgetful. Nina is very sharp and a real expert on the
Pughs (she is a lawyer and works at LSU Law school). He grew up
at Napoleonville under the shadow of Woodlawn and Madewood.
He is 60 but seems much older, she appears very much younger
but is probably about 55. They are both extremely nice and were
very helpful -- Nina gave me about 60 pages of Xerox material
about the Pughs etc. Some very good information on the Pugh
Welsh ancestry, coat of arms etc. I'm going to keep it for a while
till I clear up some questions when I next see her -- and then I'll
send it to you.
But the reason I'm writing is to ask you if you could Xerox that
letter that has the advice to the daughter about don't go near the
Irish? And anything else you think they might like -- I don't think
we can teach them anything about the Pughs -- Nina seems to
know everything. But some personal color? I am asking mainly
because it would be nice if we could give them something in
return.
... Also, the attorney in Thibodeaux (who had mentioned some
letters to you) is Judge Pugh's brother and the attorney who is
professor at LSU Law school is his other brother.
Must go, Carl"

Carl Haven McInerney writes John J McInerney,
"Th May 7, 1981 Baton Rouge
D
Many thanks for sending all the W.W. Pugh letters. Your timing
was perfect: I received them Friday in time to bring them with me
to the annual Pugh picnic held at the Woodlawn Cemetery (did you
see this when here? – W.W. Pugh is buried there, but no one else
of interest to us).
There were perhaps 30 people in attendance, including somebody
from New Orleans and somebody from Houston, but basically I'd
already met everybody with the exception of George Pugh who is
the law professor at LSU and Judge Pugh's brother.

353

Everybody was very interested in the letters -- in fact a bunch of us sat around and I read a few of them aloud. I have given them to Nina and she is making copies for some of the others. She feels that they are important enough to be given to the LSU archives so we're looking into that. I read through the letters (it is very difficult to read his writing, as I'm sure you know) and Xeroxed about 10 pages of stuff that we can keep.

As you may have noticed, the letters indicate that a certain LLewellen Pugh was the last Pugh in residence at Madewood and that after him Madewood was purchased c. 1896? The letters also refer to the fire which destroyed the sugar house and there is a real burning question about this issue -- ties in with the motives of Robert Pugh when he left Madewood to Lewellen Pugh -- remind me when I get home to tell you about it – big family scandal and a will contest.

I talked to Nina yesterday and she was so appreciative because she said that she knows of all the people that WW refers to in the letters. There was one Pugh that WW referred to as being in pretty good shape and according to Aunt Josie, she remembers him as being so drunk he'd fall off his horse all the time! - every family has its ups and downs.

I'm going to get together w George Pugh Monday next and (*sic*) has the scoop on the sugar house fire.

That's it for now,

C.

By 1984, Nina Nichols Pugh, wife of Judge Thomas Bryan Pugh had been to visit both John J. McInerney and Regina Pugh Cummings in New York.

Illustration 56 Ellen's sister, Fanny A. L. Haven's gravestone, Woodlawn Cemetery, Webster Ave., Spring Lake plot, the Bronx.

355

Lines of Descent

Following is a summary of the John Appleton Haven branch, from which Fanny and Ellen descended. Included is a letter that summarizes Ellen's ancestral branches and a chart illustrating Ellen's ancestors.

John Appleton Haven and Sarah Sherburne Langdon had three children with issue: Augusta Haven Hopkins, Ellen Eustis Haven Pugh, and Langdon Henry Haven.

Langdon Henry Haven had three children with Elizabeth Symmes: Henry Langdon, Ethan Allen and Paul Hecker Haven. Whether any of these children had issue is unknown.

Augusta DeBlois Haven Hopkins and Milt had eight children: Augusta (no issue), Ellen, Frank (no issue), Eustis (no issue), Appleton, Sarah (no issue), Louise and Caroline (aka Carrie; issue unknown)
Ellen Hopkins married Frank Iredell and had three children: Frances C Iredell, Carol Iredell, Eleanore Iredell (became Mrs Donald Warman)
Sarah L. Hopkins married Alfred Morewood (no issue)
Louise (Loulou) Alley Hopkins married Leonard Wyeth (one son, Leonard Jarvis Wyeth, b. Aug 4 1890, married Constance Priscilla Mullins Bull, died Mar 17 1968; had two children, Priscilla Mullins and Leonard Jarvis)
Eustis Langdon Hopkins married Elizabeth Stockwell (no issue)
Caroline Eustis Hopkins married Edward Griffin (issue unknown)
John Appleton Haven Hopkins (married Hilda Stone, who died, then married Allison Low Turnbull in 1901, divorced 3/1927) and had three children: Marion Louise Hopkins, married (Meyer) 4/1925; Douglas Turnbull Hopkins; J. Milton Hopkins

Ellen Eustis Haven Pugh had two children who had issue: Alice DeBlois Pugh Stone and Thomas Pugh.
Alice Pugh's children were: Jack (John Haven Stone), Ralph, Lawrence (married and had issue including Langdon Stone) and Frances (married Thomas Robinson Harris and had issue including Alyce Rossow).
Thomas Pugh's children were: Regina, Ellen, Thomas and John.
Thomas Pugh's daughter Ellen Eustis Pugh married John J. McInerney (who saved and passed on the letter collection).
As of March, 2010, John J. McInerney, age 97, lives in an Alzheimer's facility. In his room is Volume I of the Haven-Pugh Letter Collection, its cover torn off from his effort to understand what it is.
His son, John J. McInerney Jr. continues to research the Pugh and Haven genealogies.

The author hopes the younger "Thomas Pugh" generations will take an interest in their roots: Melissa, James, Thomas, Jaqueline, Beverly, Conor, Haven, another Haven, Paul, Regina, Willa, Luther, and more to come.

It seems fitting to end with a letter from John J. McInerney, in New York, to Nina Nichols Pugh, in Louisiana, written February 23, 1984. Both married a Pugh; both took a keen interest in the Pugh heritage despite having no blood relationship to the Pughs; both were lawyers; both are alive as of this writing and both are memory-impaired. The book John thanks Nina for sending is inscribed as follows:

> "To the McInerney-Pughs, the northern most post of the Thomas Pugh clan
> January 15, 1984*

> *Nina Nichols Pugh
> and
> Martin Luther King's birthdays"

John's letter to Nina Feb. 23 1984:

"Mrs. Thomas B. Pugh II
2000 Cloverdale Ave
Baton Rouge, Louisiana
70808

Dear Nina,
A thousand apologies for not writing sooner. Ice-boating season came to a sudden end and consequently, on Lincoln's birthday I went a final go around to start reviewing my Pugh family tree papers preliminary to writing you. On Monday the 13th, which was a holiday, I started at 9:30 and went through to 11 o'clock that night, taking time out for lunch and for dinner. Saturday, the 18th I spent all day and also all day Sunday, the 19th.
First of all, many thanks for sending me "Plantation Parade". I had read the chapter on "Mighty are the Pughs". Exactly where I had gotten a Xerox copy, I don't remember -- however, I had never read the rest of the book and was absolutely enchanted with it.
...I never realized that the Duc d'Orleans, who became Louis Phillippe, King of France and his two brothers, the Duc de Montpensier and Compte de Beaujolais had visited in Louisiana. It is amazing how little we know about our own country. I think that Kane writes well and really gets across what he is talking about, i.e. a way of life.
...I enclose a copy of a letter that Carl wrote his sister Kathleen in April of 1981. He does not know that I'm sending it to you. You and the judge made a great impression on Carl and I thought you would like to see what he had written about your husband.
...With regard to the Dutch side of the Pugh family I enclose copy of the document entitled "Van Rensselaer family", which Carl got from Jesse Herthum and another document showing the descent from Wouter Von Twiller and I call your attention to the fact that a mistake is made in referring to Von Twiller as the "first" Dutch

governor. My source for making that comment is "Chester's Legal and Judicial History of New York, volume 1, 1911, page 14, 23, 25, and 26 and I enclose copy of same. I also enclose Xerox copy about Von Twiller taken from "Dictionary of American Biography". You will remember that there was some discussion of Gilbert Stuart's paintings and I enclose Xerox copy from a book on Stuart giving the history of the picture made of John Haven, who was Ellen Haven Pugh's grandfather and his wife, Mrs. John Haven and also Nathaniel Appleton Haven, who was a son of Samuel Haven, to whom I will refer later on.

Ellen Haven Pugh was Ellen Eustis Haven and came from quite an illustrious family. I will start with the Haven family, which runs as follows: Richard Haven came from the West of England and settled in Lynn, Massachusetts in 1636 according to "Appleton's Cyclopedia of American biographies", although in the family tree that I have, the date is given a 1644; anyway, they settled near Flax Pond. He was a sergeant in King William's war and died in 1703. He married a woman, Susanna, and by her had among others, a son, John Haven, who was born December 10, 1656. He in turn married Hannah Hitchens and by her had a son, Joseph, who was born August 17, 1698, who married in turn Mehitabel, who was his first cousin, she being a daughter of Moses Haven, another son of the original Richard Haven. They had a son, Samuel D. Haven, class of 1749 at Harvard, doctor of divinity in 1770 from the University of Edinburgh and who also got a doctor of divinity degree in 1773 from Dartmouth. He married Mehitabel Appleton, she being the daughter of Nathaniel Appleton, they in turn had a son, John, who was born April 8, 1766 and he married Ann Woodward, they in turn had a son John Appleton Haven, Harvard, class of 1813, who married Sarah Sherburne Langdon and they were the father and mother respectively of Ellen Eustis Haven Pugh, she having married David Bryan Pugh on July 7, 1859. John Appleton Haven and his wife, Sarah, attended his 50th reunion at Harvard in 1863 according to a letter Sarah wrote to her daughter, Ellen Eustis Pugh.

With respect to the Langdon's, the first one in our country was Tobias, who married Elizabeth Sherburne on June 10, 1656. She had a child named Tobias, who was born in 1660 and he married a Mary Hubbard and they had a child named John, who was born May 28, 1707 and he married Mary Woodbury Hall, who was descended from colonial governor Thomas Dudley. According to a note she helped make the flag for John Paul Jones, which was adopted by Congress. They had two children, Woodbury Langdon, who was born in 1738 and John Langdon. John signed the U.S. Constitution and was the governor of New Hampshire. Woodbury was a member of the old Congress 1779 -- 80, president of New Hampshire Senate, judge of the Supreme Court of New Hampshire in 1782, 1786 to 1790. Woodbury Langdon married Sarah Sherburne, they had among other children, Caroline and Henry Sherburne. Henry Sherburne was born on March 11, 1766 and died on March 23, 1818 according to his daughter's letter to Ellen. He married Ann Eustis, the daughter of Dr. Benjamin Eustis and Elizabeth Hill Eustis. Her brother, William, married Henry Sherburne Langdon's sister, Caroline. He was the class of 1772 at Harvard, he studied medicine under Dr. Joseph Warren (General Warren, who was killed in the battle of Bunker Hill). He served Warren in the Revolutionary Army, was made vice president of the society of the Cincinnati, elected to the house of representatives in 1800, Secretary of War in the Cabinet of presidents Jefferson and Madison, minister to Holland in 1814, and again was a member of Congress and governor of Massachusetts.

Henry Sherburne Langdon and Ann Eustis had a daughter, Sarah Sherburne Langdon, born on March 12, 1797 and died January 17, 1876. She married John Appleton Haven and, of course, was the mother of Ellen Eustis Haven Pugh.

With respect to the Sherburne's, the first one, Henry, arrived in what was to be Portsmouth in 1632. He was born in 1612 and died in 1681. He married Rebecca Gibbons, their child Samuel, born August 4, 1638 and was killed by the Indians at Casco Bay on August 4, 1691. He married Love Hitchens and they had a child, Henry, who was born February 16, 1674 and died December 29, 1757. He was a member of the assembly and government council. He was provincial council and Chief Justice of New Hampshire in 1728. He married Dorothy Wentworth, who was the sister of lieutenant governor John Wentworth and she was the aunt of Governor Benning Wentworth. They in turn had a son, Henry, class of 1728 at Harvard, held various offices, member of the colonial Congress in Albany, etc. He married Sarah Warner and they in turn had a daughter, Sarah Sherburne, who married Woodbury Langdon, as set forth above.

William Wentworth came from England to Boston in 1632. He was the founder of Exeter, New Hampshire. He married Elizabeth Kenney, his son, Samuel, had the Dolphin Inn and later a great tavern across the valley in Portsmouth. He was one of the signers of the petition to keep Portsmouth under the government of Massachusetts. He married Mary Benning. His daughter was Dorothy Wentworth who married Henry Sherburne above.

With respect to the Appletons, the first one was Samuel, who was born in 1586 and died in 1670. He came from England to Ipswich in 1635 and became a freeman in 1636. The lands granted to him as of a few years ago were still held by his descendents. He married a Judith Everard and they had a son Major John Appleton,

who was born in 1622 and died in 1699. He married Priscilla
Glover and they had a son, Captain John Appleton, who was born
1652 and died 1739. He married Elizabeth Rogers and they had as
their son, Nathaniel Appleton, who was born in 1693 and died
1784. He had a doctor of divinity at Harvard and was a member of
the Harvard Corp. He married Margaret Gibbs, who was
descended from Elizabeth Temple, who traces her ancestry to Lady
Godiva. Their child Mehitabel Appleton was born in 1729 and she
married Samuel D. Haven, above referred to.

I do not have the chain on the Eustis family, since it was only in
the last year or so that I ascertain that there was a mistake in the
family tree of the Langdon's, as originally they had the Sarah
Sherburne Langdon, who married John Appleton Haven, as the
daughter of Woodbury Langdon and Sarah Sherburne, instead of
her being their granddaughter.

I hope I have not bored you too much with the foregoing.
We thoroughly enjoyed having dinner with you and any time you
are back in the area, please call or even better, give us advance
notice so we can make some plans. We have a lot of fun in the
summer and would like to introduce you to our Great South Bay
and swimming in the Atlantic Ocean.
Sincerely,
John J. McInerney"

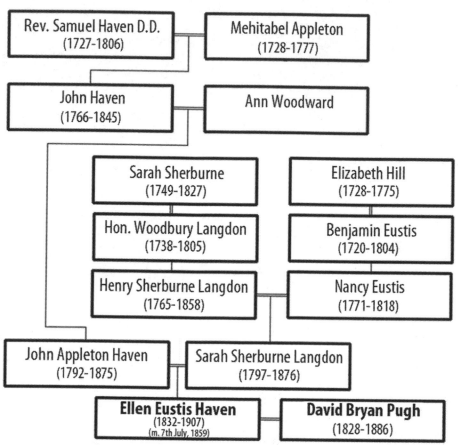

Illustration 57: Ancestors of Ellen Eustis Haven. Ellen's ancestors include prominent Portsmouth, N.H. and Massachusetts merchants, ship-builders, scholars and men who were influential during the Revolutionary War and the formation of the American government (image courtesy John J. McInerney, Jr.).

Afterword

I am privileged to live with Fanny and Ellen, to carry them with me every day, everywhere I go. We've been through a lot together. Sometimes, while transcribing letters, I was so moved by their words and their sorrow that I cried, and I had to stop working: I had to ensure no tears fell on the actual letters, and I couldn't see the computer screen through my tears.

I've met a lot of people through Fanny and Ellen. In the course of researching the hundreds of letters for clues to the people who were referenced, I reached out on the internet and to Pugh cousins through my brother. I met, by computer, Pugh relatives in the South, out west and as far away as Argentina.

My two most exciting discoveries were related to one another. First, I found someone I thought might be a relation, after studying online obituaries. After sending a letter by postal mail, I eventually connected over the computer with Alice Pugh Stone's grand-daughter, Alyce Rossow, who lives in California. She wrote, "Yes, my grandmother was Alice De Blois Pugh. I was named after her..."

After I learned that Alyce was the daughter of the woman my mother (Ellen Eustis Pugh) had occasionally but fondly referred to as "Cousin Frances", I got an email from Alyce that really knocked me out:

> "I remember the name of McInerney. I remember going for a sailboat ride with John McInerney when I was, perhaps, nine. His boat was unusual because it was wooden and the boards stretched from bow to stern as one piece not pieces pieced together. Was John your father?"

(Yes, John was my father, and Alyce was brought out to our house from New Jersey, by her mother, who was my mother's Cousin Frances. I was either a baby or not yet born).

Periodically Alyce and I exchanged questions and information by e-mail.

Then, Alyce and her husband Terry came east to visit Alyce's family, and said they were willing to come to New England to meet me. I was so excited I could hardly think straight!

My brother John and his wife Vicki came from Vermont to Portland, and we three drove to Portsmouth, N.H., to meet Alyce and Terry. We arranged to meet at the Library Restaurant in Portsmouth, at the center of which is what remains of the lovely 1785 home of Woodbury Langdon, our ancestor. Alyce, John and I thumbed through pages of information, and the five of us visited historical sites and cemeteries related to the Havens and Langdons.

Meantime, at home, I'd been through hundreds upon hundreds of letters, documents, account books, check books and registers, prayer books, newspapers, scrapbooks and photographs over the years. There were pictures of Ellen and others, but none of Fanny. Throughout Fanny's letters, she is consistent if not adamant about not wanting her picture taken. So I resolved to carry a great regret to my grave: I would never know what Fanny Haven looked like.

Then, one day, Alyce sent more pictures. Amongst them was a photo labeled "Aunt Fanny Jaffrey 1922". I cried, and cried some more. A dream come true! Not only could I finally learn what Fanny looked like, but it was, to me, the ideal of a likeness I might have hoped for: a happy, kind-looking and handsome woman standing in front of one of her vacation haunts in Jaffrey, N.H. I put a copy of Fanny's picture next to Ellen's, and to John Appleton Haven's. They are 3 peas in pod.

Based on past experience, I know that new information is around the corner, more relatives will appear, and the story will be refined over time.

These then, are some of the many rewards I have enjoyed during my years of working with the letters. I am not finished with the letters. I look forward to re-reading the entire collection, and living, laughing and crying again with the Haven sisters.

Illustration 58: Ellen late in life, possibly 1906 (photo courtesy of Della Haden-Dirickson).

365

Illustration 59: Fanny Haven, in Jaffrey, N.H. 1922, about 2 years before she died (photo courtesy of Alyce Rossow).

Made in the USA
Middletown, DE
04 June 2016